Mediation Law

In England mediation became a key part of the civil justice reform agenda after the Woolf Reforms of 1996, as disputants were deflected from litigation towards settlement outside the court system. The Civil Procedure Rules (CPR) give courts the power to 'encourage' mediation through judicial case management or use stronger measures by using costs to penalise parties who act unreasonably by refusing to use ADR or mediation. One of the effects of this institutionalisation is an emerging case law that defines how mediation is practised as it merges with the litigation process. When mediation first began to be used in England the parties either agreed to mediate by a contract before a dispute happened or decided to attempt the process as a way of resolving disagreements. Inevitably, some disputants either refused to abide by their contractual obligations or would not follow through with the settlement agreements reached through the process. This brought the authority of the law into a new area and the juridification process began.

This book explores how mediation law shapes the practice of mediation in the English jurisdiction. It provides a comprehensive examination of the legal environment for mediation, and explores the jurisprudence in order to analyse the extent that institutionalisation by the state and courts has led to the monopolisation of the process by lawyers and a further 'juridification' process results. The book includes a comparative legal methodology on the structures underpinning mediation practice in other common law jurisdictions, including the USA, Australia, and Hong Kong, in order to explicate shared or distinctive approaches to mediation.

The book will be of great interest to academics and students of legal theory and dispute resolution.

Penny Brooker is a Reader in ADR and mediation at Wolverhampton University where she is the Co-Director of the Law Research Centre. She is the co-coordinator of an International Task Group (TG 68) for the CIB (International Council for Research and Innovation in Building and Construction) which produced an edited book on international perspectives on construction mediation. She has been a member of the Academic Committee of the Civil Mediation Council since 2005.

Mediation Law

Journey through Institutionalism
to Juridification

Penny Brooker

Routledge
Taylor & Francis Group

LONDON AND NEW YORK

First published 2013
by Routledge
2 Park Square, Milton Park, Abingdon, Oxon, OX14 4RN

Simultaneously published in the USA and Canada
by Routledge
711 Third Avenue, New York, NY 10017

Routledge is an imprint of the Taylor & Francis Group, an informa business

British Library Cataloguing in Publication Data
A catalogue record for this book is available from the British Library

Library of Congress Cataloging-in-Publication Data
A catalog record has been requested for this book

ISBN: 978-0-415-61294-4 (hbk)
ISBN: 978-0-203-79662-7 (ebk)

Typeset in Garamond
by Keystroke, Station Road, Codsall, Wolverhampton

Printed and bound in Great Britain by
TJ International Ltd, Padstow, Cornwall

Contents

Table of Cases

UK Cases

Other Jurisdictions

Australia

New Zealand

United States

Table of Legislation

UK Legislation

Other Jurisdictions

Australia

Federal

1 Development of modern mediation

Introduction

Mediation defies a universal definition because of the variant ways that mediators practise[1] but there is a common understanding that it is a process where a third party neutral assists the parties to reach a 'consensual'[2] agreement about the settlement of their dispute. Mediation is not a construct of the 20th century and there is evidence of mediatory processes dating back 4,000 years to Sumerian and Chinese cultures.[3] When social cohesion is vital, 'kinship based'[4] communities from across the continents of Asia, Australasia, Africa and the Americas have mediated their disputes through 'harmony', 'moral persuasion' and 'agreement' rather than adversarial mechanisms.[5]

Mediation has a more recent history as one of a number of processes forming the Modern Alternative Dispute Resolution (ADR) Movement, which has swept, albeit at different tempos, across many countries and different legal systems from the middle of the 20th century to the present day.[6] A number of factors are responsible for the 'explosion of ADR'[7] but primarily in common law countries it is attributed to a response to dissatisfaction with litigation, which is the formal system provided by the State for citizens to access the courts for resolution of their disputes.[8]

Alternative to litigation in Common Law

Litigation in the English and Welsh jurisdiction is based on the Common Law, which uses an adversarial system where the parties bring evidence to the

---

1 See for example, Riskin (1996)
2 Genn (2012) at 82
3 See for example; Spain & Paranica (2001) at 393; Clarke (1991); Clark (2002) (2012); Pei (1999); Hensler (2003); Kovach (2006) in Alexander (2006)
4 Woolford & Ratner (2008) at 4–5
5 Bradney & Cownie (2000); Woolford & Ratner at 41; Auerbach (1983); Spain & Paranica (2001)
6 Alexander (2006); Clark (2012)
7 Nader (1988)
8 See generally Alexander (2006); Clark (2012). Commentators note that similar concerns have driven ADR developments in civil law countries.

court to 'prove' their case, which can then be challenged through cross-examination.[9] During the 18th and 19th centuries in England, litigation procedures became so technical that Holdsworth described them as 'a blot upon the legal system'.[10] The complexity of both the evidentiary and procedural rules eventually necessitated a reliance on legal professionals, which is reputed to create delay and expense, and distances people from accessing the courts.[11]

As the common law courts were centralised this was accompanied by a growth of a specialised legal profession[12] extending their 'monopoly over conflict resolution', which also inevitably led to the consequence of increasing legal cost.[13] Moreover, Woolford and Ratner observe that 'urbanisation and industrialisation' provided for an 'increasingly complex life' where it became normal for people to seek redress from legal 'neutrals', thus allowing lawyers to expand their role in an ever more complex litigation process.[14]

The confrontational aspects of litigation in many common law countries eventually led to experimentation with alternatives and the promotion of mediation, which has been tailored from a 'community based system' to a 'dispute resolution technique' used in a myriad of settings including family and commercial disputes.[15] Mediation is recognised now as the principal ADR process utilised for legal reform in many common law countries but many civil law countries have also witnessed an ADR and mediation movement in response to civil litigation problems.[16]

Problems with litigation

In England, the problems of costs and delay in court action led to countless quests to reform litigation, which Zuckerman believes have been largely ineffective because of the interests that the legal professions have in retaining the status quo and preserving their costly litigation practices.[17] Nonetheless, ADR became a key part of the civil justice reform agenda after the highly critical review of civil litigation and lawyers' activities undertaken by Lord Woolf in 1995.[18] The main objectives of the consequent Civil Procedure Rules (CPR) are to divert disputants from litigation towards settlement outside the court system.[19] The CPR provide judges with the power either to

---

9 Jacob (1985); Jolowicz (1996); Fuller (1972); Auerbach (1983)
10 Holdsworth (1938) Vol. 12 at 178–9
11 Jacob (1985); Auerbach (1983); Jolowicz (1996): Woolford & Ratner (2008)
12 Baker (2007); Holdsworth (1922)
13 Woolford & Ratner (2008) at 41
14 Woolford & Ratner (2008) at 42
15 Woolford & Ratner (2008) at 42
16 For an overview of other countries' ADR and mediation developments see for example, Alexander (2006) and Clark (2012)
17 Zuckerman (1996a) at 776
18 Woolf (1995)
19 Woolf (1996). See Roberts (2000); Genn (2010)

'encourage' the use of alternatives including mediation through judicial case management or use more 'coercive' measures by using costs to penalise parties who act unreasonably by refusing to use mediation.[20]

Government and judicial policy has led to the co-option of mediation by the court system, which has initiated a 'fledging' mediators' profession dominated by lawyers who are shaping mediation practice and styles.[21] Inevitably, the result of the close 'linkage'[22] of mediation with litigation is a developing body of 'mediation law' where the courts determine and 'institutionalise' mediation practice[23] in the English jurisdiction. The aim of this book is to explore how the courts support mediation practice and how law is delineating when the process should be initiated, upheld by the courts and institutionalised into the litigation process.

This chapter will first discuss the definitional issues surrounding both ADR and mediation. The practice of mediation is not homogenous and there has been experimentation in both process and mediator approach leading to one of the most contentious academic debates in the mediation literature, that of facilitative-evaluative practice.[24] In England and Wales, this debate is beginning to have relevance as a mediator profession emerges and as government and legal policies progressively assimilate mediation into litigation. This chapter therefore also reviews the different models of mediation and mediator's styles in order that an analysis can be made of these developments on mediation policy and mediation law.

The chapter will continue by tracing the history of the Modern ADR and Mediation Movements from their formation in the United States of America (USA) in the middle of the 20th century to their transference to the English civil system through a process of experimentation, implementation, institutionalisation and regulation.[25] The chapter will briefly review the early attempts to avoid the common law in England as an analogy for the current phenomenon of mediation development before undertaking an analysis of the factors involved in the present interest in the process, as it forms part of the civil justice reform agenda. A review will be made of the problems of civil litigation in England and Wales and the CPR designed to encourage parties to use alternatives rather than proceeding to trial. This chapter will also consider the key arguments against informalism before explaining the contention of this book, which is that developments in mediation have

---

20 Brunsdon-Tully (2009) at 219; Brooker (2009); Shipman (2006); Genn (2010) (2012)
21 Miles (2004) at 1. For a detailed analysis of the involvement of legal professions in mediation here and elsewhere, see Clark (2012)
22 Baruch Bush (2008) at 714
23 Alexander (2008a) at 104; See also Coben & Thompson (2006); Alfini (2008)
24 Riskin (1996). See for example, Stulberg (1997); Kovach & Love (1996) (1998); Stemple (2000); Lowry (2000); Lande (2000); Stipanowich (2001); Oberman (2005); Noce et al. (2002)
25 See for example, Press (2003–2004); Kovach (2006); Sanders (2007)

resulted in its juridification. The final section will review the early mediation case law following the CPR.

Definitions of ADR and mediation

ADR

Above it was noted how people sought to look for alternatives to the adversarial system of litigation in the common law. Mediation is just one of a number of procedures which come under the 'umbrella'[26] of ADR, which embraces a diverse range of dispute resolution processes, which are non-binding and private in nature, unless the parties expressly agree otherwise, but the literature in many countries include informal mechanisms where the third party neutral provides a decision. ADR procedures such as 'expert determination'[27] or 'early neutral evaluation'[28] or the 'mini-trial'[29] require the neutral to assume a more 'intrusive'[30] role, by first engaging in fact finding and then either issuing a recommendation or decision with the parties' agreement.[31]

Arbitration

Some countries' ADR histories allude to arbitration[32] as an alternative to litigation but often the law in many nations defines and oversees its management leading some writers to position it within the formal system.[33] Many international construction industries, including England, have made statutory provisions for adjudication in the built environment where adjudicators have an allocated period to hear and give a decision on a dispute, which allows the project to continue.[34]

---

26 Department of Constitutional Affairs (1999); Genn (2010) at 81
27 In expert determination, a third party neutral is appointed, sometimes through a prior contract term, to review and issue a binding opinion. For an overview of procedures used in the construction industry in England see Gaitskell (2005a, b); Kendall (2000)
28 In Early Neutral Evaluation (ENE), the parties appoint a neutral to provide a non-binding decision.
29 The mini-trial is reported to be used in large commercial cases such as construction disputes. Gaitskell (2005) (a) (b)
30 Effron (1989); Goldberg et al. (1985)
31 Brown & Marriott (2011) at 133–52 Chapter 7 Contractual Adjudication and Other Adjudication Processes
32 Hensler (2003). Hensler provides a concise history of the ADR movement in the USA including a review of the court-annexed programmes for arbitration. See also Riggs & Schenk (1990); Stipanowich (1996)
33 See Lavers (1992). See also Brown & Marriott (2011) at 109. Brown & Marriott (2011) applaud the acceptance of arbitration as part of 'mainstream ADR by practitioners'.
34 See for example, Brooker & Wilkinson (2010). Contributors from a number of countries in the review indicate that there is a preference in construction industries for adjudication, where the adjudicator provides a quick binding decision until the contract is completed, which has impinged on mediation growth.

Conciliation

Conciliation is another ADR process, which has different understandings in diverse settings. A number of taxonomies define conciliation as a procedure where the conciliator provides a non-binding recommendation or, occasionally, even a binding decision.[35] ADR literature in some contexts uses mediation and conciliation to describe the same process using the term 'interchangeably'.[36] Following a fervent debate on mediator styles prior to establishing a voluntary scheme for mediator registration, the Australian National Mediator Standards define processes where the neutral provides an 'advisory' component, or 'expert information' as conciliation or evaluative mediation.[37] However, at the consultation phase, it was recommended that mediation should refer to a 'non-advisory' facilitative process and 'conciliation' to an advisory or evaluative procedure or to a blended approach.[38]

As the mediation movement gained momentum across many different nations both in court initiatives and the private context, mediators and theorists began to develop and explain different mediation styles or models. Explicitly a divide developed between mediation champions who defend the neutral providing an 'evaluation' of the merits of the dispute to the participants and those who believed that there was only one 'true' or 'pure' form of mediation which is a facilitative process.[39]

Definition of mediation

In 1985, Goldberg et al. characterised mediation as the least 'intrusive' ADR procedure in that the mediator has no power to 'impose an outcome' on the parties.[40] In the USA, as mediation use expanded, research and commentators began to report on how the process and mediators worked in practice. Folberg and Taylor[41] categorised early mediation models by the context of practice (for example, family, labour, court-connected) or by reference to the procedures used by mediators (shuttle,[42] structured,[43] muscle,[44] or team[45]) or

---

35 See for example, Alexander (2008a) at 104
36 Gaitskell (2005b) at 292; Kendall (2000) at 84
37 National Mediator Accreditation Standards at 2(4)
38 Sourdin (2007)
39 Menkel-Meadow (1993) at 372
40 Goldberg et al. (1985) at 91
41 Folberg & Taylor (1984) at 130–46
42 Folberg & Taylor (1984) at 138. In shuttle mediation the mediator goes between the parties.
43 Folberg & Taylor (1984) at 136–7. Structured mediation has 'detailed rules of procedure' which gives a 'common set of procedural rules', which provides a sense of 'security' to the participants.
44 Folberg & Taylor (1984) at 135. Folberg & Taylor explain that in 'muscle mediation' the mediator 'acting as a closet arbitrator' 'tells the parties what is fair and appropriate' in the caucus.
45 Folberg & Taylor (1984) at 140–6. Team mediation allows the mediators to bring together more than one expert, which can 'enhance' the process.

the 'background' of the mediator[46] such as labour, therapeutic or lawyer-mediation. They describe mediation as a 'goal-directed, problem solving intervention', which is not only a 'forum for decision making' where disputes can be settled but is also a 'conflict management' tool.[47]

'Facilitative mediation' is perhaps the dominant mediator style[48] and the antecedent for models now described in the literature. In its 'purest form',[49] the mediator facilitates settlement by encouraging the parties to explore the underlying issues of their dispute and their 'needs' but also to 'acknowledge the dispute from the other side'.[50] The mediator helps the parties to generate 'consensual'[51] settlement outcomes, which do not have to be based on 'legal rights'.[52]

Rise of evaluative mediator practice

As mediation developed in the USA, a new type of practice gained recognition where the mediator role includes providing an evaluation of the parties' case or the potential outcomes of court action and proposing or developing settlement proposals.[53] The international and national literature progressively reveals that as court systems and governments 'embrace' mediation legal professions begin to recognise the opportunities this affords and embark on influencing mediation practice either as mediators or as advocates in the process.[54] Research from international and national sources suggest that the impact of legal dominance in mediation is accompanied by an escalation of evaluative mediators where the key objective for mediating becomes seeking monetary rather than party-created outcomes, which is attended by a rise in adversarial conduct in mediation as a new role emerges for legal representatives in the process.[55]

This growth in evaluative mediator practice led to criticism from facilitative adherents that it erodes the participants' self-determination, a 'fundamental' principle of mediation and one which 'distinguishes' it from adjudicatory processes.[56] Supporters of evaluative mediators countered that the practice is 'market driven' and therefore preserves party self-determination

46 Folberg & Taylor (1984) at 131
47 Folberg & Taylor (1984) at 8
48 Noce (2008); Jarrett (2009); Linden (2001)
49 Menkel-Meadow (1993) at 372
50 Alexander (2008a) at 111
51 Genn (2010) at 81
52 Folberg & Taylor (1984) at 7
53 Boulle et al. (1998) at 29
54 Roberts (1992) at 258. See Clark (2012). Clark reviews the influence of lawyers in mediation.
55 See for example, Baruch Bush & Pope (2002); Lowry (2000); Lande (2000); Stulberg (1997); Kovach & Love (1996) (1998); Menkel-Meadow (1997); Welsh (2001a,b); Clark (2012); Clark & Mays (1996); Mason (2012). For a review in England see Roberts (1992) (1993); Brooker (2007)
56 Welsh (2001b); See also Alfini (2008)

by supplying clients with a choice.[57] To address the debate and assist 'informed consent', Riskin published a framework delineating a mediator's 'orientation' to mediation, which used a grid with two crossing continuums to explain the approaches that mediators might adopt from evaluative-to-facilitative on one scale and broad-to-narrow on the other.[58] At the most evaluative point of Riskin's scale a mediator might put forward and press the parties to accept a specific settlement and at the other end the mediator uses facilitative communication techniques to encourage the parties to generate settlement options. Riskin suggests that mediators adopting a narrow orientation will consider outcomes for settlement on a 'distributive' basis, whereas when assuming a broad approach, might encourage the parties separately in the caucus to consider 'underlying interests' or future interactions between the parties or even the interests of parties outside the dispute.[59]

The publication of the grid reinforced the academic debate on the evaluative-facilitative divide in the USA, which has now manifested itself in many other countries where mediation is developing.[60] Arguments about the dangers of evaluative practice include exposing the parties to flawed recommendations without sufficient protection;[61] a lack of recognition of the different roles in training programmes;[62] constricting the mediator field to legally qualified persons;[63] threats to mediator ethics and neutrality[64] and a rise in adversarial behaviour in the process as the parties 'persuade' the mediator about their case:[65]

> The central characteristic of mediation is facilitated negotiation and the use of evaluative techniques both endangers the neutrality of the mediator and perpetuates an adversarial culture. 'Evaluative' mediation is an oxymoron. It jeopardizes neutrality because a mediator's assessment invariably favors one side over the other. Additionally, evaluative activities discourage understanding between and problem-solving by the parties. Instead, mediator evaluation tends to perpetuate or create an adversarial climate. Parties try to persuade the neutral of their positions, using confrontational and argumentative approaches. In some cases, the party whose position the mediator disfavored will simply leave the process.

---

57 See for example, Baruch Bush (2002)
58 Riskin (1996). Riskin made changes to the grid and terminology in a later article. The evaluative-facilitative continuum became directive-elicitive. See Riskin (2003) See also Alexander (2008a) at 99. Alexander explains and reviews a diverse range of mediation models.
59 Riskin (1996) at 29–32
60 See for example, Alexander (2006); Alexander (2008a, b)
61 See for example, Kovach & Love (1998); Menkel-Meadow (1997); Stipanowich (2001); Stemple (2000)
62 See for example, Kovach & Love (1996), (1998); Menkel-Meadow (1997)
63 See for example, Kovach & Love (1996) at 105
64 Kovach & Love (1996)
65 Kovach & Love (1996) at 31

Other mediation models

Mediators espouse other practices in addition to evaluative and facilitative styles and there are many categorisations of mediation models in the literature.[66] Some writers suggest the four 'primary' mediation processes are facilitative, evaluative, transformative and narrative.[67] However, the four 'paradigm models' described by Boulle and Nesic are facilitative, settlement, therapeutic and evaluative.[68] The literature complicates the understanding of mediation models by adopting different nomenclatures. For example, facilitative mediation is sometimes categorised as 'problem-solving, interest based,[69] or Harvard-method mediation'.[70] Another name given for 'settlement mediation' is 'compromise mediation'.[71] Boulle and Nesic describe transformative and therapeutic mediation as the same process and evaluative as 'advisory' or 'managerial mediation'.[72]

In the UK, there remains little publicity about mediator styles beyond facilitative and evaluative ones and little evidence that mediators use other approaches beyond these two or a combination of both in commercial non-family sectors.[73] Research suggests that the dominant style for mediator training is facilitative in the UK, although studies indicate that evaluative mediation is present in many settings and ADR organisations now offer 'advanced training', which is said to include evaluative interventions.[74] There is little evidence to suggest that mediators regularly practise or widely publicise transformative, narrative or therapeutic mediation though there may be an exception for family, community or reparation mediations[75] and in non-family civil disputes, mediators may use some of the techniques within their practice.[76]

Although commercial mediators in England usually adopt either a facilitative or an evaluative or 'blended approach' in mediation,[77] for completeness a brief description is given of other models or styles.

66 See for example, Alexander (2008b) at 8. Professor Alexander classifies six meta models: Expert Advisory, Wise Council, Tradition-based, Facilitative, Settlement and Transformative.
67 Boulle (2005). Boulle describes the key models as evaluative, facilitative, therapeutic and settlement. See also Boulle & Nesic (2001)
68 Boulle & Nesic (2001) at 31
69 Boulle & Nesic (2001) at 27
70 Jarrett (2009) at 54
71 Boulle & Nesic (2001) at 28
72 Boulle & Nesic (2001) at 28
73 Brooker (2007) notes the paucity of debate in UK mediation, apart from a few noteworthy exceptions. See for example: Roberts (2000); Dolder (2004); Genn (1998); Mulcahy (2001a); Clark & Mays (1996); Emery et al. (2005); Goriely et al. (2002). See more recently, Clark (2012)
74 See Brooker (2007) (2011)
75 Emery et al. (2005)
76 Brooker & Wilkinson (2010); Brooker (2011). Some UK mediators are accredited by the Institute of International Mediation (IMI) whose website has a search facility for mediator style. British mediators on this site indicate that they adopt a transformative style. See Brooker (2011) at 40
77 See Australian Standards of Mediator Practice (2008)

In transformative mediation, the mediator's role is one of 'empowering' the participants by supporting their 'decision-making' and enabling them to 'recognise' the other party's position.[78] Transformative mediators are more concerned with the parties 'learning' from the experience, gaining 'new skills' and an 'enhanced sense of control over their lives'.[79] A mediator using a narrative approach helps the parties to first articulate their conflict as a 'story' and then assists them 'reconstruct' it together.[80] Alexander explains that therapeutic mediators 'reject the negotiation paradigm'[81] and use 'therapeutic interventions', which are said to occur over many sessions[82] and focus on underlying conflict and 'behavioural' problems.[83]

Advantages and benefits of mediating

Quicker, less costly and less adversarial than litigation

The basis of early literature broadcast the advantages of informal procedures and highlight the problems with litigation with claims that ADR is quicker, less costly and less adversarial.[84] Advocates of mediation assert that savings in either costs or time occur by not taking a case all the way to court, or by clients restricting their legal representative's input to the mediation process, although commentators point out that comparisons are flawed because most cases settle before the expense of a court hearing.[85] One of the key promotional attributes of mediation that receives significant coverage in the literature are the high settlement rates of over 80 or even 90 per cent reported by mediators and mediation organisations, although empirical studies often suggest substantially lower rates are achieved.[86]

Party satisfaction

An important side effect of participating in mediation is that participants are reported to be more satisfied with their experience of the process and with the outcomes achieved, which are "tailor-made" to fit the 'outcome needs of the parties'.[87] Therefore, parties are more likely to stand by their settlement

---

78 Baruch Bush et al. (1996) at 729; Baruch Bush & Pope (2002). See generally, Baruch Bush & Folger (1994) (2005)
79 Hensler (2003) at 190; Noll (2001) at 83
80 Jarrett (2009) at 54. See also Linden (2001); Foster (2003)
81 Alexander (2008a) at 101
82 Oberman (2005) at 815
83 Waldman (1998). See also Emery et al. (2005)
84 See for example, Brown (1989); Carroll (1989) at 11; Douglas (1989); Gilvarry (1989); Williams (1987); Dixon & Carroll (1990); Royce (1989); Mackie (1992); Fenn (1991); Bevan (1992)
85 See for example, Genn (2010) (2012); Brunsdon-Tully (2009)
86 See for example, Genn (2010) (2012); Brunsdon-Tully (2009); Brooker & Lavers (2005a,b)
87 Goldberg et al. (1985) at 92

agreements, as they perceive them to be fair.[88] Goldberg et al. suggest that the experience of resolving their own dispute enhances their ability to resolve future problems 'without the need for external intervention'.[89]

'Consensus continuity, confidentiality and control'

The major benefits of mediation are sometimes categorised as 'consensus, continuity, confidentiality and control'.[90] There is consensus in that the parties consult with each other and agree to use the process, which provides the basis for exploring settlement and reaching mutually agreed outcomes.[91] Proponents of a non-adversarial approach maintain that it improves party relationships and by addressing a wider range of interests than just legal outcomes, presents opportunities to explore continuing commercial relationships or 'creative outcomes' such as future 'business arrangements'.[92] In contrast to litigation, mediation takes place in private and is confidential thereby avoiding adverse publicity or damage to reputations.[93]

Self-determination

One of the most important attributes is said to be self-determination because the parties can control the process from selection, design, outcome or even departure without settlement:[94]

> The vision of self-determination that inspired the contemporary mediation movement placed the disputants themselves at the center of the mediation process. They were the principal actors and creators within the process. It was assumed that the parties would actively and directly participate in the communication and negotiation that occurs during mediation, would choose and control the substantive norms to guide their decision-making, would create the options for settlement of their dispute, and ultimately would control the final decision regarding whether or not to settle their dispute in mediation. This vision of party self-determination assumed that, at the conclusion of a mediation, the parties would feel that the agreement they reached was their own.

Having reviewed the main claimed advantages of ADR and mediation the next section considers how first, the common law jurisdictions began to cast

---

88 Tyler (1988); Lind et al. (1989) cited in Zander (1995a); Goldberg et al. (1985) at 92
89 Goldberg et al. (1985) at 92
90 O'Connor (1992) at 108; Dixon & Carroll (1990)
91 Genn (2010) at 82
92 Stipanowich (2001) at 849
93 O'Connor (1992) at 108
94 Welsh (2001b) at 8

a "proprietary"[95] eye over these procedures in order to provide alternatives to litigation and then how government and court policies began a process of cementing mediation 'within' the formal process.[96]

The Modern ADR Movement in the USA

Empowerment

The Modern ADR Movement in Common Law countries started in the USA, first, Auerbach suggests, as a way of empowering local communities in the 1960s through the provision of mediators in neighbourhood and community-based 'law firms and court systems'.[97] Second, there was a growing rhetoric that the courts could not deal with the number of claims brought by an increasingly litigious people.[98] Although the perceived litigiousness of the American people is sometimes blamed for the congestion in the court system, research provides an alternative view that the cause was partly due the courts' inability to deal with the rapid expansion of the law.[99] The 'litigation explosion' was found to be more likely to be the result of an expanding body of 'new law' and 'rights law' as society became more complex.[100]

Alignment with legal reform

ADR began to have more impact in the USA when aligned with legal reform and to the 'access to justice' agenda at the National Conference on the Causes of Popular Dissatisfaction with the Administration of Justice (Pound Conference) in 1976.[101] Nader describes how the gathering of law educators and practitioners at the conference speaking on the complaints of the administration of justice centred on an 'ideology of consent' which exploited a 'harmony ideology for legal reform' in the rhetoric of ADR as a way of addressing all that was wrong with litigation:[102]

> The rhetoric of ADR builds on the ideology of consent, hiding relations of force behind the notions of persuasion and mutual accord. The drama set the stage for the alternative dispute resolution movement. Each man in turn spoke about some version of the following complaints: The courts are crowded; American lawyers are too adversarial and the American

---

 95 Roberts (1992) at 238
 96 Clark (2012) at 96
 97 Auerbach (1983) at 116–17
 98 See for example, Goldberg et al. (1985) at 4–5; Auerbach (1983)
 99 Galanter (1983) (1986); Nader (1988); Alschuler (1986)
100 Galanter (1996) (1986); Nader (1988); Galanter (1983) (1986); Alschuler (1988)
101 Nader (1988); Stemple (1996); Kovach (2006)
102 Nader (1988) at 275; Nader (1993) at 6

people too litigious; new tribunals are needed to divert cases generated by the regulated welfare state; 'cumulative tinkering' should be adopted as a strategy, a way of creeping in with reform. Furthermore, alternative dispute agencies were portrayed as agencies of settlement or reconciliation, peace rather than war.

Furthermore, Nader observed that the 'ideology of harmony' began to be believed and 'institutionalised' as a 'movement' for legal reform, which was 'anti-litigation':[103]

> The harmony law model was for some anti-law, anti-confrontation, anti-anger, and for many a response to the 'too many rights' movement. Furthermore, the ADR movement was being spearheaded by the Chief Justice of the U.S. Supreme Court.

At the Pound Conference, Professor Sanders introduced what later became a new concept of the ADR movement, the 'multi-door court house', where the courts administer a number of mechanisms for the most appropriate disposal of the case in order that the courts work 'more effectively' and cases not requiring judicial expertise are deflected to other procedures:[104]

> It is important to recognize that the ADR movement is not an anti-court movement, as is often asserted. It is an effort to have the courts more effectively doing those things that they are peculiarly fit to do, and have other institutions like arbitration and mediation dispose of those cases that don't require the specialized expertise of courts. That is the idea behind the multi-door courthouse – a comprehensive justice center where cases are screened and analyzed so that they can be referred to that process or sequence of processes that's best suited to provide an effective and responsive resolution.

Development of arbitration in the USA as an ADR process

Hensler notes that mediation was not the primary process in the early ADR movement in the USA.[105] Many state and federal court systems adopted court-annexed arbitration[106] for small claims in the early 1970s and some judges and lawyers began to call arbitration systems and settlement conferences ADR.[107] The attraction of arbitration eventually began to lose

---

103 Nader (1993) at 6
104 Sanders (2000) at 5; see Hensler (2003) at 174
105 Hensler (2003)
106 Hensler (2003) at 177. Hensler indicates that these methods included mandatory non-binding arbitration, court annexed arbitration or 'judicial arbitration'.
107 Hensler (2003) at 178

out to the more flexible process of mediation when commercial users began to complain that the procedure had become as slow and expensive as litigation as lawyers relocated their 'normal' practices into arbitrating.[108] Hensler suggests that users became less enamoured with arbitration as the courts began to take an increasingly 'rigid' approach to contractual arbitration agreements and arbitrator's decisions, which reduced the parties' rights to appeal whereas in contrast the parties retain their right to litigate if they choose mediation.[109]

The Modern Mediation Movement in the USA

Experimentation, implementation to institutionalisation

The Modern Mediation Movement in the USA is said to have increased pace from the 1970s, and then transferred to England and Australia in the 1980s and to European civil countries and South Africa in the 1990s.[110] Academics identify three phases to the movement in the USA, from experimentation, to implementation and institutionalisation, although some writers extend the final stage to incorporate regulation.[111] These phases provide an analogy with the current developments in the English jurisdiction albeit from a start date nearly 20 years on:[112]

> The dalliance with mediation in different jurisdictions, although respectively often widely divergent in terms of pace of development and time of origin, has tended to follow a similar pattern: first there is 'discovery' of the process by interested professionals; second, there is 'experimentation' by these professionals who may organise themselves into groupings to promote the practice of the process; and third, there is some form of underpinning, promotion or legitimisation by government or the formal legal system and an attendant institutionalisation of the process occurs.

Hensler charts the USA developments with mediation from the mid 1970s to the 1990s.[113] First, in the 1970s community justice centres and then small claims courts experimented with mediation. This was followed in the 1980s when mediation programmes were set up for specialised disputes such

---

108 Hensler (2003) at 182
109 See for example, Hensler (2003) at 183–4; Riggs & Schenk (1990); Stipanowich (1996)
110 Alexander (2006) at 1
111 Sanders (2007) at 599. Sanders identifies three phases to the modern ADR movement as experimentation, criticism and finally institutionalisation. See also Kovach (2006) at 390–1. Kovach describes three phases: experimentation, implementation and regulation. See also Menkel-Meadow (1991); Goldberg et al. (1985) at 6–9
112 Clark (2012) at 7
113 Hensler (2003) at 180–5

as 'child custody' and 'family law issues' and for 'money disputes' in the 1990s all with the aim of alleviating pressure from the courts.[114]

Experimentation

Experimentation was followed 'rapidly by implementation' but not, as Kovach and others observe, with an appropriate level of consideration for the 'legal, ethical and practical issues' which currently shape mediation practice in the USA.[115] State and federal courts use different 'triggering mechanisms' to implement mediation.[116] Kovach describes the divergent court approaches for initiating mediation ranging from encouraging the parties to mediate on a voluntary basis to more 'controversially' compelling attendance but the most 'widespread' method in the USA is the 'court order' which is also called 'court-annexed mediation'.[117]

Institutionalisation

As mediation became entrenched in the court systems in the USA, the next phase of development was institutionalisation. The concept has been used in a narrow context of exploring mediation court programmes, which result in 'regular and significant use of mediation'.[118] Press describes institutionalisation as when 'any entity (governmental or otherwise) which as an entity, adopts ADR procedures as part of doing business' and includes schemes for mediation in schools, government agencies and courts programmes all of which develop rules and regulations for use.[119] For Sanders the principal aim of this phase is to make the consideration of mediation a 'seamless' part of the process of dispute resolution rather than putting the onus on 'disputants' to initiate its use:[120]

> We are now in the midst of the third phase, which can be characterized under the rubric of 'Institutionalization' or 'Mainstreaming.' The principal aim of this effort is to seek ways of working mediation into the fabric of dispute resolution, so mediation will be naturally considered in the process of resolving disputes, rather than putting the burden on the disputant who wants to invoke mediation.

Kovach describes how state and federal laws have consolidated the institutionalisation of mediation in the USA through various 'court programmes'

---

114 Hensler (2003) at 182
115 Kovach (2006) at 390
116 Alexander (2008b) at 14
117 Kovach (2006) at 396–8
118 McAdoo et al. (2003) at 8
119 Press (2003–2004) at 904
120 Sanders (2007) at 599

and 'methods of court referral'.[121] Since 1998, federal courts are required to provide ADR programmes and by 2003 over half of all state courts and nearly all federal courts are reported to have mediation programmes in place.[122] Judges may refer appropriate cases from their lists or cases are diverted through 'local rules', which either mandate participation or treat it as a 'pretrial procedure' to remain on the court list, or a mediation date may be set before the parties can proceed to trial, which Kovach observes limits potential savings and time because of the late use.[123] Often courts introduce 'opt out' provisions but these also vary in design such as 'lodging objections' or identifying specific cases which are unsuitable and the parties' 'objections' are not treated the same, as they are either accepted or the judge uses 'discretion' as to whether a mediation order is still made.[124]

Effect of institutionalisation in court programmes

An influential factor in the expansion of mediation in USA has been the escalating number of court mediation schemes, which not only raised the level of awareness of potential users but also changed lawyers' attitudes towards mediating.[125] Many researchers and promoters of mediation identified the reticence of the USA legal profession to use or recommend mediation, as the chief inhibiter of mediation growth.[126] Research suggested lawyers lacked knowledge about the mediation process, feared competition in the dispute resolution market threatening their income and sometimes held perceptions about strategic disadvantages in mediating such as proposing mediation would have implied a weak case or using the process could reveal trial strategies.[127] Empirical studies demonstrate that court exposure to mediation, unsurprisingly perhaps, increases 'familiarity' with the process and experience leads to more positive perceptions about mediating.[128] However, it also established an association between the rising number of court schemes and the dominance of lawyers in the process with the consequence that participants progressively experience a reduced role in mediation.[129] Researchers found that as lawyers became more involved in court schemes and in private mediations, there was an escalation in evaluative mediator practice, where lawyers use more 'directive' approaches such as

---

121 Kovach (2006) at 397–8
122 Alternative Dispute Resolution Act 1998. See Kovach (2006) at 397; see also Hensler (2003) at 185
123 Kovach (2006) at 397–8
124 Kovach (2006) at 398. For example, Kovach identifies domestic violence as a limiting factor.
125 Hensler (2003) reports that practically all Federal Courts and half of the State courts in the USA administer mediation schemes.
126 See for example, Stipanowich (1996) (2004); Wissler (2004); Rogers & McEwen (1998)
127 Kovach (2006) at 394; Stipanowich (1996); Wissler (2004)
128 Wissler (2004); Rogers & McEwen (1998); Stipanowich (1996) (2004)
129 See Stipanowich (1996) Wissler (2004); Rogers & McEwen (1998)

predicting court outcomes or evaluating party cases and there was a prolifera-
tion of adversarial conduct from legal advocates within the process.[130]

Regulation of mediation practice in the USA

The presented picture of mediation in the USA is that of the institutionalisation
of the process, with lawyers having considerable influence over its
practice. Within this framework, Kovach reports that mediation is entering
another phase, which involves 'overt attempts to regulate practice'[131] by
either 'states or interested groups',[132] which many report is the natural
progression as a new mediators' profession develops.[133] Different state and
mediation programmes, however, evidence a plethora of systems to regulating
practitioners, which Kovach suggests are based on two approaches, one
developing ethical guidelines or codes of practice and the other establishing
standard qualifications usually based at either state or programme levels.[134]
However, training and provider organisations also provide 'conditions' for
practice, based on 'minimum levels of training, competency and continuing
developing education' and accreditation of mediators who reach these
standards.[135]

Regulation and the diversity-consistency debate

Central to regulating and accrediting practice is the challenge of finding
an inclusive definition of mediation, which encompasses different approaches
to mediating, which were discussed above.[136] Definitional debates are particularly intense when they involve regulating mediation and the development
of mediator standards of practice, which are either nationally defined (see
Australia) or specified for particular mediation programmes.[137] The tension
centres on what Alexander defines as a 'diversity-consistency debate' where
the interests of consumer protection conflict with the desire of mediators
to continue 'innovative' and 'flexible' practice.[138] It has specific implications for practice if the definition of mediation used to regulate activity
excludes evaluative interventions by the mediator as a way of preserving self-
determination. As mediation develops internationally, most countries come
to the stage of regulating activity, particularly when a mediator profession

130 Genn (1998) at 10; Nolan-Haley (1998); Brad Reich (2002); McAdoo & Hinshaw (2002);
     Thompson (2004); Wissler (2004); Hensler (2001); Menkel-Meadow (1997); Mason
     (2012)
131 Kovach (2006) at 420
132 Mosten (2004) at 293
133 See for example, Alexander (2008a, b); Mills (2005); Boon et al. (2007)
134 Kovach (2006) at 425
135 Kovach (2006) at 430
136 Hensler (2003); Alexander (2008b); Alexander (2006)
137 Alexander (2008b) at 2
138 Alexander (2008b) at 2; Sourdin (2007)

begins to develop and when different professions compete to control the market.[139]

The following section reviews the ADR movement in England and Wales where it is possible to draw an analogy to the progression of events in the USA as people sought to find alternatives as an adversarial system took grip of litigation.

ADR Movement in England and Wales

Early alternatives in England and Wales

Seeking alternatives to the formal system is not a new phenomenon in England, the origins of the Common Law date back to the Middle Ages[140] but there was "pluralistic" legal system of customary law, 'old communal courts', Ecclesiastical Courts and the Law Merchants which existed together but had their own jurisdiction.[141]

> These were not just simply separate systems with a separate technical jurisdiction. They were competitive, contending courts with an overlapping jurisdiction answerable to different authorities.[142]

The common law system 'subsumed' these alternative forums as successive kings elected to control their subjects through state regulation and state-controlled courts.[143] However, over time many groups and individuals have sought to bypass the jurisdiction of the Common Law by seeking redress from other tribunals or persons perceived to be more suited and better informed about the dispute in hand.[144] For example, Holdsworth describes how in the Middle Ages the courts of the Law Merchants provided legal codes for commercial disputes throughout Europe and the development of Courts of Equity illustrates how people avoided the rigours of the Common Law and by seeking equitable relief.[145] Behrens charts the history of Church Courts revealing that Ecclesiastical Courts from the early Middle Ages used mediation and during the Reformation after adopting the Roman law utilised an investigative 'cognitio procedure' which 'allowed' mediation to continue until an adversarial approach was introduced in 1850.[146] Arthurs describes

---

139 See for example, Alexander (2008b); Boon et al. (2007); Meyer & Leathes (2008); Clark (2012) at 74–9
140 Holdsworth (1922) Vol. 15 at 449; Baker (1988) at 155–72; Van Canegegem (1988)
141 See for example, Arthurs (1984); Bradney & Cownie (2000) at 11; Holdsworth (1922)
142 Bradney & Cownie (2000) at 11–12
143 Woolford & Ratner (2008) at 41; Holdsworth (1922)
144 See for example, Holdsworth (1922); Arthurs (1984)
145 Holdsworth (1922); Nolan-Haley (2004). Nolan-Haley discusses the similarity between equity and mediation as alternatives.
146 Behrens (2002) at 140–1

how England maintained over 300 local and specialised courts up until the 1830s but these disappeared as industrialisation increased the need for central control and increased state supervision both in the lives of its citizens and in business activities.[147]

Arbitration

One dispute resolution system that has a long history as an alternative to the common law and other courts in England is arbitration. In the USA arbitration was one of the early ADR procedures which grew to prominence in the 1970s (see above) but in the UK it has been an alternative forum to litigation dating back to Roman times.[148] It had particular appeal to business in the 19th century because of the costs and delay involved in litigating but another important factor was that commercial parties were (and still are) able to appoint arbitrators with technical expertise in the field of dispute rather than judges who may lack specialist knowledge.[149] Arthurs suggests that the business world preferred decisions based on commercial norms rather than legal precedence.[150]

A review of arbitration shows that it was not assimilated into the common law as were other tribunals and courts but was endowed with a 'legal status' through successive cases and statutes which provided for a 'symbiotic relationship with the formal law'.[151] Statute law ensured that parties who had voluntarily agreed to arbitrate could not defy arbitrators' decisions or sidestep arbitration by going straight to the court.[152] One of the most significant enactments institutionalising[153] arbitration and providing a special connection with the court was the introduction of the 'case stated mechanism', which permitted courts to stay proceedings for parties to arbitrate if they had agreed to use the procedure and gave arbitrators the "power" to ask the court for an opinion on their award:[154]

> The most important development was the Common Law Procedure Act of 1854 which gave the courts power to stay court proceedings where the parties had agreed to arbitrate disputes, and it empowered arbitrators to state their awards in the form of a special case for the opinion of the court. This was the basis of the case-stated mechanism

---

147 Arthurs (1984)

148 Abrahams (1988)

149 For a discussion on arbitration developments see for example: Ferguson (1980); Parris (1978); Lane (1986); Parker (1959); Flood & Caiger (1993)

150 Arthurs (1984)

151 Arthurs (1984); Brooker (1999) at 12

152 See An Act for Determining Differences by Arbitration 1698; An Act for the Further Amendment of the Law, and the Better Advancement of Justice 1833

153 See for example, Yarn (2004)

154 Jaffe (1989) at 185

which until 1979 provided the most important mechanism for reviewing arbitral awards.

Parker describes how arbitrators acquired enhanced statutory powers to compel attendance and examine witnesses but the court retained its supremacy through the right of reviewing arbitration for "procedural irregularities" and "mistakes of law".[155] 'Arbitration was not so much suppressed by the courts as captured by them.'[156]

Legal monopoly and juridification of arbitration

Arbitration to the present day continues as an alternative to litigation but by the 20th century it had been 'appropriated' by the legal professions, which may have been one explanation for the support given by the formal system.[157] Arthurs described how a 'powerful lawyers' lobby' was involved in statutory developments in arbitration but this close association is blamed for encroaching 'legalism'.[158] Arbitration eventually began to resemble a court procedure by mimicking adversarial litigation, where lawyers provided legal representation and even became the arbitrators.[159] By the 20th century, the problems of arbitration were manifold: Arbitrators were accused of being frightened of appeals if they departed from court-like procedures; lawyers were blamed for 'hijacking'[160] the process and 'seeking to blind [non-legal advisors] with legal science'.[161] Flood and Caiger explore how lawyers monopolised the field of construction arbitration from other professional experts, through a process of juridification where they had the 'power of appropriation' because of their 'power over legalism'.[162] The problems with arbitration eventually led to the 1996 Arbitration Act which provided arbitrators with 'the power to adopt procedures suitable to the circumstances of the particular case, avoiding unnecessary delay or expense' (cl 33(1) (b)),

---

155 Parker (1959)
156 Arthurs (1984) at 71
157 Arthurs (1984); Flood & Caiger (1993)
158 Arthurs (1984); Flood & Caiger (1993)
159 See for example, Brooker (1999); Brooker (1997) Brooker (1997) notes that in 1920 arbitrators criticised parties for bringing their lawyers to arbitration: Expensive Arbitration *The Journal of the Institute of Arbitrators* (1920)
160 Bingham (1992)
161 DAC (1996) at 153; Bingham (1992); Flood & Caiger (1993)
162 Flood & Caiger (1993) at 440. See also at 413. The authors observe Pierre Bourdieu's thesis. See Bourdieu (1987) at 817 'The juridical field is the site of a competition for monopoly of the right to determine the law. Within this field there occurs a confrontation among actors possessing a technical competence which is inevitably social and which consists essentially in the socially recognized capacity to interpret a corpus of texts sanctifying a correct or legitimized vision of the social world. It is essential to recognize this in order to take account that all "social fields" illustrate power struggles between different groups and that in the "juridical field" is the site of a competition for monopoly for the right to determine law.'

although these arrangements have not altogether increased the fortunes of domestic arbitration, particularly in the construction arena which began to face competition from statutory adjudication.[163]

Arbitration is used as an analogy for mediation developments because of its long history as an alternative before becoming inextricably intertwined with litigation with its own statutory framework and a vast body of law-delineating practice. The involvement of lawyers in mediation will be discussed below but the legal professions have been instrumental in the development of many alternatives to litigation.

Modern ADR Movement in England and Wales

Early initiatives

Apart from arbitration, before the 1990s ADR was limited to a small number of neighbourhood schemes and to established mechanisms in the construction industry such as expert determination or conciliation in the ICE contracts.[164] There was however, some experimentation, particularly in the construction field with new procedures such as mini-trials and expert panels such as those used on the Channel Tunnel development.[165] Generally there was little awareness of mediation activity in the UK other than recent 'converts' returning from training in the USA who disseminated the positive advantages of using mediation.[166]

The first ADR providers established in England in 1989–1990, IDR Europe Ltd (now ADR Group) and CEDR (Centre for Dispute Resolution), raised the profile of mediation and provided mediator training to the commercial sector.[167] The legal professions demonstrated an early 'proprietary interest' as lawyers began training as mediators and their professional bodies were involved in developing ADR policy.[168] Reports from some commercial sectors feared lawyers would 'monopolise'[169] these developments by acting as mediators or advising in the process or, more cynically, through 'defensive marketing' where lawyers assure clients that ADR is excellent for most cases except for the 'unique' features of their dispute, which requires litigation.[170]

---

163 Arbitration Act 1996 cl 33(1) (b). For a review of adjudication see for example; Kennedy & Milligan (2008)

164 Projects and organisations offering neighbourhood and community mediation began early in the 1980s. See Young (1989) who reported on findings from the Sandwell project in the West Midlands. For a review of ADR developments see Mistelis (2001) (2006)

165 See *Channel Tunnel Group v. Balfour Beatty* [1993] AC 334. The contractual arrangement was for disputes to go to a panel of experts.

166 Bucklow (2006)

167 Mistelis (2001)

168 Roberts (1993) at 238. See also Roberts (1992); Robertshaw & Segal (1993)

169 Brooker (1999) at 26; Brooker & Lavers (2000); Roberts (1992); Davies (1992)

170 Miles (1992) at 313. See Clark (2012) at 85–6

Rule 1: The strategy – keep the old products (and the fees that go with them) while manipulating the image to suggest the new service is on offer.

Rule 2: The tactic – suggest to the client that nearly every case is suitable for ADR except the one he has in front of him where unique circumstances apply requiring 'that old adversarial magic'.

Legal professions' interest in ADR

In 1991, both of the legal professional bodies, the Bar Council and the Law Society, published reports on ADR and recommended leading roles for their members in policy developments.[171] Professor Roberts was highly critical of the Beldham report for failing to take into consideration the 'diverse interests' of government and the courts and with both the Bar and Law Society for the central role that they envisaged for their members.[172] Furthermore, he voiced concerns that the 'colonisation' of mediation by the legal professions threatened the process because of the problems lawyers would have in transferring their traditional adversarial skills to those of facilitative processes:[173]

> . . . . . we must recognise the uncomfortable truth that lawyers pose a particular threat to the integrity of mediation. Facilitatory mediation of the kind envisaged by the Committee is a difficult task requiring skills and experience very different from those acquired in the practice of litigation. As active, dominant professionals, accustomed to occupying partisan advisory and representative roles, lawyers should recognise that they may have great difficulty in adapting to the posture of impartial facilitator of other peoples' decision making.

Court interest in ADR

Court practice statements and ADR initiatives

Some members of the judiciary were quick to recognise the potential ADR might have for alleviating delay in the courts and the rising number of cases.[174] In 1993, the Commercial Court issued a practice statement requiring

---

171 Beldham (1991); Brown (1991)
172 Roberts (1993); Beldham Report (1991) at 16. The report proposed that lawyers with at least seven years experience should be used as mediators. Brown (1991)
173 Roberts (1992) at 261
174 Genn (2010) at 33–7. Genn updated the case statistics from the QBD and the Country Courts previously analysed by Kritzer (2004). Her analysis shows a steep increase in trials from 1938 to 1990 followed by a decline. Professor Genn suggests that litigation growth in England up to 1990 shows a similar pattern to that observed in the USA thus supporting Galanter's theory that the rise in litigation rates are related to an increase in 'rights'. See Galanter (1983) (1986) See also, Mistelis (2001) (2006)

the parties to complete an 'amended' questionnaire before the court hearing indicating whether they had considered ADR or mediation and, specifically, whether an alternative might be used when the costs of litigation were 'disproportionate' to the dispute.[175] Other divisions of the High Court and the Court of Appeal followed suit and in 1996, the Commercial Court practice direction was updated[176] and encouraged judges to use their power to make an 'ADR order' staying proceeding until an 'early neutral evaluation' (ENE) was undertaken by a judge or other expert.[177]

From 1996–1998, the committee of the Commercial Court undertook a review of the workings of the ADR practice direction and the findings persuaded the committee that ADR had much to offer litigants in terms of costs, early settlement, 'improved range of outcomes' and continuing relationships but could, moreover, provide a 'substantial contribution to the more efficient use of judicial resources'.[178] Interestingly in view of the government proposal for compulsory mediation for financially small cases in 2011,[179] the working party rejected the court adopting either a mandatory or a more active role of investigating why parties fail to use ADR because it was felt that this would 'impinge on areas of privilege'.[180] Further, the report did not recommend the implementation of costs sanctions as it was thought that such a measure would not induce implacable parties to mediate and might lead to 'spurious' reasons for rejecting ADR which the court would have to accept if 'superficially plausible'.[181] The working party opted to continue with 'persuasive' rather than coercive action and commended the continuance of the 1996 practice direction.[182]

Modern Mediation Movement in England and Wales

Early mediation projects

ADR or more specifically mediation was slowly entering the psyche of professionals and judges in the legal arena, but despite the early rhetoric and professional training of mediators, these did not translate into large numbers of mediations taking place in England in the 1990s.[183] Professor Genn's

---

175 Practice Statement, 10 December 1993 [1994] 1 WLR 14; [1994] 1 All ER 34. See Mistelis (2006). Mistelis summarises the key events of the ADR movement in England from 1960–2006 and records the Court Practice developments.
176 Practice Direction, 7 June 1996 [1996] 1 All ER 383; [1996] 1 WLR 1024
177 Practice Statement (Commercial Cases: Alternative Dispute Resolution) 7 June 1996 [1996] 1 All ER 383. See Mistelis (2006) at 146
178 Commercial Court Working Party on ADR (1998) at (v). For a more detailed overview of the report see Mistelis (2006) at 147–8
179 Commercial Court Working Party (1998) at (i) & (ii)
180 Commercial Court Working Party (1998) at (i) & (ii)
181 Commercial Court Working Party (1998) at (iii)
182 Commercial Court Working Party (1998) at 2
183 See Genn (2010) at 98

Report on one of the first pilot schemes in the London County Court found that less than 5 per cent of invitations to take part resulted in mediation and suggested that many legal professionals lacked awareness about ADR or were sceptical about using mediation.[184] The Court of Appeal introduced a mediation scheme in 1997 but experienced similar low uptake rates with only 2 per cent of those invited mediating which totalled 39 mediations.[185] The report concluded that mediation was in all probability an unattractive option at this stage in litigation after one party had already had a successful judgment at court and both parties would have expended considerable costs to that point.[186]

Lord Woolf's review of civil litigation

At the same time that the committee of the Commercial Court reported on the ADR, the then Lord Chancellor tasked Lord Woolf to undertake a review of civil litigation, the findings of which were published in an interim report in 1995 and a final report in 1996.[187] Lord Woolf highlighted the main 'defects' of costs, time and adversarialism in litigation in the Overview to the Final Report.[188]

Criticism of the legal professions and adversarialism

In the interim report the legal professions were blamed for the 'uncontrolled nature of litigation'[189] and for their part in nurturing the adversarial system through an 'excessive(ly) combative environment',[190] where the court rules were routinely manipulated or ignored, intimidating tactics were employed and costs and delay were ubiquitous:[191]

> Such exploitation is endemic in the system: the complexity of civil procedure itself enables the financially stronger or more experienced party to spin out proceedings and escalate costs, by litigating on technical procedural points or peripheral issues instead of focusing on the real substance of the case. All too often, such tactics are used to intimidate the weaker party and produce a resolution of the case which is either unfair or is achieved at a grossly disproportionate cost or after unreasonable delay.

---

184 Genn (1998)
185 Genn (2002) at 78
186 Genn (2002) at 98
187 Lord Woolf Interim Report (1995); Lord Woolf Final Report (1996)
188 Lord Woolf (1996) at 2
189 Woolf (1995) at 1.3.1
190 Woolf (1996) at 1.4.1
191 Woolf (1995) at 5

Civil justice reform

Lord Woolf proposed three key approaches to tackling the problems: judicial control, a tiered procedural system and sanctions for non-compliance with the new rules.[192] Recommendations for reform included introducing three tracking routes for cases according to financial size and complexity (small claims under £3,000;[193] fast-track for claims under £10,000 and multi-track for complex or high-value claims) with timetables for fixed schedules and court appearances.[194] There were to be new rules for limiting discovery[195] and single expert witnesses[196] to tackle some of the abuses of the 'multi-million pound litigation support industry'.[197] Litigation was to 'be less adversarial' with an expectation that parties would 'cooperate with each other' and act reasonably in the litigation.[198] Control of the case was to be taken away from the lawyers and given to courts to 'manage' through the process of judicial case management.[199] Judges were to have powers to 'intervene and impose sanctions', not only for breaches of the rules but also when the parties conducted litigation in an 'unreasonable or oppressive manner'.[200] It was to be the judicial application of the costs rules for unreasonable conduct which would drive the agenda for settlement through using alternative procedures.

Lord Woolf's proposals for ADR and mediation

In a chapter devoted to ADR in the Interim Report, Lord Woolf acknowledged not only the benefits that the diverse procedures offered for litigants but also the advantages for apportioning civil justice resources.[201] However, the report did not recommend compulsory ADR because court provision in England was not as grave as in other jurisdictions but recommended instead that ADR should be encouraged both outside the courts prior to beginning proceedings and during litigation by providing the opening for the parties to explore settlement and consider using alternatives.[202] These recommendations were based on the practice statements 'pioneered' in the commercial court and required the parties at the case management conference and the pre-trial review 'to state whether the question of ADR had been discussed and, if not why not'.[203] Lord Woolf, however, went further than the

---

192 Zander (1997) at 211
193 The maximum for small track is now £5,000. See Practice Direction 27. Current proposals are that small claims should go up to disputes of £10,000
194 Armstrong (1995)
195 Woolf (1995) Chapter 12
196 Woolf (1995) Chapter 13
197 Woolf (1996) Final Report Chapter 12 at 2
198 Woolf (1996) Overview at 9
199 Woolf (1995) at 5
200 Woolf (1996) Chapter 6 Sanctions: Recommendations at 3
201 Woolf (1995). See Chapter 18
202 Woolf (1995) Chapter 18 at 3. See Roberts (2000)
203 Woolf (1996) Recommendation 39. See Palmer & Roberts (1998) at 456

Commercial Working Party on ADR were prepared to go by recommending that the court should be able 'to take into account the litigants' unreasonable refusal to attempt ADR when considering their conduct in litigation'.[204] The intended effect was that the court should take a more pro-active role than simply encouraging ADR to that of penalising the parties for non-use when the courts considered the parties' conduct in litigation. Litigation was not the only method of resolving disputes and not always the most appropriate and the role of the court was to raise awareness about ADR.[205] In the final report, Lord Woolf continued to believe that litigants should not be mandated to use ADR, but recommended that the court should have the power to sanction a party for unreasonably refusing a court proposal to attempt ADR or an offer to mediate and that a court should be able to take into consideration when a party 'acts uncooperatively in the course of ADR'.[206]

In the Final Report, encouraging ADR was to be a essential feature of the duty placed on judges in case management when they were expected to 'explore ADR and settlement with the parties'.[207] However, in the Interim Report Lord Woolf warned of the dangers of ADR becoming 'too institutionalised' after reviewing the experience of arbitration, which was described as 'litigation behind closed doors'.[208]

Criticisms of the Woolf Reforms

Prior to the implementation of the Civil Procedural Rules (CPR), which put into effect Lord Woolf's proposals, there was considerable academic debate about whether the reforms would engender the desired outcomes. Specific to some of the criticism was the lack of research undertaken on either the causes of the problems, or on the proposed methods for addressing them which it was argued were based on 'anecdotal' evidence;[209] there was also concern that the reforms would not be adequately financed, which might jeopardise their success.[210]

Zuckerman alleged that the reforms would be unlikely to restrain the legal professions from seeking ways to thwart the rules in order to 'maximise profits', which they had achieved in all the previous reforms.[211] Critics were sceptical about judicial case management because it would require a

---

204 Woolf (1996) Recommendation 40
205 Woolf (1996). See Chapter 18 at 1
206 Woolf (1996) Overview Chapter 18. See Recommendation 41
207 Woolf (1996) Chapter 5 at 11 (c)
208 Woolf Interim Report (1995) Chapter 18 at 22
209 See Genn (2010) at 62–5 at 62; Dehn (1995); Zander (1995a, b); Zander (1997)
210 See for example, Greenslade (1996)
211 Zuckerman (1996a); Zuckerman (1996b) at 782–3. Zuckerman provided examples of how the Reforms will 'provide incentives for exaggerating the value of claims and their complexity in order to escape the fast track'.

significant 'cultural change' for judges and involve training.[212] Jolowicz suggested that increasing the control that judges have in limiting evidence and in controlling multi-track cases might lead 'inadvertently' to managing judges adopting an inquisitorial rather than an adversarial approach.[213] There was also disquiet about the increased level of judicial discretion provided for in the rules which would lead to uncertainty and inconsistency in their application, which Zander doubted could be addressed through Lord Woolf's suggestion of judicial training because 'the discretion is the discretion to judge':[214]

> Case management means, by definition, a vast increase in judicial discretion. Over and over again in the Woolf Report one reads, 'the judge will decide', 'the judge will direct', 'the judge will have a discretion', 'the judge will have the power to . . .' I do not regard it as an improvement in the system if similar procedural issues are routinely decided by different judges in different ways . . . Inconsistent decisions will not simply increase. They will be everywhere. For me that is a considerable diminution in the quality of justice.

The Woolf Reforms involved a shift in the role of the court for providing a forum for dispute resolution between citizens to one of 'promoting settlement'.[215] Roberts contended that the introduction of case management signified the intention of government to expand court control into the private informal sphere and surmised that the legal professions would be disconcerted with judicial involvement in 'legal negotiation strategies', which would ultimately lead to a new 'unsupervised space' where lawyers explore ADR prior to the case management meeting, with a 'plausible demand for quick run through to judgment': 'So, paradoxically, the new arrangements may lead to the development of a discrete unsupervised pre-litigation phase in which serious negotiation take place.'[216]

Civil Procedure Rules 1998

Overriding objective and case management

The Civil Procedure Rules (1998) created an 'overriding objective'[217] for the courts to 'deal with cases justly',[218] which includes: 'ensuring the parties

---

212 Zander (1995b); Zander (2009). Professor Zander has recently suggested that available research on the effectiveness of case management from both the USA and Australia is 'discouraging' in relation to time, costs, satisfaction or fairness.
213 Jolowicz (1996) at 210
214 Zander (1997) at 238; Zander (1996)
215 Roberts (2000) at 739–40
216 Roberts (2000) 746–7 at 740 & 747
217 CPR 1.1.(1)
218 CPR 1.1.(2)

are on an equal footing',[219] 'saving expense',[220] 'dealing with the case pro-
portionately',[221] 'ensuring the case is dealt with expeditiously and fairly'[222]
and allocating 'appropriate court resources'.[223] The court has a duty under
rule 1.4 to further the overriding objective by 'actively managing cases' which
is defined in rule 1.4.2(a)–(j) of the rules. Settlement is a core principle of the
overriding objectives and the court must 'encourage the parties to co-operate
with each other in the conduct of the proceedings'[224] which includes using
ADR 'if the court considers that appropriate and facilitating the use of such a
procedure'.[225]

The Rules provide further powers for the court to promote ADR in rule
26.4. A party may request in writing a stay[226] and a court on its 'own initiative'
is permitted to authorise a 'stay' of proceedings while the parties attempt
ADR[227] or if all the parties make a request to the court.[228]

Pre-action protocols

Lord Woolf's final report also set out proposals for developing pre-action
protocols in specialised areas of litigation such as personal injury, medical
negligence or technical and construction disputes, which were to 'set out
codes of sensible practice' and should 'focus the attention of the parties' on the
'early but well-informed settlement'.[229] The aims of pre-action protocols are
to encourage the settlement of the dispute without starting a court action
and to support the efficient management of cases that do go to a hearing.[230]
To achieve these aims the parties are encouraged to '(1) exchange information'
about the issues and (2) consider using a form of 'Alternative Dispute
Resolution'.[231] Although the pre-action protocols and court guides are all
slightly different, in essence they require the parties to meet at a set time after
the respondent has replied in writing to the claim to discuss the possibility
of using ADR and at the first Court Management Meeting to report to
the judge on the 'efficacy of ADR, the appropriate timing of ADR and the
advantages and disadvantages of a short stay of proceedings to allow ADR to
take place'.[232]

---

219 CPR 1.1.(2) (a)
220 CPR 1.1.(2) (b)
221 CPR 1.1.(2) (c)
222 CPR 1.1.(2) (d)
223 CPR 1.1.(2) (e)
224 CPR 1.4.(2) (a)
225 CPR 1.4.(2) (e)
226 CPR 1.4.(1)
227 CPR 26.4.(2) (b)
228 CPR 26.4.(2) (a)
229 Woolf (1996) Chapter 9 at 5. See also Chapter 10
230 See for example, CPR Pre-Action Conduct 1.1
231 Pre-action Conduct 1.2
232 See for example the TCC Court Guide 2005, 7.2.3

It is now over 16 years since the implementation of CPR and there is now significant literature on the effectiveness of the rules on a wide number of matters, which is not the focus of this book.[233] This section considers the short-term effect of the rules on mediation activity and raises some of the issues which restrict its use.

Criticisms of CPR and the pre-action protocols

Successfulness of CPR

Figures immediately following the introduction of CPR did suggest a significant jump in mediation use, although this was from a relatively low base; but there was considered opinion that until judges used their powers to penalise parties who unreasonably refused to mediate under s44 it was unlikely that there would be substantial growth.[234] The first report on the new rules from the Lord Chancellor's Department intimated that the reforms had successfully reduced the number of cases issued, improved settlement, simplified litigation practice and was bringing about a change in the adversarial climate with more parties using ADR and mediation.[235] However, the Continuing Report and other studies were a little less positive.[236] For example, research undertaken by Goriely et al. in the area of personal injury, clinical negligence and housing claims indicated that CPR had improved openness to settlement but the change in culture was inconsistent, and although studies suggested that awareness about mediation had been raised by providing openings to explore settlement, there were concerns about the frontloading of costs.[237]

As a response to considerable disquiet about the costs of litigating, Lord Jackson undertook a review. Although the final report found that most of the 10 specialised pre-action protocols generally encourage earlier settlement, there was a 'high degree of unanimity' that the general pre-action protocol, which uses a 'one size fits all' approach, creates substantial delay and excessive costs and 'serves no useful purpose'.[238] The report recommended repealing sections of the general pre-action protocol but warned that this would not

---

233 Ten years on from the introduction of CPR, observers were reporting that many problems remain with litigation. For a detailed analysis, see Dwyer (2009)
234 LCD (2001) (2002); CEDR Solve reported a 14% rise in mediation appointments in the year following CPR. CEDR Solve Statistics (2002/2003); Brooker & Lavers (2000) (2001)
235 LCD (2002). See Zander (2009). Zander suggests that the improved behaviour in litigation may be disingenuousness on the part of lawyers, anxious to present a picture of co-operation to avoid sanctions.
236 LCD (2002)
237 Goriely et al. (2002); See also Brooker & Lavers (2005a) at 207–11. Interviews with commercial and construction lawyers indicated that CPR had raised the profile of ADR and mediation and brought it into settlement negotiations which are pursued through the protocols.
238 Lord Jackson (2009), Introduction at xxii

give litigants in non-specific areas 'carte blanche because the costs sanctions would continue to apply to unreasonable behaviour'.[239]

A chapter of the report was devoted to ADR where the disappointing use of mediation was singled out,[240] not only because of its potential to save costs, although it was expressly noted this was not always the case, but also because parties were not 'aware' of all the benefits of mediating, which might mean they were discounting mediating too quickly.[241] After considering the evidence and feedback concerning ADR, the report made a number of observations:[242] First, mediation and joint settlement meetings were a 'highly efficacious means' of enabling settlement; Second, small businesses and the General Public did not appreciate the benefits of mediation; Third, contrary to 'widespread' opinion, personal injury cases with 'specialist' mediators can lead to a 'reasonable outcome' and 'bring satisfaction'; Finally, there was inconsistency in the level of awareness of some judges, solicitors and counsel.

In order to address these observations, the report recommended that mediation should be 'recognised' as having a more 'significant role to play in civil justice'. Although Lord Jackson was opposed to mandating mediation or sanctioning all parties or fettering the discretion of judges in applying the rules, he did support taking action to 'change the culture' rather 'the rules' through a 'serious campaign (a) to ensure that all litigation lawyers and judges *(and not just some litigation lawyers and judges)* are properly informed about the benefits which ADR can bring and (b) to alert the public and small businesses to the benefits of ADR'.[243] In order to tackle the wide variety of information on mediation, the report recommended the production of an annual 'single authoritative handbook' by a 'neutral body', which would become the standard training manual for judges and for Continuing Professional Development.[244] However, the report found that the problem of public awareness was complicated and other than introducing a 'clear brochure' at every court, advised no other action.[245]

Mediation integration with CPR

CPR has now integrated mediation within the formal system of mediation, although the evidence still indicates that many potential litigants and their lawyers may not be as enamoured with the process as those wishing to utilise

---

239 Lord Jackson (2009) Introduction at 6.2
240 Lord Jackson (2009) part 6, 36 at 4.9
241 Lord Jackson (2009) part 6, 36 at 1.2
242 Lord Jackson (2009) Introduction at 3.1
243 Lord Jackson (2009) Chapter 18 at 3.6
244 Lord Jackson (2009) Chapter 18 at 3.6–3.7. The date set for publication was April 2013 having been extended from April 2012 http://www.judiciary.gov.uk/about-the-judiciary/advisory-bodies/cjc/working-parties/adr-mediation-handbook Downloaded on 21 February 2013
245 Lord Jackson (2009) Chapter 18 at 3.10

it in order to reform the formal system of litigation or as ADR practitioners. There is also a wide literature on the theoretical arguments against ADR and the deployment of settlement as a key objective of reforming civil justice. The following section will outline the counter arguments against ADR developments because although many proponents recommend the advantages of using alternatives, particularly in relation to cost, speed and party self-determination, there are critics of 'informalism' who question the underlying motives and ideologies of the ADR and mediation movement.[246]

Criticism of informalism

Access to justice and settlement

Palmer and Roberts simplify the 'complex' modern movements into 'two conversations',[247] which both 'crystallise and approve a powerful ideology of adjudication'.[248] The first, in the 1960s and 1970s, focuses on the lack of availability of adjudication, and 'Access to Justice' with quicker, cheaper and 'more available' adjudication.[249] The second in the 1970s centres on writings on the 'merits of settlement': this drew attention to the problems of litigation and the 'advantages' of settlement.[250] The authors illustrate that both discussions are concerned with the issue of power, which has as its basis two social theories. One founded on Marxist theory that power emanates from the 'stratification' of society and 'domination' by powerful corporations[251] and the second, based on Weber's 'power of agency' theory where 'particular' agents are able to make others act 'contrary' to 'normal'.[252]

'Institutionalism'

Palmer and Roberts identify a third movement at the start of the 1980s, which builds on 'Access to Justice and Settlement' and leads to the 'institutionalism' of ADR.[253] At this time, they observe that various areas of practice begin to align themselves to the ADR movement, 'linked only by the settlement ideology', which included new mediator professionals wanting to 'carve out a career', the legal profession who seek to influence and find new business and the judiciary who 'case manage' the new alternatives.[254]

---

246 Palmer & Roberts (1998) at 29
247 Palmer & Roberts (1998) at 25
248 Palmer & Roberts (1998) at 29. The authors provide and analyse selected readings of the 'informalism' debate from key texts.
249 Palmer & Roberts (1998) at 26. The authors state that these writing are amalgamated in Abel (1982)
250 See for example, Fiss (1984)
251 Palmer & Roberts (1998) at 29
252 Palmer & Roberts (1998) at 29
253 Palmer & Roberts (1998) at 44–5
254 Palmer & Roberts (1998) at 45

Inequalities of ADR and mediation

Owen Fiss, who is one of the leading American critics, disagrees with those who promote the outcome of ADR as the 'consensual agreement' of the parties and contends that consent may be 'coerced'.[255] He argues that settlement is based on the parties' prediction of what they will achieve at court,[256] which is 'prejudiced by inherent inequalities' and 'unequally distributed resources'.[257] Fiss identifies three ways that poorer disputants are disadvantaged by settlement: first, they may have insufficient resources to acquire the information necessary for predicting court outcomes; their financial position may necessitate a quick settlement, which richer opponents can 'exploit'; and finally, disputants may not be able to afford litigation, which their opponents can use against them calculating the costs of going to trial and then reducing the settlement offer.[258] Fiss argues that in contrast to settlement processes which recognize that there may be inequalities in 'bargaining', litigation 'struggles' against them; 'Judgment aspires to an autonomy from distributional inequalities, and it gathers much of its appeal from this aspiration'.[259]

Some critics are sceptical that the new procedures are able to protect against procedural injustices.[260] Fiss recognises the judicial process can provide 'small' protections to counter procedural inequalities such as when the judge takes steps to assist litigants who are unrepresented 'by asking questions, calling his own witnesses, and inviting other persons and institutions to participate in proceedings'.[261]

Fiss also censures settlement and ADR for its role in stifling the law and argues that the court has a 'broader' purpose than just deciding between two litigants because judges are vested with 'power', to 'explicate and give force to the values' of the law. Therefore, judgment is not the end of the court process, the role of adjudication is to 'interpret' and develop the law:[262]

> These officials, like members of the legislative and executive branches, possess a power that has been defined and conferred by public law, not by private agreement. Their job is not to maximize the ends of private parties, nor simply to secure the peace, but to explicate and give force to the values embodied in authoritative texts such as the Constitution and statutes: to interpret those values and to bring reality into accord with them. This duty is not discharged when the parties settle.

255 Fiss (1984) at 1075
256 See Mnookin & Kornhauser (1978–1979)
257 Fiss (1984) at 1076
258 Fiss (1984) at 1076
259 Fiss (1984) at 1078
260 Guill & Slavin (1989)
261 Fiss (1984) at 1077
262 Fiss (1984) at 1085

'Interest of state and capital'

Critics of informal justice argue that there are underlying motives behind ADR, which conceal the 'covert' interests of state and capital:[263] 'informal institutions neutralise conflict by responding to grievances in ways that inhibit their transformation into serious challenges to the domination of state and capital'.[264] Abel describes how states 'control' ADR mechanisms 'such as complaints' and 'grievance procedures' in order to preserve their power over these systems.[265] For these reasons, Auerbach warns of the 'seductive appeal' of state-promoted alternatives, which can avert political criticism, deter 'litigation strategies', and ultimately result in 'injustice without law'.[266]

Although much of the critical writing about ADR and mediation began in the USA, the theoretical concerns have the same resonance to developments in England and Wales. Roberts criticised the early government and court policies in the English jurisdiction, which promoted ADR and provided that the courts retain control over settlement practices at the expense of protecting prospective litigants: 'Private informal procedures which enjoy the authority of the courts, but which are stripped of the procedural safeguards of adjudication carry the risk of unregulated coercion and covert manipulation'.[267]

Recently, Professor Genn reproached government policies in the English jurisdiction, for siphoning funding from the civil courts in order to finance the ever-increasing costs of the criminal justice system.[268] Her analysis of court data found an increase in the initiation of civil cases but also more cases settling before the hearing, which does not support the view that there is an 'explosion of litigation' because the majority of people who begin actions in the English jurisdiction continue to settle before trial.[269] Moreover, she observes that government policies since the 'mid 1990s' have reproduced the 'crisis rhetoric' that nurtured ADR developments in the USA in order to cut legal aid and civil court funding to prop up the expanding criminal justice budget.[270] These policies translate into an ADR agenda of deflecting cases away from the courts and were 'facilitated by an anti-justice, anti-adjudication discourse', which she maintains the public have 'internalised' and some parts of the judiciary enthusiastically embraced.[271] In tune with other critical work, Professor Genn observes that ADR policies jeopardize the function of a civil justice system, which is concerned with 'social and economic

---

263　Palmer & Roberts (1998) at 25. See for example, Abel (1982); Auerbach (1983); Roberts (1992) (1993); Guill & Slavin (1989); Nader (1988)
264　Abel (1982) at 280
265　Abel (1982) at 270–80. See Palmer & Roberts (1998) at 33
266　Auerbach (1983) at 144
267　Roberts (1992) at 262
268　Genn (2010) Chapter 2; Genn (2012)
269　Genn (2101) at 32–5; Genn updated Kritzer's work. See Kritzer (2004)
270　Genn (2010) at 43
271　Genn (2010) at 73

stability', where society should be able to expect 'authoritative adjudication' in order to 'avoid legal risk'.[272]

In Professor Genn's analysis the emphasis of mediation policy should not be about which cases should be denied access to the courts but which cases should be heard because this is fundamental to 'developing the law'.[273] This will be a particularly relevant contention when consideration is given to the lack of consistency in the exercise of judicial discretion in sanctioning parties for not mediating, which is reviewed later in the book. Genn argues that mediation policies have been advanced on what have been largely unproven assertions that the process is better than litigation.[274] Many court mediation schemes indicate high levels of satisfaction with the 'informality', 'speed', 'lack of legal technicality' and for providing the opportunity to be 'heard', but Genn suggests that the findings do not conclusively show the process is a better option to litigation as there was little disparity between the length of time of 'mediated and non mediated cases' and cost savings were difficult to substantiate because comparisons were drawn to the expense of trial, not to the norm of settling before.[275]

Professor Genn concludes that government policies that utilize the 'Access to Justice' banner do not stand up to scrutiny because mediation does not aid access to courts, does not provide 'substantive justice' because parties give up legal entitlements to 'focus on problem solving', mediators are only concerned with assisting settlement but not the 'quality' of the outcome, and 'success' is about what the parties 'can live with': 'The outcome of mediation is not about *just* settlement it is *just about settlement*'.[276]

Despite the serious objections raised about the motives of courts and political institutions in utilising ADR, there is still strong support for mediation as an alternative when it operates as a voluntary mechanism alongside or as a 'supplement' to litigation.[277] Mediation does not stand alone as an 'optional extra'[278] and its institutionalisation has repercussions. As mediation becomes recognised as an integral part of civil justice reform we see an extension of legalisation and juridification, as reviewed below.

Legalisation, institutionalisation and juridification

Institutionalisation

The mediation movement in many legal systems evidences the phenomenon of institutionalisation[279] but also as mediation merges with the civil justice

272 Genn (2010) at 74
273 Genn (2010) at 75
274 See Genn (2010) at 108–13
275 Genn (2010) at 112
276 Genn (2010) at 117
277 See for example, Genn 2010 at 78–9; Brunsdon-Tully (2009) at 236
278 Brooker (2010b) at 150
279 Clark (2008); Alexander (2006); Welsh (2001b)

system it also experiences 'legalisation', which is defined as 'the extension of procedural rules governing the processing of disputes'.[280] This process has ultimately led to a body of mediation law emerging.[281] The terms legalisation, judicialisation and juridification are often used to mean the same things[282] and earlier in this chapter it was observed how the legal professions 'juridify' arbitration in England and Wales by appropriating 'the right to determine law' from other specialist professions.[283] One of the themes of this book is to explore the juridification of mediation.

Meaning of juridification

Blichner and Molander identify a number of descriptive explanations of juridification including 'the increase in formal law',[284] lawyers monopolising a 'legal field'[285] or the 'expansion of judicial power'.[286] With the purpose of defining the juridification process in a way that incorporates numerous meanings, they developed a framework with five 'dimensions', which they contend are the main features:[287] First, 'constitutive juridification' is a process where a new 'political order' is created and 'essential norms' are established and added to the 'competencies of the legal order'.[288] Second, juridification involves the 'expansion of law'[289] into new areas such as religion,[290] sport[291] or industrial relations.[292] Blichner and Molander describe the expansion of law as the 'core element' of juridification and include within this process the 'legal regulation of activity that was previously unregulated'.[293] A third process of juridification is an increasing resolution of conflict 'by reference to the law'.[294] This can be through 'highly specialised' judicial 'legal conflict solving' or 'legal reasoning outside the judiciary' or 'lay conflict solving'

280　Harrington (1982) at 36 in Abel (1982)
281　Coben & Thompson (2006) at 48. The authors report a 95% increase of litigation cases involving mediation in the USA from 1999–2003. See also Alexander (2006); Alfini & McCabe (2001); Menkel-Meadow (1991)
282　Blichner & Molander (2008) at fn 2
283　Flood & Caiger (1993)
284　Blichner & Molander (2005) at fn 3. Citing Habermas (1987) at 359; see also Blichner & Molander (2008)
285　Blichner & Molander (2005). Citing Brooker (1999) at fn 3. See also Flood & Caiger (1993)
286　Blichner & Molander (2005) at fn 5 citing Tate & Vallinder (1995)
287　Blichner & Molander (2005) at 4–6
288　Blichner & Molander (2005) see 5–6 at 6. They use the EU as an example of a 'new legal order'.
289　Blichner & Molander (2005) at 31 citing Habermas (1987) at 356–63. See Ruben (2002). Ruben, for example, illustrates how UK military law, which was an 'autonomous legal system', progressively integrated 'criminal law norms' through juridification.
290　See also Saunders (2002); Edge & Loughrey (2001)
291　See for example, Gardiner (2006); Gardiner & Felix (1995)
292　Blichner & Molander (2008) at 50; Xuereb (1988)
293　Blichner & Molander (2005) at 12 & 14. See also Harker et al. (2011) at fn 191. The authors contend this is the most general usage of juridification.
294　Blichner & Molander (2005) at 6

where legal reasoning is used – but not necessarily accurately – as it may involve 'mistakes, misunderstandings and misinterpretations'.[295] Their fourth feature of juridification is where the 'legal system or legal professions' receive more power, which they refer to as 'increased judicial power'.[296] Judicial and legal 'experts' attain this power when a particular case exhibits 'indeterminacy and lack of transparency', which makes it difficult to 'determine the state of law' and thus disputants have to rely on 'legal advice' to interpret the law.[297] Finally, juridification is a form of 'legal framing' whereby people regard themselves as 'legal subjects' 'with equal legal rights and duties'.[298]

Blichner and Molander do not suggest that the 'dimensions' are connected or that there is a 'cause and effect relationship' between each one but they argue any of the strands can be linked either 'positively or negatively'.[299] Even before government policies in the English jurisdiction absorbed mediation into the litigation process through CPR, judicial interest had commenced by way of court practice statements, which were followed soon after by cases brought by litigants to enforce mediation clauses and agreements. CPR is the stimulus for the expansion of mediation law as litigants bring disputes over mediating to the court for judicial determination and the legal professions become increasingly involved in explicating the emerging law.

Early case law on ADR and mediation

CPR powers

After CPR came into force on 26 April 1999, early case law reflected the attitude[300] and ideology[301] of judges to using case management and their understanding and appreciation of ADR. In *Muman v. Nagasena*, Ambedkar International Mission appealed an unsuccessful application for possession of a property, which had been used as a Buddhist temple, and for the removal of the tenant, a Buddhist monk (N), who claimed to be the acting Patron.[302] The Court of Appeal (CA) held that the judge in the first instance had erroneously decided that the mission was not the legal owner as and

---

295 Blichner & Molander (2005) at 16
296 Blichner & Molander (2005) at 19 fn 43. The authors state that when juridification refers to 'judicial power' this is often referred to as 'judicialisation' citing Neal & Vallinder (1995).
297 Blichner & Molander (2005) at 18–19
298 Blichner & Molander (2005) at 24
299 Blichner & Molander (2005) at 27–9 at 29. Not all legal and social theorists view juridification as a negative influence because in other contexts the term is used positively as 'legal order is imposed' in areas of conflict. See for example; Saunders (2001) for an analysis of juridification in religious law. Saunders (2002) at 2173–98
300 Oyre (2004)
301 Shipman (2006)
302 *Muman v. Nagasena* [2000] 1 W.L.R. 299; [1999] EWCA Civ 1742

referred the case back to the County Court for a hearing on the contested issues.[303]

In analysing the background of the case, Mummery LJ noted that the costs of the proceedings were already in excess of £90,000 and directed that a stay in proceedings should not be removed until the parties attempted 'the healing process' of mediation.[304] Neither of the parties had sought a stay from the court, which led Underhill to suggest *Muman v. Nagasena* is an early example of the court exercising its own discretion to order parties to mediate.[305] The court referred the parties to a mediation service for charitable disputes set up by CEDR and the 'National Council for Voluntary Organisations' with funds from the Home Office, to avoid wasting charitable donations on further funding litigation.[306]

A number of High Court judges signalled early enthusiasm for using 'active case management' to encourage mediation. For example, in the Chancery Division, Mrs Justice Arden in *Guinle v. Kinstreet Ltd v Balmargo Corp Ltd v. Hamam* issued an order for mediation in a case involving four parties in three different actions concerning a share dispute, breaches of contract, conspiracy and breach of duty and property on trust.[307] In a detailed section on ADR the court referred to the many benefits of mediating, such as the reduction of court time, the costs for the parties, high settlement rates, the potential to narrow the issues, the possibility of continuing relationships or achieving outcomes outside the range of the court.[308] Mrs Justice Arden was influenced by the litigation expenditure already incurred, the further costs of going to trial and the likelihood that one litigant would be unable to meet the costs of losing, necessitating the court to find a 'viable' alternative to litigation, 'which deals with the case in ways which are proportionate to the financial position of each party'.[309]

Commentators suggest that this case is surprising in its dismissal of the views of the defendants, who questioned the motive for offering mediation just before the case management meeting and refuted the likelihood the proposal was in 'good faith'.[310] Arden J rejected the defendant's argument that the court lacked 'jurisdiction' to order the parties to resolve their dispute 'before a neutral individual or panel' because the words in the 'draft ADR order' would only require the parties to 'take such steps (if any) as they think

---

303 As a charity proceedings under the Charities Act s 33(8), the parties are required to seek permission for litigation from either the Chancery Division or the Charity Commissioners in order to avoid the 'frittering' of money on internal disputes. See *Muman v. Nagasena* [2000] at 299

304 *Muman v. Nagasena* [2000] at 301

305 Underhill (2003) at 261; Dundas (2004)

306 *Muman v. Nagasena* [2000] at 305

307 *Nigel Edgar Bertrand John Guinle v. Kirreh Kinstreet Ltd v. Balmargo Corp Ltd Interfisa Management Inc v. Hamam* [1999] ADR LR 7/13

308 *Guinle v. Kirreh Kinstreet Ltd* [1999] 11–14

309 *Guinle v. Kirreh Kinstreet Ltd* [1999] at 13

310 Dundas (2004) at 151; Underhill (2000)

fit following the appointment of mediator'.[311] Dundas criticised the 'terse way' the court approached the jurisdictional issue and the failure to review case management powers under CPR rule 1.4.(e) and noted that the decision provided a precedent that the court may order mediation without the consent of both parties,[312] which was relied on in the later case of *Shirayma Shokusan v. Danova*.[313] The decision does serve to indicate the enthusiasm that some judges had for mediation in the early case law.

The Court of Appeal explored case management powers in *Dyson v. Leeds County Council*, which involved a claim of a failure of duty of care under the Occupiers' Liability Act 1957 and negligence under the common law to take adequate precautions to protect an employee against asbestos dust from May 1954 to July 1968.[314] The evidence from the parties' experts conflicted on whether occupiers of property would have known about the dangers of asbestos and therefore taken safety measures in the 1950s or by the 1970s.[315] Ward LJ held that the judge at first instance had failed to justify why he had found the evidence from the defendant's expert witness more compelling and should have given reasons as to why the occupiers had the requisite knowledge at the later rather than the earlier date.[316] Lord Justice Ward regarded the case as 'pre-eminently the category of case' where the courts should encourage ADR under rule 1.4(2) (e) because the parties had 'substantially' agreed damages and because of the 'ordeal' that would face the widow at a re-hearing.[317] Plaintiff's counsel had already tried to 'persuade' the defendant to use mediation and the court warned the parties of the 'dire consequences' of indemnity costs if they failed to take note of the court's 'encouraging noises'.[318] Both Law LJ and Woolf LJ 'associated themselves' with the remarks made about using alternatives.[319]

The Court of Appeal took the occasion to review CPR powers to promote ADR in an application for judicial review of a decision by a city council to close an old people's home in *Cowl and Anor v. Plymouth City Council*.[320] Lord

---

311 *Guinle v. Kirreh Kinstreet Ltd* [1999] at 12–13
312 Dundas (2004) at 152. Dundas argues that the court in *Shirayama Shokusan Co Ltd v. Danovo Ltd (No 1)* [2003] EWHC 3306 (Ch) erroneously used *Guinle* as authority for issuing a stay for mediation without the consent of both parties. See *Shirayama Shokusan Co Ltd v. Danovo Ltd (No.1)* 5 December 2003 [2003] EWHC 3306 (Ch); [2004] BLR. 207. See also Cornes (2007)
313 Dundas (2004) at 152–3. Dundas suggests that Blackburne J 'assumed' he had the jurisdiction relying on *Guinle v. Kirreh Kinstreet Ltd* which he says 'is a misreading of Judge Arden's judgment; she considered CPR r.1.1 only in the context of her making an order for separate trials to "enable the court to deal with the various actions justly, and thus in accordance with the overriding objective of the CPR."'
314 *Dyson v. Leeds County Council* [2000] C.P. Rep. 42 at 1–6
315 *Dyson v. Leeds County Council* [2000] at 7
316 *Dyson v. Leeds City Council* [2000] at 13
317 *Dyson v. Leeds County Council* [2000] at 15–16
318 *Dyson v. Leeds County Council* [2000] at 17–19
319 *Dyson v. Leeds County Council* [2000] at 20 & 21
320 *Cowl and Anor v. Plymouth City Council* [2001] EWCA Civ 1935

Woolf issued a forceful judgment, denying the right to judicial review, when an 'alternative remedy would cover exactly the same ground' and exhorted future courts to use the 'ample powers under CPR to ensure that the parties try to resolve the dispute with the minimum of involvement of the courts'.[321] The parties and their lawyers were criticised for not using the complaints procedure and the Court urged judges to 'deter' litigation by initiating meetings where the parties are required to explain their failure to use a complaints system or other form of ADR.[322] As a final point, Lord Woolf reminded lawyers of their 'heavy obligation' only to use litigation 'if it was really unavoidable'.[323]

Costs incentive – rule 44 CPR

Lord Woolf's strategy for persuading parties to try ADR or mediation was set down in the rules for costs in r 44 of CPR. The normal rules are that the losing party pays the successful litigant's costs and these can be awarded at a higher indemnity level if the parties' conduct is 'unreasonable to high degree'.[324] Judges when exercising their discretion in costs 'must' take into consideration 'all the circumstances' of the case which includes '(a) the conduct of the party' but the 'decisive future' of ADR expansion was perhaps situated in r 44(5) which further defines 'conduct'.[325] Judges have discretion to take into consideration the 'parties' efforts, if any, before and during the proceeding in order to try to resolve the dispute' but an amendment in 2009 added 'and in particular the extent to which the parties followed any relevant pre-action protocol'.[326]

One of the earliest cases to consider the effect of a failure to give due consideration to ADR is found in *Paul Thomas Construction Ltd v. Hyland*, which involved a small claim between a builder and the homeowners, who were dissatisfied with the quality of work completed.[327] The Technology and Construction Court (TCC) verified that unreasonably failing to 'explore' alternatives to litigation was a breach of the protocols.[328] The builder had indicated a willingness to use ADR but their correspondence exposed an 'exceedingly heavy handed approach' as they refused to provide further particulars of the claim, demanded the homeowners paid half of the money

---

321 *Cowl and Anor v. Plymouth City Council* [2001] at 14 & 2
322 *Cowl and Anor v. Plymouth City Council* [2001] at 13 & 3
323 *Cowl and Anor v. Plymouth City Council* [2001] at 27
324 CPR s 44(2) (a). See *Reid Minty v. Taylor* [2002] 1 WLR 2800. Before *Reid Minty*, the standard for indemnity costs was behaviour 'deserving of moral condemnation' or 'lacking in moral probity' (per Lord Justice May at 28) but in *Kiam v. MGN* [2002] 1 WLR 2801 the court found the standard to be reached was 'unreasonable to a high degree', (per Lord Justice Simon Brown at 12)
325 CPR r 44(4) (a) & r 44(5). Brooker & Lavers (2005a) at 162
326 Rule 44(5) was amended on 6 April 2009 by Rule 9(b). Rule CPR 44.14 & s44(5)
327 *Paul Thomas Construction Ltd v. Hyland and another* 8/3/00 CILL/01 1743 at 4–6 at 6
328 *Paul Thomas Construction Ltd v. Hyland* (2000) at 4–6 at 8

for the work done before appointing a neutral, pay all the neutral's fees and finally, threatening to pursue litigation unless their demands were met.[329] In comparison, the court noted that the defendants had taken a 'reasonable' approach, and furthermore, unlike many defendants, were not prevaricating in order to delay payment.[330]

At the time of judgment, the TCC pre-action protocol was not in place but the general pre-action protocol was, which the court took into consideration in awarding indemnity costs because the builder's conduct was 'wholly unreasonable' in commencing litigation when they 'could' or 'should have explored alternative dispute resolution'.[331] However, the judgment did not assume that ADR had to be any specific procedure and stated this could 'include sensible discussions' which did not necessarily involve a third party neutral.[332] Such a broad approach to defining alternatives to litigation may have contributed to obscuring, or at least watering down the objectives of CPR, in that it legitimates claims that lawyers and their clients have pursued settlement through legal negotiation, which is the normal course of action when disputes arise.

At the time of the *Cowl* decision in 2001, Lord Woolf implied that ADR was well documented and established: 'Today sufficient should be known about ADR to make the failure to adopt it, in particular when public money is involved, indefensible'.[333] Education and information were key objectives in the Woolf reforms, which recommended that all courts should hold information about ADR and providers. Nevertheless research and official reports, both before and after CPR, suggest a lack of knowledge was holding back mediation expansion and the position has not radically changed ten years on.[334] This brief review of the cases following CPR shows how the courts began to interpret case management powers and what steps should be taken to encourage settlement and ADR. When ADR and mediation first gained attention in the UK, commentators frequently discussed the terms synonymously, although mediation eventually gained recognition as the 'frontrunner' in developments.[335] The term 'alternative dispute resolution' is defined in the Glossary to the CPR as a 'collective description of methods of resolving disputes otherwise than through the normal trial process'.[336]

---

329 *Paul Thomas Construction Ltd v. Hyland* (2000) at 4–6 at 6
330 *Paul Thomas Construction Ltd v. Hyland* (2000) at 3
331 *Paul Thomas Construction Ltd v. Hyland* (2000) at 8
332 *Paul Thomas Construction Ltd v. Hyland* (2000) at 8
333 *Cowl* (2001) at 25
334 Woolf (1996) Overview 9(b). See for example; Genn (1998); Lord Jackson (2009) Introduction at 3.1
335 Brooker & Lavers (2000) at 357
336 Brooker & Lavers (2000). The authors report on the findings from interviews with representatives of legal organisations, ADR providers, the Judicial Studies Board and ADR specialists. Interviewees recognised mediation as the 'core-technique' but believed definitional problems existed because many sectors of the public and legal professions did not distinguish between ADR and mediation. Further, the interviewees believed that

By 2004, Dyson LJ in the Court of Appeal in *Halsey*, which remains the leading decision on the guidelines for unreasonably refusing an offer to mediate, explained that ADR is now 'usually understood as being a reference to some form of mediation by a third party'.[337]

The aim of Lord Woolf's civil justice reform was not just to foster an eclectic group of procedures, but to encourage settlement away from the courts.[338] The definition of ADR in the rules is broadly drawn and inclusive of both binding and non-binding procedures but may also include 'conventional negotiation'[339] or 'discussions' as shown by *Paul Thomas Construction Ltd v. Hyland*,[340] which has perhaps muddied the water on two fronts. First, the courts by including negotiation and 'discussions' when exercising discretion on the conduct of the parties in relation to settlement attempts before litigating has the effect of diluting the objective of promoting ADR procedures involving third party neutrals who often provide the catalyst for brokering settlement. Second, such a broad approach may include dispute resolution processes that conceal more adversarial behaviour, particularly with relevance to legal negotiations, which traditionally centre on 'legal norms' rather than problem-solving which may reduce the likelihood of party-created outcomes as lawyers begin to dominate proceedings in mediation.[341]

The early case law, however, had began to show that there were pockets of judicial enthusiasm for mediation; but as noted earlier many commentators began to suggest that litigants and their legal advisors would not take significant notice until judges used their sanctioning powers, which will be discussed in Chapter 3.

Conclusions

This chapter provided a brief history of the modern ADR and mediation movements in the USA, which were to provide a template for developments in England and many other jurisdictions. One of the primary drivers in the course of mediation development was the response to Lord Woolf's Reforms

judges were likely to have mediation in mind when they considered the suitability of cases for ADR.
337 *Halsey* [2004] EWCA Civ 576 at 5
338 Roberts (2000)
339 *Corenso (UK) Ltd v. The Burnden Group Plc* [2003] EWHC 1805 (Q.B.) at 60 "The requirement on parties is to attempt to resolve their differences without resorting to court by alternative dispute resolution. In some cases, the only available way may be mediation. In other cases, it may well be that negotiation, or attempts to use an honest broker, may be equally appropriate. So long as parties are showing a genuine and constructive willingness to resolve the issues between them, it does not seem to me that a party will be automatically penalised because that party has not gone along with a particular form of alternative dispute resolution proposed by the other side", per Reid J QC at 60. See Brooker & Lavers (2005a) at 181–2
340 *Paul Thomas Construction Ltd v. Hyland* (2000) at 8
341 See for example, Welsh (2001a) at 788; Genn (2010) at 82; Kovach & Love (1996) at 31; Clark (2012) at 4.2.1–4.2.3.2

for civil litigation. Although there had been earlier initiatives to promote ADR in the form of practice directions, the implementation of the CPR activated the growth of mediation practice by setting the scene for parties to test the boundaries of the courts' commitment to ADR and mediation. The rules have been operating in the civil courts in England and Wales for just over a decade and there is now a significant body of mediation law.

Mediation in England shows a similar pattern to arbitration, which began as an alternative forum for business people seeking determination of their disputes from experienced neutrals based on commercial practice, but ended up in an interdependent relationship with litigation as parties sought the help of the courts to enforce agreements to arbitrate or to overturn or uphold arbitrators' decisions. With case and legislative involvement, arbitration became as formalised as litigation, which resulted in party dependence on lawyers who began to 'juridify'[342] the process to prevent competition from non-legal experts. The Mediation Movement has shown an analogous story to arbitration where the legal professions from an early stage began to influence and dominate mediation developments. One theme of the book is to explore the extent to which state and court institutionalisation of mediation has led to 'juridification', both through the expansion of mediation law and by lawyers as they seek to dominate the field.

Common law jurisdictions have a shared experience of problems with litigation but some countries have taken divergent approaches to civil justice reform. For example, it has been discussed how some states in the USA have adopted mandatory mediation whereby there is a expectation that parties will mediate before litigating or have given judges the power to direct or order the parties to participate in mediation when claims are brought before the court. This book will include a comparative methodology on the legal arrangments, underpinning mediation practice in other common law jurisdictions particularly in the USA, Australia and Hong Kong.

Mediation law in England and Wales is first explored by considering the legal status of the parties' agreements to mediate as disputants tested the legality of their contractual mediation arrangements. Chapter 3 undertakes an analysis of compromise agreements reached in mediation or other ADR processes as parties sought to enforce their mediated settlements. Chapter 4 reviews the CPR 'legal framework'[343] for initiating mediation and the exercise of judicial discretion in identifying the appropriate criteria for mediating. Chapter 5 considers how the law protects the confidentiality of negotiations and events that take place in mediation. The final chapter draws together the main themes of the book in relation to the institutionalisation and juridification of mediation and considers to what extent this is influencing both mediation practice and the regulation of an emerging mediator profession.

342 Flood & Caiger (1993). See the earlier discussion.
343 See Alexander (2006) at 19–24. Alexander discusses how mediators must 'work within the framework of a legal system', at 19.

2 Initiating mediation through ADR clauses and court stays

Introduction

Chapter 1 reviewed the history of ADR and the mediation movement in the English jurisdiction and introduced the major themes of the book. An overview of the Modern ADR Movement shows how mediation has become connected to the formal system of litigation: First through court Practice Directions, which encouraged parties to consider alternative mechanisms; and second through the Civil Procedure Rules, which introduced court management duties requiring judges to 'encourage and facilitate' ADR[1] and implement a costs regime to sanction unreasonable behaviour in litigation, which includes refusing to use ADR.

In the English jurisdiction, parties initiate mediation in one of three ways.[2] A disputant can propose mediation when a dispute occurs, probably on the advice of 'enlightened'[3] lawyers but this usually does not involve the courts as the parties have voluntarily set the process in motion. This chapter is concerned with the second two ways for 'triggering'[4] mediation. First, mediation may commence through the existence of a clause in a contract identifying that the parties will use the process as a first step or 'condition precedent' to litigation when a dispute or disagreement occurs.[5] Indeed, the lack of interest in mediation in the early 1990s (and beyond) led ADR promoters to recommend that organisations and businesses insert clauses into their contracts to counter the existence of negative perceptions that proposing mediation implies a weakness in the case, which many disappointed mediation providers believed to be restricting growth.[6] The second way mediation may commence

---

1 CPR 1.4 (e)
2 Newman (1997) at 46
3 Gould & Cohen (1998) at 107
4 Alexander (2008b) at 14
5 Suter (2009) at 32; Jones (2009) at 196; Kendall (1993) at 587
6 Research on ADR experiences in the construction industry in England did not suggest that respondents believed that proposing ADR signalled a lack of confidence in the case or that its non-binding nature was a weakness. See Brooker & Lavers (2001). In contrast, Professor Genn's findings on mediation in the London County Court Scheme found that some legal representatives thought that mediation did suggest weakness in case. Genn (2002) at 2.11

is because the court issues a stay in the litigation proceedings. The court adjourns proceedings either because a party at a hearing requests that the court uphold an existing contract clause or because judges have discretionary powers to stay proceedings through an application by the parties, or on their own initiative if the case is deemed appropriate, which provides an opening for the parties to attempt settlement before recommencing the trial timetable.[7] Mackie et al. suggest there is no requirement for court proceedings to be deferred while the parties seek to organise mediation as the processes can run concurrently if the court or one party is concerned that delaying tactics are being used; but they do note costs for litigation purposes will continue to be incurred.[8]

Early research into construction mediation at the beginning of the 21st century suggested that neither contract provision nor judges in the English jurisdiction have been 'an effective force' in mediation development.[9] Nevertheless, there have been a steady stream of cases involving contractual provision for ADR, which will be reviewed before undertaking an analysis of the discretionary powers judges now have under CPR to stay proceedings for mediation to be attempted.

Contractual provisions for ADR in contracts

The first chapter explored how arbitration, an early alternative to litigation, grew to prominence in the 18th and 19th centuries but case law revealed how parties attempted to bypass contractual agreements to arbitrate or tried to ignore arbitrators' decisions. Eventually statutory enactments permitted arbitration to expand but the formal court system retained supremacy through its powers of overview. The formal system 'subsumed' arbitration and the procedure began to resemble litigation through the introduction of costly procedural arrangements and intensive legal involvement.[10] This section considers how some litigants began to try to avoid contractual agreements to use an alternative before proceeding with litigation in the same way that arbitration parties had before them which lead to applications to the court to uphold ADR clauses in contracts.

Contract clauses

It is perhaps inevitable that after a dispute arises some parties will endeavour to circumvent the agreement and try to go immediately to litigation, perhaps

---

7 CPR r 26(4). See the White Book (2013) at Section A Part 24.6.2
8 Mackie et al. (2007) at 65
9 Brooker & Lavers (2001) at 333–4. A study of commercial and construction lawyers' experience with mediation found that only 10 per cent of the reported mediations commenced through a court order and two mediations by a contract clause.
10 See discussion in Chapter 1. For a discussion on arbitration developments see for example, Ferguson (1980); Parris (1978); Lane (1986); Parker (1959); Flood & Caiger (1993)

because they perceive that this is a more appropriate method for resolution or because they believe that a court determination is necessary on a legal issue. Cheong argues that the common law's 'orthodox' approach to enforcing mediation clauses relies on 'three theoretical arguments'.[11] First, they do not have contractual force because they are merely expressions of an 'agreement to agree' which is 'void' in contract law; second they require a 'good faith obligation', which the courts cannot determine; and finally they lack 'procedural certainty'.[12] In 1993, the Court of Appeal considered a form of ADR in *Channel Tunnel (C) v. Balfour Beattie (B)*.[13] The employer and contractor agreed under clause 67 of their contract that they would refer 'any dispute or difference' between them to a panel of three persons who were required to issue a written decision within 90 days during which time the contractor was obliged to proceed with the work. However, clause 67(6) (3) permitted the parties under certain conditions to refer the dispute to arbitration in Belgium if either party was 'dissatisfied with the unanimous decision of the panel' or the 'panel failed to give a unanimous decision' or the 'unanimous decision' was 'not given effect'.

The parties were disputing the value of a variation order for a cooling system but had been unable to reach a final price with their estimates at variance between £112 million (Balfour Beattie) and £78 million (Channel Tunnel).[14] As an interim measure, Channel Tunnel agreed to pay monthly amounts based on their estimate until the parties reached consensus on the cost of the variation. This understanding was in place for seven months until Balfour Beattie demanded payment based on their valuation and threatened to suspend work.[15]

At the court of first instance, the plaintiffs (Channel Tunnel) sought an application for an injunction to prevent the suspension of work by the defendants (Balfour Beattie) and the defendants unsuccessfully requested a stay in proceedings for arbitration, although the court did not issue an order for an injunction because of their 'undertaking' that they would not stop work.[16] However, the Court of Appeal awarded the stay on the grounds that a party could not just ignore an arbitration agreement because a preliminary step was needed.[17] In the House of Lords, Mustill LJ held that by analogy with the court's discretionary power to 'enforce a foreign jurisdiction clause'[18] it has an 'inherent power' to enforce an arbitration clause or a 'dispute resolution clause', which was 'nearly an immediately effective agreement to

---

11 Cheong (2008)
12 Cheong (2008) at 195–6
13 *Channel Tunnel Group Ltd and Another v. Balfour Beatty Construction Ltd and Others* [1993] 2 W.L.R. 263; [1993] A.C. 334
14 *Channel Tunnel v. Balfour Beatty* [1993] at 348
15 *Channel Tunnel v. Balfour Beatty* [1993] at 344
16 *Channel Tunnel v. Balfour Beatty* [1993] at 344
17 *Channel Tunnel v. Balfour Beatty* [1993] at 344
18 Arbitration Act 1950 s4(1)

arbitrate, albeit not quite' and therefore the court had jurisdiction to stay proceedings regardless of whether clause 67 fell within s1 of the 1979 Arbitration Act.[19] Mustill LJ observed that 'large commercial entities' would be aware of the likely occurrence of disputes and the availability of different dispute resolution procedures when they agreed to specific mechanisms in their contracts and they should not disregard these arrangements when it ceased to 'suit their purpose': 'The fact that the appellants now find their chosen method too slow to suit their purpose, is to my way of thinking quite beside the point'.[20]

The House of Lords' decision in *Channel Tunnel* paved the way for courts to uphold contractual arrangements to use ADR in the same way that the judiciary supported arbitration clauses before statutory intervention. However, the dispute resolution clause in question involved a binding, determinative ADR mechanism, akin to arbitration, rather than a non-binding procedure such as mediation. Further, the parties had agreed to a two-tier procedure where arbitration was the final arbiter of the dispute and where the law has, in the main, settled jurisdictional issues.

Other cases eventually came before the English courts with differently defined dispute resolution clauses where one party was seeking enforcement. In *Cott v. F. E. Barber*,[21] a reference to an ADR method was placed under a heading of arbitration in the contract. The clause however, stated that the parties would submit their case to the Director General of the British Soft Drink Association (BSDA) to appoint 'an independent consultant and shall act as an expert and not as an arbiter and his decision shall be final and binding on the parties'.[22] The person appointed was an expert in the 'soft drinks industry' but not in dispute resolution and when Barber sought a stay from the court in order that expert determination could take place Cott claimed that the clause was uncertain as to which alternative 'forum', arbitration or expert determination, applied.[23]

Hegarty J held that the heading of the clause did not 'prevail' over the clause itself when the 'express wording' did not create 'ambiguity or ambiguity in construing the words of the clause' and it was clear that the clause related to a process of expert determination.[24] Further, the court held that it had an 'inherent jurisdiction' to stay the action for a clause relating to expert determination rather than under the power given in s49(3) of the Supreme Court Act 1981 for an 'effective arbitration clause' and cited Mustill LJ's observation that there were now 'changing attitudes' in the legal system to ADR.[25] Nevertheless the defendants avoided the stay because BSDA did not

19 *Channel Tunnel v. Balfour Beatty* [1993] at 352–3
20 *Channel Tunnel v. Balfour Beatty* [1993] at 353
21 *Cott v. F E Barber* [1997] 3 All ER 540
22 *Cott v. F E Barber* [1997] at 543
23 *Cott v. F E Barber* [1997] at 544
24 *Cott v. F E Barber* [1997] at 543
25 *Cott v. F E Barber* [1997] at 546

have 'rules for arbitration or any form of dispute resolution', the expert had no experience of 'these matters' and the contract did not provide 'rules and principles' to help the expert.[26]

Agreements to negotiate

The dispute resolution clauses in *Cott v. F. E. Barber* and *Channel Tunnel* both involved binding methods of dispute resolution where the third party provides a decision, rather than non-binding processes such as mediation.[27] This distinction led to a line of thought that the courts would not enforce mediation agreements because by analogy they were agreements to negotiate which the English courts traditionally were unprepared to enforce because of uncertainty:[28]

> Agreements to negotiate are clearly not binding upon the parties and it may have been suspected that since mediation is a non-adjudicative process and de facto a form of negotiation then such an agreement to mediate would likewise not be enforceable.

Agreements to agree

The common law position on the uncertainty of agreements to agree had been emphasised by the Court of Appeal in *Courtney v. Tolaini* in 1975.[29] The plaintiffs, Tolaini, planned to develop land and the defendant builders, Courtney, offered to find financiers for the project on condition that they were involved as contractors in the development.[30] Letters produced in evidence detailed Courtney's role in introducing a financial party and the arrangements to appoint Tolaini's quantity surveyor to negotiate a 'fair and reasonable contract' price, which were reproduced on demand by Courtney in a letter agreeing the 'terms specified therein'.[31]

Denning LJ disagreed with the court of first instance that an enforceable contract existed because the 'words' in the letters indicated a price had 'yet' to be agreed and this deficiency was said to be 'fundamental' to any contract but particularly contracts between builders and employers who would never commence work without this agreement.[32] Denning LJ did suggest that the matter might have been decided differently had the parties agreed for a third party or an arbitrator to settle the price but as no such 'machinery' existed in the agreement no contract was in place.[33]

---

26 *Cott v. F E Barber* [1997] at 548
27 Nesic (2001); Cheong (2008) at 197
28 See Clark (2003) at 171; Lee (1999) at 23
29 *Courtney v. Tolaini* [1975] 1 All ER 716
30 *Courtney v. Tolaini* [1975] at 297
31 *Courtney v. Tolaini* [1975] at 300
32 *Courtney v. Tolaini* [1975] at 301
33 *Courtney v. Tolaini* [1975] at 301

The Court of Appeal after giving consideration to Lord Wright's argument in *Hillas and Co Ltd v. Arcos Ltd*[34] that a right of action in contract for negotiation might exist if the parties had provided consideration, concluded that contracts to negotiate were not 'known to the law . . . because they are too uncertain to have any binding force' and, furthermore, courts would be unable to assess damages 'because no-one would know whether the negotiation would be successful or would fall through'.[35]

The House of Lords reaffirmed that the English jurisdiction does not recognise a contract to negotiate in *Walford v. Miles*.[36] The defendants had agreed to a 'lockout clause' that they would cease to negotiate the sale of their company shares and property with other parties provided they received confirmation that the plaintiff's finances were in place.[37] The plaintiffs supplied a 'comfort letter' from their bank but then received information from the defendants' solicitors that their clients had agreed a sale with a third party.

The House of Lords was unconvinced by the plaintiff's submission that an agreement to negotiate in good faith if supported by consideration is enforceable, which they based on a Court of Appeal case in the United States.[38] In Lord Justice Ackner's opinion the USA line of authority had proceeded on an 'unsustainable' argument that an agreement to negotiate is 'synonymous' with an 'enforceable agreement to use best endeavours', although the distinction was not further expanded upon.[39] An agreement to negotiate has the same effect as an agreement to agree and is unenforceable 'simply because it lacks the necessary certainty' and a court would not be able to decide if the parties had 'terminated negotiations for a proper reason' unless it gave consideration to whether this was done 'in good faith'. This concept was 'repugnant to the adversarial position of the parties in negotiations':[40]

> However the concept of a duty to carry on negotiations in good faith is inherently repugnant to the adversarial position of the parties when involved in negotiations. Each party to the negotiations is entitled to pursue his (or her) own interest, so long as he avoids making misrepresentations. To advance that interest he must be entitled, if he thinks it appropriate, to threaten to withdraw from further negotiations or to

---

34 *Hillas and Co Ltd v. Arcos Ltd* (1932) 147 LT at 515
35 *Courtney v. Tolaini* [1975] at 301–302
36 *Walford v. Miles* [1992] 2 AC 128
37 *Walford v. Miles* [1992] at 132
38 *United States Court of Appeal, Third Circuit, Channel Home Centers, Division of Grace Retail Corporation v. Grossman* (1986) 795 F 2d 291
39 *Walford v. Miles* [1992] at 137–8. See Mills & Loveridge (2011) at 529. Mills and Loveridge cite *Little v. Chance* [1995] CLC 164 and state that there is no 'logical distinction' between an agreement to negotiate in good faith and an agreement to best endeavours.
40 *Walford v. Miles* [1992] at 138

withdraw in fact, in the hope that the opposite party may seek to reopen the negotiations by offering him improved terms. [. . .] how is a vendor ever to know that he is entitled to withdraw from further negotiations? How is the court to police such an 'agreement?' A duty to negotiate in good faith is as unworkable in practice as it is inherently inconsistent with the position of a negotiating party. It is here that the uncertainty lies. In my judgment, while negotiations are in existence either party is entitled to withdraw from those negotiations, at any time and for any reason. There can be thus no obligation to continue to negotiate until there is a 'proper reason' to withdraw. Accordingly a bare agreement to negotiate has no legal content.

Nevertheless, the House of Lords accepted that agreements to negotiate for a 'specified time' with consideration are different to a 'bare agreement to negotiate'.[41] Lord Ackner drew a distinction between parties agreeing to lock themselves *out* of negotiating with other persons during an agreed period with the requisite consideration because they are not locking *into* negotiation, which would require the courts to consider whether they had negotiated in good faith, which is a concept not recognised because of uncertainty.[42] In *Walford v. Miles*, the agreement was 'unworkable because there was no way of determining for how long Miles were locked out from negotiating with any third party'.[43]

Walford v. Miles precluded the enforceability of agreements to negotiate which therefore cast doubt on whether the court would enforce mediation contracts, which are described as a form of 'structured negotiation'.[44] *Halifax Financial Services Ltd v. Intuitive Systems Ltd* considered the position of non-binding methods of dispute resolution including mediation[45] in a clause (33.1), which first stipulated that senior representatives were to 'meet in good faith and attempt to resolve the dispute' and if this meeting did not reach a settlement then under clause 33.2 the parties could propose to enter into 'structured negotiations' with a neutral adviser or mediator.[46] If the meeting with the Neutral Adviser resulted in an agreement, the parties would 'record' the outcome 'in writing', which clause 33.6 stipulated would become binding, although clause 33.7 provided that the parties could request the Neutral Adviser to give a 'non-binding but informative' opinion. Clause 33.8 stated that the parties could refer the dispute to court in the event that they had not

---

41 *Walford* v. *Miles* [1992] at 138
42 *Walford* v. *Miles* [1992] at 139
43 *Walford* v. *Miles* [1992] at 140
44 See *Aird v. Meridan Ltd* [2006] EWCA Civ 1866 at 5
45 *Halifax Financial Services Ltd v. Intuitive Systems Ltd* [1999] 1 All ER (Comm) 303; (2000) 2 TCLR 35; [1999] CILL 1467. See Nesic (2001) at 2. Nesic notes that this case was heard before CPR came into force.
46 *Halifax Financial Services Ltd v. Intuitive Systems Ltd* [1999] at 307. Clauses 33.1 and 33.2 of the contract.

reached agreement through 'structured negotiation' unless the parties agreed to refer the dispute to arbitration in London.[47]

Intuitive Systems had agreed to provide an IT system for Halifax within a specified time but claimed that this was impossible due to the demands for changes made by the plaintiffs.[48] Halifax, after a series of meetings, purported to accept the repudiation of the contract by Intuitive Systems prior to issuing proceedings in court and in response, Intuitive Systems claimed that clause 33 provided a 'condition precedent' to litigation and requested that the court stayed proceedings to allow the defined process to commence.[49]

McKinnon J did not construe clause 33 to be a 'condition precedent' which bound the parties but, if found to be wrong, was 'strongly' disposed to the opinion that the meetings had been conducted 'pursuant to clause 33' and that 'appropriate senior representatives' had been present.[50] The court found that clause 33 was not an 'arbitration agreement' or even 'nearly an immediately effective agreement to arbitrate' as was the clause in *Channel Tunnel*, but only made 'provision for the parties to negotiate hopefully to agreement' and only when negotiation failed 'at that stage' to select arbitration, which they were not 'bound' to do.[51] McKinnon J accepted the defendant's argument that there was a distinction between 'determinative' alternatives including 'arbitration clauses, binding expert valuations and third party certifications' and 'non-determinative procedures including negotiation, mediation, expert appraisal and non-binding rulings from a mediator'.[52] The parties in *Channel Tunnel* and *Cott v. F. E. Barber* had agreed to 'determinative procedures unlike the non-determinative procedure in clause 33' whereas the parties in *Halifax* had 'in fact, in no sense bound themselves to any method of determining any dispute between them' and therefore, the court would not stay proceedings.[53]

McKinnon J further opined that mediation clauses and even arbitration clauses do not 'oust the court's jurisdiction', which would be against 'public policy' but held that courts have the power, 'in appropriate cases' to stay proceedings either under the Arbitration Acts or their 'inherent jurisdiction'.[54] Clause 33 was not an agreement to use arbitration or expert determination and therefore did not come under the Arbitration Acts or the courts' more general powers to stay proceedings when the parties have agreed to a binding dispute resolution proceedings.[55] Nor would McKinnon J consider using the court's 'general discretion' to issue a stay in proceedings to

47 *Halifax Financial Services Ltd v. Intuitive Systems Ltd* [1999] at 307
48 *Halifax Financial Services Ltd v. Intuitive Systems Ltd* [1999] at 304
49 *Halifax Financial Services Ltd v. Intuitive Systems Ltd* [1999] at 307
50 *Halifax Financial Services Ltd v. Intuitive Systems Ltd* [1999] at 311
51 *Halifax Financial Services Ltd v. Intuitive Systems Ltd* [1999] at 312
52 *Halifax Financial Services Ltd v. Intuitive Systems Ltd* [1999] at 312
53 *Halifax Financial Services Ltd v. Intuitive Systems Ltd* [1999] at 313
54 *Halifax Financial Services Ltd v. Intuitive Systems Ltd* [1999] at 311
55 *Halifax Financial Services Ltd v. Intuitive Systems Ltd* [1999] at 312

'encourage settlement' because the parties had already engaged in 'months of negotiations' and 'forced negotiation would be futile'.[56]

The law up to this point acknowledged that the court has inherent power to stay proceedings where parties agreed to determinative procedures as 'condition precedent' to arbitration but the enforceability of non-binding processes remained uncertain until CPR came into force[57] and the issue was addressed by the commercial High Court in *Cable & Wireless Plc v. IBM United Kingdom Ltd* after CPR.[58] The parties were in dispute over the 'validity' of a 'benchmarking' report issued by a third party, which obliged IBM to produce a plan to 'adjust costs and compensate' Cable & Wireless.[59] Clause 41 of the contract required the parties to escalate disputes through 'negotiations between senior executives' before attempting 'in good faith' an 'ADR procedure recommended to the parties by the Centre for Dispute Resolution' but clause 41 also stated 'the ADR procedure which is followed does not prevent any party or Local Party from issuing proceedings'.[60] Clause 40 in the contract detailed the internal dispute resolution arrangement and levels for escalating the dispute.

IBM requested a stay in proceedings for ADR to commence on the grounds that the clause was 'analogous to an arbitration clause' but Cable & Wireless submitted it was an agreement to negotiate therefore unenforceable due to a lack of certainty.[61] In Justice Colman's analysis clauses 40 and 41 showed the parties had a 'mutual intention' only to litigate as a 'last resort' and he dismissed the argument that the contract allowed the parties to issue proceedings which would indicate they did not intend the dispute resolution clause to be binding.[62] The clause only provided for the parties to issue proceedings where they had 'reasonable cause to do so to avoid damage to its business or to protect or preserve any right of action'.[63]

The dispute resolution clause used in *Cable & Wireless* was distinguished from an 'agreement to negotiate' or an agreement to 'strive to settle a dispute amicably', which had been used in the case of *Paul Smith v. H & S International Holding Inc*,[64] because both gave 'insufficient objective criteria' to assess whether there had been 'compliance or breach of such a provision'.[65] In *Cable & Wireless* the parties had gone further by identifying that they would use a procedure recommended by CEDR, which had been

56 *Halifax Financial Services Ltd v. Intuitive Systems Ltd* [1999] at 313
57 See Nesic (2001)
58 *Cable & Wireless Plc v. IBM United Kingdom Ltd* [2002] CLC 1319; EWHC (Comm) 2059; 2 All ER (Comm) 1041
59 *Cable & Wireless* [2002] at 8
60 *Cable & Wireless* [2002] at 12
61 *Cable & Wireless* [2002] at 15
62 *Cable & Wireless* [2002] at 17 & 20
63 *Cable & Wireless* [2002] at 20
64 *Cable & Wireless* [2002] at 23. Citing *Paul Smith v. H&S International Holding Inc* [1991] 2 Lloyd's Rep. 127
65 *Cable & Wireless* [2002] at 25

providing 'mediation services' for over 12 years and had published a 'model procedure' for mediation.[66] Not only had the parties 'prescribed the means' for attempting ADR, the court found that CEDR's mediation model provided guidelines for attendance and engagement by the parties and also stipulated that termination could only take place after the appointment of the mediator and commencement of the process.[67] Therefore, Colman J was of the opinion that the court would be able to 'determine' a breach of the ADR clause if the parties did not 'cooperate' with the appointment of a mediator or failed to send documents to the mediator or did not attend when called for the first meeting.[68]

Colman J warned future courts and litigants that to 'accentuate uncertainty' in a contract provision would 'fly in the face of public policy' because not only was mediation now 'recognised' and 'well-developed' in the English jurisdiction but also an established part of the procedure required by CPR.[69] Where contract clauses do not provide for an 'identifiable procedure' such as existed in *Cable & Wireless*, Colman J said they should not 'necessarily fail for uncertainty' but should be examined to consider whether the clause was 'expressed in an unqualified and mandatory term'.[70]

Commentators observe that the court 'assumed' the reference referred to mediation despite the fact that the parties had not decided which ADR procedure to use.[71] Mackie, the Chief Executive of CEDR,[72] commenting on the decision, intimated that 'hypothetically' CEDR might have recommended another ADR procedure, but that the 'reference to CEDR' 'could' still have reached the test posited in *Cable & Wireless* of 'unqualified and mandatory', which required 'a minimum duty of participation'.[73] This may be an accurate reflection but it would not necessarily have solved the issue relating to non-binding ADR unless the procedure chosen was not determinative. *Cable & Wireless* was one of a number of cases heard at what some regard as the 'high point' of mediation before the more restrained CA judgment in *Halsey*.[74] Early case law in the English jurisdiction illustrated the understanding some members of the judiciary had about mediation and particularly the abilities of skilled mediators to resolve even 'unpromising' cases,[75] which was a belief exemplified in the judgment of Brooke LJ in *Dunnett v. Railtrack*:[76] 'Skilled

---

66 *Cable & Wireless* [2002] at 21
67 *Cable & Wireless* [2002] at 1 & 21
68 *Cable & Wireless* [2002] at 29
69 *Cable & Wireless* [2002] at 25
70 *Cable & Wireless* [2002] at 32
71 Suter (2009) at 30; See also Mackie (2003)
72 Professor Mackie was the Chief Executive of CEDR at the date of writing see http://www. cedr.com/foundation/downloaded on 11 December 2012
73 Mackie (2003) at 349
74 *Halsey v. Milton Keynes General NHS Trust* [2004] EWCA (Civ) 576. See Genn (2010) at 99
75 See Shipman (2006); Brooker & Lavers (2005a); Genn (2010)
76 *Dunnett v. Railtrack Plc* [2002] at 14

mediators are now able to achieve results satisfactory to both parties in many cases which are quite beyond the power of lawyers and courts to achieve'.

ADR clauses following Cable & Wireless

Even after the bullish decision in *Cable & Wireless*, the English courts have continued to examine ADR and mediation clauses. In *Flight Training International v. International Fire Training Equipment Ltd (IFTE)*, the dispute resolution clause (Article XI) stated that disputes would be submitted to the Advisory, Conciliation and Arbitration Service (ACAS) and the fees to be paid by the party 'which does not prevail at mediation'.[77] When a dispute arose, Flight Training contacted ACAS but they responded to the effect that they did not deal with commercial disputes, after which they applied to the court to 'appoint' an arbitrator but IFTE countered the existence of 'a valid arbitration clause'.[78]

Cresswell J judged that the clause was not an agreement to submit disputes to arbitration.[79] ACAS provided three *distinct* (emphasis in judgment) services of conciliation, mediation or arbitration and the clause referring to payment of the mediation fees indicated that they intended to 'select' the mediation service from ACAS.[80] Therefore, the court declined Flight Training's application to appoint an arbitrator, which led one commentator to observe that the result was that the parties had to litigate which was the one dispute resolution process that they had eschewed.[81]

In *Holloway v. Chancery Mead Ltd* homeowners made an application to the court to refer their dispute with the sellers of the property to arbitration but Chancery Mead claimed there was a 'condition precedent' in the sales contract requiring the homeowners to submit their dispute to the National House Building Council's (NHBC) dispute resolution service.[82] The homeowners and the builders of the property, which was not Chancery Mead, were part of a Buildmark agreement provided by the NHBC but some disputes were outside the scope of the dispute resolution service.[83] Despite holding that the dispute was outside the remit of the service, Ramsey J nonetheless provided an opinion on whether there was a 'binding obligation' on the parties to refer disputes to the NHBC Resolution Service had this not been so.[84]

---

77 *Flight Training International v. International Fire Training Equipment Ltd* [2004] EWHC (Comm) 2004 WL 07447 at 7
78 *Flight Training* (2004) at 13 and 18
79 *Flight Training* (2004) at 46
80 *Flight Training* (2004) at 46
81 Debattista (2005)
82 *Holloway v. Chancery Mead Ltd* [2007] EWHC 2495 (TCC) at 15
83 *Holloway v. Chancery Mead Ltd* [2007] at 44
84 *Holloway v. Chancery Mead Ltd* [2007] at 66

Ramsey J considered English authorities but specifically deliberated on the Australian case of *Aiton Australia Pty Ltd v. Transfield Pty Ltd*[85] in which Einstein J, in contrast to the House of Lords decision in *Walford v. Miles*, held that an agreement to negotiate in good faith could be binding if it is 'sufficiently precisely defined to be certain' and the parties participate with an 'open mind'.[86] Open mindedness meant '(a) a willingness to consider such options for the resolution of the dispute as may be propounded by the opposing party or by the mediator as appropriate; [and] (b) a willingness to give consideration to putting forward options for the resolution of the dispute'.[87]

Einstein J set down four criteria for the enforceability of ADR clauses from which Ramsey J considered that there must be at 'least three requirements': 'First, that the process must be sufficiently certain in that there should not be the need for an agreement at any stage before matters can proceed. Secondly, the administrative processes for selecting a party to resolve the dispute and to pay that person should also be defined. Thirdly, the process or at least a model of the process should be set out so that the detail of the process is sufficiently certain.'[88]

The HSBC clause was found to be enforceable because there were 'clear paths' for the system to be 'accepted or rejected', the 'administrative processes' for implementing the dispute resolution service were 'clear' and the process was 'sufficiently detailed for providing a dispute resolution service that is certain'.[89] Though Ramsey J opined that the clause in *Cable & Wireless*[90] would also reach these three requirements, it is difficult to see how a clause that does not stipulate the process that should be used is sufficiently certain, even where there is an identified mechanism in the contract directing the parties to an organisation, when there is still another step to be taken by a third party in selecting the most appropriate process. Parties, who were perhaps intending to select a non-binding ADR process may instead find themselves in a binding procedure, which hardly enhances party choice or self-determination.

The three-stage test was used by the commercial High Court in *Sulamerica CIA Nacional De Seguros SA & Ors v. Enesa Engenharia SA & Ors* when considering whether a clause stating that the parties would 'seek to have the dispute resolved by mediation' was enforceable.[91] The clause failed on all three grounds:[92] In the first place the parties had not made an 'unequivocal

---

85 *Aiton Australia Pty Ltd v. Transfield Pty Ltd* [2000] ADRLJ 342
86 *Holloway v. Chancery Mead Ltd* [2007] at 79
87 *Holloway v. Chancery Mead Ltd* [2007] at 79
88 *Holloway v. Chancery Mead Ltd* [2007] at 81
89 *Holloway v. Chancery Mead Ltd* [2007] at 82–4
90 *Holloway v. Chancery Mead Ltd* [2007] at 82
91 *Sulamerica CIA Nacional De Seguros SA & Ors v. Enesa Engenharia SA & Ors* [2012] EWHC 42 (Comm) (19 January 2012) at 2
92 *Sulamerica* [2012] at 27

commitment to engage in mediation' but only agreed in 'general term' to attempt the process and furthermore had not agreed to a 'particular procedure'.[93] Second, the parties had not defined any model of mediation or ADR such as that provided by CEDR, which had satisfied the court in *Cable & Wireless*.[94] Finally, the parties had not agreed on the 'identity of the mediator, the location of the mediation and the process in which the parties had to engage'.[95] Additionally, the court held that the actions of the insurers in sending a 'draft mediation agreement' was evidence that the parties had not reached agreement about how to proceed and indicated that 'there was a need for further agreement'.[96]

The three-stage test was used again in *Wah v. Grant Thornton*.[97] Before arbitrating the parties were required to take the dispute to the Chief Executive for resolution by 'amicable conciliation' and then to a three-person panel.[98] Hildyard J reiterated that 'agreements to agree' and agreements to negotiate in good faith, 'without more' are not enforceable, the court must 'strain to find a construction' where there is a 'legally enforceable contract'.[99] Each case is considered 'on its own terms' and the test is not that 'the clause is a valid provision for a recognised process' but whether the 'obligations and/or negative injunctions it imposes are sufficiently clear' for the courts to determine.[100] The test to apply in such circumstances is whether the clause is:[101]

> (a) a sufficiently certain and unequivocal commitment to commence a process (b) from which may be discerned what steps each party is required to take to put the process in place and which is (c) sufficiently clearly defined to enable the Court to determine objectively (i) what under that process is the minimum required of the parties to the dispute in terms of their participation in it and (ii) when or how the process will be exhausted or properly terminable without breach.

In *Balfour Beatty Construction Northern Ltd v. Modus Corovest*, the parties made 'homemade amendments' to a standard form contract used in the construction industry.[102] The clause stated that:[103]

---

93 *Sulamerica* [2012] at 27
94 *Sulamerica* [2012] at 27
95 *Sulamerica* [2012] at 27
96 *Sulamerica* [2012] at 27
97 *Wah v. Grant Thornton International Ltd aka Wah (aka Tang) v. Grant Thornton International Ltd* [2012] EQHC 3189
98 *Wah v. Grant Thornton* [2012] at 27
99 *Wah v. Grant Thornton* [2012] at 57 and 58
100 *Wah v. Grant Thornton* [2012] at 59–60
101 *Wah v. Grant Thornton* [2012] at 60
102 *Balfour Beatty Construction Northern Ltd v. Modus Corovest (Blackpool) Ltd* [2008] EWHC 3029 at 5 & 17
103 *Balfour Beatty v. Modus* [2008] at 13

Either party may identify to the other any dispute or difference as being a matter that is capable of resolution by mediation and, upon being requested to do so, the other party shall within seven days indicate whether or not it consents to participate in the mediation with a view to resolving the dispute or difference.

Coulson J found that the parties had only made an 'agreement to agree'[104] because the clause afforded the non-referring party with a choice whether to mediate or not when a dispute occurred,[105] which it is submitted would not pass the third certainty requirement proposed by Ramsey J in *Holloway v. Chancery*. Policy commitment to mediation or ADR does not override the need for certainty in cases where the construction of the clause does not point towards the parties 'intending' that their dispute will be removed from litigation before it arises.[106] In drawing up the clause in *Cable & Wireless* both parties intended to use an ADR procedure other than litigation or arbitration as the first port of call. In contrast, in *Balfour Beattie v. Modus* the parties had agreed to consider using mediation after a dispute arises when presumably the party declining to use it does so because they believe the process is inappropriate for the issue. In other words, the parties reserved their right of 'keeping their negotiating hands free' to select the most suitable procedure when the dispute occurs.[107]

Approaches from other common law jurisdictions to mediation clauses

Just as many common law countries are following similar paths in ADR development so too have they grappled with the problem of enforcing ADR or mediation provision in contracts.[108] Part of the problem is what remedies the courts can award when a party has breached a mediation clause, which would be 'specific performance, damages or an injunction' and the difficulties that each of these present as an effective solution.[109] It is said that there is nothing gained by ordering a reluctant party to engage in mediation, either through specific performance or an injunction, as they can simply 'frustrate' the process before arriving at court at a later stage, which 'wastes time and costs'.[110] In the English jurisdiction, agreements to negotiate are

---

104 *Balfour Beatty v. Modus* [2008] at 17
105 *Balfour Beatty v. Modus* [2008] at 17
106 *Flight Training* (2004) at 46
107 Mackie (2003) at 350
108 For an analysis of awarding damages in common law jurisdictions see for example, Katz (1988); Boulle (2001); Cheong (2008); Hong Kong Working Group Report (2010) at 7.4–7.81
109 See for example, Mackie et al. (2007) Chapter 9; Hong Kong Working Group (2010) at 7.78–7.79
110 Katz (1988) at 583; See Hong Kong Working Group (2010) at 7.73

not enforceable because the court cannot 'police' the negotiations, particularly when it has not developed the concept of good faith recognised in other jurisdictions and the process of mediation presents the same problems in view of its confidentiality.[111] The difficulty with damages is that if mediation fails to settle there is 'no loss' for the court to estimate: 'Equally they say that there can be no loss to the other party if for want of co-operation and consent the consensual process would have led to no result',[112] which Lord Denning found with negotiation agreements that 'fall through'.[113] Countering these arguments are those who believe that once parties are at mediation the process can take over and against all odds produce settlements or at the least reduce some of the issues.[114]

Mediation and non-binding ADR clauses in the USA

In the USA, despite the longevity of the mediation movement, court approaches to pre-dispute mediation contract agreements have lacked a consistent approach,[115] perhaps largely because binding arbitration, which has statutory support, was one of the first procedures adopted as part of an ADR agenda and courts had then to consider how to deal with non-binding processes. Some courts in the United States were influenced by the 'antiquated' principle of 'ousting the court's jurisdiction', which Schmitz suggests led to an 'overly' restrictive interpretation of clauses[116] and in the early days there may have been judicial 'mistrust or misconceptions about ADR'.[117] Katz reports that until the middle of the 1980s courts usually dealt with mediation and non-binding ADR clauses by refusing enforcement based on two lines of reasoning, the 'futility argument' and the 'damages argument'.[118] She suggests that equity principles support the argument that it is 'futile' to order the parties to mediate because the courts will not enforce a 'vain order' and therefore 'will not order the parties to do something that would be ineffectual'.[119]

ADR clauses however began to receive support from the judicial application of the rules in federal and state arbitration statutes.[120] Neither the Federal

---

111 *Walford v. Miles* (1992) at 138. The issues of confidentiality and the overlap with the principles of without prejudice privilege are dealt with in Chapter 5.
112 per Giles J in *Hooper v. Natcom* [2002] at 206A–C
113 *Courtney v. Tolaini* [1975] 1 All ER 716 at 302
114 Hong Kong Working Group (2010) at 7.73. See *Dunnett v. Railtrack Plc* [2002b] EWCA Civ 303 (Costs) at 16
115 Katz (1988) (2008a,b); Stipanowich (2007); Rau (2005); Schmitz (2004)
116 Schmitz (2004) at 27–8
117 Stipanowich (2007) at 463
118 Katz (1988) at 583; Katz (2008a,b). Citing *In re Estate of Ferdinand Marcos Human Rights Litigation*, 94 F 3d 539 (9th Cir. 1996); *Virginian Ry. Co. v. System Fed'n No. 40*, 300 USA 515, 550, 601 (1937).
119 Katz (1988) at 538. See also Schmitz (2004)
120 See for example, Stipanowich (2007)

Arbitration Act (FAA) 1925 nor the Uniform Arbitration Act (UAA) 1955[121] provide a definition of arbitration, which left the courts to 'reach their own conclusions' of its applicability to non-binding ADR procedures.[122] Federal and state courts began to take a 'pragmatic'[123] approach to the enforceability of non-binding ADR clauses in order to stay proceeding or compel attendance.[124] Stipanowich's analysis of USA case law indicates that ADR clauses were either not enforced because of 'irrelevant procedural distinctions' or 'interpreted to . . . extend to virtually any kind of ADR procedure, or simply applied them willy-nilly without discussion'.[125]

Katz believed that the 'breakthrough'[126] for mediation was the decision in *AMF Inc v. Brunswick Corp*,[127] when a Federal District Court held that a clause agreeing to an 'advisory opinion' was enforceable under the FAA, which led many courts to accept that mediation clauses came with the 'scope' of arbitration legislation.[128] Critics of this approach highlighted that it was not the intention of Congress to apply the FAA or the UAA to non-binding ADR processes.[129] Schmitz noted that the National Conference of Commissioners on Uniform State Law (NCCUSL) declined to revise the UAA to include summary enforcement of mediation clauses and the drafters of the Uniform Mediation Act preferred to leave enforcement to the courts, which, the author suggests, was on the assumption that courts would 'readily' do so.[130]

The issue of treating ADR clauses as if they are arbitration clauses was reviewed by the United States Court of Appeal in *Advanced Bodycare Solutions LLC v. Thione International Inc*, where the clause in question required senior personnel to negotiate before submitting the dispute to 'non-binding arbitration or mediation'.[131] The appeal court decided that the factor

---

121 UAA was revised in 2000. The UAA is 'the model' for the majority of state arbitration statutes. See Stipanowich (2007) at 842.
122 Stipanowich (2007) at 435. For a detailed review of the case-law on the definitional issues of arbitration see Stipanowich (2007). Stipanowich's analysis reveals how different State and Federal courts have considered the scope of the FAA and UAA from 'classical arbitration' where a third party neutral provides a binding decision to non-binding arbitration and non-binding ADR procedures to finally mediation.
123 Rau (2005) at 467–73
124 See Stipanowich (2007). The author gives a detailed analysis of cases of the scope of arbitration law from 'classic' binding arbitration to non-binding arbitration and ADR and eventually mediation. See also Stipanowich (2001)
125 Stipanowich (2001) at 858; See also Katz (2008a, b)
126 Katz (2008a) (not paginated)
127 *AMF Inc v. Brunswick Corp*, 621 F Supp 456, 458, 463 (EDNY 1985)
128 See Rau (2005) at 469
129 See for example, Stipanowich (2007) at 438 & fn142; Schmitz (2004); Katz (2008a, b)
130 Schmitz (2004) at 12–13; Stipanowich (2007) at 444; Leasure (2008) at 26. Leasure reviews the enforceability of mediation clauses in Kansas State and cites *Lynn v. General Electric* 2005 WL 701270, where the district court noted that both the UAA and the UMA drew distinctions between mediation and arbitration.
131 *Advanced Bodycare Solutions LLC v. Thione International Inc no 07-12309 Appeal from the USA District Court for the Southern District of Florida (11 Circuit) (2008)*

'controlling' whether a procedure is arbitration was whether it 'results in an award' and the 'bright line' distinguishing mediation from arbitration is whether the process 'purports to adjudicate or resolve a case in any way', if it does not then 'it is not arbitration within meaning of the FAA'.[132] Furthermore, clauses providing the 'option' for arbitration *or* mediation (italics provided in judgment) were not 'an agreement to settle by arbitration a controversy' and therefore were 'not enforceable under the FAA either'.[133] The aim of the Court of Appeal was not 'denigrating' mediation but encouraging its use through 'local rules to order mediation or to use their inherent powers to stay proceedings'.[134]

Although it is suggested that some courts in the USA still enforce ADR clauses through the auspices of the arbitration Acts, now other grounds are often be used.[135] For example, Stipanowich notes that many federal and state jurisdictions provide statutes for enforcement of mediation agreements and judges may use the existence of an ADR clause 'to augment the judicial prerogative' to order attendance.[136] Mediation clauses are now enforced as a 'condition precedent' to arbitration or litigation either through the 'contract provision or through statute'.[137]

Courts are reported to 'frequently dismiss' claims if the parties try to avoid their agreements to mediate but there is said to be a 'dearth of judicial authority' on what remedies will be awarded because compliance with these clauses is not expensive.[138] One informal survey found 29 enforcement decisions, which had used 'common law contract principles' by ordering 'specific performance, stays or dismissals of litigation or arbitration, damages, and sanctions, such as denial of attorney fees and costs'.[139] However, some contract provisions are ambiguous and may cause difficulties for the courts to interpret.[140] Cole et al. note three problems which impinge on the enforceability of a mediation clause: (1) 'vagueness', (2) 'conflicting provisions', and (3) 'incorrect terminology'.[141] In their analysis where there is 'vagueness' the courts will usually endeavour to uphold the clause because the settlement outcome of mediation is 'not binding' on the parties.[142] 'Sloppy drafting' reportedly creates enforcement problems, for example having different

---

132 *Advanced Bodycare Solutions LLC v. Thione* (2008) at 8–9
133 *Advanced Bodycare Solutions LLC v. Thione* (2008) at 11
134 *Advanced Bodycare Solutions LLC v. Thione* (2008) at 11
135 Cole et al. (2012) at Section 6.2
136 See Stipanowich (2007) at 447. For example, Stipanowich cites at fn 173 the Texas Alternative Dispute Resolution Procedures Act, Tex Civ Prac & Rem Code Ann § 154.001–154.073.
137 See Cole et al. (2012) at section 6.4. See also Rau (2005) at 461
138 Cole et al. (2012) at 6.1
139 Katz (2008a) at 183
140 Cole et al. (2012) at section 6.8
141 Cole et al. (2012) at section 6.8
142 Cole et al. (2012) at section 6.8. Cole et al. cite *Oglebay Norton Co. v. Armco, Inc.*, 556 NE 2d 515, 521 (Ohio 1990)

dispute resolution provisions in the same contract is said to be 'common-place', but Cole et al. note that the Supreme Court in Utah gave precedent to the arbitration rather than the mediation clause because the contract stated that the 'addendums control' conflicting provisions and an addendum contained the arbitration clause.[143] They cite a number of cases where the definition of mediation has been confusing, for example in *Oliver Design Group v. Westside Deutscher Frauen-Verein* the contract provided for 'binding mediation' but the court refused a stay for arbitration because they held that the parties intended mediation and not arbitration.[144] Finally the authors note that clauses may not be 'specific enough' as they do not provide sufficient detail about mediator appointments, participation and steps to be taken to begin the process. However, they caution against over specifica-tion other than requiring 'attendance' because this may result in 'disputes over compliance'.[145]

Australian agreements to use ADR or mediation

As noted above, courts in the English jurisdiction have chosen to develop the law on ADR clauses using persuasive Australian cases. Boulle reported that by 2001 all jurisdictions in Australia could make orders for referrals to mediation[146] and since 1997, Federal Courts use mandatory referral.[147] However, there is a significant difference in the 'structural' arrangements 'across jurisdictions' because court programmes were set up with different 'objectives' and may have arrangements to refer parties to either court schemes or to 'external' organisations'.[148] It is against this developing backdrop of mandatory mediation that Australian courts have considered the enforcement of non-binding ADR clauses.

Australian courts will stay proceedings for arbitration clauses under the common law *Scott and Avery*[149] rule and more recently under powers of the 'uniform commercial arbitration Acts' enacted by each state.[150] However, until the decision in *Hooper Bailie v. Natcon*, there had been uncertainty

---

143 Cole et al. (2012) at Section 6.8. Cole et al. cite *Central Florida Investments, Inc. v. Parkwest Associates*, 2002 UT 3, 40 P 3d 599 (Utah 2002) at 606

144 Cole et al. (2012) at Section 6.8. Cole et al. cite *Oliver Design Group v. Westside Deutscher Frauen Verein*, 2002-Ohio-7066, 2002 WL 31839158, *2 (Ohio Ct App 8th Dist Cuyahoga County 2002), related reference, 2004 WL 5199473 (Ohio CP 2004) and related reference, 2004 WL 5199474 (Ohio CP 2004).

145 Cole et al. (2012) at section 6.8

146 Boulle (2001) at 46, 46–7; Sourdin (2006) in Alexander (2006)

147 Federal Court of Australia Act 1976 (Cth) s53A and ss 53A(1), 1(A) as amended by the Law and Justice Legislation Amendment Act 1997. See Sourdin (2006) 51–8. See also Boulle (2001)

148 See Sourdin (2006) at 51–8

149 See Brown & Marriott (2011) at 598. Brown and Marriott discuss the use of *Scott and Avery* clauses in contract which make the decision of the arbitrator a 'condition precedent' before litigating. *Scott and Avery* (1856) 10 ER 1121

150 Angyal (1994); Sourdin (2006); Mead (1996)

whether courts would enforce ADR or mediation clauses.[151] Early Australian case law also exhibits two lines of reasoning against enforcement: first, an ADR or mediation clause 'ousted the court's jurisdiction'[152] and second, the courts regarded them as agreements to negotiate, which failed because of a 'lack of intention to create legal intentions and for want of certainty'.[153] In *Hooper Bailie v. Natcon*, the parties agreed to engage in conciliation in a 'letter', which was reported to have settled some issues but after Natcon went into liquidation, arbitration was restarted by the liquidators at which point Hooper Bailie requested a stay in proceeding to conclude the conciliation.[154]

Giles J after reviewing the Australian and English authorities dismissed the contention that it would be 'futile' for the court to try to enforce consent because they would not be enforcing 'cooperation and consent but participation in a process from which cooperation and consent might come'.[155] The court held that agreements to use either conciliation or mediation were not the same as 'agreements to agree' or 'agreements to negotiate in good faith', which was the approach taken in *Walford v. Miles*, and contracts with 'express' or 'implied' terms, which provide 'sufficient certainty' about the parties' 'conduct in participation' should be enforced.[156]

Giles J concluded that the court had the authority to stay arbitration proceedings, either through the Commercial Arbitration Act 1984 or through its 'inherent power' to 'prevent an abuse of process' 'namely that the court makes people abide by their contracts'.[157] Mead suggests that Giles J was 'influenced' by what conciliation had achieved before the winding up order and the potential 'value' of continuing with the process, which allowed the court to distinguish an earlier case refusing enforcement where the parties were entrenched in their positions.[158]

However, in contrast, Giles J in the later case of *Elizabeth Bay Developments v. Boral Building Services* found that the mediation clause in question was not 'sufficiently certain' to be enforced.[159] The clause required the parties to use mediation administered by the Australian Commercial Disputes Centre (ACD Centre) if they were unable to resolve the dispute within a specified

151 *Hooper Bailie Associated Limited v. Natcon Group Pty Limited & Anor* (1992) 28 NSWLR 194. See Angyal (1994)
152 Angyal (1994) at 35. Angyal suggests that this was the reasoning behind the refusal to enforce a conciliation clause in *Allco Steel (Queensland) Pty v. Torres Strait Gold Pty Limited & Ors* (unreported, SC of Qld, 12 March 1990). See also Mead (1996) at 32
153 Angyal (1994) at 35–6. The author cites *Coal Cliff Collieries Pty Ltd v. Sijehama Pty Ltd* (1992) 24 NSWLR 1
154 *Hooper Bailie Associated Ltd v. Natcon Group* (1992) NSWLR 194. See Mead (1996) at 33
155 *Hooper Bailie* (1992) at 206. See Dreadon (2005) at 71
156 *Hooper Bailie* (1992) at 209. See Angyal (1994) at 38; Cheong (2008) at 199
157 Mead (1996) at 33. Mead cites MacKinnon LJ in *Racecourse Betting Control Board v. Secretary for Air* [1944] Ch 114 at 211
158 Mead (1996) at 33 cites *Allco Steel (Queensland) Pty Ltd. v. Torres Strait Gold Pty Ltd & Ors* (unreported SC of Qld 12 March 1990) at 50
159 Mead (1996) at 35 cites *Elizabeth Bay Developments Pty Ltd v. Boral Building Services Pty Ltd* (1995) 36 NSWLR 709. For a detailed analysis see Mead (1996)

period but the contract did not contain detailed information on the procedure to follow, although the ACD Centre had written guidelines and a mediation agreement that participants sign prior to commencement.[160] Giles J accepted that both parties considered they had incorporated the guidelines into their contract but they still had to draw up a mediation agreement before starting the process, which the court noted could have taken any number of forms, therefore the clause could not be enforced because it lacked certainty in the conduct of the procedure.[161] Mead suggests the court could have corrected this shortfall by 'reference to external standards',[162] which was the approach eventually adopted in the English jurisdiction in *Cable & Wireless* (see above).

The position was clarified in the later case of *Aiton Australia Pty Ltd v. Transfield Pty Ltd* (discussed above) which had to consider the enforceability of an extremely convoluted dispute resolution clause.[163] Clause 28 included a process for a dispute notice, meetings to exchange information, mediation, legal action and expert determination; additionally, the parties agreed 'to make diligent and good faith efforts to revolve disputes in accordance' with this provision. *Aiton* includes an analysis of a 'good faith' requirement in dispute resolution, which the Lords in *Walford v. Miles* (above) considered incompatible to the adversarial nature of negotiation.

Einstein J approved the decision in *Elizabeth Bay Developments*[164] that a stay or adjournment will not be granted 'if the procedures are not sufficiently detailed to be meaningfully enforced'.[165] As discussed earlier in the review of English cases, the court held that for enforceability an ADR clause must first act as a 'condition precedent' before litigation; second it must 'be certain' with no further party agreement needed before starting the process; third 'the administrative processes for appointment and payment of the third party must be in place' or a 'mechanism' to set this in motion and finally 'the clause' should be sufficiently comprehensive for the 'process to be followed'.[166] In Justice Einstein's opinion the clause in *Elizabeth Bay Developments* failed because it did not satisfy the third condition as there was 'no mechanism' for paying the mediator's fees[167] but despite the need for careful drafting, it was recommended that ADR clauses should not be 'overly structured' as this could result in the process resembling litigation.[168] These requirements have now been crystallised in the English case of *Holloway v. Chancery Mead* and

---

160 *Elizabeth Bay Developments* (1995) at 714. See Mead (1996) at 57–8; Spencer (1995)
161 *Elizabeth Bay Developments* (1995) at 715–16. See Mead (1996); Spencer (1995)
162 See Mead (1996) at 35
163 *Aiton Australia Pty Ltd v. Transfield Pty Ltd* [2000] ADRLJ 342
164 *Elizabeth Bay Developments Pty Ltd v. Boral Building Services Pty Ltd* (1995) 36 NSWLR 709. See Mead (1996)
165 *Aiton Australia Pty Ltd v. Transfield Pty Ltd* [2000] at 44
166 *Holloway v. Chancery Mead Ltd* [2007]
167 *Elizabeth Bay Developments* (1995) at 66–7. See Spencer (1995); Mead (1996)
168 *Elizabeth Bay Developments* (1995) at 62. See Spencer (1995); Mead (1996)

applied to mediation clauses on a number of occasions. The Australian case law has also provided guidance to the Hong Kong jurisdiction.

Hong Kong agreements to mediate

When Hong Kong became a 'Special Administrative Region' in China in 1997, the 'Basic Law' derived from the 'common law, rules of equity, ordinances, subordinate legislation and customary law' remained in force.[169] Article 84 of the 'Basic Law' permits the courts to 'refer' to common law cases from other countries as precedent in their judgments.[170] Although the Hong Kong Court of Final Appeal (CFA) considers House of Lords (now the Supreme Court) and Privy Council decisions to be 'persuasive', so too are 'final appellant' decisions from other common law countries and at the 'end of the day, the courts in Hong Kong decide for themselves what is appropriate'.[171]

Hong Kong has also had an inconsistent approach to contracts containing ADR or mediation clauses and has looked to common law countries for persuasive guidance. In *Hyundai v. Vigour* the contract contained a 'lengthy' dispute resolution clause where the matter could first be referred to the architect and if any party was 'dissatisfied' with the architect's decision, then to arbitration but the arbitration clause provided for a request for conciliation where the conciliator had to issue a decision if no agreement was reached.[172] The parties were in dispute over a number of decisions by the architect when Hyundai issued a notice of arbitration after which they drew up a written agreement ('March Agreement') to relinquish their rights to 'arbitration or court action forever' and to take any unresolved issues to 'the managing directors' but if this failed, to mediation.[173] The issue before the court was whether the 'March Agreement' was contrary to public policy in that it ousted the court's jurisdiction and whether the agreements to negotiate then mediate were unenforceable for uncertainty.[174]

Reyes J did not construe the 'March Agreement' as the parties 'surrendering their right to litigation' because the parties were not 'ousting the court's jurisdiction' but only 'postponing' it until negotiation and mediation had taken place.[175] The court chose to follow USA authority and the Australian

169 See the Department of Justice: The Legal System in Hong Kong website
170 See the Department of Justice: The Legal System in Hong Kong website
171 F *Solicitor (24/07) v. Law Society of Hong Kong* [2008] 2 HKLRD 576 at 17. See Meggitt (2010) at 237. The author provides a commentary on the persuasiveness of English courts and suggests that the English Court of Appeal, which has provided more decisions on CPR than the House of Lords, would in the 'pecking order simply be one of the considerations' that the Hong Kong courts would consider.
172 *Hyundai Engineering and Construction Co Ltd v. Vigour Ltd* 2004 WL 6086 (CFI), 2004 WL 6086 (CFI), [2004] 3 HKLRD 1, [2004] HKEC 444 at (2)
173 *Hyundai v. Vigour Ltd* [2004] at 11
174 *Hyundai v. Vigour Ltd* [2004] at headnote 1 & 3
175 *Hyundai v. Vigour Ltd* at [2004] at 58 & 62

precedent in *Coal Cliff Collieries Pty Ltd v. Sijehama Pty Ltd*[176] rather than English jurisprudence by concluding that there should be no 'blanket rule' that all agreements to agree are unenforceable and that a 'nuanced approach' is adopted.[177]

Reyes J was unable to 'reconcile' Lord Ackner's 'reasoning' in *Miles v. Walford* that 'good faith negotiations were unworkable'[178] because it was questionable whether there was any 'conceptual' difference between 'best endeavours' and 'good faith' which were little different to the question of whether the parties have acted reasonably which the court 'regularly asks'.[179] This lead him to the opinion that 'English and Hong Kong courts should have no real difficulty in assessing "objectively" whether parties have acted in a spirit of cooperation and good faith'.[180]

Judge Reyes reviewed the Hong Kong case of *Kenon Engineering Ltd v. Nippon Kokan Koji Kabushiki Kaisha* where the parties had agreed to settle their disputes by a 'final and binding mediation award' but the two mediators had not been able to settle on the terms of mediation, 'the extent of the matters to be mediated' or the time frame.[181] The court in *Kenon Engineering* held a stay could not be awarded because the clause was not an 'arbitration agreement' and that 'if it was a mediation agreement it was not clear as to procedure'.[182] Reyes J approved the decision because of the inability of the mediators to reach agreement on the details of mediation but opined the case was 'limiting' because of a failure to consider Australian cases or *Cable & Wireless*.[183] He also approved the reasoning in *Cable & Wireless* because the parties had done more than agree to 'resolve the dispute in good faith' by agreeing to a procedure 'recommended by CEDR', which was enforceable because there was 'sufficient certainty' about the process to 'ascertain' whether a breach had occurred but Reyes J felt that 'one further step' could be taken.[184] Colman J had distinguished between an unenforceable agreement to negotiate and an agreement to negotiate by a prescribed procedure identified by CEDR rules[185] but Reyes J did not believe there was a 'practical distinction' between a 'negotiation pursuant to an identified procedure' or 'negotiation in good faith' or 'negotiation in accordance with such mediation procedure as the parties acting in good faith might reasonably agree on' and the courts should be able to enforce all three.[186]

---

176 *Coal Cliff Collieries Pty Ltd v. Sijehama Pty Ltd* (1991) 24 NSWLR 1
177 *Hyundai v. Vigour Ltd* [2004] at 77
178 *Walford v. Miles* [1992] at 138. See discussion above.
179 *Hyundai v. Vigour Ltd* [2004] at 83
180 *Hyundai v. Vigour Ltd* [2004] at 81
181 *Kenon Engineering Ltd v. Nippon Kokan Koji Kabushiki Kaisha* (unrep., HCA Nos 3492 and 3973 of 2002 and HCCT No 21 of 2003) at 89
182 *Hyundai v. Vigour Ltd* [2004] at 34
183 *Hyundai v. Vigour Ltd* [2004] at 91
184 *Hyundai v. Vigour Ltd* [2004] at 94
185 *Hyundai v. Vigour Ltd* [2004] at 96
186 *Hyundai v. Vigour Ltd* [2004] at 96

Reyes J concluded that there was 'no hard and fast rule' that agreements to negotiate or mediate in good faith are unenforceable 'per se' and the court should look at each case to see 'whether they can frame objective criteria' to assess whether there has been a breach of the obligation.[187] The evidence from the correspondence in *Hyundai Engineering* 'implied an obligation of cooperation and good faith' similar to *Cable & Wireless*[188] and 'the failure to identify the procedure or the time frame was not fatal' because there were 'minimum steps' that the parties could have taken, such as appointing a mediator who 'could then guide' them towards adopting a suitable procedure 'within a reasonable time frame'.[189]

This pioneering decision in Hong Kong was to be short lived and the Court of Appeal dismissed Reyes J's reasoning on a number of grounds. First, Rogers VP opined that Lord Ackner[190] had not meant that an agreement to use best endeavours to negotiate was enforceable because it was 'clear that what was being said was that a court is not in a position to determine the good faith or otherwise of negotiations because a party is entitled to negotiate any way he sees fit'.[191] Second, Reyes J had not 'sufficiently analysed' the Australian case of *Coal Cliff Collieries* which disagreed with the English authorities that 'no promise to negotiate in good faith would ever be enforceable' and the cases referred to in *Coal Cliff Collieries* concerned situations where 'the third party neutrals were authorised to settle' or 'where there was a readily ascertainable external standard'.[192] Further, Kirby J in *Coal Cliff Collieries* had not found that the clause 'to proceed in good faith to consult together upon the formulation of a more comprehensive and detailed joint venture' was enforceable, which therefore did not support the argument that the 'March Agreement' in *Hyundai Engineering* that 'the managing directors should resolve and decide any issues' was enforceable.[193]

Finally the CA held that the term 'submit to a third party mediation procedure' did not have any 'precision' about the 'steps' the parties had to take in contrast to *Cable & Wireless*, which had identified a CEDR procedure.[194] In the opinion of Roger VP the 'March agreement' was for some form of 'negotiation assisted by some unspecified party, whoever that might be' and an 'imprecise and unenforceable' provision that the managing directors should resolve the dispute.[195] Thus the Court of Appeal found that the agreement for the managing directors to negotiation in good faith and the

---

187 *Hyundai v. Vigour Ltd* [2004] at 98
188 *Hyundai v. Vigour Ltd* [2004] at 99
189 *Hyundai v. Vigour Ltd* [2004] at 100
190 *Hyundai v. Vigour Ltd* 2005 WL 10594 (CA), [2005] 3 HKLRD 723, [2005] HKEC 258, [2005] HKEC 258 at 27, *Walford v. Miles* [1992]
191 *Hyundai v. Vigour Ltd* [2005] CA at 27
192 *Hyundai v. Vigour Ltd* [2005] CA at 28
193 *Hyundai v. Vigour Ltd* [2005] CA at 29
194 *Hyundai v. Vigour Ltd* [2005] CA at 30
195 *Hyundai v. Vigour Ltd* [2005] CA at 30

mediation provision were both unenforceable because they were 'in essence' an agreement to agree.[196]

Cheong considers that the Court of Appeal in Hong Kong failed to provide sufficient reasoning by 'clinging to the orthodoxy' and neglecting to address the reasoning in new cases.[197] Nevertheless, he argues that by holding the 'March Agreement' unenforceable on the grounds of 'uncertainty' about 'the steps to take', the Court had 'impliedly approve(d)' *Cable & Wireless* signalling that carefully 'drafted' mediation clauses are enforceable and by evading an analysis of whether the courts can determine good faith leaving it 'open for later debate' by the courts.[198]

As Cheong observes the 'imprecision' of the 'March Agreement' made it a poor contender to test the validity of mediation clauses but the Court of Appeal, by focusing on 'good faith', has left it open for the future enforcement of an unambiguous clause thereby following the increasing trend in many jurisdictions to support mediation on policy grounds.[199] The argument may be academic in situations where ADR or mediation is mandated or compelled through court referrals but problems with drafting will still arise particularly when there are 'multi-tiered' dispute resolution clauses.[200] There are frequent reminders that when contracts contain glaring anomalies, such as failing to incorporate appendices that identify the process for selecting the ADR neutral[201] or when the words obviously indicate that the parties have the option of accepting or rejecting a mediation proposal then common law courts may have to review challenges to enforcement.[202] Therefore, the 'intellectual battle'[203] may be over in most common law countries but the need for parties and advisors to take adequate precautions when drafting mediation clauses remains.

Legislating for mediation clauses

One option to minimize problems with ADR clauses is to enact national legislation but there has been little encouragement despite the problems encountered with enforcement. As noted above, the drafting committees of

---

196 *Hyundai v. Vigour Ltd* [2005] CA at 23
197 Cheong (2008) at 203 & 206
198 Cheong (2008) at 208 & 207. See also the Hong Kong Working Group (2010) at 7.71. The Working Group suggests that the decision may indicate the CA general approach to mediation clauses but stated that *Hyundai v. Vigour* [2005] was decided on its 'own facts'.
199 Cheong (2008) at 207–08
200 See Jones (2009); Dobbins (2005)
201 See for example, Aibinu et al. (2010) at 40. The authors cite the Australian case of *State of New South Wales v. Banabella Electrical Pty Ltd* [2002] NSWSC 178 where the clause made provision for the parties to agree to an expert 'prescribed in the Annexure' but failed for uncertainty because the name was not in the document.
202 *Balfour Beatty Construction Northern Limited v. Modus Corovest (Blackpool) Ltd* [2008] EWHC 3029 at 5 & 17
203 Cheong (2008) at 208

both the Uniform Arbitration Act and the Uniform Mediation Act in the USA elected not to include the enforcement of ADR clauses. In Australia NADRAC 2010 did not take on proposals for legislating for this issue when making recommendations for future enactment for mediation law.[204] The report did recognise the 'benefits' of correctly drafted clauses such as providing 'up-front agreements about the allocation of costs' or allowing the contract to continue while the parties pursue settlement but also recognised that badly drafted provision can result in 'complex legal disputes' over their 'interpretation'.[205] The NADRAC report confines itself to supplying model clauses which parties can adopt or modify.[206] Hong Kong took a similar approach before implementing the Mediation Ordinance and despite acknowledging the difficulties of litigation in this area, elected not to include statutory provision for mediation clauses because of the courts' 'inherent jurisdiction to stay proceedings'.[207]

Careful drafting of mediation clauses v. flexibility of choice

To some extent, the more forceful approaches taken to compelling mediation in Australia, USA and Hong Kong are likely to minimise the necessity of legislative action. Nevertheless, the cases show the major obstacle to enforcement in common law jurisdictions is that of obtusely drafted provisions, which in most circumstances is overcome by ensuring that parties or their legal advisors take adequate precautions to avoid ambiguity. Practical advice abounds on how to avoid uncertainty in drafting ADR clauses[208] but, equally, there are cautionary tales from the cases about overly complex or technical provisions that may result in formulaic or legalistic procedures.[209] The experience of arbitration provides a warning against over-legalisation as over time the procedure increasingly came to resemble the very process that the parties wished to avoid.

In commercial contexts, such as IT or construction, there can be complicated contractual relationships or scientific issues where disputes arise, which increases the likelihood of acquiring specialist legal advice when designing dispute resolution mechanisms in contracts. This is particularly acute when there are on-going contracts. This increases the influence of lawyers in

---

204 NADRAC (2009). See Carroll (2001–2002). Carroll highlights this discussion prior to the enactment of ADR legislation in Australia.
205 NADRAC (2009) at 9.4–9.5
206 NADRAC (2009) at 9.11
207 Hong Kong Working Group (2010) at 7.79
208 Advice on drafting mediation clauses can be found in many publications and journal articles that consider mediation practice and principles. See for example Mackie (2003); Mackie et al. (2007); Boulle & Nesic (2001); Dobbins (2005); Jones (2009)
209 For example, Giles J who warned that 'overly structured' provisions may be 'counter-productive as it may begin to look much like litigation itself'. *Elizabeth Bay Developments v. Boral Building Services* (1995) at 62. See for example, Coben & Thompson (2006) at 144–5; Mackie (2003) at 350

mediation development but the contractual arrangements may also fetter the party's choice about the most suitable dispute resolution mechanism at the time the dispute arises. There are ways to ensure that litigation remains an option: for example Mackie advises that the parties can ensure that in appropriate situations they can still go to court by preserving the right to commence litigation and ADR together either for 'injunctive relief' or to 'indicate' how critical the problem is.[210] However, the possibility of leaving the choice of ADR procedure or mediation model depending on the dispute remains, in all probability, at best an agreement to agree or an agreement to negotiate.

However careful the drafting is, the cases show that in some circumstances they inevitably bear a risk of leading to litigation. Mediation is now so integral to litigation that the courts are prepared to support mediation clauses albeit not at the expense of well-defined legal principles. The inevitable result of this is to reinforce the institutionalisation of mediation. Mediation is following the same course as arbitration. First commerce recognises the process as an attractive alternative to litigation in that it provides a quick and cheaper solution to their problems or other benefits such as reaching a commercial compromise. Some parties then do not want to use mediation perhaps for the particular dispute that arises, or the clause has been drafted in such a way that it is open to interpretation, which often requires legal experts' advice, which may lead to the courts for determination.

Although contract clauses have gone some way to advancing the voluntary use of mediation, the process can also be initiated by an order from the court staying litigation until ADR is attempted when the parties have not made pre-dispute contract arrangements. Chapter 1 gave a brief review of the early cases, which followed CPR when judges began to use their case management powers to order parties to seek settlement through an ADR procedure. This next section provides a more detailed analysis on how courts exercise their discretion when issuing an ADR order to stay proceedings.

Stay in proceedings

Inherent powers to stay proceedings

The Court of Appeal and the High Court have 'inherent power to stay any proceeding that come before it'[211] for a wide range of reasons such as abuse of process or failure to comply with a court order[212] and similar powers are vested in the County Courts.[213] Section 9 of the Arbitration Act 1996 also

---

210 Mackie (2003) at 351
211 The Supreme Court Act 1981 s49(3)
212 White Book (2013) at Section 9 'Jurisdictional and Procedural Legislation' Part C at 49.3-176
213 County Court Act 1984, s76

recognises the inherent power of the court to stay proceedings when the parties have agreed to arbitrate, which is relevant to case law on ADR and mediation clauses prior to the enactment of the CPR 1998, discussed above.[214]

Before the introduction of the Civil Procedure Rules, the court had issued practice directions encouraging judicial support for staying proceedings for ADR or mediation.[215] CPR put this practice on a more formal setting with the introduction of rule 26(4):

26.4 – Stay to allow for settlement of the case

(1) A party may, when filing the completed directions questionnaire, make a written request for the proceedings to be stayed while the parties try to settle the case by alternative dispute resolution or other means.

(2) If all parties request a stay the proceedings will be stayed for one month and the court will notify the parties accordingly.

> (2A) If the court otherwise considers that such a stay would be appropriate, the court will direct that the proceedings, either in whole or in part, be stayed for one month, or for such other period as it considers appropriate.

(3) The court may extend the stay until such date or for such specified period as it considers appropriate.

(4) Where the court stays the proceedings under this rule, the claimant must tell the court if a settlement is reached.

(5) If the claimant does not tell the court by the end of the period of the stay that a settlement has been reached, the court will give such directions as to the management of the case as it considers appropriate.

The usual mechanism for prompting an ADR Order is that litigants file an allocation questionnaire (now called 'directions questionnaire') prior to court proceedings[216] and the judge will consider 'written requests' by 'all' parties for a stay while they 'try to settle their dispute by alternative dispute resolution or other means'.[217] The earlier version of CPR permitted 'the court on its own initiative' to issue a stay if it deems it 'appropriate' now under CPR 26(2A) the order may be made 'if the court otherwise considers that such a stay

214 Arbitration Act 1996 s9
215 See Chapter 1
216 Court protocols require parties to complete a form stating that they have considered ADR prior to litigation and to file this at the court. See Mackie et al. (2007) at 63. In the April 2013 CPR update 'allocation questionnaire' was changed to 'directions questionnaire'.
217 CPR r.26(4) (2) (a) changed by CPR r.26(4) (2A). See the White Book (2013). Section 14 at 14.13 Practice Direction 12.2 provides for other 'circumstances' that a judge may make an ADR order such as when the court has to make an order after judgment or has to decide on a payment order or a 'listing for a disposal hearing', when an ADR Order may also be made (r.12.2(1) (d))

would be appropriate'.[218] Parties not only have to explain their settlement attempts to the court during case settlement meetings but why ADR is not appropriate to their case.[219] Judicial consideration for making ADR Orders usually takes place in a case management conference (CMC) or when making directions to designate a case to the fast track or multi-track where there is no CMC.[220] A stay is usually granted for one month,[221] but it is worth noting that Mackie et al. suggest there is no requirement for court proceedings to be deferred as mediation can run concurrently with litigation with costs continuing, which they suggest may be expedient if the court suspects one party of using delaying tactics.[222] The situation for small claims of less than £5,000 are a little different as the parties can tick a box when lodging their claim indicating willingness to try mediation, after which the court will contact them, although current government policy is to introduce an automatic referral system where the parties will attend a mediation information meeting.[223]

Draft ADR Orders

Many of the Court Guides provide draft ADR Orders.[224] For example, the Admiralty and Commercial Court Guide supplies a Draft ADR Order which states in the rubric that each party 'shall' provide a list of three neutrals or 'additionally' or 'alternatively provide a list of one or more panels of neutral individuals'.[225] The order then requires that the parties 'in good faith endeavour to agree' on the neutral by a stated date but where this has not been achieved the CMC is 'restored to enable the Court to facilitate agreement' on the neutral or panel list.[226] The ADR Order requires the parties to 'take such serious steps to resolve their disputes' through the procedure set up but in the case of non-settlement they must 'inform the courts' in writing before 'disclosure' and 'exchange of witness statements' or 'experts reports'.[227] This

---

218 CPR 26.4(3)
219 White Book (2013) at Section 14.13
220 See White Book (2013) at 14.2–14.3. See also Mackie et al. (2007) at 65
221 CPR s26(4) (2) (b). The court normally issues a stay for one month but this may be extended when the court 'considers' it 'appropriate'. See CPR s26(4) (3). See also Cornes (2007) at 12. Cornes suggests that the judge's power does not 'extend' to ordering ADR if 'one or both parties' object
222 Mackie et al. (2007) at 65
223 A new scheme was introduced in October 2012 where small money claims for less than £5,000 will be automatically referred to the Mediation Service Pilot Scheme which is operating in the County Court Money Claims Centre if both parties have indicated agreement on their allocation questionnaire. See Practice Direction PD 51H
224 White Book (2013) at Section 14 C
225 Admiralty and Commercial Court Guide (2011) 9th Edition. See also appendix E of the TCC Court Guide (2010) 2nd Revision
226 Admiralty and Commercial Court Guide (2011) Appendix 7 Draft ADR Order at 1
227 Admiralty and Commercial Court Guide (2011) Appendix 7 Draft ADR Order at 2 & 4

Court Order, however, specifically notes at the end of the document the term 'ADR procedure' is used in order to maintain flexibility and choice for the parties.

The TCC Draft ADR Order appears simpler in design. It requires the parties to exchange a list of three neutrals for either 'mediation or ENE (Early Neutral Evaluation) or other form of ADR' prior to a specified date given in the order but when no agreement is reached 'the court will choose one of the listed individuals'.[228] Paragraph three states the length of time for the 'stay of proceedings' and obliges the parties to 'inform the court' on whether they have reached settlement. In the event of non-settlement the parties are required to 'comply' with any 'outstanding court directions' and must 'attend' another CMC by a given date.

When cases have been designated to the multi-track or there is no CMC the court may give directions, which include a court order (often called an (Ungley Order)) for ADR.[229] An Ungley Order states that the parties 'shall' by a specified date 'consider whether the case is capable of resolution by ADR' and requires that the parties file with the court a 'witness statement without prejudice save as to costs', giving reasons why they believe the case is not suitable.[230]

Halsey and court orders for ADR

The Court of Appeal in *Halsey* is primarily concerned with the criteria for penalising an unreasonable refusal to use mediation, but Dyson LJ also considered the 'impact' of CPR for the court to encourage and facilitate ADR.[231] Chapter 1 reviewed the approach to ADR orders in the early days of CPR when some judges issued orders on the understanding that they could do so without either or both parties' consent.[232] However, the steer following the Court of Appeal in *Halsey* is that the court should not 'compel' the parties to mediate or use ADR without their consent.[233] *Halsey* declined to accept that the court could order the parties to mediate 'against their will' on the grounds that it may breach a party's right to access to a court under article 6 of the Human Rights Act.[234] Furthermore, the court 'could not conceive of

---

228 TCC Court Guide (2010) Appendix E at 1 & 2
229 CPR 29.2. For an explanation of case management at this stage see White Book (2013) at Section 14.13
230 Lord Dyson reviewed the effectiveness of Ungley Orders in *Halsey*. See *Halsey* [2004] at 32–3
231 *Halsey* [2004] at 29
232 *Muman v. Nagasena* [2000] 1 W.L.R. 299; [1999] EWCA Civ 1742; *Guinle v. Kinstreet Ltd v. Balmargo Corp Ltd v. Hamam; Shirayama Shokusan Co Ltd v. Danovo Ltd (no 1)* [2003] EWHC 3306 (Ch)
233 *Halsey* [2004] at 10. See Mackie et al. (2007) at 84–90
234 The court's power to order parties to ADR is considered in detail in Chapter 4. Most commentators now suggest that this would not breach article 6 as the parties are not prevented from accessing the court as they can still go if mediation is unsuccessful. See for example Genn et al. (2007) at 15

circumstances' when it would be appropriate to force 'unwilling' participants into a 'voluntary process' because of the likely 'damaging effect' to mediation and the potential (if unsuccessful), of increasing litigation costs.[235] Although at the time of writing the legal position has not changed, Lord Justice Ward in 2013 had misgivings over the decision in *Halsey*, first on the issue of a breach of the Human Rights Act 1998, which he implied is *'obiter'*, but also that this prevents a judge from ordering a stay under CPR 26.4(2) (b) and his honour encouraged a review when the issue was next contested.[236]

Halsey recognised that the 'strongest form of encouragement' that a court can use is the Commercial and Admiralty Court's Draft ADR Order which requires the parties to take 'serious steps' to settle the dispute in ADR but 'stopped short of compelling' attendance.[237] However, Dyson LJ was clear that a refusal to engage in mediation after an ADR had been issued would *'for that reason alone . . .* be unreasonable' (italics in case) because it could be 'assumed' that the court would only make an order in 'suitable' cases.[238] The dicta in *Halsey* observes that parties are 'always at risk' of costs penalties if they refuse to 'even consider ADR' and 'particularly so' if a court order has been made.[239] ADR orders had not been issued by the courts of first instance in either *Halsey* or *Steel*, which were co-heard by the court, and therefore the Court of Appeal did not have to consider the effect of non-compliance.[240]

Halsey also confirmed the suitability of 'encouraging' ADR through 'less strong' orders based on the 'Ungley Order' because they draw the parties' attention to the importance of 'considering ADR' and alert them to the 'risk' they take in costs.[241] These types of orders are criticised because they 'relieve' the judge from evaluating whether the case is appropriate for mediation, thereby transferring the risk to the parties.[242] Shipman contends that should such orders become common practice in a wider context than clinical negligence, then the question of the reasonableness of a party's behaviour in rejecting mediation will be 'irrelevant' because court recommendations will become 'habitual' rather 'indicative' of appropriateness criteria.[243]

Case management and court orders

Although the CA in *Halsey* is authority for suggesting that courts cannot compel 'unwilling' parties to mediate, the White Book considers that

---

235 *Halsey* (2004) at 10
236 *Wright v. Michael Wright Supplies Ltd. & Anor* [2013] EWCA Civ 234 at 3. See Chapter 4 when the issue of a breach of article 6 is reviewed in more detail.
237 *Halsey* (2004) at 30
238 *Halsey* (2004) at 31
239 *Halsey* (2004) at 33
240 *Halsey* (2004) at 77
241 *Halsey* (2004) at 31. See the White Book (2013) at 14.12
242 See Mackie et al. (2007) at 87. See also Shipman (2006) at 203
243 Shipman (2006) at 203. The criteria for mediation suitability is considered in Chapter 4.

perhaps this should be read in conjunction with judicial speeches on the issue of Article 6 but also on the question of whether the courts should be able to 'direct' the parties to mediate.[244] The White Book cites two cases which indicate that some judges do believe that they have this 'power': First in *Honda Giken Kogyo Kabushiki Kaisha (A Firm) v. Neesam*[245] where Judge Fysh QC directed the parties to 'use their best endeavours' to mediate before a specified date; and the second, in *Uren v. Corporate Leisure (UK) Ltd*[246] when Smith LJ directed the parties 'to attempt mediation' before retrial.[247]

The powers of a court to issue an ADR Order in case management was reviewed in *B v. Ministry of Defence*, which involved a group action against the Ministry of Defence for alleged injuries caused during atomic testing in the South Pacific some 50 years ago.[248] Following a limitation action, Foskett J had stayed proceedings for a month with the consent of both parties after which the claimant brought three applications before the court, one of which was that the court exercise case-management powers to order a stay for mediation.[249]

Macduff J made two observations: First, he encouraged the parties to 'consider mediation'; and second, that it would not be 'helpful, nor was the case 'appropriate', to order mediation because the parties had already been encouraged to mediate and 'just as a horse can be taken to water and not made to drink, so a party can be taken to mediation without being required to mediate seriously' and the parties could anyway 'unilaterally withdraw' if they were so minded.[250] Thus, mediation was 'unlikely to achieve anything'.[251] Macduff J was not drawn on the issue of whether the courts could 'direct the parties or merely encourage' because of the futility of ordering mediation in this case:[252]

> On the question of whether the court is able actually to order mediation as opposed to encourage it, I have been referred to authority, the well known case of *Halsey v Milton Keynes General NHS Trust* [2004] EWCA (Civ) 576, of course, as well as the case of *AB & Ors v Wyeth* [1997] 8 Med LR 57 with particular reference to *dicta* of Lord Justice Steyn. I have also been referred to a speech given by Sir Anthony Clarke, then Master of the Rolls. That was a speech in which he could be taken to be saying that

244 White Book (2013) at section 14.9. See Lord Phillips (2008); Lord Clarke (2008); Sir Lightman (2007). Clarke (Sir Anthony) MR *The future of civil mediation* (2008) 2nd Civil Mediation Council, downloaded on 24 April 2013
245 *Honda Giken Kogyo Kabushiki Kaisha (A Firm) v. Neesam* [2009] EWHC 1213 (Pat)
246 *Uren v. Corporate Leisure (UK) Ltd* 2011 WL 291623
247 See the White Book (2013) at Section 14.9
248 *B v. Ministry of Defence* (aka *AB v. Ministry of Defence*) [2009] ECHC (Admin) QB at 2
249 *B v. Ministry of Defence* (2009) at 4
250 *B v. Ministry of Defence* (2009) at 17
251 *B v. Ministry of Defence* (2009) at 17
252 *B v. Ministry of Defence* (2009) at 18

mediation could be something which the court could order, over and above encourage. It was a speech made not in court, but to an invited audience in Birmingham. However, whether I have the power to order mediation or merely to encourage, I do not consider it would be helpful for me to put anything in my order.

Judicial activism[253]

It is difficult to ascertain the number of court orders made for ADR. *Dicta* in *Cable & Wireless* suggest that ADR orders were 'commonplace' in the commercial courts in the early days of CPR even when one of the parties made objections.[254] By 2004, Dyson LJ in *Halsey* stated that ADR orders were 'routinely' issued by commercial court judges,[255] but there is little empirical data to support the contention that judges are driving mediation through this process, and current opinion indicates sporadic practice across the country.[256] In 2005, research by Peysner and Seneviratne on court management (in fast track and multi-track cases) found that judges either 'rarely' issued or 'proposed' stays for mediation.[257] Judges in the study reported that they would 'more readily' agree to a stay when the claimants put in a request but were 'more cautious' when the initiative came from the defendant because of scepticism about delay and would 'probably ask the claimant's views before doing so'.[258]

Other surveys indicate that court orders have not been an 'effective force' in mediation development.[259] A study of commercial and construction lawyers' experience with ADR in 2001 found that only 10 per cent of reported mediations commenced through a court order and only two mediations by a contract clause.[260] A more recent study in the specialist Technology and Construction Court in 2008 found that 35 per cent of respondents who had issued claims resolved their dispute by mediation but that only 10 per cent were stimulated through a court order, although a further 12 per cent were prompted after an 'indication' from the judge.[261]

---

253 See Barrett (2008) at 690
254 *Cable & Wireless* [2002] at 29
255 *Halsey* (2004) at 6
256 Allen & Mackie (2010)
257 Peysner & Seneviratne (2005) at 45; See also Genn et al. (2007) at 45 & 19. Genn reports that few court orders for mediation were made during the London County Court's Automatic Referral System (ARM), which ran from 2004–2005. District judges had 'limited success' in encouraging parties to mediate at case management conferences where objections to referral were heard and only 19% of the orders were for a stay in proceedings for mediation to take place. The authors of the report blamed the failure of the scheme partly on the 'impact' of the decision in *Halsey* that the court could not compel reluctant parties to mediate. Genn et al. (2007) at 19
258 Peysner & Seneviratne (2005) at 45
259 Brooker & Lavers (2001)
260 Brooker & Lavers (2001) at 333–4
261 Gould et al. (2010) at 14 and 50

Peysner and Seneviratne's study suggested that judges may have issued stays because of fears of appeals, but this does not seem to be a regular occurrence and a recent search of case law only found one case where a party challenged a judge's failure to make an ADR order.[262] The Court of Appeal in *Punjab National Bank v. Jain & Ors* refused to grant an appeal after a deputy judge in the Chancery Division rejected the claimant's request for a mediation order.[263] The stay had been declined on five grounds: the expense of mediating; reluctance to compel mediation where one party had 'limited' funds for litigation; lack of judicial power to 'require mediation'; the unlikelihood that a mediation order would 'take the matter further' and finally, the belief that 'sensible solicitors' could, if they wanted, 'still agree to mediation'.[264] The Court of Appeal refused to 'interfere' with the 'reasons' given for vetoing the stay on the grounds they are a discretionary part of case management and no criticism was made of the judge for not making an ADR order or for not ordering the parties to 'use their best endeavours to consider mediation'.[265]

The underuse of mediation is often blamed on the legal professions but culpability is also placed on some judges, who do not actively promote mediation either through a lack of understanding[266] or their 'ideological' stance, which Shipman suggests is based on their commitment to ADR or their belief that civil justice is achieved through finding the 'correct legal outcome'.[267]

'Self styled' and 'bespoke' ADR orders[268]

Where judges are enthusiastic promoters of mediation, Mackie et al. record that they often produce 'self styled' ADR orders, which imply a more directive approach.[269] For example, they note an order from the County Court where provision was made for an 'identified' ADR provider to supply a list of mediators and an unreported Chancery case where the court named the ADR procedure to use when the parties were ordered to 'try to settle this case by mediation'.[270] In an employment case, the legal representatives were 'ordered' to approach CEDR and to 'jointly' select a mediator from their 'panel'.[271]

---

262 Peysner & Seneviratne (2005) at 45. Mackie et al. (2007) at 81–2. The authors report that Colman J is a strong supporter of ADR and observed that parties do not 'ignore ADR orders' as they had no knowledge of any case where the party returned to court to explain why mediation had not been used after the court recommended it.

263 *Punjab National Bank v. Jain & Ors* [2004] EWCA Civ 589

264 *Punjab National Bank v. Jain & Ors* [2004] at 18

265 *Punjab National Bank v. Jain & Ors* [2004] at 42

266 Lord Jackson (2009)

267 See Shipman (2006) at 181–2. This is discussed more fully in Chapter 4

268 See Mackie et al. (2007) at 76

269 Mackie et al. (2007) at 76. Two of the authors of the book were connected to CEDR as Chief Executive and Director and both are well known and experienced mediators.

270 Mackie et al. (2007) at 79–80

271 Mackie et al. (2007) at 79–80

Of course, mediation may have been the procedure of choice for the parties but Mackie et al. indicate that 'robust' judicial 'pressure' is sometimes applied in relation to 'choice of mediator and mediation machinery' by providing, for example, that the ADR provider has the 'power to nominate' the mediator if the parties failed to agree.[272]

Mediation is said to be conceptually different from litigation because the parties have the choice not only on how the process is conducted but also on the final outcome achieved.[273] When judges use a more intrusive approach by identifying the procedure to use or naming mediation providers, this encroaches on the parties' self-determination by influencing choice and implies court 'approved'[274] status to specific organisations and their panels of mediators.

Central to this discussion is the contention that judges may go beyond merely providing the opportunity for the parties to engage with mediation (or other ADR process) to endorsing ADR providers or mediators who may lean towards specific mediation models.[275] Although there are many different mediator 'orientations',[276] the escalation of evaluative practice has been associated with the institutionalisation of mediation within legal systems through court rules. This brings legal professionals within its ambit who in turn begin to influence party choice both in their representative capacity and as practising mediators.[277] Judges by their very calling are influential, and when they adopt a 'robust'[278] approach to ADR Orders, either by counselling the parties about which process or which ADR providers to use, then this endorses more than settlement negotiations through mediation as it may also promote a primacy of a particular mode of practice. ADR Orders outwardly represent the philosophy underpinning CPR by directing suitable cases to alternative procedures, but individualised draft orders may signify an unintended outcome of promoting 'approved' practice,[279] which may be at odds with the philosophical foundation of mediation, that of self-determination.[280]

Approaches in the USA, Australia and Hong Kong to staying proceedings

In the discussion above it was noted that Australia, the USA and Hong Kong have all found ways to support mediation contractual arrangements, which

272 Mackie et al. (2007) at 79
273 See for example, Welsh (2001b) at 4; See also Alfini (2008)
274 Alexander (2008b) at 10
275 Chapter 1 discussed the many mediation models but the most contentious debate on mediator approach has involved the distinction between evaluative and facilitative.
276 Riskin (1996)
277 See for example, Welsh (2001b); Alfini (2008)
278 Mackie et al. (2007) at 85
279 Alexander (2008b) at 23
280 See for example, Welsh (2001b)

denote that many common law courts are willing to exercise 'inherent power' to stay proceedings in order that the parties attempt ADR. However, both Australia and the USA have well established mandatory and referral programmes, which provide judges with the power to stay proceedings until the parties comply with these requirements. As the English jurisdiction does not mandate mediation, although there are proposals to make attendance at mediation information sessions automatic, this chapter will not engage in detailed review of USA or Australian law on judicial powers to order parties to go to mediation, but will give a brief overview for completeness. However, Hong Kong introduced very similar civil procedure rules to the English jurisdiction but consequently after implementation has taken a more forceful approach through a practice direction requiring parties to mediate prior to litigation, which stipulates that judges can stay proceedings – discussed in detail below.

USA inherent authority to stay proceedings

In the USA judges have 'inherent authority to require participation in mediation', which Kovach observes comes from two 'lines of authority':[281] First, judges have a 'duty to manage their own caseloads' and second, state and federal statutes introduced to advance ADR programmes have in the main made attendance at mediation a mandatory pre-condition to litigation.[282] It is reported that the existence of legislative and court rules have meant that there have been 'few challenges to the judicial authority' and Coben and Thompson found in their review of ADR case law there was a 'simple principle':[283]

> courts are inclined to order mediation on their own initiative, and will generally enforce a pre-existing obligation to participate in mediation, whether the obligation was judicially created, mandated by statute or stipulated in the parties' pre-dispute contract.

Although there are circuit cases revealing 'conflicting' opinions,[284] in *Re Atlantic Pipe Corporation*,[285] the Court of Appeal in the First District identified four 'sources' of judicial power to mandate mediation: '(a) the court's local rule; (b) applicable statute; (c) Federal Rules of Civil Procedure and (d) the

---

281 Kovach (2006) at 396
282 See Kovach (2006) at 397. Kovach discusses the Civil Justice Reform Act 1990 that requires Federal District Courts to 'enact a cost and delay reduction plan' including how ADR is utilised, and the ADR Act 1998, which 'authorised' ADR programmes.
283 Coben and Thompson (2006) at 105
284 Dominguez (2007)
285 *Re Atlantic Pipe Corporation (APC)* (2002) 304 Fed 135 No. 02-1339, decided September 18, 2002

court's inherent power.'[286] Despite the existence of these sources of power, the Court of Appeal found that the Puerto Rico federal dispute court could not make a 'mandatory mediation order' because it had failed to implement local rules under the Civil Justice Reform Act 1990, it had not provided an ADR programme under the ADR Act 1998, and, although the Federal Rules of Procedure provide courts with 'authority to require mediation', this was limited by the words 'authorised by statute or local rules' and no such rules existed.[287] The Court, however, opined that the Federal Rules of Procedure Act had not 'stripped' judges of the authority they had prior to enactment and the courts retained an 'inherent power to act'[288] but with the caveat, that this should only be exercised when it was 'reasonably likely to serve the interests of justice'.[289] The Court concluded that a district court has the inherent power to order mediation but these must be 'crafted' in such a way that it 'preserves procedural fairness and shields objecting parties from undue burdens'.[290]

Australian court powers to order ADR

Similarly, in Australia, commentators report that nearly all courts operate referral mechanisms to ADR 'with or without the parties' consent'.[291] In 2011, the enactment of the Civil Dispute Resolution Act required that all parties take 'genuine steps' to settle their disputes and both litigants must submit a 'statement' itemising what actions have been taken.[292] These steps include 'considering' ADR, 'agreeing' on a facilitator; and 'attending the process'.[293] As with the USA, the law is relatively settled regarding the power of the court to mandate unwilling parties' attendance at ADR, based largely on the benefits that mediation processes have over litigation.[294] Mack suggests that the 'touchstone of a referral decision' is that there is some 'prospect of success' for ADR.[295] In a similar vein to Brookes J's view in *Dunnett*, the courts have indicated that even where parties are reluctant to mediate, the process is still able to produce 'successful' outcomes and unless the 'attitudes of the parties or other circumstances' indicate otherwise the court will exercise its 'discretion'.[296] Mack's review of the case law in Australia shows that there is a 'breadth and variety' in the orders that are made, which stems not only

---

286 *Re Atlantic Pipe Corporation (APC)* (2002) at 15
287 *Re Atlantic Pipe Corporation (APC)* (2002) at 18–31
288 *Re Atlantic Pipe Corporation (APC)* (2002) at 27
289 *Re Atlantic Pipe Corporation (APC)* (2002) at 39
290 *Re Atlantic Pipe Corporation (APC)* (2002) at 40
291 See Mack (2003); Tronson (2006); Aibinu et al. (2010) at 27–30
292 Civil Procedure Resolution Act 2011 Part, 2s ss 6 & 7
293 Civil Procedure Resolution Act 2011 Part 4 (1A) 1(d) & (e) (i) (ii)
294 See Mack (2003) at 8.5
295 See Mack (2003) at 8.5. See also Tronson (2006) at 413
296 *Remuneration Planning Corporation Pty Ltd v. Fitton* (2001) NSWSC 1208 at 3. See Mack (2003) at 76

from the 'power of referral' but also from the 'courts' inherent powers' and case decisions have, for example, prohibited lawyers' attendance in ADR or awarded 'sanctions' such as a 'stay in proceedings'.[297]

Hong Kong Mediation Practice Protocol

The civil procedure rules implemented in Hong Kong were influenced by the Woolf Reforms but consequently more affirmative action has been taken in relation to mediation, which is articulated in a Mediation Practice Direction (PD 31).[298] PD 31 requires the parties and their solicitors to 'file' a signed 'mediation certificate'.[299] If a party wishes to attempt mediation, they must 'serve' a 'Mediation Notice' on the other parties, which must be responded to within 14 days.[300] If the parties have differences about any aspect of the mediation process, they must endeavour to 'reach agreement about them, which must be recorded in writing'[301] but in the event that these remain unresolved, the Mediation PD permits them to make a 'joint application for directions from the courts' or 'in the absence of willingness any party may apply'.[302]

The practice direction also reiterates the power of the court to award costs for unreasonably failing to use mediation and specifically states that sanctions will not apply 'where the party has engaged in mediation to the minimum level of participation agreed to by the parties or as directed by the Court prior to the mediation in accordance with para. 1 of this PD'.[303] Nor will the courts order adverse costs when a party 'has a reasonable explanation for not engaging in mediation' and the PD highlights 'active without prejudice settlement negotiations', although when these have 'broken down' they no longer form the 'basis' for failing to engage in mediation and the parties should then 'actively engage in some other form of ADR'.[304]

The Mediation PD does not specify 'a minimum level of participation' but provides examples in a footnote, which include agreement about the 'identity of the mediator', 'terms of appointment', 'applicable rules' and 'participation by the parties in the mediation up to and including at least one substantive mediation session (of a duration determined by the mediator) with the mediator'.[305]

PD 31 also provides the court with the power to order a stay in proceedings for mediation to take place, which can be either on the part of 'one or more of

297 See Mack (2003) at section 8.8 generally
298 Weixia Gu (2010) at 51
299 PD 31 at Part B 9
300 PD 31 at Part B 11
301 PD 31 at Part B 12
302 PD 31 at 13 (1) (2)
303 PD 31 at Part A 4. & 5. 1(a)
304 PD 31 at Part A 5.2
305 PD 31 Appendix C, fn 4

the parties' or at the discretion of the court 'in such terms as it thinks fit' but taking into consideration 'milestone dates' and 'avoiding the postponement' of court dates.[306]

Since the Mediation PD 31 came into force, the courts have considered a number of applications from parties who have been unable to resolve their differences on how to engage in mediation. In *Resource Development Ltd v. Swanbridge Ltd*[307] the parties sought help from the court with the selection of mediator, minimum participation and the suitability of a stay until the mediation was concluded. Master Lung decided that there was little between the specialist knowledge (land law) of both proposed mediators so the deciding factor was the 'discrepancy' in their fees and gave a preference for the lower rate of $2,500 an hour than that of $5,000.[308]

Regarding the minimum level of participation, one party expressed a wish for at least two sessions whereas the other preferred to leave it to the 'discretion' of the mediator and the proposed direction in the PD of 'up to and including at least one substantive mediation session'.[309] The court decided that it should not 'impose more than is necessary' on the parties because mediation is a voluntary process and if one party decided to terminate, this would be something for the 'determination of the trial judge' and therefore, the court ordered the minimum level of one substantive session the duration of which the mediator would decide.[310]

On the matter of issuing a stay, the court posited that the 'main question' is 'what is the practical effect?' and decided not to award a stay as it would not 'save any costs' because the parties were 'ready for trial' but it was suggested that while there was a 'glimpse of success' for mediation then 'a reasonable solicitor will not deliver brief to counsel'.[311] This case has since been followed by *CY Foundation Group Ltd v. Leonora Yung*[312] when the court refused to grant the defendants' request for a 90-day stay but held that there was a financial 'practical benefit' for a 'short stay' running from 'the date of filing and serving the mediation notice' because '13 parties' had not at that time 'exchanged witness statements'.[313]

In *Hak Tung Alfred Tang v. Bloomberg* the parties had agreed to mediate but the plaintiff and second defendant were unable to agree the minimum level of participation.[314] Master Lung observed that the parties should have 'confidence' in the mediator to determine the length of the mediation and

306 PD 31 Part B (3) 16
307 *Resource Development Ltd v. Swanbridge Ltd* (2010) WL 1322741 (CFI), [2010] HKEC 841
308 *Resource Development Ltd v. Swanbridge Ltd* (2010) at 6
309 *Resource Development Ltd v. Swanbridge Ltd* (2010) at 7
310 *Resource Development Ltd v. Swanbridge Ltd* 2010 at 7 & 8
311 *Resource Development Ltd v. Swanbridge Ltd* 2010 at 10
312 *CY Foundation Group Ltd v. Leonora Yung* [2012] HKEC 521
313 *CY Foundation Group Ltd v. Leonora Yung* [2012] at 21
314 *Hak Tung Alfred Tang v. Bloomberg LP* July 16 2010 WL 2214180 (CFI), [2010] HKEC 1227 at 6

they can terminate at any time; but whether their conduct would be regarded as a 'sincere and genuine attempt on mediation would be for the court to decide at the end of the trial'.[315] The court held that the parties should engage in 'at least one substantive mediation (of a duration decided by the mediator)'.[316] The court observed that agreeing to mediate is only the first step and party disputes over choice of mediator, venue and participation are not conducive to 'saving costs and time' and cautioned parties to adopt a more 'flexible and cooperative' attitude to mediation 'so as to save time and costs'.[317]

At least one judge has observed that 'lip service' is sometimes given to court suggestions for mediation and warned litigants of the potential for adverse costs orders for insincere behaviour, which does not 'constitute minimum level of participation'.[318] The early case law indicates that litigants in Hong Kong do not always comply with Civil Justice Reform (CJR) or the Mediation PD 31. For example in *Faith Bright Developments Ltd v. Ng Kwok Kuen* the parties had not submitted either the mediation questionnaire or the timetable questionnaire, which led the court to refuse to hear the case management summons and comment on current practice in the Hong Kong jurisdiction:[319]

> At the time of writing this decision, I have come across similar cases in other case management summons hearings. I have also gathered information from the Registrar of the District Court that a similar situation of non-compliance with O.25, PD 5.2 and PD 31 is prevalent in the District Court.

These cases illustrate the potential drawback of closely regulating mediation, which may of course standardise expectations but is also likely to result in satellite litigation as parties bicker over its procedural organisation. The Hong Kong Working Group believes that the introduction of PD 31 has created an 'impact' on mediation developments by providing a first step for the parties and their lawyers to enter into a 'dialogue' which will enable them to come to a consensus on the areas of 'agreement and disagreement'.[320] The Working Group believe that PD 31 will result in lawyers becoming 'increasingly immersed' in mediation practice, which may prove to be a doubled-edged sword for party involvement, as other jurisdictions have found.[321] The early case evidence indicates that there is some way

---

315 *Hak Tung Alfred Tang v. Bloomberg LP* [2012] at 12
316 *Hak Tung Alfred Tang v. Bloomberg LP* [2012] at 13
317 *Hak Tung Alfred Tang v. Bloomberg LP* [2012] at 14
318 *Colin David Jones v. Rotary International Ltd* 2010 WL 7565 (CFI), [2010] HKEC 333 at 46
319 *Faith Bright Developments Ltd v. Ng Kwok Kuen* [2010] WL 3838078 (CFI) at 2
320 Hong Kong Working Group (2010) at 1.8
321 Hong Kong Working Group (2010) at 5.105

to go in changing litigation practices and PD 31 may potentially encourage minimal engagement rather than a more open or responsive approach where real benefits are more likely to be achieved.

Commentary

This exploration of the law shows how it is expanding into mediation practice through the rules for enforcing clauses and judicial discretion in staying proceedings for the parties to mediate before accessing the courts. The English jurisdiction and most of the judiciary is standing against implementing more coercive measures than sanctioning non-compliance with CPR relating to ADR, and there may be lessons to learn, particularly from Hong Kong's short experience with PD 31 but also perhaps from the inclinations of the legal professions to influence and control how mediation works in practice.[322] Discouragingly as the law regulates practice it also increases 'judicial power'[323] – both that of the lawyers who advise on drafting and interpretation, and of the judges as they use their discretion to direct cases away from the courts but also in developing or extending legal principles to various parts of mediation practice.

Although parties are not ordered to mediate against their will, CPR highlights judicial discretion to stay litigation for a short period for attempting ADR and the threat of a costs sanction when the court has made recommendations through an ADR order is a formidable incentive to undertake mediation. Although much of the evidence is anecdotal, judges may do more than just encourage the use of alternatives and through their position may be influencing the parties' choice of process and mediator. ADR is almost exclusively thought of as mediation in the courts[324] and although some ADR orders make the distinction, the revitalisation of the Court of Appeal's Mediation Scheme (CAMS) when parties are 'informed' in cases up to £100,000 that their case is 'automatically recommended for mediation to CEDR' (which requires them to opt out), is evidence of increasing judicial acknowledgment that the CPR rules encouraging parties to use alternatives is about mediating.[325]

Perhaps more troubling is that the scheme not only limits choice but also gives authoritative recognition to one organisation.[326]

---

322 See for example, Clark (2012)
323 Blichner & Molander (2005) at 19
324 *Halsey* [2004] at 5
325 Court of Appeal Mediation Pilot Scheme (CAMS) Reference Scheme.
326 CEDR organises the Scheme for the Court of Appeal http://www.judiciary.gov.uk/media/media-releases/2012/news-release-mediation-pilot-court-of-appeal downloaded on 21 December 2012

Conclusion

The CPR rules have been responsible for changing judicial attitudes about the validity of mediation clauses in contracts and the courts will enforce them when parties draft provisions, which clearly represent their intentions to mediate before either litigating or arbitrating. However, it is axiomatic that the incorporation of mediation clauses into legal documents expands the law, by not only increasing party reliance on the drafting expertise of lawyers but also when things go wrong seeking a legal interpretation first from legal professionals and then the courts in order to avoid their 'pre-dispute' arrangements. It is inevitable that there will be occasions when one or other of the parties may have genuine reasons to prefer to take their dispute to the court or even some other dispute resolution process, but it is of course also right that parties should not be able to evade their legal obligations when they previously elect to fetter them.

The next chapter analyses how the courts approach the enforcement of agreements reached through the mediation process, when parties try to avoid the settlement either because they claim there is no consensus (and therefore that a contract is not in existence) or that there are invalidating circumstances.

3 Enforcing mediation settlement agreements

Introduction

What sets mediation apart from most dispute mechanisms is party self-determination, which is said to enhance satisfaction with the outcome achieved, which then leads to increased compliance with the mediated agreement.[1] Compliance is one criterion that some empirical research tests for mediation satisfaction, but, although the majority of studies suggest that users are satisfied with their agreed outcomes,[2] some jurisdictions report a growing trend for litigants approaching the courts to enforce agreements reached through mediation.[3] This increase may just reflect an escalation in mediation activity but the historical progression of arbitration shows the expansion of law as parties sought help from the courts to uphold the arbitrators' findings, which eventually led to a vast body of arbitration law. Court and statutory interference with private arbitration arrangements led to reports of significant dissatisfaction with the procedure and the involvement of lawyers, who dominated and influenced its practice, to the extent that it began to resemble litigation in terms of cost, speed and complexity.[4] The 'institutionalisation' of arbitration within the formal system and the 'appropriation' by the legal profession is responsible for a 'culture of legalism' as lawyers 'juridified' the procedure by establishing their dominance over the 'right to determine the law'.[5]

---

1 See for example, McEwen & Maiman (1984)
2 *ADR* Now reports that compliance in small claims schemes is nearly 100% and 'that there is hardly ever a problem' with enforcing small claims. http://www.adrnow.org.uk/go/SubPage_137.html. A report by Consumer Focus found that parties were more likely to receive payment after mediation than in small court claims. Consumer Focus (2010) at 2.18
3 Alfini & McCabe (2001); Coben & Thompson (2006)
4 See Chapter 1
5 Flood & Caiger (1993) at 440. The authors observe Pierre Bourdieu's thesis that all 'social fields' illustrate power struggles between different groups and the 'juridical field' is the site of a competition for monopoly for the right to determine law. 'Within this field there occurs a confrontation among actors possessing a technical competence which is inevitably social and which consists essentially in the socially recognised capacity to interpret a corpus of texts sanctifying a correct or legitimised vision of the social world'. Bourdieu (1987) at 817

The idea that merchants are the best judges of their own affairs has existed since at the least the middle ages. That tradition has created its own forums for dispute resolution taking account of industry norms and culture. In recent times a struggle has emerged, as lawyers seeking new areas of work have sought to capture some of these areas from business people, the architects, engineers and others who have a deep involvement in the construction industry. It results from an amalgam of causes – responses to economic cycles, demand creation, supply control, and the culture of legalism. And lawyers are in strong position to effect colonisation because of their power over the discourse of legalism. They have the power of appropriation.

Mediation, as with other alternative dispute resolution mechanisms,[6] has not been immune from incursion by the legal professions, who are accused of 'diminishing' party self-determination as they 'dominate' the process either as legal mediators or advocates in the process.[7] Empirical studies in the UK and other jurisdictions report that lawyers are influential in the choice of mediator and they often have a 'preference' for 'evaluative' rather than 'purely' facilitative mediators.[8] The premise behind facilitative mediation is that mediators assist the parties to reach mediated outcomes of their own creation, whereas 'evaluative' mediators may take a more pro-active role offering suggestions and guidance on the settlement outcome.[9] When parties, or their legal advisors, opt for 'evaluative' mediation there is less 'ownership' of the settlement and the potential for parties to be less satisfied or compliant with the outcome.[10]

When a party refuses to abide by the agreement, it may be because of a 'change of mind',[11] but within the context of mediation, events may transpire which cast doubt on the legality of the mediation settlement. In order to enforce mediation agreements courts are required to review the validity of the contract, which involves a consideration of the necessary requirements for the formation of a 'binding' contract, or evidence of what happened in the mediation that provides vitiating factors making it either void or voidable.

---

6 The Housing Grants, Reconstruction and Regeneration Act 1996 introduced statutory adjudication to provide a quick and relatively short mechanism to resolve disputes, which allows the project to continue. There are now a considerable number of legal cases defining its practice and many adjudicators are trained legal professionals. See for example; Kennedy et al. (2010)

7 See Welsh (2001a,b); For a comprehensive review of the influence of lawyers in mediation see Clark (2012)

8 Brooker (2007); Clark (2012); Genn (1998)

9 See for example, Riskin (1996)

10 Consumer Report (2010) at 101 & 50. The Consumer Report found that the party who 'won' was more likely to receive payment than successful parties in court, but that it may not be financially viable to continue to seek redress if a party refuses to comply either with a court judgment or with a mediated agreement. See for example the case studies in Consumer Report (2010) at 49

11 Cole et al. (2012) at section 7.1

A review of the events in mediation inevitably impinges on the confidentiality of the process. That is one of the key elements underpinning negotiations as parties will make either concessions or admissions confident that these are not admissible in later court or arbitration action.[12] Confidentiality is reviewed in Chapter 5. In England and other common law jurisdictions, settlement negotiations which are stipulated to be without prejudice are protected except for narrow exceptions from later court review and there is now a developing concept of mediation confidentiality.[13]

Court analysis of the enforcement of mediation settlements goes beyond contract law and the reaching of consensus, as there are implications for mediation policy, confidentiality and protecting weaker participants.[14] On the one hand, mediation or ADR policy has been implemented to accelerate settlement and reduce litigation 'balanced' against this; however, is the need to support 'legitimate concerns' about the settlement and for disputes to be brought to a close without further litigation:[15]

> Settlement negotiations and other ADR processes need to be encouraged and their confidentiality protected though inadmissibility rules. This priority needs to be balanced against the needs to encourage finality of disputes and to allow ADR agreements to be submitted as evidence of an agreement reached.

This chapter reviews the law, which deals with the enforcement of mediated settlement agreements. First, the chapter provides a brief explanation of the legal foundation of mediation settlements before an analysis is made of the emerging case law from this and other common law jurisdictions. It then considers to what extent the progressive institutionalisation of mediation is leading to 'creeping legalism' in mediation.[16]

Legal foundations of a mediated settlement agreement

No valid agreement

When a litigant has to seek court help to uphold a mediated settlement agreement, in effect the breaching party is usually claiming that there is no

---

12 Alfini & McCabe (2001) at 196; See also Mackie et al. (2007) at 113
13 See for example, Koo (2011); Wood (2008) (2009); Kallipetis (2009)
14 Deason (2005); Cole et al. (2012) at 7.1; NADRAC (2006) at 11.32–11.39; Hong Kong Working Party (2010) at 7.186–7.190; Thompson (2004)
15 NADRAC (2006) at 11.32; See Thompson (2004) at 515: 'Legitimate concerns about confidentiality or other bright-line rules should not totally deprive participants the opportunity to raise basic claims of unfair treatment'.
16 Nolan (2010) at 1

valid agreement in existence.[17] Litigation involving mediated settlement agreements therefore often concerns issues surrounding the formulation of a contract where one party claims that one or more parties to the agreement are breaching or failing to abide by the terms of the contract. It is not the place for this book to provide a detailed analysis of contract law but litigated mediation settlement agreements not surprisingly concern issues of the formulation of contracts. Treital defines a contract as 'an agreement giving rise to obligations which are enforced or recognised by law. The factor, which distinguishes contractual from other legal obligations, is that they are based on the agreement of the contracting parties'.[18]

Formation of contract

For an agreement to be binding on the parties, as every first year law student knows, the parties must intend legal relations, the agreement must be evidenced by a valid offer and acceptance, which means there has been 'a meeting of the minds' and there must be consideration on both sides.[19] A contract can, however, be either void or voidable when there are vitiating factors such as misrepresentation, mistake, duress, undue influence or unconscionable behaviour, which indicate a 'defect in the parties' consent'.[20] Sime et al. suggest that parties may claim that mediated agreements are not valid because of contractual formation problems such as a lack of agreement between the parties; no offer or acceptance; uncertain terms; a lack of consideration, incapacity, lack of writing in situations where contract or statute requires this (as for contracts for land); mistake, misrepresentation, duress or undue influence, lack of authority, illegality, frustration, performance, renunciation, impossibility, when a party has accepted a fundamental breach or through discharge by a later compromise agreement.[21]

Written agreements

At present enforcement of mediation settlements may rest on an analysis of contract law. There is no requirement that a contract has to be in writing unless it falls into specific exceptions for example, contracts for land, deeds or other 'statutory controlled' arrangements such as consumer credit agreements.[22] However, many mediation providers and mediators now require participants to sign contracts of engagement, which explicitly provide that their agreed outcomes be 'reduced' into writing and signed by the parties or their

17 See Coben & Thompson (2006) at 77; Pryles (1998); Alfini & McCabe (2001); Thompson (2004)
18 Treital (2003) at 1 (11th edition)
19 Coben & Thompson (2006) at 77
20 Spencer & Brogan (2006) at 358
21 Sime et al. (2010) at 488–9; See also Mackie et al. 2007 Section 7.7 at 132–5
22 Treital (2003) at 163

authorised representatives.[23] Some mediation agreements incorporate the rules and procedures of mediation. For example, ADR Group's 'Mediation Procedure and Rules' require the parties to sign a mediation agreement which 'governs the relationship between the parties before, during and after the mediation' and section 8.1 of the rules state that 'Any settlement reached, will not be legally binding until it has been recorded in writing and signed by or on behalf of its the parties'.[24] The CEDR Solve model agreement uses a similar clause in their mediation contract: 'No terms of the settlement reached will be legally binding until set out in writing and signed by or on behalf of each of the parties'.[25]

However, as the case law below shows even when participants take measures to diminish potential problems of enforcement this does not eradicate court involvement. Furthermore, formalising contractual arrangements expands the participation and influence of the legal professions at both stages of commencing and concluding mediation, which inevitably leads to escalating levels of legalism and juridification as lawyers are engaged to act as mediation advocates with responsibilities for drawing up the terms of the contract and litigants seek advice on the determination of the law regarding mediation activity.[26]

Policy grounds for upholding compromise agreements

When parties agree to settle their disputes the courts will uphold their compromise agreements on policy grounds of 'avoiding litigation' and encouraging resolution.[27] Where the parties have arrived at a 'clear compromise' agreement, the position taken by the Court of Appeal in 2008 in a family law case is unequivocal that as a 'matter of policy' they will be 'robustly upheld':[28]

> The Court of Appeal ADR scheme has a relatively low take up from family appeals but an encouragingly high success rate; and as a matter of policy it is important that this court should signify that if the parties arrive at a compromise, a clear compromise, within the mediation process, then that compromise will be robustly upheld by this court.

Application for proceedings and Tomlin Orders

If one party refuses to comply with the mediated settlement reached recourse to the court may depend on whether the parties has begun litigation or not.

---

23 See for example, CEDR Model Mediation agreement 13th edition clause 7 (2012)
24 ADR Group's 'Mediation Procedure and Rules' at 2.1 & 8.1
25 CEDR Model Mediation agreement 13th edition (2012)
26 Blichner & Molander (2008)
27 Anson (2002) at 101; See Roebuck (2006). Roebuck describes how mediated compromises were upheld and legislated for in Aethelred's reign.
28 *Rothwell v. Rothwell* (2008) EWCA Civ 1600 at 8

If the parties mediate before beginning litigation they can begin proceeding for a court order to enforce the mediation agreement, which would require the courts to establish the legality of the agreement through the principles of contract law.[29]

Conversely, if the parties have begun litigation but reached settlement Sime et al. list the number of ways the agreement can be recorded with the court which may depend on the 'complexity' of the agreement.[30] For example, the parties can enter judgment for payment of an agreed sum or through an 'endorsed counsel brief' or a consent order informing the court of the agreed settlement; or by 'staying proceedings on the agreed terms' or for 'no order' except for costs.[31] However, the court must have jurisdiction of the case and the order must be in terms based on the 'cause of action of the case'.[32] Where the terms of agreement are outside the 'powers of the court or the issues of the case' Sime et al. and others recommend using a Tomlin Order.[33]

Tomlin Orders

A Tomlin Order can be used when the parties have begun litigation but then engage in mediation either because the court has stayed proceedings for ADR (or mediation) to take place or the parties mediate on their own initiative.[34] A compromise agreement can then be recorded in a Tomlin Order, which has the effect of staying proceedings.[35] The Order is usually addressed in the following terms:[36]

> The claimant and the defendant having agreed to the terms set out in the schedule hereto, IT IS ORDERED THAT all further proceedings in this claim be stayed except for the purpose of carrying such terms into effect. Liberty to apply as to carrying such terms into effect.

The terms of the mediation agreement can be attached in a sealed schedule to the Tomlin Order but does not make an application to the court to enforce the schedule for an injunction or an order for specific performance.[37] The White

---

29 See for example, Pryles (1998); Spencer & Brogan (2006); Sime et al. (2010); Mackie et al. (2007); Newman (1997)
30 Sime et al. list a number of routes that can be taken to record compromise settlements (which may or may not have been through mediation) which may depend on the complexity of the agreement reached after proceedings have been initiated. Sime et al. (2010) at 327–38
31 See Sime et al. (2010) at 327–38
32 Sime et al. (2010) at 331–2
33 Sime et al. (2010) at 332; Mackie et al. (2007) Chapter 5; Newman (1997)
34 CPR 26(4). See discussion in Chapter 2
35 White Book (2013) at Part 40.6.2
36 White Book (2013) at Part 40.6.2; Mackie et al. (2007); Sime et al. (2010); Newman (1997) at 51
37 White Book (2013) at Part 40.6.2

Book records three orders made by the court in conjunction with the Tomlin Order: '(i) That the proceedings be stayed to enable the agreed terms to be put into effect. (ii) That, if the agreed terms require it, there be payment out of monies paid into court and provision for accrued interest thereon. (iii) For costs to be assessed, whether between the parties or out of public funds.'[38] Since the implementation of the Civil Procedure Rules and the emphasis on settlement, the number of Tomlin Orders is reported to have increased.[39] However, as the evolving case law below indicates, disputes may still arise even when the parties have recorded their settlement agreements as a contract and even after lodging them with the court.

Uncertain terms

The Court of Appeal had to consider the meaning of the terms of a mediation settlement agreement in *Sargeant (S) v. Macepark (Whittlebury) Ltd* (M) when a landlord had permitted the lessee access to landlocked property but both parties under the lease paid a contribution to the upkeep of the access road.[40] There had been considerably more traffic on the road than expected necessitating repairs and following mediation the parties agreed on the costs that each would contribute and the procedure for appointing a contractor.[41] It was the responsibility of Sargeant to employ a contractor based on the average of three tenders but not exceeding the average quotation.[42] One quotation was submitted after a delay of four months and a contractor (R), who had quoted the lowest tender, was asked to confirm his quote, which although revised with an increased price was still the lowest.[43]

As required by the settlement agreement, Sargeant sent a letter to M detailing the quotations with the new revised price for R's tender and confirming the appointment of R but R had informed Sargeant in a letter that part of the work might be liable to a £10,000 supplement.[44] On completion of the work, the invoice was at the higher quoted price but included the £10,000 supplement and Sargeant requested M's share of the payment.[45]

On appeal, the court considered whether the settlement agreement meant that the price paid would be the 'quoted price or the invoiced price (with the £10,000 supplement)' but the 'crucial question' was whether any price could be charged as long as it did not go above the cap (i.e. the average of the three quotations).[46] The Court read the clause in the

---

38 White Book (2013) at Part 40.6.2
39 White Book (2013) at Part 40.6.2
40 *Sargeant v. Macepark (Whittlebury) Ltd* [2008] EWCA Civ 1483 at 3
41 *Sargeant v. Macepark (Whittlebury) Ltd* [2008] at 4
42 *Sargeant v. Macepark (Whittlebury) Ltd* [2008] at 4
43 *Sargeant v. Macepark (Whittlebury) Ltd* [2008] at 6–12
44 *Sargeant v. Macepark (Whittlebury) Ltd* [2008] at 10
45 *Sargeant v. Macepark (Whittlebury) Ltd* [2008] at 13–14
46 *Sargeant v. Macepark (Whittlebury) Ltd* [2008] at 24

settlement agreement to mean that Sargeant was entitled to choose the contractor but had to discuss the appointment with M (which they had done) and that the only 'constraint' on the choice of contractor was that the price must not exceed the average of the three quotations.[47] The court did not read the clause to mean that the average of the quotation was the cap and they could expect payment up to the cap. The court held that the 'disclosed quotations' could not be overtaken or 'substituted by an undisclosed tender' but Sargeant were entitled to the 'percentage' of the 'disclosed quotation', which had been at the revised higher price but they were not entitled to a percentage of the 'invoiced figure at the higher sum' (which had included the undisclosed supplement).[48]

This case shows the inherent dangers that exist when drawing up mediation settlement agreements and the problems when terms are imprecise. Although mediators may be involved in drafting the final agreement, this is an important role for legal advocates at the end of the mediation and as Mackie et al. note where disputes are commercially complex this may require specialist 'transactional lawyers', but additionally in some cases a legal team of experts, which is only too likely to increase the overall legal costs of mediating:[49]

> Bearing in mind the complex commercial cases which might settle may well require sophisticated drafting and foresight as to what is required, this might justify having a transactional lawyer in attendance with the litigation specialist, who is there (and vitally so) to advise on what the litigation alternative might hold if the dispute does not settle.

Lawyers representing clients in mediation are advised to take particular care when drawing up settlement agreements in order to avoid 'uncertainty' of terms due to 'vagueness or ambiguity'[50] or that the parties have only reached an 'agreement to agree' or that 'pre-conditions' such as 'drawing up a consent order' are done.[51] Where there is concern about consideration Mackie et al. suggest that the agreement should be executed by deed.[52] Sime et al. advise that the agreements should be 'comprehensive and accurate' and include 'all practical details' which would include 'payment dates' or 'enforcement options' such as 'interest on late payment' or 'foreseeable events'.[53] Regardless of how careful drafters of settlement agreements are the cases show the difficulties that arise as parties regret their arrangements and either seek to re-negotiate or avoid altogether.

47   *Sargeant v. Macepark (Whittlebury) Ltd* [2008] at 26
48   *Sargeant v. Macepark (Whittlebury) Ltd* [2008] at 26
49   Mackie et al. (2007) at 293. See also Sime et al. (2010) at 323–4
50   Sime et al. (2010) at 323–4 at 324
51   Mackie et al. (2007) at 274–5 at 274
52   Mackie et al. (2007) at 275
53   Sime et al. (2010) at 323–4 at 324

No concluded agreement

Chapter 5 considers *Brown v. Rice & Patel* in relation to the effect of without prejudice statements and confidentiality in mediation, but it is examined here in the context of whether the parties had reached a concluded settlement in mediation and the effect of a mediation contract, which required any settlement agreement to be signed in writing.[54] Mrs Rice, who had an individual voluntary arrangement (IVA) for insolvency had agreed to sell her property to Mrs Patel but had not informed the supervisor of the IVA which led to a bankruptcy petition.[55] Mr Brown (the trustee in bankruptcy) began an action against Mrs Patel in relation to the alleged undervalue of the property. However, prior to the court hearing they agreed to mediate and both parties signed a written mediation agreement.[56] The mediation session lasted 13 hours but failed to reach a settlement. The applicant (Brown) alleged that they had accepted an offer made by Mr Patel (on his wife's behalf) after the mediation had ended, which had been left open until midday the next day.[57] Mr Patel maintained that neither he nor his wife believed they were making 'any terms of settlement' by which they could be bound and that the offer was to be discussed with family and friends before being confirmed by midday the next day.[58]

Mr Evans, who was acting for Mr Brown, contended that Mr Patel had confirmed that the offer still stood in a telephone call close to the 12 o'clock deadline, which had been cut dead due to a signal loss. Mr Patel on the other hand claimed he had said there was no offer and to proceed to trial.[59] Regardless, Mr Evans faxed an acceptance of the offer to Mrs Patel's solicitor. In a second telephone call before the deadline, Mr Evans accepted in cross examination that Mr Patel had said he was not 'minded' to accept Mr Evans's offer and would go to trial but 'considered this to mean' that he would not 'budge' from the final offer. However, following this conversation Mr Patel did instruct his solicitor to proceed to trial.[60]

Isaacs J explained that in making an analysis of whether an offer had been made the court is required to adopt an 'objective test' to establish

---

54 *Brown v. Rice & Patel* [2007] EWHC 625. One of the exceptions to without prejudice statements includes allowing evidence to show that the parties have reached a concluded agreement.
55 *Brown v. Rice & Patel* [2007] at 1
56 *Brown v. Rice & Patel* [2007] at 3
57 *Brown v. Rice & Patel* [2007] at 3
58 *Brown v. Rice & Patel* [2007] at 34
59 *Brown v. Rice & Patel* [2007] at 37
60 *Brown v. Rice & Patel* [2007] at 42

whether the party intended to be bound but an 'apparent intention may suffice'.[61] The court concluded that regardless of what the Patels 'thought, objectively they had put forth an offer', although it was accepted that Mr Patel may have believed that he was only considering making it after discussions with 'friends and family' although he had failed to make that clear to Mr Evans.[62]

However, the court accepted the defendants' argument that the 'offer, if made, was incomplete' because there was no certainty on how the settlement would be 'effected', which could have been either through a Tomlin Order or through a court judgment, which might have been a 'matter of some importance' to the litigant.[63]

> The manner in which litigation generally is to be disposed of by a settlement agreement may be a matter of some importance to the parties to the litigation. The consequences of a judgment against Mrs Patel as opposed to a Tomlin Order would differ. In my judgment, the absence of any provision as to the manner of disposal of the litigation does make the offer incomplete. Its purported acceptance would not give rise to a complete agreement.

A further reason there was no binding contract was the inclusion of clause 1.4 in the agreement to mediate, which required any outcome to be 'reduced into writing and signed by or on behalf of the parties' and the parties could not have 'intended to be bound by their agreement until it was drawn up and signed by both parties'.[64] The court did not accept the applicant's argument that providing a time for accepting the offer waived clause 1.4 because that would give 'no meaning to the offer': 'The acceptance period is relevant to whether there was a settlement at all': Had the time lapsed there would have been no settlement 'on which clause 1.4 *could* bite' but if accepted in the time period then there was a settlement on which 'clause 1.4 *would* bite' and the court concluded that the acceptance could not have been effective because it 'would not have resulted in a concluded settlement' as it was incomplete until reduced into writing.[65]

The court went on to consider one further matter. The applicants had tried to get around the problem of clause 1.4 by arguing that the mediation had ended in the evening and therefore the offer was not made 'in mediation' – which meant there was no requirement for a signed agreement.[66] The court

---

61 *Brown v. Rice & Patel* [2007] at 50. The court referred to *Chitty on Contracts* (29th edition 2004 Vol. 1 at 2-002
62 *Brown v. Rice & Patel* [2007] at 34
63 *Brown v. Rice & Patel* [2007] at 51
64 *Brown v. Rice & Patel* [2007] at 53
65 *Brown v. Rice & Patel* [2007] at 67
66 *Brown v. Rice & Patel* [2007] at 61

recognised that this issue did not need to be 'determined' because there was no settlement agreement but because of the 'importance to the mediation world' a review was made of the practice of leaving settlement offers 'on the table' after the mediation had concluded.[67] The court suggested that this was done to 'enable the parties to reflect' on the settlement offers or for the mediator to 'continue discussion with the parties individually'.[68] Mr Isaacs judged that acceptances made after the mediation hearing are 'just as much made in the mediation as if it was made at the hearing itself' and therefore had there been a valid offer and acceptance in the instant case there would have been a 'settlement reached in mediation' within the meaning of clause 1.4.[69]

This view may be at odds with current mediation agreements, for example CEDR Model Mediation Agreement, states that 'No terms of settlement reached *at* the Mediation will be legally binding until set out in writing and signed by or on behalf of each of the parties' and although the courts may interpret this to mean the same as *in* the mediation process, it could at some point become a matter of contention.[70] Practically mediators and the parties (or their representatives) may want to reduce their final offer into writing with time frames for acceptance when disengaging from the mediation session: this would at least preserve the offer and any confidentiality or without prejudice issues could be documented. Conversely, the parties may want to acknowledge formally in writing that the mediation has ended. However, these actions again introduce a level of formality and legalism into what is essentially an informal process, which future litigants may ask the court to review.

Establishing when mediation begins or ends may have particular relevance to the statutory limitations for litigation.[71] At present when the parties elect to mediate before litigating the statutory time limitations continue to run, leading Mackie et al. to suggest that if the 'expiry' date is close then it may be practical to commence proceedings at the same time or alternatively enter a 'binding agreement' to postpone their operation.[72] The EU Mediation Directive has made specific provision for 'limitation and prescription periods' for cross border disputes so that parties are not 'prevented from initiating judicial proceedings or arbitration'.[73] The directive has been implemented by statutory instrument, which also specifies a time frame for mediation.[74] For limitation purposes a cross border mediation 'starts' when the parties and

---

67 *Brown v. Rice & Patel* [2007] at 62
68 *Brown v. Rice & Patel* [2007] at 63
69 *Brown v. Rice & Patel* [2007] at 63
70 CEDR Model Mediation Agreement (2012)
71 Mackie et al. (2007) at 190
72 Mackie et al. (2007) at 190
73 EU Mediation Directive 2008, Article 8
74 Cross-Border Mediation (EU Directive) (Statutory Instrument 2011 No. 1133)

the mediator enter into the 'agreement to mediate' but the ending is prescribed by a number of possible situations:[75]

(a) the parties reach an agreement in resolution of the relevant dispute;

(b) a party completes the notification of the other parties that it has withdrawn from the mediation;

(c) a party to whom a qualifying request[76] is made fails to give a response reaching the other parties within 14 days of the request;

(d) the parties, after being notified that the mediator's appointment has ended (by death, resignation or otherwise), fail to agree within 14 days to seek to appoint a replacement mediator;

(e) the mediation otherwise comes to an end pursuant to the terms of the agreement to mediate.

At present the question of when a mediation ends has been specified for cross border disputes but commentators note if the courts are going to make 'incursions' into mediation for enforcement purposes there might need to be 'some kind of definition of its parameter' for domestic disputes. However government proposals in 2012 to extend the EU provisions have to date not been progressed.[77]

Illegality

The legality of a compromise mediation agreement was at issue in the High Court Chancery division in *Thakrar v. Ciro Citterio* when family members of a company who were in dispute negotiated an agreement that the company would buy out Kirit's shares.[78] Statutory requirements limit the circumstances that a company can buy out its own shares and the matter was further complicated when the Ciro Citterio (the company) went into liquidation as any arrangements had to be authorised through the administrators and approved by the creditors' committee.[79]

Mediation took place with the administrators, resulting in a signed settlement agreement which was 'approved by five members of the Creditors' Committee' and then drawn up into a Tomlin Order.[80] The Court of Appeal

---

75 Cross-Border Mediation (EU Directive) (Statutory Instrument 2011 No. 1133) see s8(4) and s8(5)

76 Cross-Border Mediation (EU Directive) (Statutory Instrument 2011 No. 1133) s8A. (6) 'For the purpose of subsection (5), a qualifying request is a request by a party that another (A) confirm to all parties that A is continuing with the mediation'.

77 Mackie et al. (2007) at 135. See also Birch (2006)

78 *Thakrar v. Thakrar* [2002] EWHC 1975 Ch at 4

79 *Thakrar v. Thakrar* [2002] EWHC at 9; See also at the Court of Appeal *Kirit Lalji Thakrar, Trustee in Bankruptcy of Rasik Lalji Thakrar v. Rasik Lalji Thakrar, Urmila R Thakrar, Vinod Lalji Thakrar, Manjula Thakrar, Nilesh Rasik Thakrar, Surbhi Thakrar, Reena Thakrar* [2002] EWCA Civ 1304 at 48

80 *Thakrar v. Thakrar* [2002] HC at 18 & 20

declined to enforce the Tomlin Order because of the 'high risk' that no court would 'approve' and it might indicate 'apparent approval', which could influence potential 'challenges' from 'aggrieved unsecured creditors or the administrators'.[81] The issue of the validity or illegality of the mediation settlement was remitted to the administration court where Kirit sought a declaration that the company was bound by the mediation agreement but the company claimed that any agreement was 'conditional on the making of the Tomlin Order';[82] or if not 'then unenforceable for illegality'.[83]

The claims of illegality were based on s143(1) and s151(1) of the Companies Act 1985.[84] Under s143 companies are not permitted to 'acquire their own shares' albeit subject to limitations, which include if the purchase is made 'in accordance with Chapter VII' through a contract 'approved' by a 'special resolution of members of the company and is made out of distributable profits'.[85] Section 151(1) does not permit a company to give 'financial assistance either directly or indirectly' to assist the purchase of shares but this section does not apply when they are made in 'accordance' with Chapter VII.[86]

The two issues on legality considered by the court were first, whether there were 'distributable profits' with which to buy out the shares; and second, whether the 'participation of all the members was to be treated as the equivalent of a special resolution'.[87] On the second issue, the court concluded that this had been decided previously when the Court had permitted an appeal on Judge Boggis's order. But the time for appeal had expired and as the order had not been set aside it remained valid, which 'did not give rise to an illegal transaction'.[88]

---

81 *Kirit Lalji Thakrar, Trustee in Bankruptcy of Rasik Lalji Thakrar v. Rasik Lalji Thakrar, Urmila R Thakrar, Vinod Lalji Thakrar, Manjula Thakrar, Nilesh Rasik Thakrar, Surbhi Thakrar, Reena Thakrar* [2002] EWCA Civ 1304 at 50–51

82 *Thakrar v. Thakrar* [2002] HC at 27. The court held the agreement was 'not conditional on the making of the Tomlin order' (at 38). First, because the compromise included issues outside of the claim to the CA and the parties would not 'wish' them to be 'conditional on a stay for proceedings' (at 33). Second, the mediation agreement depended on 'two conditions' (a signed document and the agreement of the majority of the creditor's committee) both of which had been 'satisfied' and there was no evidence that a 'third condition' (a stay) was needed (at 34). Third, the terms of the schedule were complete apart from reference to the order in paragraph 2 but the court did not 'accept' that this 'justified the imposition of a third condition' (a stay) (at 35). Fourth, the 'recital' in the Tomlin Order referred to 'the parties having agreed the terms set out in the schedule' which showed an 'intention' that they had 'already made a contract in those terms' and although the recital used the 'standard terms of a Tomlin Order', the court 'regarded' this 'recital' to be an 'express confirmation' that the agreement was both 'prior and independent' of the making of the order (at 36). Fifth, as the schedule was 'independent' of the order, the order had 'additional' requirements not only to enforce the schedule but to 'limit the effect of the order' (at 37).

83 *Thakrar v. Thakrar* [2002] HC at 28

84 *Thakrar v. Thakrar* [2002] HC at 41

85 *Thakrar v. Thakrar* [2002] HC at 42–4. Companies Act 1985, s143 (3) (a) and (c)

86 *Thakrar v. Thakrar* [2002] HC at 44

87 *Thakrar v. Thakrar* [2002] HC at 45

88 *Thakrar v. Thakrar* [2002] HC at 46

On the first issue, the court recognised that there had been 'common ground' that there were 'sufficient distributional profits' to cover the purchase of the shares, which the Court of Appeal had referred to, and an expert witness report at the mediation also confirmed there were sufficient funds.[89] The High Court found that the mediation agreement was one that could be enforced by relying on *Binder v. Alachouzos*.[90] In *Binder* the Court of Appeal rejected an argument that a compromise agreement with an unregistered moneylender was unenforceable for illegality under the Moneylenders Act, because the purpose of the Act was to protect borrowers and courts would ensure they had not been attained through an 'unfair advantage' and would enforce if 'satisfied that the terms are fair and reasonable'.[91]

The High Court held in *Thakrar v. Ciro Citterio* that the compromise mediation agreement was one that the 'court can and should uphold' because it was reached through a 'genuine' mediation which had been conducted 'on a proper commercial basis' and each side was 'represented by experienced solicitors and had the assistance of skilled accountants'.[92]

Thakrar v. Ciro Citterio considered the illegality of a compromise mediation agreement, which if successful would have meant that the contract was void but other case law has also considered mediation settlements where there are claims that the agreement is invalid due to vitiating factors that allow a party to rescind the contract.

Misrepresentation and 'alleged repudiation'

The Chancery Division of the High Court in *Crystal Decisions (UK) v. Vedatech* reviewed the enforceability of a mediated settlement agreement, which the defendants argued was invalid due to misrepresentation.[93] Mr Subramanian, the second defendant and managing director of Vedatech, claimed to have relied on financial statements made by Crystal Decisions that they were making losses when agreeing to settle at a lower rate.[94] Although Vedatech unsuccessfully claimed for payment under the contract, Jacob J awarded costs on a 'reasonable basis' but intimated that an enquiry was needed as to quantum and stayed the proceedings for a mediation to take place.[95] The parties signed a mediation agreement incorporating CEDR's model procedure into the terms of the contract, which stipulated that any settlement agreement was not legally binding until reduced into writing.[96] Mr Subramanian signed the mediated agreement as Vedatech's representative and was required to provide

89   *Thakrar v. Thakrar* [2002] HC at 47–8
90   *Binder v. Alachouzos* [1972] 2 QB 151
91   *Thakrar v. Thakrar* [2002] HC at 49
92   *Thakrar v. Thakrar* [2002] HC at 78
93   *Crystal Decisions (UK) v. Vedatech Corp* [2007] EWHC 1062 (Ch)
94   *Crystal Decisions (UK) v. Vedatech Corp* [2007] at 1–3
95   *Crystal Decisions (UK) v. Vedatech Corp* [2007] at 3
96   *Crystal Decisions (UK) v. Vedatech Corp* [2007] at 5

Crystal Decisions with bank details to allow payment of the settlement. It did not supply them, however, stating in an email that he had information that the agreement had been reached fraudulently.[97] He indicated that an application would be made to the court for the settlement to be set aside unless Crystal Decisions reopened the mediation.[98] Before the application was heard Mr Subramanian purported to 'self-rescind' the settlement agreement on the 'basis of misrepresentation, innocent or otherwise'.[99] At the case management hearing Jacobs J warned the applicant that the mediation settlement could only be set aside on 'proof of fraudulent misrepresentation' because under Clause 11 of the mediated agreement the parties had agreed that there would be no right of action for 'any statements or representation . . . unless fraudulently made'.[100] Mr Subramanian refused to discontinue his allegations of fraud, and the court stayed proceedings for a new action and a court order required both parties to pay money into court for security.[101] Crystal Decisions was permitted to apply for judgment on the 'validity' of the mediation agreement because of the defendants' failure to make a payment order into the court, which debarred them from making a defence to the application but the court agreed to hear Mr Subramanian on the 'nature and scope of the relief' sought by Crystal Decisions.[102] The claimants at first sought a declaration from the court that it rejected Mr Subramanian's rescission of the Settlement Agreement but accepted that this would require the court to try the 'remaining allegations of misrepresentation and duress', therefore they 'simply' requested the court to declare the 'Settlement to be valid, enforceable and binding on the defendants'.[103]

The Court held that there was 'nothing in the agreement' to challenge its enforceability and the defendants were not permitted to give evidence that the notices of rescission had been served because the signed mediation agreement did not permit rescission 'on innocent or negligent misrepresentation'.[104] Further, the court did not accept that Crystal Decisions had 'repudiated' the settlement agreement when they stated in a letter that they would take action to 'set off their costs from the settlement sum' if the claim was 'pursued and failed'.[105] Set off was not permitted by Clause 4 of the mediation agreement but in the view of the court, Crystal Decisions's letter did not 'evince an

97 *Crystal Decisions (UK) v. Vedatech Corp* [2007] at 12
98 *Crystal Decisions (UK) v. Vedatech Corp* [2007] at 10–11
99 *Crystal Decisions (UK) v. Vedatech Corp* [2007] at 17
100 *Crystal Decisions (UK) v. Vedatech Corp* [2007] at 19. A fraudulent misrepresentation is one that is made 'knowingly, or without belief in its truth or recklessly, careless whether it be true or false'. See *Derry v. Peek* (1889) 14 App Case 337 at 374
101 *Crystal Decisions (UK) v. Vedatech Corp* [2007] at 20
102 *Crystal Decisions (UK) v. Vedatech Corp* [2007] at 44–5
103 *Crystal Decisions (UK) v. Vedatech Corp* [2007] at 46
104 *Crystal Decisions (UK) v. Vedatech Corp* [2007] at 52
105 *Crystal Decisions (UK) v. Vedatech Corp* [2007] at 55–6

intention not to be bound by the agreement (in fact of the contrary)'.[106]
Nor had Crystal Decisions repudiated the mediation agreement by failing
to make the settlement payment after receiving the bank details because
Mr Subramanian had 'qualified' this by sending another letter which had 'in
effect' said that payment would not be accepted.[107]

The Court of Appeal also refused to allow rescission of a compromise agreement in *Trustees of Morden College v. Mayrick* when the applicant claimed that
the mediated settlement had been gained through misrepresentations about
evidence of ownership both before and in the mediation.[108] Morden College
had leased out land owned through a 'long and undisturbed possession'
but had no documents of title.[109] They sought possession from Mr Mayrick,
who had gained a registered possessory title.[110] Following a mediated agreement both parties agreed to transfer 'parcels of land' to each other but Mr
Mayrick refused to complete the exchange claiming that the College had
failed to provide 'documentary evidence of title'.[111] He asserted that the
College had leased the land to a Housing Association, which had gained title
through 'adverse possession', which was then transferred to him.[112] In effect,
he was claiming that he already had a registered title to the land and that the
College had misrepresented that they had 'unregistered documentary evidence', which could be transferred to him thereby giving him a 'documentary
title'.[113] The Court held that Mr Mayrich could not go to trial on a claim of
misrepresentation 'unsupported by evidence' which had only been raised for
the first time in the Court of Appeal.[114] Furthermore the Court should not
permit the reopening of a compromise agreement when a party knew he had
ownership but had 'chosen' not to bring it up because this would encourage
litigious behaviour: 'Unless a firm negative answer is given to that question
countless compromises intended to avoid further litigation would prove to be
little more than an irresistible invitation to yet later proceedings'.[115]

Economic duress

Crystal Decisions and *Morden College* involved the courts' approach to mediation
agreements gained through claims of misrepresentations. Another vitiating
factor was considered in *Farm Assist Ltd (FAL) v. Secretary of State for the
Environment, Food and Rural Affairs* (DEFRA), when the claimants sought to

---

106 *Crystal Decisions (UK) v. Vedatech Corp* [2007] at 56
107 *Crystal Decisions (UK) v. Vedatech Corp* [2007] at 57–8
108 *Trustees of Morden College v. Mayrick* [2007] EWCA Civ 4
109 *Trustees of Morden College v. Mayrick* [2007] at 2
110 *Trustees of Morden College v. Mayrick* [2007] at 14–17
111 *Trustees of Morden College v. Mayrick* [2007] at 24
112 *Trustees of Morden College v. Mayrick* [2007] at 24
113 *Trustees of Morden College v. Mayrick* [2007] at 60
114 *Trustees of Morden College v. Mayrick* [2007] at 55
115 *Trustees of Morden College v. Mayrick* [2007] per Mr Justice Lindsay at 65

set aside the mediated outcome on the grounds of economic duress.[116] For the courts to be satisfied that a contract was entered into through economic duress '. . . there must be pressure: (a) whose practical effect is that there is compulsion on, or lack of practical choice for, the victim; (b) which is illegitimate; and (c) which is a significant cause inducing the claimant to enter into the contract'.[117] Factors which might be taken into account to show economic duress include threatening to breach a contract; acts of bad faith; whether the victim had any 'realistic alternative' than to enter the contract; or whether the victim had made an 'affirmation of the contract'.[118]

It was alleged that DEFRA had engaged in 'illegitimate pressure' in relation to the stance taken to the valuation of FAL's account.[119] The conduct included a failure to 'take a structured, reasoned, bilateral, or bona fide approach' 'and/or bad faith in relation to DEFRA's conduct of the mediation and/or the contents of its mediation statement'.[120] The court held that the 'interests of justice' required that the mediator should be compelled to attend as a witness 'because the allegations concern what was said and done in the mediation and this necessarily involves the evidence of what FAL says was said and done by the mediator'.[121] The proceedings were not pursued and therefore the courts did not review the allegations of economic duress[122] but the decision to order the mediator to attend tacitly recognises that a mediation agreement may be invalid where it has been obtained by coercion in the form of economic duress, which thereby treats it as any other compromise agreement reached through negotiation.[123]

Common law approaches to enforceability in the USA, Australia and Hong Kong

USA

In the USA, which has a longer experience of modern mediation than England and Wales, the case law has been developing exponentially as federal and state

116 *Farm Assist Ltd (FAL) v. Secretary of State for the Environment, Food and Rural Affairs* (DEFRA) [2009] EWHC 1102 (TCC)
117 Dyson J in *DSND Subsea v. Petroleum Geo-Services* [2000] BLR 530 at 131; see *Universal Tankships Inc of Monrovia v. International Transport Workers' Federation* [1983] 1 AC 366 at 400B–E and *Dimskal Shipping Co SA v. International Transport Workers' Federation* [1992] 2 AC 152 at [165 G].
118 *DSND Subsea v. Petroleum Geo-Services* [2000] BLR 530 at 131; see *Universal Tankships Inc of Monrovia v. International Transport Workers' Federation* [1983] 1 AC 366 at 400B–E and *Dimskal Shipping Co SA v. International Transport Workers' Federation* [1992] 2 AC 152 at [165 G].
119 *Farm Assist Ltd* [2009] at 51
120 *Farm Assist Ltd* [2009] at 51. For an analysis of the case see for example, Allen (2009); Brooker (2010a); Cornes (2008). This case is considered in the chapter on confidentiality.
121 *Farm Assist Ltd* [2009] at 53(1)
122 See Allen (2009)
123 *Farm Assist Ltd* [2009] at 53

policies encourage or increasingly mandate usage.[124] A 303% increase in mediation cases was reported in the USA between 1999–2005, of which 43% concerned 'enforcement issues' involving 'contract interpretation' (23%), including: whether there had been a 'meeting of the minds' (13%); whether 'agreement had been reached' (7%); whether 'specific formalities had been met' (11%);[125] and the remainder implicated 'contract deficiencies' such as fraud (8%), duress (6%), mutual mistake (5%) or unilateral mistake (3%).[126] Cole et al. note that a 'specialised law of mediation' or a 'common law of mediation' has come to fruition as contract law principles are applied to 'specific issues unique to mediation', particularly those relating to mediator 'behaviour' such as 'misconduct', 'bias' or 'undue influence' as well as the conduct of legal representatives.[127]

The common law in the USA also uses the formation of a contract and specific defences to test the legality of mediation agreements not controlled by legislation, but parties wishing to avoid enforcement have an 'uphill battle' as critiques of the case law suggest there is virtually a 'presumption of validity'[128] about mediated settlements.[129] It would be impossible to review all the case law in the USA on how the courts have applied the common law principles relating to contract formation or the vitiating factors. Furthermore commentators in the USA who have considered the opinions on enforcement have concluded it is 'difficult to exact general principles' that can be drawn 'in a uniform manner' across the numerous state and federal jurisdictions.[130]

> The wide variety of views about the purpose of mediation, the scope of confidentiality, and how the mediation process ought to be treated differently from a negotiation, make it difficult to extract general principles of law that would be applied in a uniform manner across the many jurisdictions in the United States.

---

124 Coben & Thompson (2006); Alfini & McCabe (2001)
125 These can include the requirement for agreements to be written and signed.
126 See Cole et al. (2012) at 7.1 reporting on the finding in Coben & Thompson (2006)
127 See Cole et al. (2012) at 7.1. The authors cite Menkel-Meadow (1991 at 1) and Press (2003 at 58) who discuss the development of a 'common law ADR' and a 'common law of mediation' respectively.
128 See Cole et al. (2012) at section 7.2; Thompson (2004) at 523
129 See Cole et al. (2012) at 7.2 fn6. Cole et al. cite for example, *Chappell v. Roth*, 141 NC App 502, 539 SE 2d 666, 668 (2000), opinion rev'd, 353 NC 690, 548 SE 2d 499 (2001), reh'g denied, 354 NC 75, 553 SE 2d 36 (2001) at 500 where the North Carolina Court of Appeals stated that there should be a 'strong presumption that a settlement agreement reached by the parties through court-ordered mediation under the guidance of a mediator is a valid contract that serves to minimize the expenditure of time and money by the parties, and to bring the benefit of final resolution to our jurisprudence'. Cole et al. (2012) report that from 1999–2005 enforcement was refused in only 18% of the cases.
130 Cole et al. (2012) at 7.20

Agreements reached in mediation will be enforced in the USA if they 'objectively manifest an agreement to be bound', however as Cole et al. note this objective 'focus' 'impedes self determination'.[131] They cite, for example, the USA Court of Appeal decision to enforce a signed agreement in *Fidelity and Guar. Ins. Co. v. Star Equipment Corp* despite the belief held by one party that a 'final' document still had to be drafted after the mediation.[132] Furthermore, the courts are prepared on occasions to 'supply missing terms' where contracts lack clarity based on other criteria such as 'course of dealings' or 'usage of trade'.[133] An objective standard is used when parties claim they did not reach agreement or have only reached an 'agreement to agree' as in *Calderon v. J.B. Nurseries* where it was held that the signed agreement was 'voidable at the other parties' election, but not void'.[134] Cole et al. warn counsel to ensure that the agreements are drawn up at the end of the mediation session and if not finalised to clearly record 'the status' of the agreement to that point:[135]

> In the interest of finality and avoiding future litigation, attorneys who believe they have reached a mediated settlement would be well advised to have all parties sign off on the terms of any release before leaving the mediation session. If parties must leave the mediation session before agreeing on the language of the unresolved term, the parties should make clear, preferably in a signed writing, the current status of their negotiations.

Mediated oral agreements can be enforced in the USA, although in many court-annexed schemes there is often a requirement that the settlement outcome is a signed written document (sometimes with legal counsels' signatures) and in some jurisdictions must be recorded with the court.[136] Cole et al. observe that enforcing agreements 'strains confidentiality' but that the confidentiality rules make enforcement of oral agreements 'virtually impossible to prove', which assists the courts but does not protect parties who

---

131 Cole et al. (2012) at 7.3 citing for example, *City of DeQuincy v. Henry*, 25 So 3d 237 (La Ct App 3d Cir 2009), writ granted, 34 So 3d 296 (La 2010)

132 Cole et al. (2012) at 7.2 citing *Fidelity and Guar. Ins. Co. v. Star Equipment Corp*, 541 F 3d 1 (1st Cir 2008)

133 Cole et al. (2012) at 7.3; See Sussman (2006)

134 Cole et al. (2012) at 7.4 citing *Calderon v. J.B. Nurseries, Inc.*, 933 So 2d 553 (Fla Dist Ct App 1st Dist 2006), reh'g denied, (Mar 15, 2006) at 544

135 Cole et al. (2012) at 7.4

136 Cole et al. (2012) at 7.5. For example the authors make reference to the Missouri Supreme Court Rule 17. See 17.01 (d) which states 'All alternative dispute resolution processes shall be non-binding unless the parties enter into a written agreement as provided in Rule 17.06(c).' A written agreement shall be binding to the extent not prohibited by law'. 17.06(c) states 'Settlement shall be by a written document setting out the essential terms of the agreement executed after the termination of the alternative dispute resolution process'.

are unaware of the need for formalities.[137] Parties can 'back out' of agreements when the courts 'strictly' apply 'formality requirements' but Cole et al. cite cases where a more flexible approach has been taken to 'effectuate the intent of the parties': For example, in *Yaekle v. Andrews*, despite the fact the parties had not signed the agreement as required by statute, it was enforced because their 'actions and representations' demonstrated that they had reached a settlement.[138]

Sussman believes that the requirement for signed mediation agreements, particularly as states adopt the Uniform Mediation Act, 'will ultimately be the rule throughout the USA' and oral evidence will be precluded to show that agreement has been reached.[139] The Uniform Mediation Act 2001 is primarily concerned with protecting the confidentiality of mediation but permits evidence of written mediation settlement agreements but not oral agreements for enforcement purposes.[140] The drafters took this approach because, although it might disadvantage 'less legally sophisticated parties', it is 'common practice' in state legislation, and admitting oral evidence would lead to the parties being 'less candid' if they thought their negotiations would be 'admissible' in court.[141] The Uniform Mediation Act places the burden on the 'proponent' to persuade the court that 'the need for the evidence outweighs the confidentiality interest' and s6(b)(2) permits evidence for enforcing mediation settlement agreements in order to 'preserve the contract defences'.[142]

Parties may resist enforcement based on the common law defences, but only in 'extreme cases' have these succeeded because, it is suggested, the rules are based on the understanding that parties are able to make agreements 'in their own interest'.[143] Cole et al. treat 'fraud, misrepresentation and non-disclosure' together because the case opinions 'usually' have not distinguished between the 'concepts'.[144] Fraud has a 'high standard of proof' and misrepresentation requires a party to show that a misrepresentation is made, 'induced agreement', and it is 'reasonable to rely' on it.[145] In *Re Patterson* the Washington Court of Appeal rejected a claim of fraud because a party can make their 'own appraisal' of information and in *Chitkara v. New York Telephone Co.* the party

---

137 Cole et al. (2012) at 7.5

138 Cole et al. (2012) at 7.5. The authors cite *Yaekle v. Andrews*, 169 P 3d 196 (Colo. App. 2007)

139 Sussman (2006) at 34

140 Uniform Mediation Act (2001) s6(a) (1)

141 See Uniform Mediation Act 2001 (Amendments) s6(b) (2), Commentary on s6

142 Uniform Mediation Act 2001 (Amendments) s6(b) (2), Commentary at 33

143 Cole et al. (2012) at 7.6

144 Cole et al. (2012) at 7.7

145 Cole et al. (2012) at 7.7. The authors observe that the difficulty of succeeding in fraud and misrepresentation is shown by the fact that only 9 out of 80 cases were reported to have succeeded.

should not have relied on a statement made by the mediator, which they could have 'reasonably' checked for themselves.[146]

The courts in the USA take an uncompromising approach to mediation agreements when there are claims of mistake. No successful claims were reported for a unilateral mistake because the claimant must show that the mediation settlement agreement is 'unconscionable' or that the party knew or had 'somehow caused the mistake' and that there was no agreement to take the risk or that the risk 'should not be reasonably allocated to the proponent'.[147] Mutual mistakes have 'rarely' been upheld because a party must show that it forms the basis of what the parties agreed and the agreement will not be void if the party took on the 'risk of the mistake'.[148] Cole et al. illustrate how careful parties must be in mediation, when in *Leff v. Ecker*, the agreement was valid because the plaintiff took the 'risk' of mediating despite not having a 'clear picture' of the insurance 'policy limits' and only made an 'all out effort' to check the facts after the agreement had been reached: 'The doctrine of mutual mistake was not created to relieve litigants of agreements entered into improvidently'.[149]

Generally cases on duress are not reported to involve physical intimidation but economic duress where the claimant must prove there was no 'choice' but to enter into an 'unfair' agreement and that on an 'objective' analysis there was no alternative 'reasonable' course of action that could have been taken.[150] Between 1999–2005 there was only one successful case of duress, where a wife threatened to send under-aged sex pictures to the prosecutor to gain an advantageous settlement from her husband which was held to be a 'fraud on the court' rather than a finding of duress.[151] Many of the complaints involving duress and undue influence involved mediators giving court predictions or the use of coercive pressure by either mediators[152] and/or legal representatives, which were not successful in the main because, when participants are legally represented the court 'assumes' this provides protection.[153] Coben and

---

146 Cole et al. (2012) at 7.7. The authors cite *Re Patterson*, 93 Wash App 579, 969 P 2d 1106, 1110–11 (Div. 1 1999) and *Chitkara v. New York Telephone Co.*, 45 Fed Appx 53, 55 (2d Cir 2002)

147 As an example, Cole et al. (2012) at 7.8. The authors cite *ABA Consulting, LLC, v. Liffey Van Lines, Inc.*, 67 AD 3d 401, 889 NYS 2d 540 (1st Dep't 2009) where the claim of a unilateral mistake was unsuccessful because it was not shown that the settlement agreement had been 'induced' by a fraudulent 'false representation'.

148 Sussman (2006) at 35; Cole et al. (2012) at 7.8

149 Cole et al. (2012) at 7.8. The authors cite *Leff v. Ecker*, 972 So 2d 965 (Fla Dist Ct App 3d Dist 2007), reh'g and reh'g en banc denied, (Feb. 7, 2008) at 966

150 Cole et al. (2012) at 7.9

151 See Cole et al. (2012) 7.9; Coben & Thompson (2006) at 82 who cite *Cooper v. Austin*, 750 So 2d 711 (Fla Dist Ct App 5th Dist 2000), reh'g denied, (Feb. 9, 2000)

152 See Sussman (2006) at 33. Sussman cites *Vela v. Hope Lumber & Supply* 966 P 2nd 1196 (Okla Civ App Div 1 1998) where it was claimed the mediator used bullying tactics to get a settlement agreement

153 Cole et al. (2012) at 7.9. The authors cite *Chitkara v. New York Telephone Co.*, 45 Fed Appx 53 (2d Cir 2002) when the court enforced the mediation agreement because

Thompson report 13 opinions on undue influence and cite the discussion in *Olam v. Congress Mortgage Co* where the mediation agreement was enforceable despite complaints of ill health during a 15-hour mediation and pressure from the mediator and her own and the defendant's lawyers.[154] Sussman provides a list of the types of complaints made under the head of 'undue pressure', which includes: settlement discussions at 'unusual or inappropriate times' or 'places'; repeated 'demands' to conclude the settlement; 'extreme' threats about the 'consequences of delay'; 'absence of third party advisors'; and 'statements' to the effect that there is 'no time to consult financial advisors'.[155] Where the courts are concerned about mediators' tactics or other forms of coercion, they have to remit the case back to the court for an 'evidentiary hearing'.[156]

Other claims for non-enforcement have involved for example 'lack of authority' to settle but where this involves the parties' legal representatives courts have been inclined to 'presume' legal authority[157] or that 'apparent authority existed'.[158] Parties who wish to claim 'incompetence or incapacity' have the burden of proof because there is a 'presumption of competence' and Sussman reports that even in 'striking cases' such as 'severe depression, memory loss, brain fog'[159] or 'mental incapacity' mediated agreements have been found to be valid.[160] There may also be claims that mediation settlement agreements should not be enforced because of illegality or because the contract is against public policy.[161]

Australia

Australia has had relatively few cases on the enforcement of mediation agreements, which Spencer and Brogan suggest may be indicative of a number of 'unlimited factors' ranging from a 'lack of funds' to litigate or a 'willingness'

the mediator's predictions could be 'verified' but they cannot be 'relied' on when the legal representative is 'present'.

154 Coben & Thompson (2006) at 84; Cole et al. (2012) cite a number of cases where the defence has been successful for example: *Randle v. Mid Gulf, Inc.*, 1996 WL 447954, *2 (Tex App Houston 14th Dist 1996), writ denied, (Apr. 18, 1997)

155 Sussman (2006) at 34

156 Sussman (2006) at 34

157 Sussman (2006) at 35. Sussman cites *Inwood Intern. Co. v. Wal-Mart Stores, Inc.*, 243 F 3d 567 (Fed Cir 2000)

158 Sussman (2006) at 35. Sussman cites *Little v. Greyhound Lines Inc* 2005 WL 2429437 (DS NY 2005)

159 Sussman (2006) at 34. Sussman cites *Domangue v. Domangue*, 2005 WL 1828553, *4 (Tex App Tyler 2005)

160 Sussman (2006) at 34. Sussman cites *Alexander v. Naden*, 130 Wash App 1036, 2005 WL 3150323, *3 (Div. 1 2005); See also Cole et al. at 7.14 & 7.17

161 See Cole et al. (2012) at 7.17. The authors cite *In re Kasschau*, 11 SW 3d 305, 312–14 (Tex App Houston 14th Dist 1999) which involved an agreement to engage in an illegal act of destroying property and *Pettyjohn v. Estes Exp. Lines*, 124 Fed Appx 174, 177–79 (4th Cir 2005) where there was a claim that the mediated agreement contravened public policy.

to mediate with 'good faith' in a 'voluntary' process and skilled mediators using 'good reality testing' or 'inserting clauses' that participants return if problems arise.[162] However one reason they suggest may be mediators restraining from using 'too evaluative' conduct thus creating a framework for 'commitment' to the final agreement.[163]

NADRAC has undertaken regular reviews of ADR developments and in 2006 reported on the need for legislative provision for ADR settlement agreements.[164] Whether the courts will enforce an oral mediated settlement depends on what prompted the parties to mediate and whether there are specific statutory requirements for the settlement outcome.[165] Where mediation is initiated through a court-annexed programme there is usually 'statutory provision' for enforcement orders although not all legislation requires that the settlement agreement must be in writing.[166] For example, section 26 of the Civil Procedure Act 2005 (NSW) permits the court to order attendance at mediation and under section 29 'make an order to give effect to any agreement or arrangement arising from a mediation session'. Section 29 also permits a party to 'call evidence as to fact that an agreement has been reached' but does not state that the agreement must be in writing. Conversely, under section 34D of the Administrative Appeals Tribunal 1975 if '(a) in the course of an alternative dispute resolution process under this Division' the parties reach agreement it will be enforced 'provided the terms of the agreement are in writing'.[167]

Australia as with other common law countries also affords privilege to without prejudice negotiations, which includes the exception to show that an agreement has been reached and this has been extended to cover the admissibility of mediation settlement agreements.[168] These common law rules have substantially been 'mirrored' in the 'uniform' Evidence Act s131, which protects settlement communications from admissibility in court and although the section does not specifically mention mediation, NADRAC reports that there is a general understanding that it is applicable to settlements reached through ADR processes.[169] However, the report notes where 'statutory privileges' are given to court-ordered mediation, they 'override

---

162 Spencer & Brogan (2006) at 347
163 Ibid.
164 See NADRAC (2006) at section 11
165 See NADRAC (2006) at 11.2 fn 273. The reporters comment that the Victorian Civil and Administrative Tribunal Act 1998 (Vic) legislates for the enforcement of mediated agreements though the rubric does not suggest a written requirement is needed; but the court in *Hart v. Cuna* [1999] VCAT 626 at 17 suggested that the 'scheme of the Act is such that the agreement must be in writing'. See also Spencer & Brogan (2006) at 371–6
166 See for example, Administrative Appeals Tribunal Act 1975 s34D although parties after 'lodging' the agreement have 7 days to withdraw. See NADRAC (2006) at 11.5
167 See Appendix 4 NADRAC (2011) for a list of state and federal legislation covering admissibility of mediation communications
168 NADRAC (2011). See Chapter 4
169 NADRAC (2006) at 11.10. See Australian Law Commission Final Report on *Evidence Law* (2005)

the common law' exceptions and special mediation provisions take precedent over the more 'general provisions' in the Evidence Acts.[170]

Challenges to enforcement show that the courts will analyse the evidence using contract law to establish if there is a binding contract.[171] In *Norbert Christian Weimann as Trustee for the Weimann Family Trust No. 3 Applicant and Allphones Retail Pty Ltd*, McKerracher J held that the mediated outcome was not enforceable because on careful questioning he found the parties had not intended to create legal relations and there was 'uncertainty of the alleged agreement'.[172] The parties had drawn up an 'Agreed Outline of Mediation Settlement – New Agreement', which only the mediator had signed.[173] The representative for the franchisees indicated that she needed to 'contact the clients to let them know the deal' because they were not at the mediation and, although she was found to have the authority to settle, the court was 'left with the impression that at that stage no one was prepared to bind them-selves, commit or lock into the arrangements that had been reached such as they were'.[174] Furthermore, the 'Agreed Outline' lacked certainty in a number of areas for example, it had not been decided whether the 'terms of release' were to be 'mutual', further negotiation on the 'territory' of the franchises was required and the purported agreement had 'additional issues specified' that were uncertain as to 'whether they had been resolved' or were 'excluded'.[175]

The vitiating factors have also been a matter of court review but there are also statutory protections for consumers, which might become relevant in the mediation context such as 'misleading and deceptive conduct' and 'unconscionability' provisions in the Trade Practices Act 1974.[176] In *Abriel v. Australian Guarantee Corporation Ltd*[177] the applicants claimed that the settlement reached after mediation had been attained through 'pressure' brought on them after their counsel had been influenced to withdraw from representing them by the opposing counsel and that the respondents had taken advantage of this, which was 'unconscionable conduct' under s51AA of the Trade Practices Act.[178] Dowsett J found that it was 'inherently unlikely' that an experienced counsel would act this way or that the defendants 'plotted

---

170 NADRAC (2011) at 4.3
171 *Tapoohi v. Lewenberg* [2003] VSC 410 at 35 & 37. One party claimed he told the mediator 'repeatedly' that he did not wish to be bound by the agreement that had been drawn up and signed but the case was 'dropped' on this issue. See Spencer & Brogan (2006) at 352
172 *Norbert Christian Weimann as Trustee for the Weimann Family Trust No.3 Applicant and Allphones Retail Pty Ltd* ACN 261 ALR 343, 2009 WL 3650008, [2010] ALMD 3534 at 111
173 *Norbert Christian Weimann* [2010] at 1 & 72
174 *Norbert Christian Weimann* [2010] at 78
175 *Norbert Christian Weimann* [2010] at 100–102
176 Ss 52, 52AA, 51AB, s51AC. See Spencer & Brogan (2006) at 358–9; NADRAC (2006) at 9.24, 11.25, 11.40
177 *Abriel v. Australian Guarantee Corporation Ltd* [2000] FCA 1198
178 *Abriel v. Australian Guarantee Corporation Ltd* [2000] at 55

to provoke her withdrawal' with their legal counsel.[179] The court did not accept the applicants only signed the agreement on the reliance of their counsel's advice as they had time to seek other guidance after the mediation and had done so.[180]

In *Pittorino v. Meynert*, the court upheld the mediation agreement because the evidence provided by the plaintiff was found to be 'grossly exaggerated' for the reason that 'she had become so intensely emotionally involved' in the dispute.[181] One of the plaintiff's claims was that she had been legally unrepresented during the mediation, which the court did not uphold.[182] Her complaints that the pain from a 'burst cyst' during the mediation were unsubstantiated by medical evidence provided some months later and it was found to be 'remarkable' that she had not confided in her sisters or got 'medical help'.[183] Although the court accepted that she might have been 'confused' because of her 'emotional involvement' she would have been 'aware of the value of the offers made' including the one 'accepted after discussion with her solicitors'.[184] Nor had the plaintiff established that the Registrar acting as the mediator had ignored her complaints about illness, or made comments on the strength of the financial offer for a person of her age, which were in fact attributed to her sister, and it was not believed that the mediator had improperly hugged her.[185] After signing the agreement, Scott J believed that she had 'slept on it' and changed her mind.[186] The court noted that the mediated agreement was signed and although the plaintiff claimed she had 'lost confidence' in her legal representatives this was 'not apparent' on the document.[187] The claim did not succeed on 'grounds of unconscionability' because the plaintiff failed to 'establish' that the defendants had knowledge of 'her disability' or her 'loss of confidence in her solicitor' or that she was 'disadvantaged'.[188] Scott J recognised that it would be wrong for a mediator to put 'improper pressure' on a party and although even 'body language' or expressions can convey a mediator's views on a settlement in this case, the registrar had 'acted with the utmost propriety'.[189] The court did not accept the claim that the defendant had not provided 'proper accounts of the assets' and the plaintiff had brought along her own valuations.[190]

After NADRAC's review of the application of the common law defences it was observed that Australian courts have taken a firm approach to claims

179 *Abriel v. Australian Guarantee Corporation Ltd* [2000] at 55 & 68
180 *Abriel v. Australian Guarantee Corporation Ltd* [2000] at 69
181 *Pittorino v. Meynert* [2002] WASC at 80
182 *Pittorino v. Meynert* [2002] at 82
183 *Pittorino v. Meynert* [2002] at 88–9 at 88
184 *Pittorino v. Meynert* [2002] at 95
185 *Pittorino v. Meynert* [2002] at 100 & 103
186 *Pittorino v. Meynert* [2002] at 105
187 *Pittorino v. Meynert* [2002] at 113
188 *Pittorino v. Meynert* [2002] at 125
189 *Pittorino v. Meynert* [2002] at 127
190 *Pittorino v. Meynert* [2002] at 130

concerning 'duress, lack of capacity because of impaired intellectual ability or physical illness, or lack of legal representation or legal advice' as they may illustrate a "change of heart" and they cited Spencer's analysis:[191]

> The conclusion drawn from these cases is that duress must be proven to be illegitimate. Lack of capacity can only be successfully pled if the other parties to the mediation are aware of the diminished capacity due to ill health or intellectual impairment. Lack of legal representation is not a defence of itself but could cause a court to overturn a mediated settlement agreement if it can be proven that the party claiming it as a defence was unable to understand the settlement documents without legal assistance.[192]

Following a consideration of the cases involving defences and a review of various proposals for 'expedited' procedures for enforcing mediation agreements,[193] NADRAC recommended that although there may be 'some benefit for statutory rules on enforcement in some circumstances' they preferred to retain the status quo and leave claims for non-enforcement to the 'common law'.[194] In view of the policy issues between confidentiality and finality of litigation, the report merely proposed that the parties 'resume' negotiation when disputes arise about the terms of the settlement agreement.[195]

NADRAC's later review of ADR in 2011 found that the law surrounding confidentiality was 'unclear' and recommended the introduction of legislation for mandatory ADR, which would not permit disclosure of communications to 'non-participants' with a number of exceptions, one of which is 'to enforce an outcome', although they made no recommendation for legislation when ADR is undertaken voluntarily.[196] The recommendations for the admissibility of evidence from ADR was 'informed' by their decision on confidentiality and in order to 'encourage frank discussions' the report suggested that legislation should be introduced making 'ADR communications' inadmissible 'before a federal court or tribunal'.[197] However, the court or tribunal should have 'leave' to allow disclosure after considering 'the rights or interests in the

---

191 NADRAC (2006) at 11.26–11.28 at 11.26 citing *Morbane Securities v. McTaggart* [2001] FMCA 40; *Tapoohi v. Lewenberg* (no 2) [2003] VSC 410; *Hart v. Kuna* [1999] VCAT 626 and *Pittorino v. Meynert* [2002] WASC 76; NADRAC base their enquiry on Spencer's review of case law. Spencer (2005). For an analysis of the approach of Australian courts to mistake see for example Hunter-Schulz & Boulle (2006) at 2. Hunter-Schulz & Boulle note that *Merigan-James v. James* [2006] VSC 34 'illustrates' how the courts analyse the evidence by observing that the defendant was 'unimpressive' and that both parties had mediated on a 'pragmatic commercial basis'.

192 NADRAC (2006) at fn300. The report summarises the conclusion of Spencer's review of the enforceability of ADR agreements. See Spencer (2005) at 129

193 NADRAC (2006) at section 11; See Deason (2005)

194 NADRAC (2006) at 11.28

195 NADRAC (2006) at 11.42

196 NADRAC (2011) at 3.9.1–3.9.3

197 NADRAC (2011) at 4.7.1–4.7.2

exceptions to confidentiality', 'general public interest in maintaining confidentiality' and 'whether the admission or disclosure would serve the administration of justice', the last of which would 'allow admission or disclosure of evidence for the purposes of enforcing an outcome of ADR'.[198]

Hong Kong

Compared to both Australia and the USA the modern mediation movement in Hong Kong has been a relatively recent phenomenon and to date there is little developed jurisprudence on mediation law, particularly in the area of enforcing mediated agreements. Hong Kong uses the same common law contract formation principles and treats mediated outcomes like other settlement agreements.[199] In *Champion Concord Ltd v. Lau Koon Foo*, which is claimed to be 'one of the first cases' concerning the enforcement of a mediated agreement,[200] the court had to consider whether to uphold the sale of a house reached after the master had recommended the parties mediate. The vendor agreed to 'render all necessary assistance' in gaining consent from the DLO (District Land Officer) and a date was given for completion in 10 months (Long Stop Date) but a further 12 months if certain circumstances occurred.[201] Champion had paid the required fees, and Mr Lau had to sign a 'Toleration Letter', which he refused to do because under the terms of the settlement agreement the sale was 'automatically cancelled'.[202] Clause 15 expressly provided for the automatic cancellation of the sale if the relevant consent had not been obtained from the DLO by the 'Long Stop Date' but this was subject to the exception in Clause 16 if the DLO 'decided not to consent' and Champion 'decided to contest' the decision 'on or before that date'.[203] Despite the argument that adopting a 'sterile literalisms' would counter the 'clear object of and purpose of the settlement agreement', Stone J held that for the extended period to come into place two things had to transpire, that the DLO refused consent and the decision was 'contested' which had not occurred.[204] The alternative would have been to take a 'broad' interpretation of the clause to mean that the extended period would have effect in the 'absence of any consent', which in the view of the court the parties had not intended.[205] Regardless of the 'reluctance' to take this narrow reading, particularly in view of Mr Lau's conduct in 'concealing correspondence with the DLO' before the mediation,

---

198 NADRAC (2011) at fn200
199 *Champion Concord Ltd v. Lau Koon Foo* [2010] HKEC 984 'the Settlement Agreement means what it means, no more or less, and its construction one way or another is no reflection of the process giving rise to it', per Stone J at 34
200 *Champion Concord Ltd v. Lau Koon Foo* [2010] at 34
201 *Champion Concord Ltd v. Lau Koon Foo* [2010] at 24
202 *Champion Concord Ltd v. Lau Koon Foo* [2010] at 26–7
203 *Champion Concord Ltd v. Lau Koon Foo* [2010] at 43 & 41
204 *Champion Concord Ltd v. Lau Koon Foo* [2010] at 55
205 *Champion Concord Ltd v. Lau Koon Foo* [2010] at 59 & 67

Stone J held that the 'clear words' of the clause meant that the contract had automatically expired and any earlier conduct was 'subsumed within the settlement agreement'.[206]

The Hong Kong Working Party's report on the introduction of a mediation ordinance has decided not to legislate specifically for the enforcement of mediation settlement agreements.[207] It was noted that some countries have adopted 'separate enforcement mechanisms', which provide a quick, 'low-cost' method, but the Working Party concluded that 'sophisticated parties' might benefit from these systems at the expense of the 'weaker or uninformed' and the report also rejected an enforcement procedure with a 'cooling off period'[208] because of the danger in encouraging disputants to 'continually rescind and defer' settlement.[209] As compliance with mediated settlements is high, the Working Party felt there would be little to be gained from implementing legislation because it would require 'exceptions' to be developed such as 'duress, undue influence, misrepresentation' which would necessitate 'court proceedings' akin to what is already required when enforcing a mediation agreement.[210] It was the view of the Working Party that mediators have a role in 'ensuring' that the settlement reached is 'reasonable', which they achieve by engaging in 'effective reality testing'.[211] The Hong Kong Mediation Ordinance came into force in January 2013 and makes 'mediation communication' confidential with exceptions, which must have leave from the court, one of which is for the 'purpose of enforcing or challenging settlement agreements'.[212]

EU Mediation Directive* – enforcement of settlement agreements

There is no specific enforcement mechanism for mediated settlements between parties from different EU countries in England and Wales. The United Kingdom has been required to implement Article 6 of the Mediation Directive, which obligated member states to enact statutory provision for the enforcement of 'written' settlement agreements reached in mediation in cross border disputes. Article 7 provides for the confidentiality of mediation by requiring member states to 'ensure' that mediators or parties involved in administrating the process 'shall not be compelled to give evidence' in either court or arbitration proceedings regarding information 'arising out of or in connection with the mediation' but subsection (b) specifically provides an exception when 'necessary to implement or enforce that agreement'.

206 *Champion Concord Ltd v. Lau Koon Foo* [2010] at 64 & 67
207 Hong Kong Working Party (2010) at 7.188–7.190
208 See for example, Welsh (2001b) at 6–7
209 Hong Kong Working Party (2010) at 7.187
210 Hong Kong Working Party (2010) at section 7.190
211 Hong Kong Working Party (2010) at 7.189
212 Hong Kong Mediation Ordinance (2012) at 8(3) (a)

The directive is now implemented in Practice Direction (PD) 78 and under PD 78.24 a party can apply to the court for a 'mediation settlement enforcement order' (MSEO). The rules require an application under 78(1) (a) to include the 'application notice, the mediation settlement and the explicit consent of all the parties involved in the mediation including those not part of the application. It has been suggested this can be realised by including an explicit consent clause into the written settlement agreement which is then signed by all the parties, which Fender-Allison believes will lead in practice to 'drafting clauses' expressly stating that 'the agreement results from mediation'.[213]

The mediation agreement must be attached to the claim form when an application is made for an MSEO but confidentiality is provided by an amendment to CPR 5.4.C(1) (Court Documents) which does permit 'disclosure or inspection' 'without the court's permission'.[214] However, Allen remarks that there is no 'guidance' on this matter and there is less protection for 'accidental disclosure' by the 'court officials' in cross border mediation compared to a Tomlin Order, which does not require the mediation settlement until default on the agreement.[215]

Proposals to extend mediation enforcement orders

The government proposed to extend the rules for cross border mediation agreements to domestic mediation agreements.[216] The consultation proposal for a 'fast track enforcement procedure' was positively endorsed by 'mediators, mediation service providers, the legal professions and advice centres' but the judiciary response was negative on the grounds that there are 'adequate rules' already in place and compliance is high.[217]

Commentary

The common law courts' approach is to manage the enforcement of mediation agreements in the same way as negotiated settlements, yet as Thompson observes the process and parties' expectations in each of the processes are very different.[218] In negotiation, all the parties 'should assume' that everyone is

---

213 Fender-Allison (2011); See also Johnson et all (2010)
214 Where application for a mediation settlement enforcement order is made under rule 78.24(1) (a), 'a copy of the application notice, mediation settlement agreement and evidence of explicit consent must be served on all parties to the mediation settlement agreement who are not also parties to the application'. See Allen (2011)
215 Allen (2011)
216 Ministry of Justice (2011) *Solving disputes in the county courts: creating a simpler, quicker and more proportionate system: A consultation on reforming civil justice in England and Wales Consultation paper*
217 Ministry of Justice *The Government's Response* (2012) at 207
218 See Thompson (2004) at 555–7 at 557; Coben & Thompson (2006); Welsh (2001b); Alfini & McCabe (2001); Hong Kong Working Party (2010); NADRAC (2006)

'acting in self interest' and only agree to terms 'if they intend to be bound', which is the basis on which courts uphold agreements.[219] In contrast, mediation is about 'empowerment and self-determination', where the parties are encouraged to be 'candid' and to 'trust the neutral, the process and all the participants' to reach a mutually agreed settlement.[220] Thompson observes that the parties may place undue reliance on 'representations' made in mediation, feel more pressurized to settle in a 'compressed time frame' or because discussions are not at 'arms length' experience 'intimidation, coercion or duress'.[221] Moreover, he maintains that as mediation becomes 'institutionalised' this increases 'the mediator's power to extract, facilitate, influence or coerce agreement',[222] and parties may think that the settlement outcome has 'court approval'.[223]

> Because of the heightened expectations of candor and cooperation, parties may be less guarded and more susceptible to relying on representations coming from the adverse party. In the typical caucus-style mediation, statements of fact or representations are filtered through the court-sanctioned, neutral mediator, which gives the representations added significance and integrity in the eyes of the party. The compressed time frame and physical proximity of the participants also may contribute to an enhanced possibility of intimidation, coercion, or duress. Bilateral negotiation and court-ordered mediation present substantially different contexts, which affect the parties' expectations and behavior in different ways.

The clash between the 'core value of self-determination' in mediation versus the argument for 'judicial economy and settlement'[224] is particularly a cute when participation is mandated or 'less voluntary', which is associated with a high level of evaluative mediator activity and less compliance the outcome.[225] Thompson notes that most commentators recommend keeping the status quo by leaving contract defences to deal with enforceability issues as they arise.[226] For example, Burns maintains contract law principles are 'flexible' enough to deal with enforceability on a case by case basis rather than introducing an increased level of 'legalisation' though specific legislation, which is likely to detract from the 'values of mediation':[227]

219 Thompson (2004) at 556 citing Burns (1986); Alfini & McCabe (2001)
220 Thompson (2004) at 556
221 Thompson (2004) at 557
222 Thompson (2004) at 517–18
223 Thompson (2004) at 557; See also Alfini & McCabe (2001)
224 Alfini & McCabe (2001) at 173
225 See Nolan-Haley (2012) at 87
226 Thompson (2004) at 537; See also Alfini & McCabe (2001); Coben & Thompson (2006); Nolan-Haley (2012)
227 Burns (1986) at 115. Burns comments on Fuller's argument that when 'legalisation' forces the parties in family disputes to concentrate on enforceability issues it 'destroys trust'. Fuller (1971) at 330–32

No persuasive general argument exists for giving the mediated nature of an agreement necessary legal consequences. Contract law provides a flexible set of considerations relevant to the issue of enforceability that more adequately structure deliberation about that issue than could any single general rule. The interrelation of mediation and litigation poses special problems for both forms of social ordering, but only a procedural purist would drive a sharp wedge between them, a wedge that would, in the contexts where contract law provides for enforceability, probably reduce the value of mediation.

However, other commentators recommend that the common law defences be supplemented with 'specific bright line rules', which take account of the 'differing values' of mediation and litigation.[228] For example, Deason makes a number of recommendations which include, a 'presumption of authority' in 'court annexed' mediation and only permitting challenges to validity to signed settlement agreements in these programmes or that courts review invalidity claims 'on the pleadings' when they may either 'fail as a matter of law' or not reach 'the necessary burden'.[229] In order to 'safeguard' confidentiality, she recommends the implementation of a 'comprehensive mediation privilege' that 'precludes testimony on oral mediated settlements' and creates a 'threshold' for written agreements for enforcement purposes.[230]

Deason observes that introducing enforcement procedures may 'disentangle mediation' from the 'contract defences' but 'ironically' such moves 'integrate' the process within litigation.[231] She addresses the concerns that expedited enforcement mechanisms disregard self-determination because by upholding 'fair agreements' they may 'support not undermine' the core 'values of mediation'.[232] Her recommendation is that any proposed enforcement system only applies to specific mediation agreements, such as where the parties have been legally represented, as this provides 'effective safeguards' for the less informed or weaker parties.[233]

Welsh proposed changes to the contract law defences and recommends providing 'cooling off periods' before enforcing mediation settlement agreements.[234] She suggests a 'modification' to 'the presumption' that everyone has a 'free will' to enter mediated agreements so that the party only has to show a 'probable cause standard' for coercion plus 'evidence of the mediator's negative evaluation or strong support for a particular settlement'.[235] If satisfied, the burden passes to the mediator to 'prove' there was no 'coercive'

---

228 Thompson (2004) at 547
229 Deason (2005) at 92
230 Deason (2005) at 74
231 Deason (2005) at 586
232 Deason (2005) at 587
233 Deason (2005) at 587
234 Welsh (2001a); (2001b) at 6
235 Welsh (2001a) at 83

conduct and that the 'agreement was free and voluntary'.[236] She also recommends a 'change of focus from coercion to undue influence' which would 'recognise' that parties often 'assume a fiduciary relationship' exists with the mediator but she acknowledges that 'codes of practice' would have to be changed to emphasise this 'duty'.[237] Welsh also suggests that there should be a 'change to the presumption' of enforcement by stipulating rules that require a 'three day cooling off period' to protect participants, particularly after experiencing 'high pressurised' evaluative mediation with 'muscle mediators' in the context of court annexed programmes.[238] She accepts that a 'cooling off period' might lead to poorer settlement rates as parties attempt to 'back out' of agreements and even lead to a decreased use of mediation but she maintains that the 'fundamental principle underlying mediation is self determination not settlement', which should 'outweigh' any drawbacks to her proposal.[239]

In the English & Welsh jurisdiction, apart from cross border disputes, policy decisions not to enact a specific enforcement mechanism for domestic law may lead to an increase in cases using the common law 'defences' as parties attempt to evade their mediated agreements. There have now been a number of applications to the English courts seeking to set aside mediation agreements based on the formation or validity of mediation outcomes, and if the experience in the USA is replicated these are likely to increase as the process becomes 'less voluntary' and policy moves make mediation or mediation information sessions a precondition to litigation.[240]

To counter potential problems with enforcement mediation providers began to formalise contracts of engagement in order to create confidence and certainty for potential users. It is now common practice for mediation providers to work using their own mediation contracts, which attempt to clarify the legal position of settlement agreements and cover such matters as payment, confidentiality, jurisdiction, what documentation or evidence the parties should produce and the roles taken by the mediators, mediation advocates and the parties.[241] However, as the cases illustrate, the courts carefully review the effect of these contracts to establish the 'objective intentions' of the parties and these have on occasions excluded either contract formation or contract defences. The current strategy to formalise engagement before mediating may become a double-edged sword because although providing clarity and assisting participants in commencing mediation, as binding contracts they may in future provide a rich seam for litigation.

---

236 Welsh (2001a) at 83
237 Welsh (2001a) at 84
238 Welsh (2001b) at 7. Welsh draws the comparison of mediation to 'high pitched' selling tactics employed by some home sales representatives. See also Welsh (2001a)
239 Welsh (2001a) at 91. NADRAC (2006) observe that s34D of the Administrative Appeals Tribunal Act 1975 permits the parties 'seven days to withdraw' from a settlement agreement 'lodged' with the court. See NADRAC (2006) at 11.5
240 Nolan-Haley (2012) at 87
241 See for example, ADR Group's Rules and Procedures. Brooker (2011)

Furthermore, the formalisation of mediation contracts has perhaps led inexorably to an escalating legalism of the process.[242] There is now a developing body of mediation law revealing that as the process becomes progressively a feature of dispute resolution for civil cases the boundaries of mediated agreements are tested as lawyers and the courts are required to interpret the legal rules.[243] Mediation as an evolving 'juridical field',[244] just like arbitration before it,[245] attracts the 'interests' of legal professionals who are then implicated in an escalating level of 'the formalism of legal procedures', which leads to a greater reliance on 'their own services'.[246]

> In short, a process of circular reinforcement goes into action: every step toward the 'juridicization' of a dimension of practice creates new 'juridical needs,' and thus new juridical interests among those who, possessing the specific qualifications necessary (knowledge of labor law in this case), find in these needs a new market. Through their intervention, such practitioners cause an increase in the formalism of legal procedures, and thereby contribute to increasing the need for their own services and products, to the practical exclusion of laypeople. Laypeople are obliged to have recourse to the advice of legal professionals, who little by little will come to replace the complainants and defendants. The latter in their turn become nothing more than a group of individuals who have fallen under the jurisdiction of the courts.

Conclusion

The case law indicates how entwined mediation is with contract law as judicial policy establishes it within the framework of civil litigation and as the process connects to law there is an increase in legalism. Policy in the English jurisdiction presently eschews the introduction of expedited enforcement rules for domestic mediation and the validity of mediated agreements remains in the purview of the courts. Problems with enforcement involve legal input from lawyers at the invitation of the parties, but this involvement has expanded at both the beginning and at the conclusion of the process, which erodes the parties' autonomy and contribution to mediation.

Enforcement issues are complicated by the common law rules of without prejudice, which protect negotiations but the institutionalisation of mediation has led to a growing debate in England and Wales on whether confidentiality in mediation requires wider protection from the law, which Chapter 5

---

242 Newman (1997) at 35
243 Alexander (2008a, b); Coben & Thompson (2006); Blichner and Molander (2008)
244 Bourdieu describes a juridical field as 'the basis of the supply of legal services arising from professional competition'. Bourdeau (1987) at 841
245 Flood & Caiger (1993) at 411
246 Bourdieu (1987) at 836–7

addresses. The next chapter reviews the legal framework for directing suitable cases to ADR introduced by the Civil Procedure Rules and examines how reform of the civil justice system has led to the integration of mediation with litigation, which is increasingly leading to the strategic interaction between both processes.

Notes

*   During the production of this book a new EU directive on ADR for consumers was published: Directive 2013/11/EU of the European Parliament and the Council of the 21st May 2013 L165/63 (18.06.2013). By 2015 Member States must comply with the requirements of the directive and have in place 'ADR entities' which provide consumers with 'access to effective, fast and fair ADR procedures' (Article 1). The directive is made 'without prejudice' to the Mediation Directive of 2008 (Forward, 19). Article 2.4 allows Member States to decide whether the ADR entity may 'impose solutions' and under Article 5.4 the state can 'permit' the entity to 'make rules'. However, under Article 7 any rules and procedures must be transparent to the consumer and drawn to their attention if 'binding'. Article 6 requires that ADR Entities ensure that 'ADR natural persons' have sufficient 'expertise and skills in the field of alternative or judicial resolution of consumer goods'. Article 7 makes provision for the 'enforceability of ADR decision'. ADR Entities may introduce a variety of ADR procedures including mediation but the directive is concerned with the use of processes which involve a third party neutral either adjudicating between the consumer and trader or providing a binding decision.

4 Legal 'framework' for mediating

Introduction

Lord Woolf's recommendations for ADR and the resultant Civil Procedure Rules (CPR) has led to the progressive institutionalisation of mediation as the process connects to the courts through an application of the rules in the cases. The early cases reviewed in Chapter 1 revealed how senior judges began to 'educate' lawyers on the advantages of using ADR and the need to incorporate mediation into their practice.[1] Following CPR judges began observing in their judgments that parties should have used mediation or they advised litigants during court applications or directions to consider ADR or mediate before proceeding further.[2] Despite authoritative statements by senior judges such as Lord Woolf in *Cowl* reminding the judiciary to utilise their 'ample' powers to encourage ADR and discourage litigation, mediation remained on the 'periphery' of dispute resolution.[3] Mediation advocates began to suggest that growth would not occur until judges became 'interventionist' and used their discretion to drive the ADR agenda by sanctioning parties in costs for unreasonably failing to mediate.[4] This eventually happened in the seminal decision of *Dunnett v. Railtrack* in 2002, a judgment which was to reverberate through the professional literature.[5] *Dunnett* set the scene for mediation to become more fully incorporated into the litigation process.

This chapter considers the legal 'framework'[6] and rules that initiate or promote ADR in non-family civil cases when there are no contractual arrangements in place prior to the dispute arising. Chapter 1 reviewed the historical developments of mediation and the reforms made to the Civil Justice System to deflect cases from the courts following Lord Woolf's review of litigation

---

1 Shipman (2006) at 187–8; *Cowl* [2001]
2 See for example, *Dyson and Field (Executors of Lawrence Twohey deceased) v. Leeds City Council* (1999) CP Rep 42, 1999 WL 1142459, (1999) LAWTEL (Nov. 22, 1999) (unreported elsewhere); *Paul Thomas Construction Ltd. v. (1) Damian Hyland (2) Jackie Power* (2001) CILL 1748, 18 Const. LJ 345 (2001). See Brooker & Lavers (2005a) at 174–5
3 *Cowl* [2001] at 2. See Brooker & Lavers (2000) at 368
4 See Brooker & Lavers (2000) at 360
5 *Dunnett* [2002] EWCA Civ 303. See for example, Dundas (2002); Lind (2002)
6 Alexander (2006) at 19–24

and provided a commentary on the early judicial decisions on ADR in the immediate aftermath of CPR. The following two chapters reviewed how courts approach pre-existing ADR or mediation clauses and the rules governing upholding agreements reached through the mediated process.

The objective is to analyse how the case law, educed by CPR, is delineating mediation practice, particularly in relation to the suitability and timing of the process. In both these areas, case decisions have the effect of bringing mediation within the purview of the courts' jurisdiction thereby further institutionalising and legalising the process. First, CPR has led the courts to formulate criteria for mediating and there is now an understanding, evidenced in case decisions, that particular disputes are more suitable for mediation and should be directed away from the courts rather than depleting 'scarce' judicial resources.[7] Second, the courts, by analysing optimum timing for mediating, are establishing mediation practice within the scope of litigation.[8] The effect of this institutionalisation is that the courts are determining how mediation 'interplays' with litigation and is normalising practice[9] in relation to 'which' cases should be mediated, 'when' the process should be attempted and further, how the developing law is leading to tactical dispute resolution strategies by lawyers (or their clients).[10] This chapter analyses how establishing mediation in the Civil Justice System has led to an increase in 'legal conflict solving' and a rise in 'judicial power' through an expansion of mediation law, which is providing the opportunity for the legal professions to influence the practice of mediation.[11]

Mediation is now one of the leading (if not the foremost) ADR procedures in use in the English jurisdiction and although the courts often refer to the ADR, the legal rules and guidelines in case law most frequently allude to mediation.

The acronym, ADR, is often referred to in judicial statements but many members of the judiciary now regard mediation as the frontrunner. That said, some cases developing the rules and court protocols or Court Guides still make reference to 'collective' ADR procedures and others specifically mention mediation.[12] For example the Chancery Court Guide states that the court will 'readily grant a stay to accommodate mediation or settlement negotiation' and its 'Standard Case Management Direction allocating cases to the Multi Track' assert that the parties should give 'serious consideration to using mediation'.[13]

---

7 Shipman (2006) at 181
8 Brooker (2009) (2010a); Brunsdon-Tully (2009); Shipman (2006)
9 Allen (2008); Brunsdon-Tully (2009) at 22
10 See for example, Brooker (2010a) at 148
11 Blichner & Molander (2005) at 16 & 19; See for example Roberts (1992); Clark (2012)
12 *Halsey Milton Keynes General NHS Trust, Steel v. Joy, Halliday* [2004] EWCA Civ 576 at 5. See *Practice Direction – Pre Action Conduct* 3.1.3
13 *Chancery Court Guide* (2001 Amended in 2011) at 3.3; Model Standard Case Management Direction allocating cases to the Multi Track Form MT3 (CHY) at 2

Judicial sanctioning power

Despite promotional activities by ADR organisations, mediators and supportive recommendations by the judiciary, the uptake on mediation in most sectors remains 'stubbornly low'.[14] Some of the criticism for the lack of interest in mediation was laid at the feet of the legal professions, who were seen to be instrumental in swaying their clients' decision not to use mediation, either because of a lack of knowledge about its practice or because of a fear about a loss of income.[15] This changed dramatically after the decision in *Dunnett v. Railtrack* when the Court of Appeal (CA) declined to award the successful party costs because they had unreasonably rejected an offer to mediate.[16] The immediate effect of *Dunnett* was a significant increase in mediator appointments and innumerable publications warning the legal professions to take note.[17]

Dunnett v. Railtrack

Mrs Dunnett sued Railtrack for £9,000 for the death of three of her horses, which had strayed onto the rail line through an unlocked gate, and for post-traumatic stress disorder.[18] At the hearing on costs the Court of Appeal noted that her first legal team had dropped 'potentially their best point of claim', which was that Railtrack or their 'agents' had been negligent in not installing an adequate system when replacing the old 'automatically'-closing gate with one that did not 'self-close'.[19] At the time of installation, Mrs Dunnett had asked the contractor if she could keep a key at her premises thus giving her control to open the gate on request but Railtrack's agent refused because it would be illegal.[20] Before trial, the court requested 'skeleton arguments' and Mrs Dunnett's legal representative reduced the claim to one of 'vicarious liability' for a 'breach of duty of care' through their agent.[21] However, Railtrack were exonerated because they had satisfied their statutory duty to maintain the gate under the Railway Clauses Consolidation Act 1845 by providing one that was 'not defective' and were under no 'duty to take reasonable care' that their agent had given the 'correct' legal advice.[22] Schiemann LJ, after granting leave to appeal, suggested that Mrs Dunnett explore ADR with Railtrack,

---

14 Genn (2010) at 98. The Government report that mediations in small claims are in the many thousands.

15 See for example, Genn (1998); See also Clark (2012) at 40–46

16 *Dunnett v. Railtrack Plc* [2002a] EWCA Civ 302; *Dunnett v. Railtrack Plc* [2002b] EWCA Civ 303 (Costs)

17 CEDR Statistics (2003)

18 *Dunnett* [2002a] at 1

19 *Dunnett* [2002a] at 6

20 *Dunnett* [2002a] at 4

21 *Dunnett* [2002a] at 12

22 *Dunnett* [2002a] at 13 & 4

which they 'unequivocally' refused but also advised their solicitors to oppose a late extension of time.[23]

On appeal, Mrs Dunnett's new legal representative based the case on the type of gate installed, which was 'not self-closing' and therefore breached 'the defendant's duty of reasonable care'.[24] Counsel suggested this came within the remaining pleadings of negligence and that the replacement gate was not 'adequate' but the Court did not find 'any material' in the reduced claim that the trial judge could have decided in Mrs Dunnett's 'favour' and after this success Railtrack appealed for their costs.[25] Railtrack's explanation for rejecting the mediation offer was that they were unwilling to consider further expenditure more than the £2,500 already offered, were confident of winning the appeal, getting their costs and claimed Mrs Dunnett could have reduced any further stress if she had accepted the offer.[26] Brooke LJ responded by stating that Railtrack misunderstood the 'purpose of ADR' on and the outcomes experienced mediators could achieve, which are not attainable by the court, but which the parties can 'shake hands' on and 'live with'.[27] In particular, the court noted the power of an apology in clinical negligence or 'claims against the police', where the 'money side of the matter falls away'.[28]

The Court of Appeal concluded that Railtrack should not have an order for costs because they refused to use ADR after the court had recommended it, which struck a note with the professional legal journals who warned litigants to give serious contemplation to ADR particularly when it has been recommended by the court.[29] *Dunnett* remains an important CA decision because the judgment recognises that mediation may be appropriate at any stage of litigation even after one party has successfully argued their case at trial, which therefore extends the period of the law's involvement in mediation practice and the potential for lawyers to influence the process.

Dunnett remains a perplexing case in terms of the appropriateness of mediation and the most suitable timing for mediating. It is not possible to predict the mediated outcome with any certainty and there is no requirement that the parties have to settle. One of the benefits of mediation is that the outcome does not have to be based on legal rights but can be created by the parties but it is impossible to know whether Mrs Dunnett would have accepted an apology or whether she may have wished for compensation to replace her horses. An apology may have gone some way to reduce the tension

---

23 *Dunnett* [2002b] at 7 & 8
24 *Dunnett* [2002a] at 17
25 *Dunnett* [2002a] at 20–21
26 *Dunnett* [2002b] at 14
27 *Dunnett* [2002b] at 14
28 *Dunnett* [2002b] at 14
29 *Dunnett* [2002b] at 16. See Genn (2010) at 98–9; Brooker & Lavers (2005a) at 174–5. Brooker & Lavers observe the messages promoted by professional journals. See for example, Dundas (2002); Lind (2002); Stewart (2002); Dyke (2001)

between the disputants thereby improving the likelihood of a mediator facilitating settlement. Mrs Dunnett, however, was legally unrepresented at various stages, which may have been the case in an early mediation when she could have found herself in a vulnerable or weak negotiation position against a corporate party, which a mediator may or may not have been able to address.[30]

Appropriateness factors

Limited court guidance

The immediate response to *Dunnett* was an increase in mediation appointments reported by ADR providers but this was not sustained, despite ample warnings in the professional literature highlighting the dangers of refusing offers to mediate.[31] Uncertainty remained about when judges would exercise their discretion on costs and which cases were appropriate for ADR or mediation. At the time CPR came into force, the 'preceptors'[32] for mediation selection were unclear and largely unproven[33] although the literature began to identify conditions for using ADR and the Commercial Court produced a list of factors indicating unsuitability:[34]

Unwillingness to compromise
Requirement for a legal precedent
Requirement of injunction
Business or personal reputation in dispute
Litigation deterrent to other actions
Ease of quick summary judgment
Confidentiality would 'cause adverse publicity'
Strategic use of 'free discovery'
Fraud.

At first there was limited guidance from the court other than statements made in case by judges supportive of the new procedures. But pioneering judges began to comment on the lost opportunity for mediating, which may have helped the parties reach a resolution without the costs, time or 'stress' (*Dunnett*) of litigation.[35] There was ambiguity about appropriateness criteria for ADR or when cost penalties would be given for not utilising an alternative

---

30 See Fiss (1984). Chapter 1 reviews the objections raised by Professor Fiss to legal policies supporting settlement when one party has less resources to fight their claim.
31 See for example, Lind (2002); Wilcock (2002/2003)
32 Brooker & Lavers (2000) at 361; See also Brooker & Lavers (2000) (2001)
33 Genn (2010) at 108–113; See also Genn (2012); Brunsdon-Tully (2009) at 228
34 See for example, Gaede (1991); Hill (1996); Cooper (1992); Costello (1998); Shapiro (1999); Soo (2000). For an overview see Brooker & Lavers (2000)
35 *Dunnett* [2002]. See Shipman (2006)

before litigating. This confusion was heightened by a number of cases approving mediation in circumstances which had previously been regarded as indicators of unsuitability.

The decision in *Hurst v. Leeming* implied that virtually the only criteria that the court would accept for refusing to participate in mediation is when one party exhibits extreme or 'disturbed' behaviour.[36] Lightman J in giving his judgment indicated that few factors existed that would make a case unsuitable for mediating because 'what appears to be incapable of mediation before the mediation process often proves capable of satisfactory resolution later'.[37] The decision was criticised at the time because it imbued mediators with skills which overcome even 'unpromising' cases, whereas empirical evidence showed that the key reason for mediation failing is usually the attitudes of the parties.[38]

Mr Hurst unsuccessfully sued his former partners on the dissolution of their partnership and his counsel for professional negligence but after various court hearings it was observed he had 'waged an obsessive campaign', been unwilling to face up to reality and was 'so disturbed' by the dispute that he had been 'incapable of a balanced evaluation of the facts'.[39] Mr Leeming as the successful party was entitled to costs but Mr Hurst submitted that no order should be issued because he had offered to mediate 'before and after' proceedings and the court therefore had to decide whether the refusal to mediate had been justified.[40]

In giving his judgment, Mr Justice Lightman found only one 'critical factor' to be relevant to the appropriateness of mediating, which was whether 'objectively viewed', mediation had any 'realistic prospect of success'.[41] The court did not accept Mr Leeming's contention that mediation was not suitable because it involved a 'serious allegation of professional negligence' because professional negligence claims are 'always serious', and should be taken into account in the negotiations.[42] Similarly, the court rejected the defendant's claim that mediation was inappropriate because of the high costs already expended in litigation because these costs could form part of the discussions in mediation, and rejected his belief the case was 'watertight' because parties often hold that 'frame of mind' and nor could it be argued that the claimant's case had no substance.[43] Lightman J doubted Mr Hurst's assertion that had a mediator explained the weakness of his case mediation would have settled the dispute because the evidence suggested that he would have been 'unable to make a balanced evaluation of the facts'

---

36 *Hurst v. Leeming* [2002] EWHC 1051 (Ch) (9th May, 2002) at 16 & 14
37 *Hurst v. Leeming* [2002] at 15
38 See for example, Brooker & Lavers (2005a) at 178
39 *Hurst v. Leeming* [2002] at 16
40 *Hurst v. Leeming* [2002] at 9 & 13
41 *Hurst v. Leeming* [2002] at 15
42 *Hurst v. Leeming* [2002] at 13
43 *Hurst v. Leeming* [2002] at 13 &14

and 'exceptionally' the decisive aspect in the case was the attitude of Mr Hurst.[44]

Mr Justice Lightman provided five grounds for coming to this conclusion. First, Mr Hurst was unable or unwilling to accept any explanation about the case.[45] He had taken out two 'vexatious claims'.[46] He was bankrupt and 'had nothing to lose' if he mediated.[47] He was unable to let go of his belief that his partners had been fraudulent, his legal advisors had 'let them get away with this' and finally, he was only prepared to settle for a 'substantial' figure when he was 'entitled to nothing'.[48] All of which indicated that he would not have been able to adopt the necessary approach in mediation, which required a willingness to negotiate and compromise and for these reasons the refusal to mediate was both 'justifiable' and reasonable.[49] The High Court only accepted that Mr Hurst's attitude to the dispute made it reasonable to refuse to mediate but future litigants were warned that adopting this 'high risk strategy' would be 'severely punished' if mediation had 'a good prospect of success' because it helps the parties to adopt a 'more conciliatory attitude' which enables an analysis of the relative strengths of the case.[50]

Shortly after *Hurst v. Leeming*, the Chancery High Court in *Bank of Canada v. Secretary of State for Defence* held that a case involving a 'question of law' was appropriate for mediation despite the general understanding that this criteria indicated unsuitability.[51] The government had refused several offers by the claimant to mediate a dispute involving an 'interpretation of a lease'.[52] Lewison J acknowledged the government department had succeeded at trial but held mediation had been unreasonably rejected even though 'technically' the 'interpretation of contracts' was 'a question of law rather than a question of fact' but this was only because it was 'traditionally' the approach used.[53] One factor influencing the decision was the failure of the government office to 'abide by its formal pledge' to use ADR.[54] Interestingly the court in *Bank of*

44 *Hurst v. Leeming* [2002] at 16
45 *Hurst v. Leeming* [2002] at 18
46 *Hurst v. Leeming* [2002] at 19
47 *Hurst v. Leeming* [2002] at 20
48 *Hurst v. Leeming* [2002] at 21 & 22
49 *Hurst v. Leeming* [2002] at 23
50 *Hurst v. Leeming* [2002] at 15
51 *Royal Bank of Canada v. Secretary of State for Defence* [2003] EWHC 1841 (Ch). See above.
52 *Royal Bank of Canada* [2003] at 9
53 *Royal Bank of Canada* [2003] at 6 & 9
54 *Royal Bank of Canada* [2003] at 10 & 12. The CA in *Halsey* [2004] did not afford such significance to the government's pledge stating: 'In our judgement, the judge was wrong to attach such weight to the ADR pledge. The pledge was no more than an undertaking that ADR would be considered and used in all suitable cases. If a case is suitable for ADR, then it is likely that a party refusing to agree to it will be acting unreasonably, whether or not it is a public body to which the ADR pledge applies. If the case is not suitable for ADR, then a refusal to agree to ADR does not breach the pledge. It is, therefore, difficult to see in what circumstances it would be right to give great weight to the ADR pledge', per Lord Justice Dyson at 35

Canada offered no opinion on whether 'mediation would, or would not, have succeeded'.[55]

In contrast the Court of Appeal in *Leicester Circuits Ltd v. Coates Brothers Plc* did give consideration to the likely success of mediation when considering costs after refusing to order a new trial because the applicants failed to prove that they had 'sufficient opportunity to present their case'.[56] During the early part of the dispute in 1999 and 2001, the parties had made Part 36 offers and then by 'mutual consent' considered mediation.[57] In 2002, Leicester's solicitors wrote indicating that their clients were prepared to mediate and the correspondence indicated that a date and venue were in place, but arrangements did not progress other than submitting mediation statements to the mediator, after which he wrote to both parties saying that Coates had withdrawn 'at the insistence of their insurers'.[58] The Court declined to accept the defendant's attempt to suggest that the process had been nothing more than a 'form of negotiation which came to nothing' because the 'whole point' of agreeing to mediate and proceeding with it, 'is that the most difficult problems can sometimes, indeed often are, resolved'.[59] Neither did Judge LJ accept that mediation had 'no realistic prospect' of succeeding because it did not behove those who consent to mediate to then claim it would not be successful and the withdrawal was only because of the insurer's instructions rather than an 'acknowledgement that they had agreed to something which was pointless'.[60] The Court held that after agreeing to mediate, the 'unexplained withdrawal' had 'significance to the continuing of litigation', which was not to say that mediation 'would have succeeded' but 'there was a prospect' that it might have and therefore, Leicester, as the unsuccessful party, was ordered to pay costs up to the time of the agreed mediation but not the period after that.[61]

Canada Bank and *Hurst v. Leeming* illustrate an early commitment on the part of some sectors of the judiciary to forward an ADR agenda and both cases are now recognised as the 'high water mark' of mediation.[62] In contrast, a number of cases began to demonstrate how some judges were not persuaded to make '*Dunnett* type'[63] orders because of 'evidence' indicating that the parties had made 'reasonable offers' to settle the dispute or proposed 'round

55 *Halsey* [2004] at 12
56 *Leicester Circuits Ltd v. Coates Brothers Plc* [2003] EWCA Civ 333, WL 1610252 at 1–5
57 *Leicester Circuits v. Coates* [2003] at 10
58 *Leicester Circuits v. Coates* [2003] at 12–13
59 *Leicester Circuits v. Coates* [2003] at 16
60 *Leicester Circuits v. Coates* [2003] at 18
61 *Leicester Circuits v. Coates* [2003] at 27–8
62 Genn (2010) at 99
63 *Ronald Keith McCook v. Aloysius Lobo, London Seafood Ltd, (sued as London and Seafood Poultry Ltd)* [2002] EWCA Civ 1760 (CA) at 34

table' discussions.[64] Reid J in *Corenso (UK) Ltd v. The Burnden Group Plc* accepted that other methods of dispute resolution involving negotiation or an 'honest broker' might be sufficient for CPR requirements[65] but these decisions created a lack of certainty surrounding the suitability of mediation, which was addressed by the Court of Appeal in *Halsey v. Milton Keynes General NHS Trust, Steel Joy, Halliday* ('*Halsey*').[66]

The High Court judgment in *Hurst v. Leeming* and the rigid approach taken to the government pledge in *Royal Bank of Canada* were relatively short-lived. An objective analysis of whether a case has any prospect of success remains a relevant criteria but is now only one of six (non-exclusive) guidelines provided by the Court of Appeal in *Halsey* for weighing the factors for determining the reasonableness of rejecting an offer to mediate. Although *Halsey* provides a more extensive list of the criteria of mediation appropriateness begun in *Hurst v. Leeming*, the High Court judgment still has resonance in that it provides an illustration of how parties, and later their legal advisors, strategically use mediation within the litigation process. The court suggested that Mr Hurst was not interested in engaging in mediating in order to compromise and would not settle unless he made a sizeable financial gain. Cases and empirical research began to indicate that the CPR rules encouraged the 'strategic interplay' of mediation within litigation strategy.[67]

Developing strategic use of mediation and CPR

As the judgments show after *Dunnett* mediation was increasingly in the psyche of judges but they also reveal that the CPR rules were providing legal advisors and their clients with ammunition to pressurise and even 'browbeat' their opponents.[68] The professional literature provided anecdotal evidence that mediation could be strategically used to put clients in the 'driving seat'[69] or that some litigants were engaging in 'endless correspondence' about the timing, venue or the selection of mediator in order that the trial date arrives and mediation ceases to be an option.[70] Research into lawyers' mediation

64 *Alan Valentine v. (1) Kevin Allen (2) Simon John Nash (3) Alison Nash* [2002] EWCA Civ 915 at 4, 5 & 6. The CA was influenced by the statement made by the trial judge when considering costs who stated 'failure to go to mediation is of no cause and effect'.
65 *Corenso (UK) Ltd v. The Burnden Group Plc* [2003] EWHC 1805 (QB). Read J stated that 'ADR is not synonymous with mediation' and suggested that 'negotiation' or using 'an honest broker' might be evidence of compliance with CPR *Corenso* [2003] at 60. See for example Brooker & Lavers (2005a) at 181
66   See for example, Oyre (2004); *Halsey* [2004]
67   See for example, Brooker (2009) (2010a)
68 *Societe Internationale de Telecommunications Aeronautiques SC v. The Wyatt Company (UK) Ltd, Watson Wyatt Partners (A Firm), Watson Wyatt SARL The Wyatt Company (UK) Ltd, Watson Wyatt Partners (a firm), Watson Wyatt SARL v. Maxwell Batley (a firm)* [2002] EWHC 2401 (Ch) at 14. ('*Wyatt v. Maxwell Batley* [2002]')
69 Lind (2002). See also Wilcock (2002/2003) at 44, 44–5. For a discussion see Brooker & Lavers (2005a) at 202–5
70 Turner & Gammack (2003) at 2–4. See also Brooker & Lavers (2005a) at 176

experience in construction and commercial disputes suggested that *Dunnett* had acted as a catalyst for tactical offers where lawyers attempted to 'use costs' to 'bluff' and 'counter bluff' each other as one solicitor explained in an interview:[71]

> I have had a number of experiences of solicitors writing letters to me on the basis of saying, 'Let's mediate, and if you don't agree to this, we'll show this letter to the court.' In other words, it's being used as a costs tactic. In which case, I may, if I am in the same frame of mind, i.e. I think we can do it now; I will call their bluff if I think they are bluffing. I may say, 'Yes that's fine, let's do it.' Or, I may write back and say, 'Well, I don't know enough about my client's case to make this meaningful but, as soon as I do, then I'll get back to you.'

One case illustrating the manipulation of CPR and the strategic use of mediation is *Societe Internationale de Telecommunications Aeronautiques SC (SITA) v. The Wyatt Company (UK) Ltd Wyatt v. Maxwell Batley ('Wyatt v. Maxwell Batley').*[72] Wyatt first asked Maxwell Batley to join them in a mediation with SITA, who were suing Wyatt for erroneous legal advice.[73] The mediation took place in the January without Maxwell Batley but failed to reach an outcome because the parties were over £20 million apart.[74] Wyatt then invited Maxwell Batley to join a second mediation in the April, which they also refused to attend, but which reached a successful settlement with SITA at £35 million.[75] Wyatt made a third offer to mediate after issuing a Part 20 claim against Maxwell Batley for a contribution of costs but no mediation took place and Wyatt, which was unsuccessful at trial, then claimed Maxwell Batley should be denied of 'some of their costs' for refusing to participate in three mediations.[76]

Park J first dealt with the third mediation offer by noting that Wyatt had 'tacitly accepted' that the invitation to mediate 'three weeks' before the hearing was too close to trial which meant that the question rested on whether Maxwell Batley had unreasonably refused the first two offers to mediate about which the court made five points.[77] The refusal of the first offer was reasonable because there was insufficient time between the proposal and the mediation for Maxwell Batley to sift through the evidence produced over several years in what was a 'very large case'.[78] Second, Wyatt had only invited Maxwell Batley to participate in the mediation with SITA in order

---

71 Brooker & Lavers (2005a) at 204
72 *Wyatt v. Maxwell Batley* [2002]
73 *Wyatt v. Maxwell Batley* [2002] at 4
74 *Wyatt v. Maxwell Batley* [2002] at 5
75 *Wyatt v. Maxwell Batley* [2002] at 7
76 *Wyatt v. Maxwell Batley* [2002] at 8 & 1–2
77 *Wyatt v. Maxwell Batley* [2002] at 9–10
78 *Wyatt v. Maxwell Batley* [2002] at 11

to 'put pressure' on them to make a 'large contribution'.[79] Third, Wyatt did not invite Maxwell Batley to mediate because there was a 'dispute between them' but because they wanted them to 'come up with some money to bridge the gap'.[80] Fourth, the pressure that Wyatt put on Maxwell Batley to mediate was 'disagreeable and off-putting' and was described as 'brow beating and bullying' with threats to their 'reputation', which led the court to judge that costs should not be awarded against them for 'refusing to be dragooned into the mediation'.[81] The fifth and final point was evidence from a meeting suggesting that Maxwell Batley had been informed that the mediator was 'motoring against them'.[82] For all of the five reasons the court held that it would be a 'grave injustice' to find that Maxwell Batley had acted unreasonably in refusing the 'self-serving invitations ('demands' would be a more accurate word) to participate in the mediation'.[83]

Although not evidencing the same level of 'costs terrorism'[84] seen in *Wyatt v. Maxwell Batley*, the Court of Appeal declined to award costs for rejecting a mediation offer in *Cressman v. Coys v. Randall McDonald* because the correspondence did not evidence an intention to use mediation.[85] The parties were sent letters informing them of the Court of Appeal's mediation scheme after Waller J had indicated that the case was 'potentially fit for mediation' by 'ticking a box' after the trial.[86] The appellant's solicitors did not reply to the court within 14 days but sent a letter to the defendant asking if they were 'prepared to adopt the CA scheme', which Thorpe LJ found did not reveal where they stood regarding mediation as it was not 'implicit' that they were in favour because otherwise they would have made a 'wholehearted and unreserved commitment' to the process.[87] The Court of Appeal held that the defendant's response to the letter asking for the 'whereabouts' of his client as a signal of 'good faith', was not unreasonable and the case was 'distinguishable' from *Dunnett* because there was no 'clear commitment to the court's scheme' by the party offering mediation.[88]

The tactical interplay between mediation and litigation will be returned to later in the chapter when the timing of mediation is reviewed and when further consideration is given to mediation offers, which show no serious

---

79 *Wyatt v. Maxwell Batley* [2002] at 12
80 *Wyatt v. Maxwell Batley* [2002] at 13
81 *Wyatt v. Maxwell Batley* [2002] at 14
82 *Wyatt v. Maxwell Batley* [2002] at 15
83 *Wyatt v. Maxwell Batley* [2002] at 16
84 Brooker & Lavers (2005a) at 210, Brooker & Lavers (2005b). Research into construction and commercial lawyers' experience with mediation found that lawyers used the threat of costs after *Dunnett*.
85 *Harry Gordon Cressman, Barbara Gordon Cressman (Personal Representatives of Thomas Ashley Cressman (Deceased)) v. Coys of Kensington (Sales) Ltd v. Randall McDonald* [2004] EWCA Civ 133; 2004 WL 229242 at 7
86 *Cressman* [2004] at 3
87 *Cressman* [2004] at 4–5
88 *Cressman* [2004] at 6–7

intent to engage in the process. The early cases following CPR and *Dunnett* began to indicate that there was considerable unease about the application of the rules and when the court might penalise a party on costs for refusing to consider mediation. This was addressed by the Court of Appeal in *Halsey*, which has had a substantial influence on mediation policy and practice in the English jurisdiction, but also in other common law and civil law countries.[89] The decision reverberated throughout the mediator and legal communities and has been minutely analysed particularly in relation to comments made on compulsory mediation.[90] However, *Halsey* has also provoked significant criticism because of the remaining ambiguity produced by the guidelines but also because of the negative impact the decision had on the voluntary use of the process, which Genn describes as 'turning back the tide' of mediation development.[91]

The Court of Appeal in *Halsey*

Halsey involved two appeals where the Court of Appeal had to determine when to impose costs on a successful party after they have rejected an offer to use ADR and it is notable that because of the 'importance' given to the issue, four 'interveners' were invited by the court to give submissions including two of the oldest ADR providers (ADR Group and CEDR), the Law Society and the Civil Mediation Council.[92] Dyson LJ, who gave the leading judgment, has since been called 'a mediation sceptic' but his stance on compelling or mandating parties to attend ADR has been perhaps one of the most contentious issues debated in the literature and public forums.[93] The Court of Appeal was clear that it is inappropriate to 'order' 'truly unwilling' parties to mediate not only because this would deny them their rights of access to court enshrined in Article 6 of the European Convention on Human Rights but also because it would reduce mediation's 'effectiveness' as a voluntary process.[94] In Dyson LJ's view to 'compel' attendance at mediation merely 'adds' to both the parties' costs and time before the courts finally hear the case.[95]

89 See for example, Hong Kong Working Party Report (2010); Irish Law Commission Report (2010)
90 See for example, Shipman (2006) (2011); Brunsdon-Tully (2009)
91 Genn (2010) at 101; See also Brooker (2009); Shipman (2006); Brunsdon-Tully (2009)
92 *Halsey* [2004] at 1 & 2
93 See for example, Genn et al. (2007) at 101 Brunsdon-Tully (2009); Lord Phillips (2008); Lord Clarke (2008); Sir Lightman (2007)
94 *Halsey* [2004] at 9
95 *Halsey* [2004] at 10

Halsey and Article 6 Human Rights

Before moving on to the *Halsey* guidelines a brief review is given on Dyson LJ's *obiter* comment on compelling mediation. After *Halsey*, there was significant academic and extrajudicial debate on the position of mandating mediation. A number of senior judges gave speeches disputing Lord Justice Dyson's analysis of the legal position on Article 6 and many proponents of mediation, some disappointed with the lack of expansion in use, argued that compelling mediation does not oblige the parties to reach a settlement and therefore mandating mediation would only postpone a party's right to go to court.[96] Dyson LJ has since clarified his *obiter* position on Article 6 following the EU decision in *Rosalba Alassini*.[97] The European Court of Justice held that Italian law requiring parties in dispute to engage in mediation before accessing the court did not infringe Article 6 and furthermore the Italian government had proved that it was a 'legitimate objective' to provide a quicker and cheaper alternative to judicial determination.[98] While some argue that *Rosalba Alassini* definitively settles the question that mandatory mediation does not infringe Article 6,[99] Lord Dyson recently suggests that 'compulsory' rules might 'breach' the right to access the court if, for example, the cost of mediating is not 'free' or not part of a 'nominal fee' scheme because parties may have no real option of continuing with litigation if mediation fails.[100] The Court of Appeal returned to this issue in *Wright v. Michael Wright Supplies* when Lord Justice Ward criticised the inability of the court to 'shift intransigent parties to the parallel tract of mediation' because of the possible *'obiter'* decision in *Halsey* on EU law.[101] Furthermore, His Honour doubted that a court stay under CPR 26.4(2) (b) would be an 'unacceptable obstruction to the parties' right of access to the court' and was hopeful that a 'bold judge' would take on the 'invitation to rule on *Halsey*' on this point.[102]

Halsey Guidelines

Although Dyson LJ recognised the 'value' of ADR by exhorting the legal professions to 'routinely consider' alternatives, he nonetheless observed that some researchers do not believe the efficacy of mediation has been 'sufficiently demonstrated', but continued from the starting point that

---

96 Sir Anthony Clarke M.R. (2008); Lord Phillips (2008); Lightman, Sir (2007)
97 *Rosalba Alassini v. Telecom Italia SpA* (Joined Cases C-317-320/08) [2010] 3 CMLR 17 ECJ
98 For a more detailed analysis see for example, Ahmed (2012); Dundas (2010); Colvin (2010); Shipman (2011)
99 Dundas (2010)
100 Lord Dyson (2011) at 339
101 *Wright v. Michael Wright Supplies Ltd. & Anor* [2013] EWCA Civ 234 at 3
102 *Wright v. Michael Wright* [2013] at 3

'most cases are suitable for mediation'.[103] Courts were directed to take a 'robust' approach to encouraging ADR in appropriate cases but not to implacably accept a litigant's view against mediating without exploring the reasons given.[104] After *Halsey*, the losing litigant has the burden of proving that the successful party 'unreasonably' refused their offer to mediate because it is a 'departure from the general rule' that the unsuccessful party pays the cost of the winning party.[105] The Court of Appeal did not accept the Civil Mediation Council's suggestion that there should be a presumption in favour of mediating reversing the burden of proof because the court acknowledged the Law Society's 'submission' that mediation is not suitable for all cases.[106]

Lord Dyson went on to present six non-exhaustive factors the courts could take into consideration when exercising discretion to award adverse costs but specifically emphasised that 'no single factor' was decisive:[107]

(a) The nature of the dispute;
(b) The merits of the case;
(c) The extent to which other settlement methods have been attempted;
(d) Whether the costs of the ADR would be disproportionately high;
(e) Whether any delay in setting up and attending the ADR would have been prejudicial; and
(f) Whether the ADR had a reasonable prospect of success.

(a) Nature of case

The Court of Appeal in *Halsey* began from the basis that 'most cases are not by their nature unsuitable' but that some disputes may be 'intrinsically unsuitable' for ADR.[108] Dyson LJ cited the findings of a Commercial Court Working Party in support of this contention, with the most 'palpable reason' given that a party wants a court determination on 'issues of law or construction' when it is crucial for future business or trading arrangements or an 'on-going' contract.[109] Other 'unsuitability' factors include evidence of 'fraud or other commercially disreputable conduct', where a 'binding precedent is useful', where an application is made for 'injunctive relief' or 'other relief to protect the position of the party'.[110]

103 *Halsey* [2004] at 11 & 6
104 *Halsey* [2004] at 11 & 10
105 *Halsey* [2004] at 13. See CPR r44.2(2) (a)
106 *Halsey* [2004] at 16
107 *Halsey* [2004] at 16
108 *Halsey* [2004] at 17
109 *Halsey* [2004] at 17. See for example, Mistelis (2006) at 146–7
110 *Halsey* [2004] at 17

(b) Merits of the case

The guidelines also recognise that another valid consideration is a party's belief that they have a 'strong case' otherwise they would be at the mercy of parties making 'costs threats' with 'weak cases or speculative claims' and courts were warned of the vulnerability of large companies or 'public bodies' to 'cynical'[111] claims where pressure is put on them to make 'nuisance-value offers to buy off the cost of mediation'.[112] There is of course another side to the coin, which is where financially large organisations offer mediation in order to drain an opponent's financial resources or to press acceptance of artificially low settlement offers.[113]

There are inevitably problems in assessing the merits of any case and the financially larger or more complex the dispute the more likely parties will seek advice from lawyers; but at a hearing on costs the court has the benefit of 'hindsight'.[114] Where a case is not 'clear-cut' Dyson LJ suggests that 'little or no weight' should be given to a party who 'thought that he should win' and in borderline cases there must be 'significant countervailing factors which tip the scales the other way', some of which are likely to be from the other five criteria.[115] The decision in *Hurst v. Leeming* was 'qualified' in that a belief in a 'watertight case is no justification for refusing mediation'; such a 'belief' must be 'reasonably' held because if it is an unreasonable conviction 'it is not justified'.[116]

(c) Other settlement methods attempted

The Court of Appeal suggested that making 'settlement offers' may be 'relevant' because it might indicate either an 'effort to settle' by one party or 'unrealistic views' about the strength of a case; and because mediation 'often succeeds when other attempts to settle have failed'.[117] Even though this factor might appear innocuous, it provides a party or their lawyers with ammunition for tactical litigation practices and may even discourage the take-up of mediation. Rather than encouraging the parties to attempt the process it validates settlement negotiations, which lawyers often conduct using 'traditional' adversarial negotiation practices rather than 'principled' negotiation.[118] A number of jurisdictions have found that as legal professions

---

111 Brooker (2009) at 87
112 *Halsey* [2004] at 18. See Brooker (2009) at 87
113 See Brooker & Lavers (2005a) at 181. See Fiss (1984). Professor Fiss argues forcefully against a policy of settlement when vulnerable parties are at the mercy of those with better resources. See Chapter 1
114 See Shipman (2006) at 204. See also *Brent Ltd. and another v. Black & Veatch Consulting Ltd* [2008] EWHC 1497 (TCC) at 43
115 *Halsey* [2004] at 19. See Brooker (2009) at 87
116 *Halsey* [2004] at 19
117 *Halsey* [2004] at 20
118 See Menkle-Meadow (1993) at 363. See also Fisher et al. (1991); Clark (2012). Chapter 1 of this book explores the increasing level of legal involvement in mediation developments in the USA and England.

become more familiar with mediation, largely because of court rules encouraging or mandating activity, lawyers become more adversarial within the process, which researchers correlate to an increase in the selection of evaluative mediators.[119]

(d) Costs of mediation

The *Halsey* guidelines emphasize that the costs of mediating may be relevant particularly when the litigated sum is 'comparatively small' but the appeal case shows that ten years ago it was appreciated that this expense may be comparable to a 'day in court' because each party is usually responsible for paying the mediators' fees 'regardless of outcome'.[120] Furthermore, when court rules connect mediation to litigation, more parties bring legal advisors to the process and sometimes attend with both solicitor and counsel.[121] CEDR's 2012 Mediators' Audit reported that fees for experienced mediators had risen by a staggering 24 per cent to on average £4,279 a day and the daily rate for even less experienced mediators is over £1,500.[122] The Court of Appeal in *Halsey* was concerned that a settlement outcome in mediation is 'not predictable' thereby making the costs of the process relevant for the successful litigant because they may have to pay for the 'abortive' costs of mediating.[123]

(e) Delay

Lord Dyson's pithy statement on delay was that it was a factor to be taken into consideration when deciding whether the party's refusal was reasonable because it may delay the trial and final determination.[124] Subsequent case law (noted below) shows that the timing of mediation becomes a 'balancing act' for litigants with little clarity from the cases to assist this appraisal and CPR now fosters the strategic 'interplay' between litigation and ADR as parties make tactical mediation offers.[125]

(f) Reasonable prospect of mediation success

The Court of Appeal did not place the same critical significance on the 'prospect of mediation success' as Lightman J did in *Hurst v. Leeming* but

---

119 See Chapter 1 for an overview of this phenomenon in the United States and in England. For a recent analysis of the influence that lawyers have in mediation internationally see Clark (2012).
120 *Halsey* [2004] at 21
121 See for example, Brooker & Lavers (2005a,b); Genn (1998) (2002); Shipman (2006) at 147–8
122 CEDR Mediator Audit (2012). CEDR report that over a third of mediators earn under £1,250 or work pro bono (8.5%) and only 13.6% earn over £4,001.
123 *Halsey* [2004] at 21
124 *Halsey* [2004] at 22
125 See Brooker (2010a) at 148. See generally, Brooker (2009) (2010a); Brunsdon-Tully (2009); Shipman (2006)

whilst *Halsey* acknowledges that this factor might be relevant it is not 'necessarily determinative to the fundamental question' of whether a party's rejection of the offer was 'unreasonable'.[126] *Halsey* provides two scenarios to explain this factor: First, the court may find it is unreasonable to believe there is 'no reasonable prospect of mediation success' when confronted by the other side assuming 'a position of intransigence'.[127] In the second example, the court might conclude that there is 'no reasonable prospect' of mediation settling the dispute when one party is immovable on their position but a successful litigant is not allowed to 'rely' on his unreasonable 'obdurate' behaviour under these 'circumstances'.[128] Shipman points to the illogicality of the situation where a person's 'intransigence' is because of a 'reasonable belief in a strong case' which suggests that it would be impossible to claim that mediation has a good chance of succeeding, which would 'appear to undermine the overriding objective of CPR' to encourage settlement and save 'court resources'.[129] Factors such as considering that you have a 'strong case' or a legal point that needs a court determination do not 'evoke a picture' of overt unreasonable behaviour when pursuing litigation but what converts this belief to unreasonable conduct is that 'the party unreasonably holds that belief'.[130]

The most difficult disputes to appraise are 'borderline cases', which *Halsey* suggests are likely to be 'suitable' and that 'little weight' should be given in such cases 'unless there are countervailing factors' (which Dyson LJ does not explicate but probably involve the presence of the other *Halsey* factors).[131] The most sensible approach in 'borderline cases' may be to mediate rather than take the risk of an adverse costs penalty.[132]

Unreasonable behaviour in *Halsey*

None of the parties in *Hurst v. Leeming* or the two appeals before the Court of Appeal in *Halsey* successfully proved that their offers to mediate had been unreasonably rejected.[133] The facts of all three cases also show elements of how the parties or their legal advisors attempt to tactically use, or abuse, mediation now that it is institutionalised through the CPR rules governing litigation.[134] 'Exceptionally' the court found that Mr Hurst's uncompromising attitude to what he wanted to achieve in mediation (a significant sum when he was 'entitled to nothing') and his emotional state, signified little hope for

126 *Halsey* [2004] at 25
127 *Halsey* [2004] at 25
128 *Halsey* [2004] at 26
129 Shipman (2006) at 215
130 See Brooker (2010a) at 151
131 *Halsey* [2004] at 22. See Brooker (2009) at 87–8
132 Brooker (2009) at 87
133 See Mackie et al. (2007) at 104–6
134 *Dunnett* [2002a] at 22. See generally Brooker (2009) (2010a)

mediation to succeed.[135] In *Halsey*, the Court of Appeal upheld the decision to award costs to Milton Keynes General Area Health Trust because the facts illustrated that the claimant had used a tactical and adversarial use of ediation and had 'come no-way near' to showing that the Trust had been unreasonable.[136] Both the subject matter (medical negligence) and the Trust's belief that it had a 'strong' defence to the claim were reasonable.[137] Moreover, the Court was highly critical of the conduct of the claimant's solicitor which revealed an 'early attempt to extort a sum of money' and five letters asking the Trust to mediate for what was 'at best' a 'speculative claim'.[138] It was 'highly relevant' that the costs of mediating would have been 'disproportionately high' to the value of the claim and the claimant failed to prove that mediation had a 'reasonable' prospect of success.[139]

In *Steel v. Joy and Halliday*, the second defendants had refused the first defendant's offer to mediate because they believed that their contribution to the claimed damages involved a legal point on causation and that the offer was very late in the litigation process.[140] The Court of Appeal found that the defence involved a question of law and that the defendants had not acted 'unreasonably' in wanting a court determination on the issue, which made the case 'intrinsically unsuitable' for mediation.[141] The first defendant had failed to show that mediation would have a 'reasonable prospect' of success because the second defendant had taken a 'reasonable' 'stand on the point of law' and the Court was persuaded that mediating would have resulted in 'excessive' expense compared to a two-hour trial, although the estimate of mediating at £20,000 seemed startling.[142] All of these 'factors' led the Court to hold that the first defendant had not proved that the second defendant had unreasonably refused their offer to mediate.[143]

Mediation and litigation strategy

Six years on from his judgment in *Halsey* Lord Justice Dyson denies that he is an 'ADR sceptic' and maintains that the guidelines were correct.[144] His Lordship continues to believe that the majority of cases are suitable, such as 'family, personal injury, clinical negligence and most contractual dispute' but stresses that parties who want a legal point decided by the courts should not be prevented from litigation because there is 'public interest' in 'developing

135 *Hurst v. Leeming* [2003] at 16 & 22
136 *Halsey* [2004] at 50
137 *Halsey* [2004] at 51
138 *Halsey* [2004] at 50
139 *Halsey* [2004] at 51 & 52
140 *Halsey* [2004] at 80
141 *Halsey* [2004] at 78
142 *Halsey* [2004] at 79
143 *Halsey* [2004] at 81
144 Lord Justice Dyson (2011) at 337

the law'.[145] The *Halsey* guidelines remain the benchmark for judges consider-ing the suitability of mediation during 'case management meetings' and is the reference point for lawyers to assess with their clients whether to mediate or not.[146] However, the immediate detrimental effect of *Halsey* was that a pilot project for automatic referral of cases to mediation became virtually inoperable as parties elected not to mediate.[147] Moreover, there has been sub-stantial critical debate on the continuing ambiguity that parties face on the judicial exercise of the guidelines. The guidelines provide disputants with working criteria to assess the suitability of mediation or perhaps to 'gauge' how their decision will be viewed by the court should they unsuccessfully litigate their case.[148] However, Shipman argues that judges have 'significant discretion' on how they address adverse costs for refusing to mediate and may be more 'influenced' by their own beliefs of the merits of ADR or by an 'ideo-logical adherence to a justice on merits approach to civil justice'.[149] Therefore her analysis of cases show that where there are conflicting legal positions, or where one party refuses to mediate on the strength of their case, the deci-sion may reflect a judge's 'commitment to and understanding of ADR'.[150] A judge who believes that mediation might help the parties in 'continuing business relationships' or creative or 'appropriate outcomes' (such as an apology) may decide strongly in favour of ADR whereas when judges believe that a 'correct legal solution' is necessary, mediation will not be encour-aged.[151] Correspondingly, judges are more likely to support or recommend ADR when they are 'committed' to the 'overriding objectives of CPR' and believe courts should be the 'last resort' regardless of whether they are inclined to follow a 'justice on the merits' approach.[152]

A review of cases reveals a number of 'themes' that reoccur in the judgments. First, there are sometimes 'facts' or 'circumstances' which the court finds makes the case unsuitable for mediation. Second, there are specific 'types' of case that are regarded as especially appropriate for mediation and parties run the 'risk' of adverse costs unless there are 'countervailing factors' indicating unsuitability.[153] Third, there are circumstances at the time of the mediation offer or the rejection which either impact on the 'prospect of success' for mediating, or justify a decision to refuse to mediate until 'a party knows the case' against them, which will 'militate' against the finding that the refusal is

145 Lord Dyson (2011) at 338. Lord Dyson LJ cites Professor Genn
146 Shipman (2006) at 248. See also Brunsdon-Tully (2009); Tronson (2006); Shipman (2006); Brooker (2009) (2010a)
147 Genn et al. (2007); Genn (2010) at 107–8
148 See for example, Brooker (2009); Shipman (2006); Brunsdon-Tully (2009)
149 Shipman (2006) at 182
150 Shipman (2006) at 211
151 Shipman (2006) at 182 & 211
152 See Shipman (2006) at 181 citing Zuckerman (2003) at 26–30 & 18–20
153 *Halsey* [2004] at 22; See Brunsdon-Tully (2009); Tronson (2006); Shipman (2006); Brooker (2009) (2010a)

unreasonable (at that time).[154] This theme connects to the appropriate or most suitable timing for mediation. Fourth, there is evidence before the court that some ADR or mediation offers are not 'genuine' which suggests that there is 'no serious intent' on the part of the unsuccessful party to engage in an ADR process.[155] Finally, some of the cases disseminate a strong 'anti-litigation message' when publicizing the benefits of mediating.[156] What these themes have in common is that since CPR and the integration of ADR into the formal process of litigation, the courts are contributing to 'normalising' mediation practice,[157] which might be to 'encourage' use but the effect is also negatively impacting on how it is being strategically used. As CPR and the pre-action procedures binds mediation to litigation it comes further into lawyers' area of interest where they traditionally control dispute resolution and are therefore in the position to influence practice.[158]

Specific 'facts' or circumstances indicating unsuitability

Lack of merit in claims

The first theme explored is that the courts sometimes find specific unsuitability factors, which may indicate inappropriateness for mediation. In *Daniels v. Metropolitan Commissioner for Police*, the Court of Appeal had to consider whether the successful party should be deprived of any of their costs because of an 'absolute determination' to have the matter resolved at court and an 'adamant refusal to contemplate any form of negotiation'.[159] Daniels had sued the Commissioner for negligence, after sustaining injuries from a police horse during training and alleged that the trainer told her to ride despite knowledge about the animal's 'unreliable and impulsive nature' and had ordered her to remove a martingale which would have prevented the head rising.[160] After a day of the trial, damages were agreed at £7,000 but Collins J held that the defendants had won 'comprehensively on all issues of liability' because Daniels was a more competent rider than she claimed and had asked to ride the horse.[161] The defendants had refused two Part 36 offers first at £7,500 and then at £5,000 and confirmed in correspondence their intention to take the claim to court.[162] Ordinarily when a successful party does not

---

154 Brooker (2010a) at 154
155 See for example, *Re Midland Linen Services Ltd., Chaudhry v. Yap* [2004] EWHC 3380 (Ch) at 56
156 Genn (2010) at 121; Brunsden-Tully (2009)
157 Allen (2008) (pagination not given online)
158 See Chapter 1 generally for a review of the literature on the influence of lawyers in mediation.
159 *Daniels v. Commissioner of Police for the Metropolis* [2005] EWCA Civ 1312 at 3
160 *Daniels* [2005] at 2
161 *Daniels* [2005] at 6
162 *Daniels* [2005] at 9

achieve a greater amount than the Part 36 offer, a judge can exercise discretion and not award all the costs; but despite amassing nearly £50,000 in pursuing litigation Collins J found the defendant was 'justified in taking the stance'.[163] First, because the Commissioner of Police faced other similar cases, which would put the authority in a vulnerable position if settled; and insurance companies might decide to settle for small amounts even when claims have no merit.[164] Second, the Commissioner was 'entitled' to test the case because otherwise there was risk of other 'mounted police officers' bringing proceedings.[165] Further-more there was evidence that Daniels had brought another claim for 'bullying' which had been settled and that another 17 claims had been brought by 'mounted police' in a period of three to four years, ten of which were concerned with falls from horses.[166] Finally, the defendant had 'taken the view' that it was 'either an accident' or negligence and if they accepted liability it would open a 'flood of claims', leading Collins J to conclude, 'in the circumstances the branch took the view that the question of principle was worth the expense'.[167]

Daniels v. Metropolitan Commissioner did not involve an offer to mediate but Dyson LJ applied the '*Halsey* Rules' to the refusal of a Part 36 offer by asking when a 'refusal to negotiate is unreasonable'.[168] The court noted that the 'Glossary to the CPR' described ADR as 'collective descriptions of methods of resolving dispute' other than 'normal trial', which could be taken as 'extending to negotiation'.[169] Dyson LJ referred to two *Halsey* factors in the judgment. The first criteria given consideration was 'the merits of the case' and it was 'entirely reasonable' for a 'public body' to fight what they reasonably believed to be an 'unfounded claim' even if 'speculative claims' are sometimes paid off to 'avoid the trouble and expense'.[170] Furthermore, a court should 'be slow to characterise such conduct as unreasonable if [the] party is ultimately successful'.[171]

The second *Halsey* factor was the prospect of mediation success, but this criteria is not 'necessarily determinative of the fundamental question', which is whether the party acted unreasonably.[172] Ward LJ observed that just because the 'costs' outstripped 'the sum' did not mean that the party had engaged in litigation unreasonably because those who believe they have a 'good prospect of success' at court are 'entitled to fully and properly advance his or her case or defence'.[173] Nevertheless, His Honour drew attention to the

163 *Daniels* [2005] at 12
164 *Daniels* [2005] at 12
165 *Daniels* [2005] at 12
166 *Daniels* [2005] at 14
167 *Daniels* [2005] at 14
168 *Daniels* [2005] at 25–6
169 *Daniels* [2005] at 27
170 *Daniels* [2005] at 30
171 *Daniels* [2005] at 31
172 *Daniels* [2005] at 32
173 *Daniels* [2005] at 36

role of the court in 'encouraging mediation' as early as possible, particularly in what might appear to be an 'unseemly, or at least un-commercial squabble' to those 'outside' the legal world[174] but 'unreasonable conduct' will 'inevitably depend on all the circumstances of the case', which the judge should 'investigate'.[175]

Halsey moderated the position in *Hurst v. Leeming*, which had suggested that a belief in a 'watertight' case was never justified if there was a 'good prospect' that mediation would succeed, to requiring judgment on the 'merits' of a case and the reasonableness of the belief in the strength of one's case. In 2012, the Court of Appeal had to consider whether the judge had correctly applied the *Halsey* criteria to a refusal to use mediation in *Swain Mason & Others v. Mills & Reeve* and returned to the issue of claims having no merit.[176] The defendant had not given advice to the claimants on the 'tax consequences' of death, which meant that the sale of shares in a company were subject to inheritance tax.[177] The Court held that the defendants had no duty to provide this 'advice' because the information on the medical information was only received in an email they had been copied into about 'bank subordination' and although aware of the father's ill health, the email did not contain any information that the operation 'carried any significant risk'.[178]

In relation to costs one issue concerned the defendant's refusal to mediate, which had been suggested by the claimant 'at various stages' and encouraged by the court at two hearings, but refused because there was no belief in the 'merit' of the claim.[179] At the hearing for costs, the trial judge found that the defendant had won on the issue of breach of duty but not all the matters in dispute and was therefore not 'universally accurate' on the 'merits of the case'.[180] It was noted that the case was appropriate for mediation in relation to the 'check list' provided in *Halsey* for (a), (c), (d) and (e) but was also suitable because it would provide the defendant with an advantage in preventing 'collateral reputational damage'.[181] The judge was satisfied that there was a 'reasonable prospect' that mediation would have succeeded and that the parties would have understood the 'weaknesses of their own case'.[182] The defendant was found to have taken an 'intransigent refusal at every stage even to contemplate the possibility of mediation' and consequently, the claimants were only ordered to pay 5 per cent of their costs.[183]

---

174 *Daniels* [2005] at 37
175 *Daniels* [2005] at 38
176 *Swain Mason & Others v. Mills & Reeve (A Firm)* [2012] EWCA Civ 4928
177 *Swain Mason* [2012] at 23–4
178 *Swain Mason* [2012] at 51–2
179 *Swain Mason* [2012] at 62
180 *Swain Mason* [2012] at 63
181 *Swain Mason* [2012] at 64
182 *Swain Mason* [2012] at 65
183 *Swain Mason* [2012] at 66

In giving the judgment of the Court of Appeal Lord Justice Davies found himself 'troubled by the trial judge's approach' to the defendant's conduct.[184] First, the judge had suggested that the defendant had only been 'vindicated' on the issue of duty but this position had been 'maintained throughout' the case and was therefore 'justified' and 'determinative'.[185] The trial judge failed to explain what the weaknesses of the 'respective cases' were but suggested that these would have come to light in mediation and would have 'led to a mediated settlement'.[186] The relevance to 'the avoidance of collateral reputational damage' was criticised because the Court recognised that 'professional defendants' might want to defend their reputation at a trial once it has been 'aired by the commencement of proceedings' and it would be undesirable if future claimants were 'encouraged to think' that this 'consideration would enhance their bargaining power'.[187] Davies LJ did not believe that mediation had a good chance of success because the parties were a 'hundred miles apart' and the claimants had always believed their case was strong on the duty issue whereas it was in fact 'weak' and they lost on this.[188] The trial judge was wrong to imply that the defendant's refusal to mediate was 'intransigent' because there had been nothing during the dispute to make them reassess their position and their 'reasonable refusal' to contemplate mediation did not transform into an unreasonable refusal because they it was 'steadfastly . . . maintained'.[189]

In the view of Davies LJ, *Halsey* had made it clear that the courts should be 'astute to the danger' of claims that no 'merit' where 'the threat of costs sanctions' are used to 'extract a settlement'.[190] Lord Dyson's guidelines suggest that a reasonable belief in a 'watertight case' may be justified and in *Swain Mason* the defendant's belief in the strength of the duty issue was 'correct', the claimants failed to show that their offer to mediate had been unreasonably rejected and the judge was 'wrong' to penalise their 'attitude to mediation'.[191]

Amount in dispute

The problem of paying out more than a case was worth because of the possible threat of 'cost consequences' was reviewed in *Hickman v. Blake Lapthorn* when

---

184 *Swain Mason* [2012] at 73
185 *Swain Mason* [2012] at 74
186 *Swain Mason* [2012] at 74(2)
187 *Swain Mason* [2012] at 74(3)
188 *Swain Mason* [2012] at 75
189 *Swain Mason* [2012] at 75
190 *Swain Mason* [2012] at 74(3). See *Halsey* [2004] at 18
191 *Swain Mason* [2012] at 77. See also: *Euroption Strategic Fund Ltd v. Skandinaviska Enskilda Banken AB* [2012] EWHC 749 (Comm) at 5 & 18. The HC awarded indemnity costs against the claimants for a claim that was 'speculative', 'grossly exaggerated' and 'opportunistic'. The defendants were not penalized for rejecting mediation because there was 'no reason' why they should have to 'pay the additional costs' of mediating.

an applicant successfully sued his legal representatives for advising settlement at too low a value following a road accident causing head injuries.[192] In the subsequent hearing, before Hon. Mr Justice Jack, costs had spiralled to £435,000 on a judgment for £130,000 and one issue before the court was the first defendant's claim that the second defendant pay all the claimant's cost from the date that they refused to 'negotiate and to enter into mediation'.[193] The court was not being asked to award costs against the successful party for refusing to mediate but to award 'all the claimant's costs including the first defendant's costs' against the second defendant because they had refused to mediate, and in a 'novel' twist on *Halsey* this 'included' a refusal to negotiate.[194] The claimant had reduced his claim from £250,000 to £150,000 and Jack J observed that at this point there was a 'strong probability' that negotiation or a mediation would have achieved a figure close to that achieved at trial because the first defendants were taking a 'commercial view'.[195]

The amount being claimed by the claimant was 'three times' what the second defendants were prepared to pay but their assessment had been undertaken by 'experienced solicitors and counsel' and was not judged to be 'unreasonable'. The question before the court was whether they had made an 'unreasonable estimation' of what could have been achieved in negotiation or mediation.[196] Unlike the first defendants, the second defendant's insurers were not prepared to take a 'commercial view' but the court did not find this unreasonable in view of the 'potential threat of cost consequences' being used to 'extract more than a claim is worth'.[197]

Both *Daniels* and *Hickman* illustrate the realities of negotiating settlement and although there was no suggestion by the court that mediation would have been unable to resolve the matter, the refusals to mediate were not unreasonable because the litigants faced specific circumstances where the costs rules potentially put them under pressure either because of exposure to claims with no merit or to paying more than their value.

Fraud

Although the empirical evidence fails to support the contention that particular cases or types of parties are more appropriate for achieving settlement in mediation, lists drawing up suitability criteria frequently identify fraud as an excluding factor which was acknowledged in *Halsey*.[198] Despite this, a few days after *Halsey*, Ward LJ gave the judgment in *Couenbergh v. Valkova*, which

---

192 *Hickman v. Blake Lapthorn, David Fisher* [2006] EWHC 12 (QB) at 1
193 *Hickman* [2006] at 11
194 *Hickman* [2006] at 25–6
195 *Hickman* [2006] at 19
196 *Hickman* [2006] at 28–30
197 *Hickman* [2006] at 30
198 *Halsey* [2004] at 17. See for example *Second Report of the Commercial Court Committee Working Party on ADR.* (1998); Gaede (1991); Hill (1996)

at first blush is difficult to comprehend because it involved an alleged fraud.[199] Brown and Marriott[200] suggest that this decision 'negates' the proposition that mediation is not appropriate when fraud has been claimed, although it should be noted that where such allegations exist the rules of without prejudice or confidentiality might result in the court ordering disclosure of evidence of what take place during the process.[201] A more detailed analysis of the facts reveals the thinking behind Lord Justice Ward's decision.

Mrs Adam made a will in the 1970s in favour of family members and Mr Couenbergh but visits were rare and she became friendly with Dr Valkova who organised arrangements for a second will where she was the beneficiary.[202] The first solicitor approached had 'suspicions' about the circumstances and asked for confirmation about Mrs Adam's competency but a second solicitor made a visit along with notes which supported the contention that she did wish to make a new will in favour of her friend.[203] The will was drawn up by a third solicitor, who did not visit Mrs Adam, but was witnessed by neighbours, the 'Doyles', however after concerns about 'attestation' (Mr Doyle had signed on a second page which did not contain Mrs Adam's or his wife's signature) a third will was signed by two Italian brothers: The Italian will.[204] After Mrs Adam's death, Mr Couenbergh unsuccessfully 'challenged' both the 'Doyle' and 'Italian' wills and the court awarded costs against him to the tune of £105,000.[205]

Following a 'freezing order' on Mr Couenbergh's assets by the Legal Services Commission, which had borne the costs of the case, there was a police investigation into Mrs Adam's death.[206] Mr Couenbergh successfully applied for both orders to be stayed until after the investigation, which found there were a number of discrepancies with the Italian will including information that the Italian brothers had 'signed a document not knowing what it was' and 'did not recall Mrs Adam's signature at the bottom of the will'. The case was 'listed' for appeal because of the 'risk' that fraud had been 'perpetrated on the court' and a 'real prospect' that a 'substantial injustice' had been done to the appellant. Lord Justice Ward also took the opportunity to reiterate the advice given by the court for the parties to consider mediation:[207]

> The parties had it, and still have it, in their power to alter the destiny of this appeal and this sad case. We urged them, and continue to urge them,

---

199 *Couenbergh v. Valkova* [2004] EWCA Civ 676
200 Brown & Marriott (2011) at 92 (5-075)
201 See Chapter 5
202 *Couenbergh v. Valkova* [2004] at 4–9
203 *Couenbergh v. Valkova* [2004] at 10
204 *Couenbergh v. Valkova* [2004] at 10–11
205 *Couenbergh v. Valkova* [2004] at 13 & 16
206 *Couenbergh v. Valkova* [2004] at 19
207 *Couenbergh v. Valkova* [2004] at 52

to do so through mediation. It is a case crying out for alternative dispute resolution.

One of the factors complicating the opportunity for mediation was the involvement of the Legal Aid Commission which may have had to fund a retrial and may have 'obstructed mediation'.[208] Lord Justice Ward admonished the attitude of the 'authorities' and asked that in any future costs order that the Court of Appeal 'observations' about their failure to mediate after court encouragement and their 'intransigence' be taken into account.[209] Furthermore, the court requested that a copy of the judgment be sent to the Chief Executive of the Legal Aid Commission.[210]

The inappropriateness of mediation where a party has used fraud would seem an obvious criteria militating against its use. If one party suspects that another is acting fraudulently this may not instil confidence that this will not reoccur in the mediation and consequently settlement may not transpire. However, when permission for a retrial is because of the possibility of fraud and the Court of Appeal recommends mediating, these factors may diminish the prospect of further fraudulent conduct as the parties are aware of the court's knowledge of the situation (and, presumably, the mediator would have notice as well). One of the purposes of the rules governing the making of wills is to protect the vulnerable in society and although Dr Valkova's actions may not have been exemplary, they probably reflected the true intentions of Mrs Adam. However, when the court is identifying suitability criteria for mediating, the decision does not aid clarity and may potentially create ambiguity in mediation practice with the danger of further injustices occurring. Rather than removing fraud from the list of limiting factors for mediation, it may be better to assume that this criterion is influential if suspicions of deceit caused a party to reject mediation before trial rather than after the court hearing when the danger of fraud has been aired and probably removed.

Appropriateness criteria

Building and construction cases

One type of case that judges identify as being most suitable for mediation is a small building dispute, many of which eventually end up in the specialised Technology and Construction Court (TCC). A number of judges in the TCC are well-known supporters of mediation and steer parties towards mediating because of the perceived suitability of building and construction cases, although there is empirical evidence suggesting relatively high numbers of mediations fail to settle and that construction disputes settle significantly less

---

208 *Couenbergh v. Valkova* [2004] at 55, 54–5
209 *Couenbergh v. Valkova* [2004] at 54–5
210 *Couenbergh v. Valkova* [2004] at 54–5

often than commercial ones.[211] Mediation continues to be 'routinely' used at various stages during litigation but negotiation is still the primary dispute resolution mechanism for construction parties.[212] Recently, Lord Justice Jackson reaffirmed with 'vigour' the value of mediating 'low cost construction cases' when negotiation has failed to reach settlement.[213]

Shortly after *Halsey*, the Court of Appeal in *Burchell v. Bullard* deemed an acrimonious small building case particularly suitable for mediation.[214] The claimant homeowners had entered into a contract with the builder for an extension but refused to pay the third instalment until defects in the roof constructed by a sub-contractor were corrected.[215] After a number of 'confrontations', the builder was ordered off site and began a claim for payment of completed work and lost costs; Mr and Mrs Bullard counterclaimed for defective work which the builder joined as a Part 20 defendant with the sub-contractor.[216]

The Bullards refused to mediate at an early stage in the proceedings on the advice of their surveyor that the case was too 'technically complex' and not 'appropriate' for mediation.[217] At trial both parties were found to be 'at fault' in the way they conducted the litigation but the builder's approach was deemed 'more reasonable'.[218] At the court of first instance, Burchell was found not to have repudiated the contract but the defendants won just over £5,000 for their counter-claim for defective work although the builder was at fault for only £79.80.[219] The court awarded costs to Burchell for his successful claim and the defendants for their counter-claim but on appeal the judge was found to have 'erred' by not using judicial 'discretion' under CPR 44.7 to proportion costs.[220]

Ward LJ considered whether the defendants had unreasonably refused the offer to mediate by highlighting four of the relevant factors identified in *Halsey*: 'the nature of the dispute', 'the merits of the case', 'whether the cost of ADR would be disproportionately high and whether the ADR had a reasonable prospect of success'.[221] Mediation was appropriate on each criteria: First, small building cases were 'par excellence' suitable for mediation.[222] The 'merits of the case favoured mediation' and the defendants' conduct was unreasonable if they believed that their case was 'so watertight' that they did not need to contemplate 'any attempts at settlement'.[223] Furthermore, the

211 Brooker (2009) at 89–90; Brooker & Lavers (2002)
212 Gould et al. (2009)
213 Lord Justice Jackson (2009) at 467
214 *Burchell v. Bullard* [2005] EWCA Civ 358
215 *Burchell v. Bullard* [2005] at 2
216 *Burchell v. Bullard* [2005] at 2
217 *Burchell v. Bullard* [2005] at 3
218 *Burchell v. Bullard* [2005] at 20
219 *Burchell v. Bullard* [2005] at 7, 15 & 16
220 *Burchell v. Bullard* [2005] at 30
221 *Burchell v. Bullard* [2005] at 40
222 *Burchell v. Bullard* [2005] at 41
223 *Burchell v. Bullard* [2005] at 41

defendant's counterclaim for defective work was close to the completed contract price and not 'so watertight' that there was no room for the 'give and take' required for settlement plus it was 'nonsense' to suggest that the case was 'too complex' to mediate.[224] Neither was the cost of mediation considered a valid reason for refusing mediation as it would have been significantly less than litigating the matter.[225] Finally, the Court of Appeal took the view that the attitude of the claimant and his willingness to 'shoulder the blame' indicated that mediation would have had a good prospect of settling the dispute and the defendants should not be allowed to use their 'obstinacy' to suggest that mediation would not succeed.[226] However, the Court did not sanction the defendants because although the *Halsey* guidelines had been 'established' they had relied on advice from their 'surveyor' rather than a legal adviser and at the time of the dispute (2001) the law was not as 'clearly developed' as it was after the *Dunnett* and *Halsey* decisions.[227]

The Court took the opportunity to warn lawyers not to take mediation lightly because it has a 'stamp of approval' from the courts, a successful 'track' record in achieving settlement and the Construction Engineering Protocols 'requires' them to consider if 'some form of ADR' would be 'more suitable than litigation'.[228] Rix LJ concurred with Lord Justice Ward's judgment that the case was suitable for mediation, particularly at an early stage of the dispute, because of its 'merits, its structure and the risks in fighting it to its conclusion' but was less convinced that reliance can be placed on professionals or even legal advisors about mediating, which places substantial pressure on the parties when considering whether to mediate.[229] *Halsey* is concerned with successful parties rejecting mediation but Lord Justice Rix suggests that the question might 'arise in many different situations' including where the defendant had been 'the overall loser' and had 'exaggerated their counter-claim' and in such cases it would be 'easier' to apply the test of whether the rejection had been 'unreasonable'.[230]

The Court of Appeal returned to the suitability of small building cases for mediation in *Rolf v. De Guerin* in 2011 when the failure to mediate was seen as a 'lost opportunity' because the dispute was financially small and between a homeowner and builder.[231] There were problems with the work because of the alleged 'aggressive and interfering role' of Mrs Rolf's partner, which the defendant maintained led to him effectively losing control over the work.[232] Eventually the contract broke down when 'weekly payments' for the work

---

224 *Burchell v. Bullard* [2005] at 41
225 *Burchell v. Bullard* [2005] at 41
226 *Burchell v. Bullard* [2005] at 41
227 *Burchell v. Bullard* [2005] at 42
228 *Burchell v. Bullard* [2005] at 43
229 *Burchell v. Bullard* [2005] at 50
230 *Burchell v. Bullard* [2005] at 50
231 *Rolf v. De Guerin* [2011] EWCA Civ 78 at 1
232 *Rolf v. De Guerin* [2011] at 4 & 6

was stopped – at which point Mrs Rolf claimed £50,000 from Mr De Guerin for having to engage another builder to correct defects and complete the work.[233] Mr De Guerin counter claimed that the contract was not with him but with his company and that the claimants had repudiated the contract by ceasing to make any payments.[234]

What followed might politely be called horse-trading with the figures. Mrs Rolf made a Part 36 Offer for £14,000 including reasonable costs and issued another invitation to mediate but there was no response to this or other letters until Mr De Guerin asked for further information and indicated that his claim for repudiation of the contract was based on the cessation of payment for his work.[235] Mrs Rolf made a higher Part 36 offer with costs (£21,000) and again offered to mediate; Mr De Guerin did not respond, leading Mrs Rolf to issue another Part 36 offer.[236] Just before trial, Mr De Guerin's solicitors offered £14,000 over three years and Mrs Rolf counter offered with £21,000 and again suggested mediation.[237] Finally, Mr De Guerin's solicitors replied accepting £14,000 over three years and agreeing to mediate or attend settlement meetings but by this time the defendant was in a 'Debt Management Programme' and the offer was therefore 'unrealistic'.[238]

The trial eventually took place and Mr De Guerin, who had no legal representation, lost on the issue of the identity of the party to the contract but won on the issue of repudiation.[239] Mrs Rolf only won one of the three claims for defects for which she was awarded £2,500.[240] On the issue of costs for failing to mediate, unlike *Dunnett*, the court in *Rolf v. De Guerin* had not recommended mediation, nor had Mr De Guerin provided Mrs Rolf with reasons for refusing the offers to mediate or to attend 'roundtable meetings'.[241] Mr De Guerin's explanation for not mediating was that it would be 'admitting his guilt', he would not have been able to 'persuade the mediator' about what Mrs Rolf's partner was like, which the judge 'needed to see that for himself' and he 'wanted his day in court'.[242] The Court of Appeal held that these justifications did not 'bear real examination and were unreasonable'.[243] Furthermore the Court was persuaded by *Burchell v. Bullard* and Lord Jackson that mediation was appropriate for 'low value construction claims'.[244] On the 'facts' of the case the Court was satisfied that mediation or negotiation would

233 *Rolf v. De Guerin* [2011] at 6
234 *Rolf v. De Guerin* [2011] at 18
235 *Rolf v. De Guerin* [2011] at 21 & 22
236 *Rolf v. De Guerin* [2011] at 23
237 *Rolf v. De Guerin* [2011] at 26
238 *Rolf v. De Guerin* [2011] at 27
239 *Rolf v. De Guerin* [2011] at 28
240 *Rolf v. De Guerin* [2011] at 29
241 *Rolf v. De Guerin* [2011] at 48
242 *Rolf v. De Guerin* [2011] at 32
243 *Rolf v. De Guerin* [2011] at 48
244 *Rolf v. De Guerin* [2011] at 48 & 47; see Jackson (2009) at 4.6

have had 'reasonable prospects of success' but elected to not make any costs order because this would provide 'substantial justice between the parties'.[245]

The building cases discussed above were all relatively small in financial terms but there was strong judicial encouragement for mediation in *Brookfield Construction (UK) Ltd v. Mott MacDonald Ltd*, which involved a series of disputes over the building of the National Stadium.[246] The claimants were seeking huge damages from Mott for claims including: 'inadequate design information' (£13 million); 'design failure' (approximately £28 million); 'increased costs' (£4 million); 'delay and disruption' (approximately £100 million); 'settlement with other follow-on sub-contractors' (£41 million); 'additional claims for delay and disruption' (in excess of £60 million) and for 'invalid and/or over-valued-variations' (£2.7 million).[247] The building work had been the subject of previous litigation with *Cleveland Bridge UK Ltd* (CBUK)[248] but Coulson J was determined that the continuing action would not mirror events, so, following two Case Management Conferences (CMC) he recorded the 'principle matters' as an *'aide memoire'* with the stated aim of ensuring 'a sensible cost/benefit ratio for both parties'.[249]

Both parties were asked to 'estimate' their 'maximum likely recoverable costs' which Mott put at £27,494,500 and the claimants at £45,695,000 after which they were not to be able to recover beyond that amount.[250] To avoid the costs taking 'on an expensive life of its own', both litigants were advised to abandon the 'lack of co-operation' and 'solicitors and counsel were told to meet 'regularly' to resolve 'minor differences' thereby 'leaving only significant' issues to the court.[251] This advice was given with a 'robust encouragement to explore' ADR or mediation, particularly because such a 'large dispute' ('finance and documents') was 'ideally suitable for mediation'.[252] Both litigants were warned to consider ADR or mediation, 'sooner rather than later with an experienced construction practitioner' and should they fail to take the 'ADR option' this 'unwillingness' would be taken into account at the end of the sub-trial.[253]

Neighbourhood disputes

Another area of dispute that the courts have recommended ADR is between neighbours and families because the parties usually have to continue to live in close proximity ideally with a 'continuing relationship', which some models

---

245 *Rolf v. De Guerin* [2011] at 48
246 *Brookfield Construction (UK) Ltd. v. Mott MacDonald Ltd.* [2010] EWHC (TCC) 659 at 1
247 *Brookfield v. Mott* [2010] at 3
248 *Cleveland Bridge UK Ltd. v. Multiplex Constructions (UK) Ltd* [2010] EWCA Civ 139
249 *Brookfield v. Mott* [2010] at 6
250 *Brookfield v. Mott* [2010] at 48 & 49
251 *Brookfield v. Mott* [2010] at 52
252 *Brookfield v. Mott* [2010] at 53
253 *Brookfield v. Mott* [2010] at 53

of mediation may help to repair or at least permit an understanding 'of each others' perspectives'.[254] Disputes between neighbours often create 'extreme acrimony',[255] which blights people's lives resulting sometimes in physical illnesses or even, in extreme situations, in death.[256] Local councils, police authorities and housing associations now actively promote mediation as one way of tackling community disputes and judicial statements approve using alternatives to litigation, which is perceived to aggravate the problem. Mummery LJ began his opening statement in *Bradford v. James* by drawing attention to the devastating effect of neighbour disputes and recommended the use of 'local mediators', in this case practitioners experienced in 'legal and surveying skills', long before accessing the courts.[257] The dispute involved the transfer of ownership of a small 'cobbled area' alongside a converted barn when the title deeds had not clearly shown whether the land was included in an earlier sale of the property.[258] The court issued a 'salutary warning'[259] to mediate early before the parties become resistant to mediation and the dispute turns 'nasty and becomes expensive', particularly when the value of the dispute does not match the expense of litigation:[260]

> ... By the time neighbours get to court it is often too late for court-based ADR and mediation schemes to have much impact. Litigation hardens attitudes. Costs become an additional aggravating issue. Almost by its own momentum the case that cried out for compromise moves onwards and upwards to a conclusion that is disastrous for one of the parties, possibly for both.

In *Shah & Anor v. Joshi* the High Court emphasised the negative impact of litigating both in relation to the costs and the detrimental effect on the sibling relationship in a 'contentious probate' case where costs were sought at the indemnity level.[261] The defendants 'flatly refused' the claimants' invitation to mediate prior to proceedings, although just before trial there was an unsuccessful mediation.[262] Mr John Randall QC (Sitting as a Deputy Judge of the High Court) was 'struck' by the 'extreme desirability' of settlement when litigation costs outweigh the amount in dispute and when the 'familial

---

254 Noce et al. (2002) at 50–3
255 *Bradford v. James* [2008] EWCA Civ 837 at 2
256 See for example, Dignan et al. (1996); Brown et al. (2003); Mulcahy (2000)
257 *Bradford v. James* [2008] EWCA Civ 837 at 1
258 *Bradford v. James* [2008] at 2, 2–4
259 *Vale of Glamorgan Council v. Roberts* [2008] EWHC 2911 at 6. Lord Justice Mummery warned neighbours that they should mediate, although it is noted that in the *Vale of Glamorgan* case one of the parties was a council, which is rather removed from the close proximity of neighbours.
260 *Bradford v. James* [2008] at 1 & 9
261 *Shah & Anor v. Anupma Anil Joshi* [2008] EWHC 1766 (Ch) at 1–2
262 *Shah v. Joshi* [2008] at 4 & 7

relationship' remains 'unrepaired'.[263] The court gave an 'extended adjournment' for the parties to try to reach settlement after which it was revealed that the claimant made a 'significant move' by offering to divide the estate and let the defendants live in the house, whereas in contrast the defendant's counter offer was 'less generous and in the opposite direction'.[264] The court found that the claimants had evidenced more 'willingness to look at reasonable settlement proposals' but indemnity costs were only awarded from the 'second day of the trial onwards'.[265] The claim for indemnity costs based on the defendant's first refusal to mediate were not given because of the difficulty in assessing whether the mediation would have settled when the process two years later had failed, though it was doubted that this was likely on the 'combative performances' of the parties during proceedings.[266]

Although the courts consider building, neighbourhood or family disputes to be particularly suitable for mediation, *Halsey* and other cases generally suggest that most disputes are appropriate and unsuitability relates more to specific circumstances such as the requirement of evidence to defend claims, which connects to the timing of mediating. The court doubted that an early mediation would have succeeded in *Shah v. Joshi* because of evidence at the trial of the parties' attitude to the dispute two years after the proposal to mediate but of course their stance at this point may have had more to do with the consequences of engaging in litigation than mediating.

Delay and timing of mediation

The *Halsey* guidelines give weight to whether participating in mediation would unnecessarily delay a court hearing, which is relevant to whether a refusal has been reasonable, although Mackie et al. observe that there are advantages to engaging in the process even at a late stage as it can save court costs if issues are narrowed.[267] A number of court decisions have deliberated on the 'appropriate' timing for mediation, which comes down to 'balancing' whether the parties have enough information about the dispute in order to mediate effectively or whether it is reasonable for a party to wait until there is sufficient disclosure of evidence to respond to the claims against them. The

---

263 *Shah v. Joshi* [2008] at 7
264 *Shah v. Joshi* [2008] at 8 & 9
265 *Shah v. Joshi* [2008] at 10–11
266 *Shah v. Joshi* [2008] at 11
267 Mackie et al. (2007) at 107, 106–8. The authors discuss the benefits of mediating even when the process does not reach settlement because it can open up 'communication'; provide opportunities to assess the case or clarify 'misunderstandings. See Brooker & Lavers (2005a, b). Research in construction and commercial mediations suggest that settlement is only one benefit from mediating. See also Gould et al. (2007). Research into mediation in the TCC by Gould et al. reveals that there are a number of 'pinch points' when mediation settlement most commonly occurs: 'exchange of proceedings'; 'during or as a result of discovery'; after 'payment into court' and just before trial. Gould (2007) at 2.

pre-action protocols drive the litigation process through the exchange of pleadings, discovery of evidence and witness statements and entangle the timing of mediation within this framework.

There are a number of problems attached to delaying mediation until after the parties have fully engaged in the pre-action protocols and case management process. First, the protocols require litigants to consider or explore settlement but the expense of complying with the protocols can become a major obstacle hampering settlement because of the frontloading of costs.[268] Second, there is evidence from the cases that when lawyers or their clients find themselves in 'costs difficulties' sometimes strategic ADR or mediation offers are made.[269] Additionally, although *Halsey* confirms that the costs of mediating may be recoverable, the position of 'pre-action mediation' is less certain, which may influence when parties mediate.[270] The issue of delaying mediation is also frustrated because there are 'financially diminishing returns' the later in litigation that it takes place, although some parties prefer mediating once legal action has started because the process offers 'benefits' such as 'testing witnesses or evidence or narrowing issues'. Waiting to mediate may not present the best opportunity for a mediated settlement.[271]

The High Court gave an analysis about the timing of mediation in *Sixth Duke of Westminster v. Raytheon* when ordering a stay for mediation to take place in the USA after a claimant brought an action for 'negligent maintenance' of a Cessna plane in the English jurisdiction and proceedings against Cessna in Kansas for 'faulty design'.[272] Judge Wax in the Kansas court ordered mediation and asked the High Court if the defendants could be ordered to the same mediation.[273] Gross J first observed that the English courts can 'facilitate and encourage' mediation but not mandate attendance – although consideration can be given in costs if a party refuses a mediation offer.[274] The court provided three reasons for encouraging the parties to mediate: First, there were no grounds to believe that because mediation had been mandated in the USA that Cessna would not 'participate responsibly and constructively'.[275] Second, the claimant was 'on the face of it the innocent party' which made it desirable to bring all the parties together.[276] Finally, Gross J noted that mediating later in litigation might enable a clearer understanding

268 Lord Jackson (2009). See also; Lord Chancellor's Department (2002); Turner (2000); Goriely et al. (2002); Simmons & Howell-Richardson (2001); CEDR Civil Justice Audit (2000); Burr & Honey (2001)
269 *Wates Construction Ltd. v. HGP Greentrue Allchurch Evans Ltd* [2005] EWHC 2174 (TCC) at 29
270 *Halsey* [2004] at 21. See the discussion below on recovering the costs of mediating.
271 Brooker & Lavers (2005a) at 192. See also Brooker (2009) at 91; Gould et al. (2009); Mackie et al. (2007) at 106–8
272 *Sixth Duke of Westminster v. Raytheon* [2002] EWHC 1973 at 1
273 *Sixth Duke of Westminster v. Raytheon* [2002] at 2
274 *Sixth Duke of Westminster v. Raytheon* [2002] at 7
275 *Sixth Duke of Westminster v. Raytheon* [2002] at 10(1)
276 *Sixth Duke of Westminster v. Raytheon* [2002] at 10(2)

although it would increase costs of the dispute; but there was a 'trade off' between saving costs in an early mediation or participating with more information.[277] Judge Gross was in favour of early mediation despite the argument that the proceedings in the UK had been brought just before the hearing because the defendants had been aware of the dispute for some time, had been in receipt of the expert's report for over a year and had attended 'various tests and inspections' and furthermore 'key documents' could be provided before mediating.[278]

The court deliberated on the timing of a mediation offer in *Barnett v. Inland Revenue*, which involved a request for judicial review of a decision by the Inland Revenue.[279] Davis J did not find the facts of the case appropriate for mediation because the claim involved 'a very legal point' concerning overturning a decision by the Inland Revenue and the refusal to mediate would have been justified because it had been 'raised late in the day'.[280] In contrast, the court refused an application for a 'preliminary hearing' on an 'uncertain area of law' involving 'trade mark infringement' in order to avoid any delay in mediating in *Honda Giken Kogyo Kabushiki Kaisha (A Firm) v. Neesam*.[281] Fysh J considered that 'on balance' it was unlikely to appreciably decrease time at the final hearing, was likely to create a 'series of appeals' and could jeopardise the forthcoming mediation, which both parties had agreed to.[282] Furthermore a hearing on preliminary points was unlikely to enable the parties to 'narrow the gap' so that the planned mediation would have a 'realistic' chance of success and mediation which failed to settle would put the parties in a 'worse position than if the preliminary point had not been ordered'.[283] Therefore, the court refused the application because it 'would be likely' ('although no higher than that') to 'delay any mediation' and an order was issued for the parties to use their 'best endeavours' to mediate and to report progress to the court.[284]

In *Reed Executive Plc v. Reed Business Information Ltd*, (RBI) the Court of Appeal reviewed whether costs should be given for not using mediation on two possible occasions, first after it had been raised by the trial judge and then after Reed Employment suggested using the Court scheme after successfully winning the 'trade infringement and passing off case'.[285] At the time it was mentioned at trial most of the costs had been incurred and neither party made

---

277 *Sixth Duke of Westminster v. Raytheon* [2002] at 10(3)
278 *Sixth Duke of Westminster v. Raytheon* [2002] at 10(3)
279 *Barnett v. Inland Revenue (on the application of Barnett) v. Inland Revenue Commissioners* [2003] EWHC 2581 (Admin) at 5
280 *Barnett v. Inland Revenue* [2003] at 5 & 95
281 *Honda Giken Kogyo Kabushiki Kaisha (A Firm) v. Neesam (also known as Honda Motor Co Ltd v. Neesam)* [2009] EWHC 1213 (Pat) at 4
282 *Honda v. Neesam* [2009] at 22
283 *Honda v. Neesam* [2009] at 29
284 *Honda v. Neesam* [2009] at 39
285 *Reed Executive Plc v. Reed Business Information Ltd* [2004] EWCA Civ 887 at 41. This case is reviewed further in Chapter 5 in relation to without prejudice and confidentiality.

an offer to mediate but Reed Employment suggested the Court mediation scheme after winning the decision.[286] At this point Jacob LJ did not find RBI had unreasonably refused to negotiate when there was a metaphorical 'foot on their neck' and furthermore, a factor to be taken into consideration was the 'lateness in proposing ADR' and it 'was very late' at this point.[287] The Court of Appeal held that it was 'entirely reasonable for RBI to pursue the appeal' as they had a 'reasonable belief' of winning, which they were justified in holding.[288] They were facing disputes in 'other jurisdictions' and the case was 'full of novel points of law' making it 'tricky to formulate any deal', consequently, the possibility of ADR was 'not relevant' to the questions on costs.[289] The decision is in 'stark contrast' to *Dunnett* when the timing of the mediation offer was also just before an appeal but Railtrack was penalised for refusing the invitation after the court recommended its use, whereas no adverse award was issued in *Reed*, which Shipman suggests makes a party's belief in the 'strength' of a case 'influential' but not necessarily 'significant' on the early timing of ADR.[290] However, it does make it difficult for litigants and their legal advisors to predict the court's response to any refusal to mediate based on when the offer is made.[291]

The Court also reported that some parties use late mediation offers as a tactical ploy to deflect adverse costs in *Wates Construction Ltd v. HGP Greentrue Allchurch Evans Ltd.*[292] After a roof of a retail building collapsed, Wates Construction was sued for over half a million pounds in damages for 'negligent design' under a 'design and build contract'.[293] Wates denied liability but brought a Part 20 action against the architects, HGP, which was discontinued on the morning of the hearing following the experts' reports that the accident was caused by the failure of Wates to follow the architects' design.[294] HGP sought a costs order at the indemnity rate for the whole time or at the standard rate up to the time of the experts' reports and then at the higher rate when it was 'confirmed there was no case against' them.[295] Wates was not found to have conducted litigation in an unreasonable way up to the experts' reports, despite claims that they had failed 'to comply with pre-action protocols', failed 'to deal with disclosure properly', failed 'to plead a proper case', failed 'to address the fact they had deviated from HGP's design' and, finally, failed 'to pay the costs ordered' by the judge.[296] None of these shortcomings justified indemnity costs but Wates was ordered to pay at the higher costs'

286 *Reed* [2004] at 42–4
287 *Reed* [2004] at 45
288 *Reed* [2004] at 46
289 *Reed* [2004] at 46 & 47
290 Shipman (2006) at 198
291 See for example, Brooker (2009) (2010a); Shipman (2006); Brunsdon-Tully (2009)
292 *Wates Construction Ltd v. HGP Greentrue Allchurch Evans Ltd* [2005] EWHC 2174 (TCC)
293 *Wates Construction v. HGP* [2005] at 4 & 1
294 *Wates Construction v. HGP* [2005] at 5 & 6 & 20
295 *Wates Construction v. HGP* [2005] at 21
296 *Wates Construction v. HGP* [2005] at 11

rate for the period after the experts' reports when it had become 'apparent' that they had 'no claim against HGP' and they should have terminated the Part 20 proceedings.[297]

Coulson J did not take into consideration the mediation offer in the cost order but did make reference to the practice of lawyers making 'belated offers' when they found themselves in 'costs difficulties' and legal counsel were cautioned about pursuing this strategy.[298] The court gave a warning shot that attempts to strategically offer mediation just before trial is not the object of mediating nor is it 'in accordance' with the CPR rules and the assumption will be that a party refusing a late offer to mediate will have acted reasonably:[299]

> In the context of offers made, I have been referred to an offer by Wates' solicitors, on 21 September, of a possible mediation. Mr Nichol wisely did not push that point too hard. The mediation was proposed far too late for it to have any prospect of success, particularly given the impregnable position in which HGP found themselves so close to the start of the trial. Too often, in my recent experience, solicitors facing costs difficulties try to avoid them by making belated offers of mediation. That is not what mediation is for, and it is not a practice in accordance with the CPR.

The timing of mediation was at issue in *Witham v. Smith*, when the designers were eventually found to be liable for £1,683 for a 'design fault', which led Coulson J to cast doubt that the 'elaborate and expensive' process of litigation was appropriate for a dispute involving such 'modest sums' when the difference between the parties had been 'under £110,000'.[300] At the cost hearing, the court had to consider the 'novel' question whether the defendant's failure to mediate constituted unreasonable behaviour not because it was an outright refusal to mediate but because the agreement came very late in the litigation process when substantial costs had arisen.[301]

After reviewing the correspondence, Coulson J concluded that the defendants had not refused mediation out of hand but had 'consistently' indicated that they would mediate when the 'claim was properly set out' against them.[302] The court suggested the defendant had not unreasonably refused to participate in a 'pre-litigation offer' to mediate when the 'details of the claim' were not forthcoming and which had then been 'radically' amended before court action.[303] Coulson J observed that it was 'common practice' for claimants to make 'early' mediation offers but those defending

297 *Wates Construction v. HGP* [2005] at 11–12 & 25
298 *Wates Construction v. HGP* [2005] at 29. See for example, Brooker (2009) (2010a, b)
299 *Wates Construction v. HGP* [2005] at 29
300 *Nigel Witham Ltd. v. Smith & Anor* [2007] EWHC 3027 at 2 & 13
301 *Nigel Witham Ltd. v. Smith & Anor* [2007] at 9
302 *Nigel Witham Ltd. v. Smith & Anor* [2007] at 31
303 *Nigel Witham Ltd. v. Smith & Anor* [2007] at 31

require 'proper information' to enable an analysis of the 'commercial risk' before mediating.[304] It was also noted that 'premature mediation simply wastes time' and financial resources, and if unsuccessful runs the risk of both parties becoming entrenched in their 'positions'.[305] Conversely, leaving mediation until after 'full' discovery is also 'doomed to fail' because the costs at that point may themselves become the 'stumbling block'[306] for settling the dispute in mediation.[307] Parties are in the awkward position of having to 'identify the happy medium', when enough detail is known about the 'claim and response' but when costs are not so prohibitive that settlement becomes unlikely.[308]

In *Witham*, Coulson J doubted that an early mediation would have succeeded because of the claimant's 'uncompromising attitude' to both the 'claim and the defendants'.[309] Evidence from the documents revealed that Mr Witham had informed the mediator that the first defendant was a 'donkey' whom he had 'under enormous pressure', that they were 'clients from hell'.[310] The court acknowledged that both parties may have missed the 'critical moment' and that the settlement conference failed because both sides had significant costs and their 'attitudes had hardened' but blame could not be apportioned to either side and certainly not to the defendants for refusing an early mediation.[311] Coulson J did accept that in an 'exceptional case' the *Halsey* criteria would apply when an unsuccessful party 'unreasonably delayed' but on the facts the defendant had agreed to a settlement conference in a reasonable time and had mediation taken place the claimants' 'uncompromising attitude' precluded any 'prospect of success'.[312]

The Court of Appeal took the same approach to the timing of the offer in *S & Ors v. Chapman & ANR* (*Chapman*) when the defendants claimed that mediation would have been 'premature' before the 'exchange of documents, witness statements or expert evidence'.[313] Lord Justice Ward stated that he was in favour of mediating even before action had started but refused to criticise the respondents because they were 'entitled to see how the claim' for failing to provide adequate education was 'eventually made' and to 'take a stand accordingly'.[314] The Court held that the defendants' conduct in rejecting

---

304 *Nigel Witham Ltd. v. Smith & Anor* [2007] at 32
305 *Nigel Witham Ltd. v. Smith & Anor* [2007] at 32
306 *Charles Church Developments Ltd. v. Stent Foundations Ltd.* [2007] EWHC 855 (TCC) at 34
307 *Nigel Witham Ltd. v. Smith & Anor* [2007] at 32. See for example, *Samuel Smith Old Brewery (Tadcaster) v. Philip Lee* [2011] EWHC 1879 at 164. Mr Justice Arnold observed in a postscript that the costs were 'out of proportion to what was at stake', litigation had only served to entrench the parties' positions and they ought to have tried mediation at an 'early stage'.
308 *Nigel Witham Ltd. v. Smith & Anor* [2007] at 32
309 *Nigel Witham Ltd. v. Smith & Anor* [2007] at 36
310 *Nigel Witham Ltd. v. Smith & Anor* [2007] at 34
311 *Nigel Witham Ltd. v. Smith & Anor* [2007] at 33
312 *Nigel Witham Ltd. v. Smith & Anor* [2007] at 36
313 *S & Ors and Chapman & ANR (Chapman)* [2008] EWCA Civ 800 at 47
314 *Chapman* [2008] at 3 & 49

the first offer to mediate was reasonable because the particulars of the claim were 'wholly inadequate' and agreed with the argument that it was 'premature' before the attainment of adequate information.[315] The defendants refused the second mediation proposal because there was no 'reasonable arguable claim', which the Court of Appeal held was justified because the parents had 'unreasonably failed to respond to the perfectly proper request for further information' and also did not reply to an enquiry asking whether there were 'non-legal remedies' they might wish to pursue.[316] The claimants had 'swathes of particulars' cut out by the Master and the respondents achieved success on all the remaining claims which evidenced the reasonableness of their refusal to mediate and the Court confirmed the *Halsey* guidelines that it may be relevant to the reasonableness of conduct in refusing mediation if a party believes that they have a strong case.[317]

When considering whether the party has unreasonably refused to mediate the court will examine whether there is any 'prospect of success' for mediation at the time of the proposal.[318] In *Corby Group Litigation v. Corby DC* the claimants made an application for an interim order for costs estimated at over £4 million for a claim involving 18 people born with deformities after their mothers had been 'exposed to toxic materials' during work undertaken by Corby Borough Council (CBC).[319] The High Court declined to award costs at indemnity level because CBC had not 'acted reprehensibly in defending the case' and because it 'was difficult to understand on any sensible analysis what the Claimants' case truly was'.[320]

After reviewing the guidelines in *Halsey*, the court found the defendants were justified in rejecting the mediation offer until after expert evidence had been exchanged at which time they wrote to say 'there was no common ground between the parties', 'no reason to make any concessions' and mediation was 'highly unlikely to be productive'.[321] CBC dismissed another invitation to mediate three months later because their expert evidence backed their position and, although this analysis was later proved wrong, Akenhead J held the refusal is 'judged' when it is made and at that point the defendants were not unreasonable to think the parties would not reach settlement when mediating, particularly when the claimants used a 'scattergun approach' to the litigation.[322]

---

315 *Chapman* [2008] at 47
316 *Chapman* [2008] at 49
317 *Chapman* [2008] at 48
318 *Corby Group Litigation v. Corby DC* [2009] EWHC 2109 (TCC) at 23
319 *Corby Group Litigation v. Corby Borough Council* [2008] EWCA Civ at 1
320 *Corby Group Litigation* [2009] at 15
321 *Corby Group Litigation* [2009] at 23
322 *Corby Group Litigation* [2009] at 23. See Suter (2010) at 177–8. Suter suggests that the court should not have said that mediation had no prospect of success because mediating would have helped the council to understand the claims better.

Costs problems

There are cases where the legal costs eventually 'outstrip' the disputed liability and others which involve vast financial claims engendering eye-watering costs.[323] As costs escalate they can become the problem preventing settlement which leaves parties with the only perceived option of litigating to the end, in order to recover the legal expenditure of fighting the case – which was the issue in *Charles Church Developments Ltd v. Stent Foundations Ltd*.[324] Stent made an application for interim costs before the parties took part in a 'stayed' mediation.[325] Ramsey J found that the claimants had seriously breached the TCC pre-action protocols resulting in costs which 'might otherwise not have been incurred' and furthermore had failed to make an application for directions after issuing proceedings, which had prevented the case being settled without litigation.[326]

The claimant argued that Stent was trying to achieve 'a tactical advantage' in asking for costs at this stage of the proceedings because the parties could deal with this issue in the mediation but the court were persuaded by the defendant's argument that the mediation was 'more likely to fail if the question of costs is not resolved'.[327] Ramsey J noted that the parties were about to mediate with the additional costs 'incurred in context of (court) proceedings' rather than the lower 'pre-action protocol costs' and therefore awarded costs against the claimants at the greater rate to reflect the 'higher-cost atmosphere of court proceedings'.[328] The court considered that making an interim order before the mediation would eliminate the problem of higher costs to 1, allowing the parties to mediate in a way that more 'closely mirrors mediation at the end of a pre-action protocol procedure'.[329]

The courts are unlikely to find a party has unreasonably rejected mediation close to the trial when the offer has been made strategically to defend a likely costs order or has been proposed before the claim is set out and evidence exchanged. However, the question relevant to mediation practice remains. When should the parties mediate now that it is an integral part of CPR and the court protocols?[330] The timing may be crucial to a successful outcome in mediation though there is little research confirming when this point arrives.

---

323 See for example, *Brookfield Construction (UK) Ltd. v. Mott MacDonald Ltd.* [2010] EWHC (TCC) 659 at 1, 49. The dispute between the parties involved the building of the National Stadium and both parties had been asked to 'estimate' their 'maximum likely recoverable costs' (48) which Mott put at £27,494,500 and the claimants at £45,695,000 (49).
324 *Charles Church Developments Ltd. v. Stent Foundations Ltd. & Peter Dann Ltd.* [2007] EWHC 855 (TCC) at 34
325 *Charles Church Developments Ltd. v. Stent* [2007] at 15. See Barrett (2008) at 153–4. Barrett provides a detailed analysis of this case and others in relation to court decisions on the working of the CEPP protocols. See also Brooker (2010a) at 153–4
326 *Charles Church Developments Ltd. v. Stent* [2007] at 24–5, 31. See Practice Direction 2.3
327 *Charles Church Developments Ltd. v. Stent* [2007] at 34
328 *Charles Church Developments Ltd. v. Stent* [2007] at 46
329 *Charles Church Developments Ltd. v. Stent* [2007] at 35–6
330 Brunsdon-Tully (2009); Brooker (2009) (2010a)

However, there is evidence from some studies that settlement is more likely when the parties have a good comprehension of the issues.[331] For example, Henderson found that construction mediations in the USA were 'nearly twice' as likely not to settle if discovery has not taken place.[332] A more recent study of construction mediation in the TCC court in England found three 'points' when mediation settled: first when the parties exchanged pleading, second 'during' or shortly after disclosure and finally 'just before trial' which led to the recommendation that the court should not prescribe a time frame for mediation.[333]

Wates, *Witham* and *Charles Church Developments* illustrate 'the strategic interplay' between litigation and mediation on the issue of the most appropriate timing for mediation, which leads to a lack of certainty in the application of the *Halsey* guidelines.[334] Brunsdon-Tully believes that the *Halsey* criteria are not only 'vague' but leave the parties with no clear idea of 'whether' or 'at what point' they should mediate which may result in settlements that 'should never have occurred'.[335] Sorabji suggests that the ambiguity produced by the guidelines restricts the promotion of a 'settlement culture' under CPR and does little to advance mediation practice.[336] He recommends judges should pro-actively require parties to have 'properly particularised' their case at an early stage of proceedings to ensure adequate disclosure takes place to enable an analysis of the case and that indemnity costs should be awarded if a successful party fails to litigate in a way that 'facilitates the identification of the critical moment'.[337] In view of the difficulties that judges experience in identifying the correct time it is hardly beholden on the court to expect the parties to establish the best time, 'if it ever existed' and this failure may have catastrophic results in ratcheting up costs.[338]

Recovering mediation costs

The cases reviewing the application of adverse costs clearly support the justification of rejecting an offer when it is too early, before the party has a good appreciation of the case against them or so late that the parties are too entrenched to compromise or, as the *Halsey* criterion highlights, engagement will merely delay the trial. However, *Halsey* also reinforces the point that it may be possible to recover 'abortive' costs of an unsuccessful attempt at mediation.[339] The White Book raises three relevant matters on the recoverability of mediation costs: First, the general rules relating to recoverability of costs,

---

331 See for example, Kakalik et al. (1996); Henderson (1996)
332 Henderson (1996) at 145
333 Gould et al. (2009) at 31
334 Brooker (2010a) at 148; See also Brunsdon-Tully (2009); Sorabji (2008)
335 Brunsdon-Tully (2009) at 230
336 Sorabji (2008) at 430
337 Sorabji (2008) at 430
338 Per Coulson J in *Nigel Witham Ltd. v. Smith & Anor* [2007] at 33
339 *Halsey* [2004] at 21

second, the contractual arrangements made by the parties prior to mediating and third, whether the parties have engaged in pre action mediation or after commencing litigation.[340]

General rules on recovering costs – post action mediation[341]

When mediation forms part of the action, such as when the parties have begun proceedings and the court issues a stay for an attempt at ADR, then the successful party may be able to recover mediation costs.[342] Under s51 of the Supreme Court Act 1981,[343] the Court of Appeal, the High Court and the county courts have discretion to award costs that are 'of or incidental to the proceedings'. The position of recovering costs for 'post action' mediation[344] was confirmed in *Chantrey v. 'Convergence Group'* when a firm of chartered accountants issued proceedings for unpaid fees and the defendant counterclaimed for damages for professional negligence.[345] The court ordered a stay for mediation, which was unsuccessful after which the court found the defendant to be an 'evasive and untruthful witness' who knew that Chantrey was not the cause of the failure of the project.[346] Mediation costs were awarded discretionally under s51 of the Senior Court Act and because the 'overriding objective' of CPR requires the judge to 'manage cases actively' including 'encouraging' settlement through ADR procedures and 'facilitating' this through ordering a stay for mediation to take place.[347] Furthermore, the court referred to paragraph 17.3 of the Chancery Guide, 2005, which stipulates that an order may include the costs of an ADR procedure and to *Eagleston v. Liddel* where the Court of Appeal included mediation costs in a personal injury case.[348]

Contractual arrangements for fees

In *National Westminster Bank v. Feeney* ('*Feeney*'), the court observed that 'it is common ground that in principle' parties can claim for mediation costs because they are 'analogous' to costs incurred 'in connection with negotiations with a view to settlement' which under r 4.6 of CPR Part 23 are recoverable at the discretion of the judge.[349] The parties had agreed to settlement following mediation but the Tomlin Order did not expressly itemise the costs

---

340 White Book (2013) Section 14–19
341 *Lobster Group Ltd v. Heidelberg Graphic Equipment Ltd (and Another)* [2008] EWHC 413 (TCC) at 17
342 Supreme Court Act 1981 s51
343 Amended by Senior Court Act 1981
344 *Lobster* [2008] at 17
345 *Chantrey v. 'Convergence Group'* [2007] EWHC 1774 (Ch) at 1
346 *Chantrey v. 'Convergence Group'* [2007] at 218
347 *Chantrey v. 'Convergence Group'* [2007] at 226
348 *Chantrey v. 'Convergence Group'* [2007] at 227; *Eagleston v. Liddel* [2001] EWCA 155
349 *National Westminster Bank Plc v Feeney & Anor* [2006] EWHC 90066 (Costs) (30 November 2006) at 20 & 21

of mediating which had been undertaken through a CEDR Solve agreement whereby both agreed to pay the costs of the mediation 'equally' and their own expenses.[350] CEDR guidance notes in the contract advised that parties could alter the payment arrangements, perhaps to encourage one party to mediate or 'to take into account any court order' but no amendments had been made.[351] The court did not accept the bank's claim that the Tomlin Order 'overrode the terms of the Mediation agreement' because if the parties reached any agreement concerning the costs of mediating then they should have documented this as an 'express term'.[352]

Pre-action mediation

Both *Chantrey* and *Feeney* involved 'post-action mediation' but in *McGlinn v. Waltham* the parties had engaged in an unsuccessful 'pre-action' mediation involving allegations of defective work.[353] The claimant had 'correctly' followed the TCC's Pre-action protocol which involved mediating but, after the action was continued, dropped some of the claims, which led to a hearing for an 'interim payment' for the costs involved in responding to the discontinued claims.[354] In giving his judgment, Coulson J noted that there was 'no direct authority' on recovery of costs 'incurred in compliance with Pre-Action Protocols' but placed reliance on the Court of Appeal decision in *Callery v. Gray*,[355] when Lord Woolf CJ observed that they could be included, and held that costs 'incidental' to subsequent proceedings may be 'recoverable' depending on an 'assessment' of the facts by the court 'on each occasion'.[356] In *McGlinn*, the expenditure involved in the abandoned claim concerned an 'allegation of over payment', which was not regarded as 'incidental to proceedings' because it bore 'no relation' to defective work.[357] In the opinion of Coulson J, to hold otherwise would frustrate the objective of the pre-action protocol, which is to 'narrow the issues and allow a prospective defendant, wherever possible, to demonstrate to a prospective claimant that a particular claim is doomed to fail'.[358]

When the parties engage in 'pre-action' mediation then two considerations may be relevant: First, the contractual arrangements regarding the fees that the parties agree to (see *Feeney* above), second, whether the parties mediated as a response to the pre-action protocols.[359] *Lobster Group Ltd v. Heidelberg*

---

350 *Feeney* [2006] at 3 & 11
351 *Feeney* [2006] at 12, 13
352 *Feeney* [2006] at 19, 23–4, 28 & 33
353 *McGlinn v. Waltham Contractors Ltd* [2005] EWHC 1419 (TCC) at 1
354 *McGlinn v. Waltham* [2005] at 2 & 4
355 *Callery v. Gray* [2001] 1 WLR 2112 at 54
356 *McGlinn v. Waltham* [2005] at 8
357 *McGlinn v. Waltham* [2005] at 13
358 *McGlinn v. Waltham* [2005] at 14
359 See the White Book (2013) at Chapter 14.19

Graphic Equipment Ltd and Another involved an application for 'security costs', which included the costs of a 'pre-action' mediation.[360] Relying on the decision in *McGlinn*, Coulson J reiterated that costs incurred in complying with a pre-action protocol may be recoverable but when the 'pre-action period was lengthy' the further away the claimed costs are from commencing litigation the more likely that the 'losing party' will be able to 'dispute liability'.[361] The parties had agreed to pay their own costs in the CEDR-arranged mediation and Coulson J declined to include the 'pre-action mediation' costs because they were 'separate' to the 'pre-action protocol' costs and could not be described as 'cost of and incidental to the proceedings'.[362] The decision was influenced by the fact that the mediation had taken place 'two and half years' before trial and was seen to have 'no connection' to the court proceedings.[363]

Coulson J suggested that there may be exceptions for 'pre-action mediations' where an 'expert's report' is prepared for mediating and later used in court when it may be considered for the 'purposes' of 'materials ultimately proving of use and service in the action' but would require the parties to agree to the 'specific costs', which had not happened in *Lobster*.[364] Coulson J based his decision on the parties' agreement to pay their own costs of mediating because it would be wrong to 'upset or alter' what they had consented to.[365]

Coulson J gave further consideration on the recoverability of 'pre-action' mediation costs in *Roundstone Nurseries Ltd v. Stephenson Holding Ltd*.[366] The court ordered a stay for mediation but little progress had been made before proceedings were recommenced because of limitation problems, at which point a second stay was ordered at the parties' request.[367] By the time mediation was organised, Stephenson's expert report indicated that the defective floor was due to a design fault and they asked the designer to attend the arranged process, which they refused to do until they had more information.[368] Roundstone continued to ask for a reply to their letter of claim, which stated that they needed to comply with the pre-action protocol, but Stephenson refused because it would be in their position paper for mediation.[369] Both parties eventually exchanged position papers for mediating but the designer declined to participate and Stephenson withdrew from the

---

360 *Lobster* [2008] at 1–3
361 *Lobster* [2008] at 11–12
362 *Lobster* [2008] at 15–16
363 *Lobster* [2008] at 16
364 *Lobster* [2008] at 17: 'In such a situation the costs may be recoverable, in accordance with the principle set out in *Pecheries Ostendaises v. Merchants' Marine Insurance Co* [1928]' *Pecheries Ostendaises v. Merchants' Marine Insurance Co* [1928] 1KB 750, [1928] All ER
365 *Lobster* [2008] at 19 & 20
366 *Roundstone Nurseries Ltd. v. Stephenson Holding Ltd.* [2009] EWHC 1431
367 *Roundstone Nurseries Ltd.* [2009] at 7
368 *Roundstone Nurseries Ltd.* [2009] at 14
369 *Roundstone Nurseries Ltd.* [2009] at 15

mediation just under a week before it was due to take place.[370] The court refused to award a judgment 'in default of defence' because when a party knows that a defendant has a 'real prospect' of defending the claim the application was not made in a 'proper manner' and consequently the claimant should 'face the costs consequences'.[371]

Roundstone was seeking indemnity costs, which included a failure on the part of Stephenson to comply with the pre-action protocols by 'withdrawing' from the mediation and not providing a response to the letter of claim.[372] Coulson J, however, accepted Stephenson's argument that the response was set out in the mediation papers which was reasonable.[373]

The cancellation of the mediation was difficult because it raised a number of matters.[374] The court reiterated that where parties have organised a pre-action mediation and agreed to share the costs then this will 'not normally' be regarded as 'cost of or incidental to the proceedings' (*Lobster* considered)[375] but the parties could recover costs incurred during the 'pre-action protocol process' (*McGlinn* considered).[376] Therefore, it was necessary to consider whether the organised mediation was a 'standalone' or part of the 'pre-action process' and both parties had considered their arrangements to mediate were an 'attempt to comply with the Pre-Action process'.[377] Coulson J found it of significance that the TCC pre-action process is the only protocol that requires the parties to meet 'without prejudice' and the absence of discussion on without prejudice meetings suggested to the court they regarded mediating 'as part of the Pre action Protocol Process'.[378] Furthermore their contractual arrangements for mediation had not stipulated that the parties would 'pay their own costs' or that the costs could not be 'subsequently sought' at a future court hearing and therefore, in *Roundstone* the abortive mediation costs were 'recoverable in principle'.[379]

Coulson J concluded that, first, the defendants were wrong to call off the mediation because it was a 'part of the pre-action process', second, without mediating neither party could have 'fulfilled' their requirements under the protocol, which required engagement in a 'without prejudice meeting', third, when the mediation was organised there was no thought of 'inviting' the designer and Stephenson should have proceeded with the arrangements.[380] Finally, it was 'not unreasonable' for the designer to refuse to attend the mediation because of the late date of the expert's report.[381] Costs, however,

---

370 *Roundstone Nurseries Ltd.* [2009] at 22
371 *Roundstone Nurseries Ltd.* [2009] at 36
372 *Roundstone Nurseries Ltd.* [2009] at 43–4
373 *Roundstone Nurseries Ltd.* [2009] at 44
374 *Roundstone Nurseries Ltd.* [2009] at 45
375 *Roundstone Nurseries Ltd.* [2009] at 46
376 *Roundstone Nurseries Ltd.* [2009] at 48
377 *Roundstone Nurseries Ltd.* [2009] at 49 & 50
378 *Roundstone Nurseries Ltd.* [2009] at 51
379 *Roundstone Nurseries Ltd.* [2009] at 52 & 53
380 *Roundstone Nurseries Ltd.* [2009] at 54(a) & 54(b) & 54(c)
381 *Roundstone Nurseries Ltd.* [2009] at 55

were not awarded on the indemnity basis because Stephenson had made a '*bona fide* but not correct decision' to withdraw from the mediation which had 'perhaps' not been properly thought through.[382]

The White Book observes that mediations are now 'increasingly carried out pre-proceedings', although some research suggests that parties wait until proceedings are commenced. The timing has implications for when the parties can recover costs and is likely to influence the legal advice on when the process should take place.[383] The cases which favour delaying mediating until after evidence is compiled in order that the defendant can address the claims against them and the unlikelihood of recovering 'pre-action' mediation costs 'militates' against early attempts at mediation and does little to encourage a change of approach to dispute resolution or negotiation practice prior to beginning court action.[384]

The case law on the timing of mediation and the recovery of costs for unsuccessfully mediating illustrate how CPR and the protocols bring mediation resolutely into litigation rather than operating as a voluntary process before the parties contemplate court action.[385] Mediation cannot truly be described as a 'track to a just result running parallel with that of the court system'[386] but rather as process, which has a symbiotic relationship with litigation, such as developed with arbitration and the law.[387] The law is 'normalising'[388] mediation practice through an application of the rules governing litigation and as the process is instituted in the Civil Justice System this permits a 'tactical interplay' between both procedures.[389] Both *Witham* and *Wates* exemplify the 'token notice' that some litigants exhibit towards CPR requirements for party cooperation and how the institutionalisation of the process within litigation has made it possible for some parties to use it tactically as 'evidence apparent compliance' with the rules.[390] The next section explores further case evidence that lawyers and their clients employ mediation offers to counter adverse costs.

No serious intent to use ADR or mediation

Just before *Halsey*, the Court of Appeal in *Cressman* refused to award costs because on the evidence there was no serious commitment to engage in mediation. The courts have returned to his theme on a number of occasions when parties' communications do not evidence a 'genuine intention' to use

---

382 *Roundstone Nurseries Ltd* [2009] at 55
383 White Book (2013) at Chapter 14.19; Gould et al. (2009); Brooker (2010a) at 154
384 Brooker (2010a) at 154; Brunsdon-Tully (2009)
385 Brooker (2009) (2010a). See also Brunsdon-Tully (2009)
386 *Burchell v. Bullard* (2005), per Lord Justice Ward at 43
387 This relationship is similar to that developed between arbitration and litigation. See Chapter 1. See for example, Yarn (2004) at 939; Flood & Caiger (1993); Lane (1986); Abrahams (1988); Parris (1978)
388 Allen (2008); Brunsdon-Tully (2009)
389 Brooker (2010a)
390 See for example, Brooker (2010a) at 153; Clark (2012) at 5

ADR or mediation.[391] What such conduct does show is that parties and/or their legal advisors are negatively exploiting CPR and how the institutionalisation of mediation permits the strategic exploitation of the costs rules. In other words, the parties are merely paying lip service to the CPR in order to avoid future costs penalties.

In *Re Midlands Services Ltd*, the HC discerned that the mediation offer was not genuine and the reason for making it may have been to delay proceedings.[392] The respondents (Midlands Linen) asked the court to take into consideration a refusal of a settlement offer made at the time of the Employment Tribunal, which was the same amount as the final Part 36 offer, and the rejection of 'consistent offers to mediate' or 'take part in settlement negotiation'.[393] The court noted that the trial had taken one and a half days and had accrued costs of £60,000 to 'recover' £80,000.[394] The Court of Appeal considered that when exercising discretion on costs under CPR 44.3 the question was whether the petitioner as 'the successful party' had 'unreasonably' refused to mediate or 'abide by a suggestion' of 'the Registrar' that the 'case was suitable for mediation'.[395] In reviewing the correspondence the court noted mediation had been rejected because of the solicitors' belief that the offer was only made to 'further attempt to delay matters and prevaricate'.[396] Midland Linen's offers to mediate contained no 'specific proposals' about the 'appointment' of a mediator or communications with the ADR provider, only repeatedly mentioned mediation but then 'let it drop'.[397] The rejection was reasonable because the respondents failed to prove that they 'seriously intended' to engage in the process and had not taken 'steps' to set it in motion.[398] Furthermore, they had exhibited a 'pattern . . . of making and withdrawing offers', which led the court to conclude that the 'atmosphere' did not exist for a 'successful' outcome in mediation.[399]

In *Vale of Glamorgan Council v. Roberts* the High Court had to assess whether the council should be denied some of their costs after winning all but one section of a boundary dispute when the defendant claimed they had refused to engage in 'serious settlement negotiations or to mediate'.[400] Lewison J noted

---

391 See *Cressman* [2004] above
392 *Re Midland Linen Services Ltd, Chaudhry v. Yap* [2004] EWHC 3380 (Ch) at 1. See Shipman (2006) at 203. Shipman suggests that the offer was just a 'delaying strategy' and observes the comments made by solicitors in Genn's mediation study in 2002. Genn (2002)
393 *Re Midland Linen Services Ltd* [2004] at 6
394 *Re Midland Linen Services Ltd* [2004] at 7
395 *Re Midland Linen Services Ltd* [2004] at 14, 32 & 40
396 *Re Midland Linen Services Ltd* [2004] at 44
397 *Re Midland Linen Services Ltd* [2004] at 53
398 *Re Midland Linen Services Ltd* [2004] at 56
399 *Re Midland Linen Services Ltd* [2004] at 59–60. See Shipman (2006) at 203. Shipman suggests that when the court is aware of 'deliberate delaying tactics' this should be relevant to any prospect of success in mediation.
400 *Vale of Glamorgan Council v. Roberts* [2008] EWHC 2911 at 2

that many of the offers made by the defendant were in reality 'assertions of the merits of his own case or offers to buy the land in the dispute' and the council was under no 'obligation' to sell, was entitled to take the stance it did against the claim and, because the offer to mediate had not been 'positively' made, was not penalised for not acting on the 'suggestions for mediation'.[401] A party cannot claim that it has offered to mediate unless it is clear that this is what it has done and judges are unlikely to be swayed by a party attempting to massage tentative suggestions of settlement or negotiation into proposals to mediation in order to escape some or all of their costs.

The court was equally unimpressed in *Alexandra Wills v. Mills & Co Solicitors* when the unsuccessful litigant contended that she had asked the judge to take into consideration both her own and her solicitor's attempts to 'resolve the matter' and the defendant's lack of interest in any settlement.[402] After reviewing the case, Mance LJ did not accept the applicant's assertion that the judge had recommended that the parties attempt mediation at the end of the trial when he used the following words:[403]

> That will give you time to tell them and negotiate, or whatever it is, but you may, it is not for me to tell you, think it appropriate to get some form of legal advice. I know you are a lawyer yourself. It is a matter for you.

Nor was it clear that there had been 'conversations' between the solicitors to the effect that the defendant 'was not interested in mediation' but His Honour did recognize that it would have been better had the judge explained why the successful party was not penalised for failing to mediate.[404] Although *Halsey* identifies that court encouragement of ADR is relevant when considering adverse costs, the Court of Appeal did not accept that the judge's words had encouraged mediation 'or if it did, it was extremely weak encouragement' and had not been 'recorded in the order'.[405] After reviewing the case the Court held the defendants had not refused to mediate unreasonably because there was no 'prospect' of mediation success and the defendants were 'entitled to know the case before them' and after knowing this to take 'the view that the application was bound to fail'.[406]

---

401 *Vale of Glamorgan Council* [2008] at 8
402 *Alexandra Wills v. Mills & Co Solicitors* [2005] EWCA Civ 591 at 50
403 *Alexandra Wills v. Mills* [2005] at 53
404 *Alexandra Wills v. Mills* [2005] at 63–4
405 *Alexandra Wills v. Mills* [2005] at 66; See *Barr & Ors v. Biffa Waste Services Ltd* [2012] EWCA Civ 312. There had been discussion at the appeal hearing on the possible alternatives for ADR but the CA observed that until the judgment had been seen by both parties it was 'understandable' that no decision had been taken but a recommendation to use the CA Mediation Scheme required this to be put in an order. *Barr v. Biffa* [2010] at 49
406 *Alexandra Wills v. Mills* [2005] at 68–9

In *Colman v. General Medical Council* the claimant, a doctor and trained barrister, brought a case with 'no merit' against the GMC and others, in what was described as 'obsessive litigation'.[407] The successful defendants would be awarded their costs but the claimant cited the *Halsey* principles and other 'authorities' to support her contention that the court should use their discretion to consider 'what efforts have been made to resolve the dispute' and the 'risks' for not using ADR or mediation.[408] Royce J found that the defendants had 'behaved perfectly reasonably' and had 'taken steps to bring the litigation to an end' whereas the claimant had been 'happy to launch proceedings' for 'misconceived and spurious allegations' regardless of implications for 'costs consequences'.[409] The High Court was unprepared to use its discretion in this case because of the unreasonable way that the claimant had conducted litigation in comparison to the defendants and in effect suggested that her allegations were not justified because she herself had not evidenced any desire to settle her dispute through any method (discussion, negotiation or mediation) other than litigation. A party cannot just claim that the other litigant refused mediation or other methods of resolving a dispute when the evidence indicates that the offer is specious.

The court had to consider the claim that a failure to give any response to a mediation offer was not a rejection and an allegation that the proposal to mediate had not been genuine in *PGF 11 SA v. OMFS*.[410] The claimants accepted a Part 36 offer the day before trial when they became aware that the defendants were amending their defence to deny liability because the 'defect in the air-conditioning' did not come within the terms of the 'repairing obligations' in the 'under-lease'.[411] They had made the first offer to mediate when responding to a Part 36 offer but the defendants did not reply to this or to an invitation to use mediation two month later.[412] The claimant asserted that had mediation taken place the issue relating to the 'under lease' would have become known during 'preparations for the mediation'.[413] The claimant alluded to all of *Halsey*'s six criteria in the application, which illustrates how the guidelines are used to mount a claim that an offer has been unreasonably rejected.[414] It was contended that the case was suitable for mediation, there was 'nothing' to suggest the defendant believed the case was 'so strong that it was reasonable to refuse', they had engaged in 'negotiations' through Part 36 offers, neither party was 'unrealistic' about the 'merits' of its case, 'the cost' of mediating would not have been 'disproportionately high' nor would it create

---

407 *Colman v. General Medical Council* [2007] EWHC 1090 (QB) at 5 & 17
408 *Colman v. GMC* [2007] at 15 & 16
409 *Colman v. GMC* [2007] at 17 & 20
410 *PGF II SA v. OMFS Co* [2012] EWHC 33
411 *PGF II SA v. OMFS Co* [2012] at 4
412 *PGF II SA v. OMFS Co* [2012] at 19
413 *PGF II SA v. OMFS Co* [2012] at 23
414 See for example, Brooker (2009) (2010a)

delay and the process had a 'reasonable prospect' of succeeding.[415] Furthermore, the claimant argued that the mediator would be able to apply his or her skills to tease out 'seemingly intractable positions'.[416]

The defendant counter argued that there were considerable variations in the amount claimed and they had to wait for 'full disclosure' to discover whether the work done was 'repair or upgrading work', which meant they were 'unable to engage in reasonable discussions'.[417] They contended that a failure to respond did not mean that they were refusing to mediate and there was no 'reasonable prospect' of the mediation being successful.[418] The defendant also maintained that it was reasonable to refuse mediation because of the claimant's behaviour in a previous mediation but the court gave this short shrift for two reasons:[419] First, the claimant had not waived privilege in connection with the mediation[420] and second, had the claimant's previous conduct been the reason for the refusal, the court would have expected this to have been given in a reply. By not responding the defendant failed to establish 'evidence' that this behaviour was the reason for rejecting the offer. The court held that it was unreasonable 'not to respond' to the offer or agree to mediate because the *Halsey* criteria were present in this case including a 'reasonable prospect that the mediation would have been successful' even should the information about the 'under-lease' not have been available because the mediation would have involved 'commercial parties' with 'experienced lawyers'.[421]

The final argument made by the defendants to justify refusing mediation was that the offer was not 'genuine' because it was only made to 'pressurise' them into settling at a higher amount and had only been issued 'at the last moment' to avoid costs for their 'unreasonable failure to accept an eminently reasonable offer'.[422] The court did not believe that the 'claimant was merely going through the motions' nor that they would not have mediated should the defendant have agreed to their offer.[423] A 'warning' was issued to future courts to be 'wary' of 'retrospective' 'arguments' produced without evidence such as the need for reports, which are only raised to bolster reasons for not mediating because they are 'easy to put forward and difficult to prove or disprove' and should be made at the time of the offer when they might be 'overcome'.[424]

---

415 *PGF II SA v. OMFS Co* [2012] at 25
416 *PGF II SA v. OMFS Co* [2012] at 25
417 *PGF II SA v. OMFS Co* [2012] at 30
418 *PGF II SA v. OMFS Co* [2012] at 31–2
419 *PGF II SA v. OMFS Co* [2012] at 29, 32 & 44
420 See Chapter 5 for a discussion of without privilege. *Farm Assist Ltd. (in liquidation) v. The Secretary of State for the Environment, Food and Rural Affairs (No. 2)* [2009] EWHC 1102 (TCC)
421 *PGF II SA v. OMFS Co* [2012] at 42
422 *PGF II SA v. OMFS Co* [2012] at 45.2 & 34
423 *PGF II SA v. OMFS Co* [2012] at 45.2
424 *PGF II SA v. OMFS Co* [2012] at 44

Allen sees this as a 'gloss' on Halsey, which makes it more probable that costs will be awarded when the '*Halsey* criteria' are met:[425]

> This is a gloss on *Halsey* which does much to remind us that *Halsey* actually decides that costs sanctions are permissible against a successful party who either ignores a judge's recommendation or another party's genuinely intended invitation to mediate, so long as the *Halsey* criteria are met. *Halsey* read through the eyes of this decision seems somewhat more daunting than before.

Normalising practice and utilising the *Halsey* guidelines

Although one of the objectives of the *Halsey* guidelines is to help extrapolate which disputes are appropriate for mediation, cases such as *PGF v. OMFS* reveal that a by-product of producing criteria has led many litigants to use mediation as part of their litigation strategy.[426] In effect, the parties, or perhaps more accurately their legal advisors, use the criteria as an 'armoury' to mount or lead arguments against adverse costs.[427] A typical example of how this is achieved is found in *P4 v. Unite*,[428] which was heard by the TCC.

P4 v. Unite

Ramsey J found that *P4 v. Unite* was a 'classic example' of an appropriate case for mediating because it would have provided the opportunity to explore missing evidence and discuss the confusion over information, which was central to reaching a resolution to the dispute.[429] P4 contended that Unite had installed lighting provided to Unite's sub-contractor, who had become bankrupt, knowing that there was a 'Retention of Title' clause and although they won the case, they were only awarded £387 of the £70,000 claimed, which did not exceed any of the Part 36 offers.[430] Unite were claiming costs at 'indemnity basis' but P4 argued that such an order would be 'unjust' because the defendants had unreasonably rejected their offer to mediate.[431]

P4 had made requests to Unite to provide evidence that they had paid for the lighting but the information they received did not itemise P4's goods which only became available after 'disclosure' when the court found that the

---

425 Allen (2012)
426 See for example, Brooker (2009) (2010a); Shipman (2006)
427 Brooker (2010a) at 151
428 *P4 Ltd v. Unite Integrated Solutions Plc* [2006] EWHC 2924 (TCC)
429 *P4 Ltd v. Unite* [2006] at 46
430 *P4 Ltd v. Unite* [2006] at 7 & 1
431 *P4 Ltd v. Unite* [2006] at 3–4

'property had passed to Unite'.[432] Unite claimed that this issue was 'not determinative' but Ramsey J observed that had this information been available 'during the pre-action protocol' then it would have altered 'P4's approach' because it would have assisted their appreciation of 'Unite's case', which would have helped 'to resolve the dispute'.[433]

After the second Part 36 offer P4 made an offer to mediate or 'preferably to have a meeting' but Unite's solicitors rejected the offer stating that their clients wanted 'to defend it (any claim) vigorously', which the court found was a rejection of a proposal to mediate.[434] P4 made a second offer to use ADR after issuing proceedings, which was rejected by Unite as a 'cynical attempt' to escape costs by using *Halsey*, and was 'not in the spirit of CPR and the practice directions' and at this time they asked P4 why they had not offered to mediate before issuing proceedings.[435] Unite's solicitor continued by saying that they would be 'prepared to mediate' but did 'question whether it would be a worthwhile exercise' as they had 'already considered ADR' which was evidenced by a without prejudice offer.[436]

Unite's legal representatives provided further reasons for rejecting mediation which were based on the *Halsey* guidelines:[437] First, Unite believed that they had a 'very strong case' because they had a 'complete defence' based on s25 on the Sale of Goods Act 1979; their clients had tried 'other settlement methods' such as offering £10,000 which P4 rejected and were not taking a 'stubborn and entrenched stance'; mediation was too 'expensive' in relation to the costs of the case and they did not believe there was a 'reasonable prospect' of success because there was a 'fundamental disagreement' over 'an issue of law' about the 'meaning of notice' and an 'issue of fact' relating to the 'terms and conditions of the contract', both of which needed 'final determination by the judge'. Finally, Unite alluded to P4's increasing offers for settlement, which did not indicate they had 'adopted the correct mind set' for successful mediation or were prepared to 'compromise'.[438]

In 'submissions' before the court Unite claimed that their response to mediation had been reasonable because first, the 'nature of the dispute' was that they were in a long-term relationship and there were 'allegations of bad faith' which *Halsey* suggested were factors making the case unsuitable.[439] The 'merit' of their case was that they had a 'strong case' as success at trial had proved. They had made other 'settlement offers' which P4 refused and 'as in *Halsey*' they had made 'efforts to settle' but P4 had an 'unrealistic view' about

432 *P4 Ltd v. Unite* [2006] at 8 & 9
433 *P4 Ltd v. Unite* [2006] at 9–11
434 *P4 Ltd v. Unite* [2006] at 15–16
435 *P4 Ltd v. Unite* [2006] at 18
436 *P4 Ltd v. Unite* [2006] at 18
437 *P4 Ltd v. Unite* [2006] at 20
438 *P4 Ltd v. Unite* [2006] at 20
439 *P4 Ltd v. Unite* [2006] at 26

their case.[440] Unite claimed that the 'costs of mediation would be disproportionately high' and that there was little prospect of success because P4 'unreasonably increased' their offers. The only factor that they did not use in their defence was that mediation would have caused any delay.[441]

P4 also ran through the *Halsey* factors to show that Unite had behaved unreasonably in refusing to mediate. First, the nature of the dispute involved 'dispute facts' which Dyson LJ had said were 'intrinsically suitable for resolution by mediation' and had the parties mediated they would have been able to 'elicit and evaluate what was being said by the other side'.[442] They argued there were 'no countervailing factors' under the 'merit' criteria indicating the unsuitability of mediation because a 'belief in a watertight case is no justification' and 'borderline cases are likely to be suitable'.[443] P4 drew attention to the fact that Unite had not made suggestions for 'any without prejudice process' nor showed any 'willingness to compromise' and they disputed Unite's view that mediation would have been too costly compared to the hearing that had taken place when a one-day mediation would have sufficed.[444] They agreed with Unite that mediating would not have created any delay because they made the proposal 'before proceedings were issued' and finally had either mediation or a 'pre-action meeting' taken place the necessary information for resolving the disputes would have been 'exchanged' and this 'failure' was created by Unite's unreasonable behaviour.[445]

In coming to this judgment, Ramsey J noted the *Halsey* factors 'are not exclusive' and it was 'not' a case where there was a 'long-term relationship' requiring a 'resolution of a point of law'.[446] The issues of the case, whether the 'retention of title clause' had been incorporated, how many 'unfixed lighting fittings were on site' and 'whether Unite had paid its sub-contractor', all made *P4* a 'classic' case for mediation at the 'pre-action phase'.[447]

Unite's belief on the 'retention of title' point was not 'watertight' as claimed and only became 'stronger' 'during proceedings' when it was found that P4 had faxed over the contract without the 'terms and conditions on the back'.[448] At the time that P4 proposed mediation, Unite could not 'reasonably have thought that they had a watertight case' as they 'had risks on a number of issues'.[449] Although Ramsey J noted that P4 had increased their Part 36 offers indicating an 'increasingly unrealistic view' of their case, which might have been relevant to any refusal, the most pertinent criterion was whether

440 *P4 Ltd v. Unite* [2006] at 26
441 *P4 Ltd v. Unite* [2006] at 26
442 *P4 Ltd v. Unite* [2006] at 31; *Halsey* [2004] at 78
443 *P4 Ltd v. Unite* [2006] at 31
444 *P4 Ltd v. Unite* [2006] at 31
445 *P4 Ltd v. Unite* [2006] at 31 & 32
446 *P4 Ltd v. Unite* [2006] at 34
447 *P4 Ltd v. Unite* [2006] at 34
448 *P4 Ltd v. Unite* [2006] at 35
449 *P4 Ltd v. Unite* [2006] at 36

mediation would have succeeded.[450] Solicitors' letters containing offers of settlement were not a 'substitute' for ADR procedures where a 'mediator' assists the parties to have a 'realistic' view of their case.[451] The costs of mediation would not have been 'disproportionate' because they were negligible compared to the costs of proceedings and the commercial costs of dealing with the dispute both of which should have been taken into account.[452] Unite were wrong to suggest that P4 had not offered to mediate before trial, which indicated that they were not 'seriously considering ADR'.[453] Finally, Ramsey J considered whether mediation would have had a 'reasonable prospect of success' which required an analysis of the 'objective view of the facts' and the 'subjective approach of the parties'.[454] In this case there would 'not only have had a reasonable prospect, but a good prospect of succeeding' even if the letter suggested the parties were 'intransigent' because this often changed when they come 'face to face' with a mediator.[455] The case was a suitable case for mediating, particularly when the parties had a commercial history and P4 had been 'looking to develop' this relationship.[456] Had Unite explained that they had 'paid' their sub-contractor for the lighting this would have altered P4's 'perception' of the case and therefore the defendant's refusal to agree to 'any face by face meeting' was found to be 'unreasonable'.[457] Unite were not deprived of all their costs but 'justice was served' by sanctioning their unreasonable behaviour in refusing mediation and awarding P4 costs 'up to the time of the Part 36 order'.[458]

The *Halsey* criteria forms the basis of the costs arguments for both successful and unsuccessful litigants but following the decision in *PGF v. OMFS*, Allen suggests that litigants should not 'ignore good faith invitations to mediate' and if there are reservations about mediating these should be put 'in writing, setting out reasons fully in a way likely to appeal to judges later'.[459] Correspondence and without prejudice communications are now likely to be scattered with observations about why the party has not chosen to mediate to strengthen later attacks on costs and statements rejecting mediation, or putting the decision on hold, and should include references to requiring more information or disclosure before mediating. Before taking that route, Allen cautions future litigants that Mr Recorder Furst QC remarked in *PGF v. OMFS* that settlement before trial is often before all the evidence has been established and that participants in mediation either 'know or are prepared to

---

450 *P4 Ltd v. Unite* [2006] at 37
451 *P4 Ltd v. Unite* [2006] at 38
452 *P4 Ltd v. Unite* [2006] at 39
453 *P4 Ltd v. Unite* [2006] at 40
454 *P4 Ltd v. Unite* [2006] at 41
455 *P4 Ltd v. Unite* [2006] at 44
456 *P4 Ltd v. Unite* [2006] at 45
457 *P4 Ltd v. Unite* [2006] at 46 & 44–5
458 *P4 Ltd v. Unite* [2006] at 49
459 Allen (2012)

assume' that during the process the 'information is likely to be available'.[460] Comments about whether the offer to mediate is genuine are easy to make and a party who has real concerns about mediating should raise it contemporaneously but be aware that the court will not take it at face value.

The problem remains for potential litigants that there is a delicate balance when considering any mediation offer. Although, practically it may be safer to agree to mediation even if there are any residual doubts about the timing or the completeness of evidence, this option has been dictated by linking mediation within the litigation phase and effectively provides disputants with limited self determination or choice.

Anti-litigation rhetoric and mediation ideology

One theme that reoccurs in the judgments is the view that mediation would have been a better option than litigating, often as a reaction to the confrontational and adversarial approach in litigation, which is perceived to result in exorbitant costs, delay, stress and sometimes neither litigant gaining significant advantages from seeking a court resolution. Judges, who are devotees of mediation, impart vigorous criticism on lawyers and their clients who fail to appreciate mediation.[461] Commentators question whether the level of approval given to mediation is redolent of an 'anti-litigation'[462] stance similar to that propounded at the Pound Conference[463] in the USA, which presented a 'jaundiced' picture of litigation where an increasingly litigious society brought cases with little merit and juries awarded vast damages in an 'arbitrary, unpredictable, berserk, demented' civil system which had 'spun out of control'.[464] The federal judiciary in the USA was reported to have 'adopted an anti adjudication and pro-settlement agenda'[465] where the potential outcomes of ADR processes were portrayed as being better than the legal outcome of a court decision where only one side wins:[466]

> Substantive law is perceived as frustrating creative results and causing undesirable 'winner-take-all' outcomes. Compromise, rather than application of substantive principles, seems the ADR norm and the basis of the claim that ADR is qualitatively superior to litigation.

---

460 *PGF II SA v. OMFS Co* [2012] at 45.1. See Allen (2012)
461 See Genn (2010) at 96–103; Shipman (2006) at 188–9
462 Genn (2010) at 119–20. See also Genn (2012); Thornberg (2011); Brunsdon-Tully (2009)
463 See for example, Resnik (1998); Galanter (1998); Thornberg (2011)
464 Galanter (1998) at 717, discussed in Chapter 1
465 Resnik (1998) at 995
466 Brunet (1987) at 4–5

More cynically an anti-litigation stance is said to stem from 'corporate inter-ests' seeking to protect themselves from 'litigation' and 'regulation'[467] and from the state deflecting dissatisfaction[468] away from the courts through a 'harmony' rhetoric.[469] In the English jurisdiction case law and extra judicial speeches indicate that some judges have not been immune to delivering an anti adjudication 'message'.[470] Judgments are dispersed with negative com-ments about litigation where legal arguments have consumed party or court resources, or where costs of the action have swamped the initial claim, when mediation might have resolved the dispute through compromise at a tiny proportion of the final expenditure. Genn queries if this is indicative that judges in the English jurisdiction have a 'loss of belief in their own authority' or a 'loss of appetite for adversarialism' or, perhaps, have themselves joined the new mediator profession.[471] On the other hand, she suggests that judges may have been swayed by the ADR ideology because they are 'overwhelmed' by the lack of civil court resources as funding is directed towards the criminal justice system, leading them to be persuaded to divert cases 'into the hands of private dispute resolution'.[472]

Adversarial attitudes

McMillan Williams v. Range illustrates the 'active part' taken by some members of the judiciary in presenting 'anti-litigation' rhetoric.[473] The Court of Appeal disapproved the approach taken to litigation by both parties who were from the legal profession. The litigants had entered into a contract agreeing to pay the defendant assistant solicitor on a commission only basis, based on an expectation of billing £66,000 a year but Ms Range resigned at the end of two years at which time there was a shortfall of £17,000 against what should have been earned in commission.[474] Part of her defence was that the firm had 'negligently misrepresented' how much she would be able to bill and that the contract came under the Consumer Credit Act 1974 as it was 'credit on commission' which was 'unenforceable' due to the claimants' 'non-compliance with formalities'.[475] The Court held that the contract did not come under the Act as it was a 'contract for services' but was dismayed that costs had escalated to over £50,000 even before the negligence argument was resolved.[476] This led Lord Ward to state that the parties should have written

---

467 Thornberg (2011) at 76. See also Abel (1982)
468 Abel (1982); Auerbach (1984); Roberts (1992); Robertshaw & Segal (1993); Guill & Slavin (1989)
469 Nader (1993); Abel (1982)
470 Genn (2010) at 119
471 Genn (2010) at 120
472 Genn (2010) at 119
473 *McMillan Williams v. Range* [2004] EWCA Civ 294. See Genn (2010) at 120
474 *McMillan Williams v. Range* [2004] at 4
475 *McMillan Williams v. Range* [2004] at 6
476 *McMillan Williams v. Range* [2004] at 29

to each other, saying that the judge has recommended the 'splendid idea' of mediation rather than indulging in 'argumentative correspondence' where both sides claimed to be reasonable but obdurately would not 'compromise'.[477] The appellant finally refused to mediate two days before trial because of the unwillingness of either side to alter their stance but both parties had to pay their own costs 'for their frolic in the Court of Appeal' because they had ignored the court's recommendation to consider ADR and because of the 'posturing and jockeying' that had taken place.[478] In LJ Ward's opinion, 'the lesson to be learned' is that it is impossible to know the 'bottom line' until the mediation has ended.[479]

Excessive litigation costs

The courts are particularly critical of parties who fail to use mediation or ADR when costs spiral out of control, leading at least one judge to question whether the 'elaborate and expensive process' of litigation can ever be warranted in the TCC when the dispute between the parties is 'under £110,000'.[480] Even in a construction dispute which engendered colossal amounts, the lawyers and their clients in the TCC were firmly directed not to let the costs 'take on an expensive life of its own' and to try mediation 'with an experienced construction practitioner' before an organised sub-trial.[481] The Court of Appeal drew negative comparisons to the costs of pursuing litigation in *Ghaith v. Indesit* when in a 'postscript', Lord Justice Longmore criticised Indesit's 'inadequate response' to the court's recommendation to mediate because the costs already outstripped the 'amount at issue' and would only escalate after a 'full day' in the Court of Appeal.[482] The court drew attention to the new Court of Appeal pilot scheme for PI (personal injury) and contract claims less than £100,000 in the hope that this would reduce the number of 'comparatively small claims' being heard.[483] In concurring with the judgment, Lord Justice Ward observed that appeal is only given when there is a 'real prospect of success' but that does not necessarily mean that the appellant will be successful so both parties had much to gain from mediating

---

477 *McMillan Williams v. Range* [2004] at 29
478 *McMillan Williams v. Range* [2004] at 29
479 *McMillan Williams v. Range* [2004] at 30
480 *Nigel Witham Ltd v. Smith & Anor* [2007] at 3
481 *Brookfield Construction (UK) Ltd v. Mott MacDonald Ltd* [2010] EWHC (TCC) 659 at 53
482 *Ghaith v. Indesit* [2012] EWCA Civ 642 at 26
483 *Ghaith v. Indesit* [2012] at 26. Lord Justice Rix, who was involved in setting up the Court of Appeal Mediation Scheme compared the 'corrosive effect' of litigation: 'Judges regularly see cases in the Court of Appeal which could easily have been resolved at an earlier stage through the use of mediation. Parties may not be poles apart, but litigation can have a corrosive effect for which mediation can provide a balm. Mediation in the Court of Appeal can save a great deal of money and anxiety'. http://www.judiciary.gov.uk/media/media-releases/2012/news-release-mediation-pilot-court-of-appeal   Downloaded on 5 November 2012

with an 'experienced mediator' who often have a 'canny knack of transforming the intractable into the possible'.[484]

In *Shovelar v. Lane* the claimants estimated that the costs of litigation had exceeded the amount that the litigants were 'battling over' when they admitted 'spending of over £320,000 fighting over a £134,000 estate'.[485] Lord Justice Ward expressed his 'horror' and the likely 'horror' of the 'Great British Public' at the way that the litigants had 'conducted' litigation when the parties could have avoided the 'awful costs consequences' if they had mediated at the 'earliest stage'.[486]

Although the failure to use mediation was not under consideration in *Camertown Timber v. Sabrinder Singh Sidhu Kas* the Court of Appeal drew attention to the trial judge's view on the suitability of mediation.[487] The case took five days to try, involved eight bundles of evidence and had ratcheted up costs of £150,000 for claims of £71,000 which led Collins J to suggest that mediation would have been an appropriate forum because of the costs involved in litigating when there was a 'doubtful outcome' at court.[488] The question before the Court was whether the parties had so tested the 'judge's patience' that he had failed to 'adequately try the case before him' but although Collins J was criticised for not providing a more detailed explanation in his judgment on costs the appeal court did not displace his discretion because both sides had 'exaggerated' their claims.[489] When a veteran judge[490] does not exercise his discretion on costs because of the conduct displayed by the parties, it is difficult to appreciate how even an experienced mediator would effectively encourage a different attitude. It would require significant expertise on the part of a skilled mediator to encourage a more cooperative and candid approach.

Commercial awareness

Another factor commented on by the courts is the failure of litigants to take a 'commercial' view when electing to use litigation rather than mediating. In *Whitecap Leisure Ltd v. Rundle Ltd* the appellant had not successfully dismissed all of Whitecap's claims but Lord Ward considered the case appropriate for mediation because 'commercial' parties should 'look at their balance sheet

---

484 *Ghaith v. Indesit* [2012] at 29
485 *Shovelar v. Lane* [2011] EWCA Civ 802 at 54
486 *Shovelar v. Lane* [2011] at 61
487 *Camertown Timber Merchants Ltd. Gurpartat Singh Bhullar v. Sabrinder Singh Sidhu Kas & Co Ltd.* [2011] EWCA Civ 1041 at 2
488 *Camertown v. Singh* [2011] at 1–2
489 *Camertown v. Singh* [2011] at 3 & 34
490 *Camertown v. Singh* [2011] at 35, per Lord Justice Ward: 'The question is whether Homer has nodded and totally failed to bear those matters in mind. I find it impossible to accept that he fell into such a basic error. As a former Director of Studies of the Judicial Studies Board who went about teaching judges how to do their job, it seems impossible to my mind that this venerable grandmother needed to be taught how to suck the eggs'.

rather than the pleadings'.[491] Whitecap had made a 'gesture to drop its hands' and made mediation offers but the defendants chose to litigate when the Court of Appeal observed that the sensible approach would have been to shun litigation because it is more 'expensive than one's worst fears'.[492] After reviewing the conduct of the parties both litigants at times had been as 'bad as each other' and taking an overview the costs of the claim were set against the costs of the appeal.[493]

Even where mediation is not at issue, the Court of Appeal has expressed views on the suitability of mediation over litigation because of the detrimental effect litigating can have on the parties. For example, in *Mercedes Travis Brewer v. Stanley Mann Fortis Lease UK Ltd and Stanley Mann Racing Ltd* the case involved the sale of a vintage car where the sale documents recorded the vehicle as a 1930s Bentley but the finance contract called it a '1930 Bentley Speed Six car', which lead the buyer to claim that the seller had misrepresented the car.[494] The trial judge found in the claimant's favour but also found on points not at issue namely that the dealer had been 'dishonest' and the appeal concerned whether a draft judgment had 'an appearance of bias'.[495] The Court of Appeal observed the appropriateness of mediation because there was uncertainty about the 'outcome' of litigation, there were 'numerous issues' involving questions of 'facts, of opinion and law' and a need to 'reconstruct' unrecorded discussions, expert evidence, the extent of liability and whether the seller had 'made the promise'.[496] Lord Justice Rix was particularly struck by the 'small sums' that the parties should have been able to settle at compared to litigation and found it regrettable that the court had not exercised its 'responsibility to warn the litigants' of the *dangers and difficulties of pursuing their case through the courts* (my emphasis).[497]

To date Genn argues that mediation policy has been disseminated by 'setting it up in opposition to litigation', which the judges have 'reinforced' through an 'anti-adjudication anti law discourse'.[498] She criticises some of the judiciary for 'playing into the hands of the government' whose policy is to secure financial savings in the civil courts by 'rationalising' supply, 'reducing' legal aid and diverting cases to mediation.[499] Genn argues that by presenting mediation not as an alternative but as an 'equal or even preferential' way of resolving disputes, government policy, judicial speeches and court pronouncements minimize the importance of the Civil Justice System, which

---

491   *Whitecap Leisure Ltd v. John H. Rundle Ltd* [2008] EWCA Civ 1026 at 8
492   *Whitecap v. Rundle* [2008] at 2 & 8
493   *Whitecap v. Rundle* [2008] at 6
494   *Mercedes Travis Brewer v. Stanley Mann Fortis Lease UK Ltd and Stanley Mann Racing Ltd* [2012] EWCA Civ 246
495   *Mercedes v. Stanley Mann* [2012] at 14 & 11
496   *Mercedes v. Stanley Mann* [2012] at 341
497   *Mercedes v. Stanley Mann* [2012] at 110 & 341
498   Genn (2012) at 409–10
499   Genn (2012) at 413

is to promote 'social and economic wellbeing'[500] through the rule of law and to protect[501] a citizen's right to access justice.[502] In her analysis, using mediation as part of the 'Access to Justice' agenda, is not about 'substantive justice' because the parties have to 'relinquish their legal rights' and the mediators' role is not about justice but is one of facilitating a settlement that the 'parties can live with', therefore, mediation may not provide 'a *just* settlement but *just a settlement*'.[503]

Commentary

Hong Kong's approach

As both Australia and the USA have adopted a mandatory regime for mediating, it is not intended to review the case law from these two jurisdictions. Since ADR policy in Hong Kong has closely followed that of England and Wales, however, a short review will be undertaken of the cases which define the appropriateness of mediation both before and after the introduction of the Civil Justice Rules (CJR) in 2009.[504] There are relatively few cases on the suitability factors for mediating, but similar themes occur in both the High Court and judgments in Hong Kong, which expressly encourage the parties and the legal profession to explore the advantages of mediation over litigation even before the rules came into effect.[505] For example, in *Ansar Mohammad v. Global Legend Transportation Ltd* the High Court rejected the defendant's argument that no consideration be given to their refusal to mediate because CJR was not in place and the 'jurisprudence and practice of mediation was only developing' because the courts had 'repeatedly sent out strong messages' concerning ADR.[506]

The Court of Appeal in Hong Kong took a similar stance to that of the English courts in supporting the use of ADR in *iRiver Hong Kong Limited v. Thakral Corporation (HK) Limited*, particularly when litigation costs are huge.[507] Yeung JA dismissed the appeal but was disappointed that the parties had not tried mediation to resolve their differences over the existence of a contract where

500 Genn (2012) at 371
501 Lord Neuberger of Abbotsbury (2010)
502 Genn (2012) at 411
503 Genn (2012) at 411
504 See for example, Weixia (2010); Cheung (2010a, b)
505 See *Ansar Mohammad v. Global Legend Transportation Ltd* [2011] HKEC 645. See Order 22 rule 5 Rules of High Court ss22/5/5 and *Pacific Long Distance Telephone v. New World Telecommunications Ltd* [2012] HKEC 732. The parties refused mediation before CJR came into Force.
506 *Ansar v. Global Ansar Mohammad v. Global Legend Transportation Ltd* [2011] HKEC 645 at 44
507 Weixia (2010) at 55

the damages were over $1 million and the legal costs $4.7 million.[508] The Court of Appeal cited *Dunnett* with approval and concurred with Lord Justice Brooke that the parties may have benefited from mediating with a 'skilled mediator' and even if 'full settlement' had not been reached, it may have enabled them to settle at a later stage.[509] Mediation was established in Hong Kong and the parties should have taken the opportunity to use a 'more cost benefit means' to resolve their dispute, furthermore litigants and legal representatives were cautioned to take heed of the comments about ADR and the impending rules requiring them to 'assist the court to further the underlying objectives'.[510]

The courts in Hong Kong also acknowledge the weight given to judicial recommendations to mediate and in *Supply Chain & Logistics Technology Ltd v. NEC Hong Kong Ltd* the High Court confirmed that 'in line with the English authorities of *Dunnett* and *Halsey*' failing to use mediation could be taken into account when it had been suggested during 'proper case management' review because it indicated the appropriateness of mediating.[511] There were no significant costs because the claim had been discontinued but the court was satisfied that not responding to the 'mediation notice' should be taken into account when considering 'non-compliance with the direction of the court'.[512] The defendant had 'completely' failed to respond to two offers to mediate and because the court had emphasised the importance of mediation since 2008 the defendant should 'not be excused' for not using a 'cost-effective way' of settling the dispute.[513] The explanation that both parties' offers were too far apart was also rejected because 'the court had repeatedly stressed' that mediation does not have 'to reach complete settlement' and because the defendant was 'disputing every issue'; there was a prospect of at least some matters settling.[514] The defendant was 'deprived of 20 per cent of its costs' and warned that had the 'mediation regime' been in place then the 'entire costs' might have been lost.[515]

After the introduction of the CJR, the High Court considered the *Halsey* guidelines in *Golden Eagle International (Group) Ltd v. GR Investment Holdings Ltd* when it held that costs should be awarded against the defendant for unreasonably refusing to mediate despite their claim that the case was not suitable.[516] Lam J held that although the Hong Kong jurisdiction gives 'respect' to *Halsey* because of the similarity of the rules, it was not binding on

---

508 *iRiver Hong Kong Ltd v. Thakral Corp (HK) Ltd* [2008] 4 HKLRD 1000, [2008] HKEC 1337 [2008] HKEC 1337*River* [2008] at 98
509 *iRiver* [2008] at 99 and 103
510 *iRiver* [2008] at 106, 104–6
511 *Supply Chain & Logistics Technology Ltd v. NEC Hong Kong Ltd* [2009] HKEC 135 at 12 & 11
512 *Supply Chain* [2009] at 15–16
513 *Ansar v. Global* [2011] at 59 & 58
514 *Ansar v. Global* [2011] at 61
515 *Ansar v. Global* [2011] at 65
516 *Golden Eagle International (Group) Ltd v. GR Investment Holdings Ltd* [2010] HKLRD 273

the courts but nevertheless he examined the criteria raised by the defendant.[517] First, the nature of the case was suitable because it was a 'simple contract dispute' and was not one that 'required the determination of the court'.[518] There was no issue on any point of law, which would 'provide guidance for the future', nor was 'injunctive or other protective relief sought' to 'justify' refusing mediation.[519] Judge Lam accepted Lord Justice Dyson's argument that a 'reasonable belief' in the strength of a case might justify a refusal because of the 'threat of costs sanctions to extract a settlement' but this had to be read in connection with the 'rationale' for this factor, which was that large com-panies are susceptible to 'nuisance claims'.[520] The court doubted this could happen in Hong Kong because the sanction is based on a different rule: First there is 'only' a cost penalty for refusing to mediate, but not if the parties are unable to reach settlement after 'making a reasonable effort in mediation'; second, under PD 31 the parties are only required to attend the 'agreed minimum level of participation'; third, the costs of mediating in Hong Kong were not so exorbitant that they would 'encourage such nuisance claims'; and finally, the costs of the mediation can be recovered 'by the successful party if the mediation is unfruitful'.[521] Therefore the High Court left it open whether the parties' 'belief in the strength of its case' could justify a refusal but doubted that the defendant could have believed that this case was any more than a 'borderline' one.[522]

The court also reviewed the other *Halsey* criteria raised by the defendant's counsel and noted that the defence had made an unrealistic offer to settle and although Lord Justice Dyson had said settlement offers might be evidence of the prospect of success when mediating, he also said that the process 'often settles when other attempts have failed'.[523] The court also observed that a 'party cannot rely on his own unreasonable obdurate attitude' and despite 'correspondence' indicating the parties' views towards settlement it is not possible to 'assume' mediation would not have settled or would have been a 'waste of time'.[524] On the final claim that the cost of mediating would have been too high the court estimated that two days' mediation with an experienced mediator in Hong Kong would cost about $80,000 and this was not considered to be 'disproportionate' to the estimated costs of $600,000 for the plaintiff and $700,000 for the defendant.[525]

Most noteworthy was the fact that the High Court in *Golden Eagle* did not follow *Halsey* on which party has the burden of proving that mediation would

---

517 *Golden Eagle* [2010] at 21
518 *Golden Eagle* [2010] at 23
519 *Golden Eagle* [2010] at 26
520 *Golden Eagle* [2010] at 27
521 *Golden Eagle* [2010] at 29
522 *Golden Eagle* [2010] at 30–31
523 *Golden Eagle* [2010] at 32–4
524 *Golden Eagle* [2010] at 35–7
525 *Golden Eagle* [2010] at 38–40

have a good prospect of success. Johnson Lam J specifically noted Lord Phillips' speech when concluding that a more 'robust' approach was needed otherwise the costs sanctioning powers would be weakened.[526] Paragraph 4 of the Practice Direction 31 permits the court to take into account the 'unreasonable failure' of the party to engage in mediation and s5(4) explains how the parties can avoid this sanction which is either by participating to a 'minimum level' or by providing an explanation of why they had not done so.[527] Costs were awarded against the defendant because no 'reasonable explanation' had been given for not mediating.[528]

Hong Kong has taken a more vigorous approach to mediation policy and although the cases indicate that litigants and the judiciary may refer to Lord Dyson's guidelines, the reversal of the burden of proof requiring the refusing party to justify their explanation for not mediating may go some way to reduce the tactical use of mediation at the time of costs, although this may only be replaced by court hearings before mediating as parties argue over how to comply with PD 31. The requirement that parties only need to take 'minimal' steps after the 'mediation notice' may do little to encourage genuine and open participation in the process which was experienced at the beginning of the modern mediation phenomenon.

Criticism of *Halsey* and adverse costs

The adverse costs penalties for refusing to engage in mediation created by the CPR and the *Halsey* guidelines have not gone critically unscathed. The current rules in the English jurisdiction, although not making mediation compulsory, do significantly pressurise parties into mediating, which often obligates an attempt at a process the participants may not have voluntarily chosen. Brunsdon-Tully disapproves of the CPR penalties, which virtually 'coerce' parties to mediate, particularly litigants seeking legal aid under the current restrictive rules who have little choice other than to look outside the courts for the resolution of their disputes.[529] Genn notes that legal aid funding may not be available if other alternatives exist such as complaints or ombudsmen schemes or small claims mediation, some of which have been elevated to an 'equal' status with litigation.[530] Where parties have no real choice but to mediate, Brunsdon-Tully argues they may also feel pressed to settle, thereby leading to settlements which may not have come about and may not be 'just given the strength of the legal case which they sought to advance'.[531] Parties may also have little alternative than agreeing to settlement once they have

526 *Golden Eagle* [2010] at 43–5
527 *Golden Eagle* [2010] at 43
528 *Golden Eagle* [2010] at 44
529 Brunsdon-Tully (2009) at 218 & 228
530 See Genn (2012) at 403. See the Funding Code Criteria (2011); Brunsdon-Tully (2009); Genn (2010) at 103–8
531 Brunsdon-Tully (2009) at 225–6 & 230; See also Genn (2010)

begun mediation if their finances do not permit the continuation of litigation. Many scholars observe that the financially vulnerable in society are the most likely to lose out by not being able to gain access to the courts, as a 'two-tier system' develops where the courts are reserved for the wealthiest in society and others are designated to 'second class forms of justice'.[532]

The *Halsey* criteria developed in the wake of CPR have also engendered extensive academic and practical debate, foremost of which is criticism that the guidelines create uncertainty in practice.[533] The case law to date illustrates that there is ambiguity about 'the key conditions' for mediating, which 'lends itself to either abuse or costs injustices'.[534] Tronson is critical of the doubt created by judicial discretion when applying *Halsey*, which is particularly acute in borderline cases, because the factors do not have to be applied in every case thus reducing the decision to mediate in the English jurisdiction to a 'gamble'.[535] In comparison, she draws attention to Australian states, which mandate participation where the benefit is that the parties address their arguments against mediating at the time of the 'interlocutory hearing' rather than at the final hearing, which may create added costs but prevents the 'sword of Damocles hanging over their head'.[536] Tronson notes a 'striking similarity' between the *Halsey* guidelines and mediation suitability identified by Einstein J in *Idoport* which include costs; timing; 'factors' such as apologies; 'sensible commercial compromise' and 'the issues in dispute' which she suggests is comparable to the 'nature of the dispute'.[537] Australia is reported not to have had excessive challenges to the courts' power to mandate mediation but Tronson contends that the uncertainty of the *Halsey* guidelines would lead to 'satellite litigation' and increased costs which is perhaps supported by the cases referred to above where parties are using Lord Dyson's criteria to launch their arguments or appeals on costs.[538]

Commentators further object to the *Halsey* guidelines and subsequent cases because they are based on 'judicial assumptions' about what mediation can achieve.[539] Analysis of the survey data in England and the USA suggests that mediation policy and judicial rhetoric is often propagated on 'questionable assumptions'[540] and 'unverified empirical data'[541] that mediating saves time

---

532 Brunsdon-Tully (2009) at 226. Brunsdon-Tully notes Abel's argument that a two-tier system will develop. Abel (1982). See also Genn (2010) generally and at 114–19; Fiss (1984); Abel (1982)

533 See for example, Brunsdon-Tully (2009); Shipman (2006); Tronson (2006); Brooker (2009) (2010a)

534 Brooker (2010a) at 154. See also Brunsdon-Tully (2009); Brooker (2009)

535 Tronson (2006) at 416

536 Tronson (2006) at 415

537 *Idoport Pty Ltd v. National Australia Bank* [2001] NSWSC 427 at 27. See Tronson (2006) at 413–14

538 Tronson (2006) at 417

539 Brunsdon-Tully (2009) at 231; Genn (2010) at 108–13; Shipman (2006)

540 Hensler (2002) at 81; See Genn (2010) at 108–13; Genn (2012) at 404–5; Brunsdon-Tully (2009) at 231–2

541 Genn (2012) at 404

and money or that the parties prefer non adjudicatory or non adversarial processes.[542] Genn observes that the high levels of satisfaction with mediation in court schemes in England might be due to the participants comparing the process to how they envisage a trial to be when one of the 'main tools' mediators use to facilitate settlement is to remind the parties about the 'dangers' and the 'unpleasantness' of court.[543] Survey findings have also not conclusively proved that 'mediated and non-mediated' cases differ in 'case duration and savings in costs' because comparisons are usually drawn to proceeding to trial and most actions settle before the hearing.[544] Additionally, as Genn and others observe, mediated outcomes are virtually always financial rather than 'creative' thereby undermining the basis of judicial encouragement that a key attribute of mediation is the ability of mediators to facilitate non-legal outcomes such as apologies or future business arrangements.[545]

Drawing attention to high settlement rates is also problematic in view of the disparity across different surveys.[546] It is difficult to estimate the number of mediations taking place annually or settlement rates when there is no official list of mediators operating in the English jurisdiction and settlement in small claims mediation schemes can vary from 86 per cent (Manchester) to 58 per cent (Exeter).[547] A survey of lawyers' experience with mediation found significantly lower settlement rates for construction compared to commercial mediations, although the construction sector recorded more incidences of partial settlement.[548] ADR providers and mediators claim settlement occurs between 70–80 per cent on the day of the mediation but most figures used in promoting mediating include those that settle 'shortly after' the process has concluded.[549] There is little empirical evidence to explain what factors

542 See Genn (2010) (2012); Brunsdon-Tully (2009); Shipman (2006)
543 Genn (2012) at 404
544 Genn (2012) at 405. See also Shipman (2006) at 199–200
545 Genn (2010) at 113; See Brooker & Lavers (2005a) at 198–200. Construction and commercial mediations also rarely result in creative outcomes and the parties often do not wish to engage in 'continuing' commercial relationships once business transactions have broken down.
546 Genn (2012) at 406
547 See for example, Brooker (2011); Boon et al. (2007). For a review of mediation in small claims see for example, Enterkin & Sefton (2006); Prince & Belcher (2006); Doyle (2006); Genn (1998)
548 Brooker & Lavers (2005a) at 188
549 CEDR Mediators' Audit 2012 at 7. CEDR report a settlement rate of just over 70% on the day of the mediation and 20% shortly after giving an aggregate of 90% but there is also a 'shift' of 5% not settling on the day; ADR Group state the average rate for settlement is 80% on the day or shortly after. http://www.adrgroup.co.uk/section/3/1/commercialn Downloaded on 11 April 2013. However, rates as low as 52% on the day of mediation have been reported after ADR orders. See Genn (2002) at ii. Brooker & Lavers's study found settlement rates of 81% for commercial mediations and 70% for construction mediations. Brooker & Lavers (2005a) at 188. Professor Roberts reports a settlement rate of 66% in the Mediation Scheme operating in the Mayor's and City of London Court Mediation Scheme. Roberts (2012)

pressurise a party to settle shortly after mediating but with CEDR Mediator Audit reporting the average fees for less experienced mediators have risen by over 9 per cent (to approx. £1,500) and over 24 per cent for experienced mediators (approx. £4,500),[550] this may weigh heavily on continuing with litigation. If up to one in five mediations in non-family cases do not settle then this expense has to be added to the costs involved in continuing with litigation, whether settlement is achieved before trial or not, which may do irreparable damage to the long-term development of mediation and create 'disillusionment' with the process.[551] This may be particularly so if some parties are tempted to engage in mediation for appearance or tactical gain rather than a serious intent to seek settlement.

Judges have not been able to explain with exactitude when cases are ready for mediating, which may be a decisive factor in the mediation achieving a settlement outcome.[552] There is little empirical evidence confirming the most advantageous time to start mediation, although some studies suggest that settlement may depend on the level of evidence that has taken place[553] but weighed against this is the association of the mediating parties' attitudes to compromise or entrenchment, which are likely to harden the longer the dispute is lived with.[554]

Strategic use of mediation

Critics of ADR policy often suggest that mediation does have an important place in dispute resolution strategy running alongside litigation as it may promote 'accelerated settlement'[555] or produce many other benefits such as clarifying areas or reducing the numbers of issues in dispute which may lower trial costs.[556] There are other advantages beyond settlement, which the opportunity to mediate may present such as providing the opening for a realistic analysis of one's case and when mediating on a voluntary basis it offers parties a choice of process if negotiation fails.[557] Nevertheless mediating can also be part of a more calculated stratagem such as exhausting the opponent's litigation fund, delaying settlement or testing the other party's evidence or observing how witnesses will perform at trial.[558]

550 CEDR Mediators' Audit (2012) at 5
551 See for example, Brooker (2002) at 114; See Brooker & Lavers (2001) (2002); Brunsdon-Tully (2009) at 236
552 See Brunsdon-Tully (2009) at 223 & 230; Brooker (2010a) at 152–4
553 For example, see Henderson (1996)
554 *Bradford v. James* [2008] at 1, 8–9
555 Genn (2012) at 204
556 Genn (2012) at 204. See for example, Brunsdon-Tully (2009); Genn (2010); Brooker & Lavers (2005a,b); Clark (2012)
557 See for example, Brooker & Lavers (2005a,b); Brunsdon-Tully (2009) at 236; Mackie et al. (2007) at 106–8
558 See for example, Brooker & Lavers (2005a); Brooker (2007); Clark & Dawson (2007)

There may be numerous factors involved in reaching a settlement in mediation such as area of practice, mediation rules, timing or even mediator skills but most empirical research indicates that a significant influence on success is the parties' attitudes.[559] If participation is for tactical reasons or to show compliance with legal rules or for 'costs terrorism' activity, then this may discourage enthusiasm, further deflate settlement rates and in the end reduce voluntary engagement.[560] The cases show that judges are already observing that litigants are not making genuine offers to mediate, which they address by not penalising the refusing party but this may have a limited effect on encouraging mediation use. 'Skilled mediators' may be able to generate a climate where parties are stimulated into finding a solution to their dispute or are able to produce the elusive 'apology', particularly where 'one shotters' are involved, but it may be more challenging with 'repeat players' or where the participants are legally represented by professionals trained in adversarialism.[561]

Legal involvement and evaluative mediation

Chapter 1 explored the interest of the legal professions in ADR developments and most jurisdictions link the institutionalisation of mediation to an increase in lawyers' involvement as they act as representatives in the process or train as mediators.[562] Research and observers report that associated with this development is a change in practice as many mediators move from a facilitative orientation to incorporate more evaluative techniques.[563] Critics and researchers observe that evaluative mediation reduces the parties' self-determination as their legal advisors and mediators take more control over the process, and moreover this approach is said to increase adversarial conduct and the process ceases to be 'true alternative' to litigation.[564] As litigants face increasing compulsion to use mediation, or risk adverse costs, this engenders a reliance on lawyers to advise and represent the parties, which brings a level of legal formality into the procedure, particularly as evaluative models are used.[565] ADR providers and mediators publish their own procedural rules and mediation agreements, some of which loosely replicate the litigation process by requiring the parties to provide, within a time frame, 'positional papers' and evidence, albeit not as much as required for litigation.[566] These

---

559 See for example, Stipanowich (1996); Henderson (1996); Brooker & Lavers (2005a) at 164; Genn (1998)
560 See Brooker (2009) (2010a); Brunsdon-Tully (2009)
561 Brunsdon-Tully (2009) at 231. See for example, Menkel-Meadow (1993)
562 For an overview of different jurisdictions see Clark (2012)
563 See for example, McAdoo & Hinshaw (2002); Wissler (2004); Hensler (2001); Welsh (2001a, b)
564 See for example, Hensler (2001a) at 788 and 858. See also Brunsdon-Tully (2009); Brooker (2007); Clark (2012); Kovach & Love (1996) (1998)
565 See for example, Brooker (2007); Clark (2012); Kovack & Love (1996)
566 See Brooker (2011)

mediation 'rules' sometimes stipulate how the process will progress with opening statements and rebuttal time which may be reminiscent of a 'truncated' court procedure.[567] At present, there is no central regulation of mediators in England and Wales, although ADR organisations have been involved in developing standards of practice and more recently, the Civil Mediation Council has promoted more consistency of a practice through their membership rules.[568] ADR policy rather then fostering a new way to tackle dispute resolution through a process that has the potential to change how people negotiate, or even 'transform'[569] how they interact, is developing mediation law which is cultivating a more evaluative process of mediation which those who promulgated Civil Justice Reform may not have intended.[570]

Interplay with litigation

Since the CPR, the cases have raised the spectre of the tactical interplay of mediation with litigation.[571] The judicial comments in *Wyatt* and *Halsey* are clear warnings that the courts are vigilant that mediation should not be used as a 'litigation tool' to seek advantages over opponents, however, research evidence indicates that mediation has become a calculated part of the dispute resolution process as parties make strategic offers to mediate.[572] The rules requiring both judges and parties to consider alternatives to court action, or staying proceedings for the parties to attempt ADR inserts mediation within the litigation framework and thereby creates the environment for a more 'cynical' approach to mediating, which the courts inadvertently foster by supporting mediation policies, which might in the long-run damage its future development.[573]

'Paradoxically' the strategies to promote civil justice reform through ADR[574] result in mediation no longer being a separate entity from the court. It has become 'court sponsored' and through this process institutionalised and legalised.[575] Genn observes the 'interdependency' between courts and ADR whereby without the 'backing of coercive power' the parties would not be brought to the 'negotiation table'.[576] Just as arbitration was able to thrive through its 'symbiotic relationship' with litigation, which provided that the

---

567 Brooker (2011). See for example, Stemole (1996) at 354
568 See for example, Brooker (2011); Boon et al. (2007); Clark (2012). Chapter 6 of this book reviews the development of a mediator profession in England and Wales.
569 See for example, Baruch Bush & Folger (1994)
570 Brunsdon-Tully (2009) at 227; See also Brooker (2007); Roberts (2000); Dolder (2004); Genn (1998)
571 See Brooker (2010a)
572 McAdoo & Hinshaw (2002) at 493
573 Brooker & Lavers (2005a); Genn (2010) (2012)
574 Genn (2010) at 116
575 Roberts (2009) at 460; Roberts (2000)
576 Genn (2010) at 125

courts retain an overview of arbitrating, mediation is also developing a reciprocal association with the formal system, which is 'shaping' how the process is developing.[577] However, mediation, like arbitration before it; is showing evidence of juridification as the law begins to delineate practice and the legal professions begin to dominate developments.[578] Legal policy and the CPR may have done a disservice to mediation by institutionalising a process that may have had more to offer disputants outside the formal system of litigation.[579]

Conclusion

The criteria for mediating remains illusive but may be driven by conjecture on the part of the judiciary or their 'ideological beliefs',[580] which leaves disputants to assess what risks they are prepared to take. Many in society may find that they have little or no choice because they are unable to fund litigation,[581] but those who have resources have the option of not mediating and risking adverse costs or engaging in the process to show 'apparent compliance' with the rules, which is likely to affect both the experience of mediation and its success.[582] However, as the next chapter explores, the rules on mediation confidentiality preclude extensive court control over the parties' or their legal representatives' conduct in mediation, and therefore the future may bring additional disillusionment about the process and negate the potential that 'voluntary' mediation has.[583]

577 See for example, Brooker (1999); Brooker (2010a) at 157; Alexander (2006) at 19–21
578 See Flood & Caiger (1993) for an analysis of the juridification of arbitration.
579 Genn (2010); Brunsdon-Tully (2009)
580 See Shipman (2006) at 182
581 See Genn (2010) (2012)
582 Brunsdon-Tully (2009) at 230–1; Genn et al. (2007) at 47
583 Brunsdon-Tully (2009) at 236

5 The law surrounding mediation confidentiality

Introduction

One of the 'philosophical tenets' underpinning mediation is said to be confidentiality.[1] It is this principle that allows parties to negotiate settlement of their disputes in the understanding that their negotiations will not be used in legal proceedings should they fail to settle.[2] Some mediation advocates argue that confidentiality is so 'critical that without it the process will not work'[3] because it encourages the parties to make concessions and compromise proposals or even admissions as to liability when exploring settlement options.[4] Confidentiality also implies there is no publicity, which may provide significant benefits to commercial parties who desire to keep their disputes out of the public domain.[5]

Kovach observes that the concept of mediation confidentiality concerns different interests for the parties, their legal representatives, mediators and the process itself which raises issues about 'who' is being protected: The parties must feel assured that all persons present at the mediation will keep 'in confidence' any information they divulge.[6] Lawyers and other representatives have interests in protecting information and from acting as witnesses in court.[7] Finally, mediators are concerned with confidentiality because it 'encourages disclosures' and 'builds trust' between themselves and the parties, which facilitates the settlement outcomes.[8] Bevan said that in mediation the

---

1 Spencer & Brogan (2006) at 312; See also Deason (2001) at 35. See Alexander (2009) at 229; Burnley & Lascelles (2004); Koo & Zhao (2011) at 264
2 Toulson & Phipps (2006) at 15.016. This statement is reinforced by Toulson & Phipps: '. . . it would destroy the basis of mediation if, in the case of the mediation failing, either party could publicise matters which had passed between themselves or between either of them and the mediator'.
3 Kovach (2006) at 439
4 Koo (2011)
5 Mackie et al. (2007) at 206. The authors note that a company which is in litigation with a number of parties may wish to settle with one party without the others being aware of the details of the settlement, which might involve an 'admission' about liability.
6 Kovach (2006) at 439
7 Kovach (2006) at 429
8 Kovach (2006) at 438–9

caucus (individual/private meetings with the mediator) is the 'engine room' which is the catalyst for reaching settlement,[9] where assurances of confidentiality allow mediators to get insight from the parties of their 'positions, interests and options' thereby enabling movement towards resolving the dispute.[10] Legal rules requiring mediators to report or 'testify' on events in mediation are said to compromise their 'neutrality' as they move to a refereeing role,[11] which some argue affects the parties' conduct in mediation as they attempt to 'persuade' the mediator about the strength of their case and leads to increasing adversarial conduct.[12]

Confidentiality, however, involves two competing policies, one concerning settlement without litigation, which makes possible the efficient use of judicial resources, and the second that courts should have all the necessary evidence to determine the case – although there are concerns that taking too 'broad' an approach can 'sterilise' mediation if information is deliberately divulged to prevent disclosure at court.[13] In the English jurisdiction mediation is recognised as a form of third party assisted negotiation and issues of confidentiality have been addressed through the application of the without prejudice rule which protects statements and admissions made while trying to negotiate a settlement from later being used in the courts.[14] As court rules place more pressure on disputants to explore settlement before litigating, the question of how to protect prejudicial negotiating positions that occur in mediation has become a critical issue to the practice of mediation.

Bevan recognised in the early 1990s that the courts would eventually be required to review how the without prejudice rule operates with mediation but he also observed that there would be tension between how the law institutionalises confidentiality and mediation's 'procedural flexibility'.[15] This chapter will first review without prejudice privilege and analyse how the courts have dealt with disclosure of information from mediations as it is raised in the case law. Consideration will then be given to the principle of confidentiality, which parties usually commit to in their contractual arrangements for mediation.[16] As mediation becomes more commonplace because of the requirements of CPR, this chapter investigates the argument

---

9 Bevan (1992) at 19. In a mediation caucus the parties meet separately with the mediator.
10 Mackie et al. (2007) at 123–4
11 Kovach (2006) at 439
12 Kovach & Love (1996) at 31
13 Spencer & Brogan (2006) at 314–15. Citing Rogers CJ in *AWA Limited v. Daniels (t/a Deloitte Haskins & Sells)* (1992) 7 ACSR 463 who made reference to *Deloitte Haskins and Sells* (1992) 1 ACSR 462 '. . . it would be entirely too easy to sterilise otherwise admissible objective evidence simply by saying something about it in the course of the Mediation, even if the subject be irrelevant to the mediation discussion'. See also Burnley & Lascelles (2004); Deason (2006)
14 *Aird v. Prime Meridian Ltd* [2006] EWCA Civ 1866. See Bevan (1992) at 30–31
15 Bevan (1992) at 30–32. See also Burnley & Lascelles (2004) at 28–36 'Enshrining mediator confidentiality in law or guidelines would be another step towards the institutionalisation of mediation, the effectiveness of which is its procedural flexibility'.
16 See Mackie et al. (2007) at Chapter 7

for developing a 'unique mediation privilege' to protect confidentiality being infringed by the court and proposals for greater protection or immunity for mediators.[17]

Without prejudice

Although mediation is often endorsed on the grounds of its confidentiality; legal protection for the statements in mediation in common law countries has been for the most part through an application of the without prejudice rules. Negotiations between disputing parties are denied later disclosure in the courts first on the grounds of public policy of promoting settlement before court action[18] and, second, because the parties have 'impliedly agreed' to non-disclosure.[19] By providing without prejudice protection to statements the parties are encouraged to negotiate 'freely and frankly' in the knowledge that any admissions of liability will not be used against them should the dispute continue to court.[20]

Although many mediators consider mediation to be a more 'dynamic' and complex process than negotiation,[21] it is 'understood' by the courts to be a 'form of assisted without prejudice negotiation' which was confirmed in *Aird v. Meridian Ltd*. Consequently 'what goes on in the course of mediation' cannot be referred to or relied on in subsequent court proceedings.[22] The Court of Appeal in *Aird* had to consider whether a joint experts' report ordered by the TCC under CPR rule 35.12 and subsequently used in a stayed mediation was protected by the without prejudice rule.[23] The Court held that the status of a court order is not altered because it has been prepared 'with an eye to assisting a contemplated mediation'.[24] The 'discussions of the expert meetings', 'the discussion at the mediation about the experts' discussions and their statements' all came within the 'without prejudice rule' but the finished experts' report was not protected because it was a court order and 'it did not acquire a privilege by being used in the mediation'.[25] The Court in this decision recognised the standing of mediation but did not elevate the process above the court in much the same way that judges supported arbitration by allowing it to flourish but not to 'oust their jurisdiction'.[26] Without prejudice

---

17 See for example, Briggs (2009b); Kallipetis (2011)
18 See Koo (2011); Altaras (2010); *Rush & Tompkins Ltd v. Greater London Council* [1989] AC 1280; *Cutts v. Head* [1984] Ch 290 and *Unilever Plc v. The Procter and Gamble Co* [2000] WLR 2436
19 *Muller v. Linsley & Mortimer* [1996]; See Koo (2011) at 194
20 *Cutts v. Head* (1984) at 306. See Koo (2011); Parke & Bristow (2001); Zamboni (2003); Bingham (2008); Cornes (2008); Altaras (2010); Brooker (2010a); Brookes (2009)
21 Kallipetis (2009); Briggs (2009b)
22 *Aird v. Prime Meridian Ltd* [2006] EWCA Civ 1866 at 5
23 See for example, Allen (2008); Sorabji (2008)
24 *Aird v. Prime Meridian Ltd* [2006] at 24
25 *Aird v. Prime Meridian Ltd* [2006] at 31 & 29
26 Cornes (2007) at 14

statements in mediation will be protected by the common law but the courts' jurisdiction takes precedence.

Exceptions to the without prejudice rules

The principle of without prejudice is however not 'absolute' and the common law provides exceptions to the general rule, which were identified by Robert Walker LJ in *Unilever v. The Procter and Gamble.*[27] The courts have not considered all of the exceptions in relation to mediation (at the time of writing), but they act as guidance to the likely approach when the 'facts fit' in future mediation litigation either when litigants seek to engage the courts to enforce mediation agreements or more cynically when parties are seeking to escape from disadvantageous compromises.[28]

The court may order disclosure of without prejudice statements when the following conditions apply:[29]

1) To provide 'evidence that without prejudice communication has resulted in a concluded compromise'.[30]
2) To provide 'evidence of an estoppel' where a 'clear statement' is made on which 'the other party is intended to act and does in fact act'.[31]
3) To provide 'evidence that the concluded agreement should be set aside on the ground of misrepresentation, fraud or undue influence'.[32]
4) To provide 'evidence of what the other said or wrote in without prejudice negotiations if the exclusion of the evidence would act as a cloak for perjury, blackmail or other unambiguous impropriety'.[33]
5) To provide 'evidence of negotiations in order to explain delay or apparent acquiescence' ('for instance, on an application to strike out proceedings').[34]
6) To provide 'evidence as to whether the claimant acted reasonably as to his loss in his conduct'.[35]
7) The 'exception (or apparent exception)' for an offer expressly made 'without prejudice except as to costs'.[36]

---

27 Koo (2011) at 197. *Unilever Plc v. The Procter and Gamble Co* [2000] WLR 2436
28 Brooker (2010a) at 155; See for example, Cornes (2008); Kallipetis (2009); Wood (2008)
29 *Unilever Plc v. The Procter and Gamble Co* [2000] at 2444
30 Walker LJ at 2444 cites; *Tomlin v. Standard Telephones and Cables* [1969] 1 WLR 1378
31 Walker LJ at 2444 cites; Neuberger J in *Hodgkinson & Corby v. Wards Mobility Services* [1997] FSR 178 at 191
32 *Unilever* [2000] gives as an example *Underwood v. Cox* (1912) 4 DLR 66 and *Hodgkinson & Corby v. Wards Mobility Services* [1997] FSR 178, 191
33 Walker LJ at 2444 cites; *Forster v. Friedland* (unreported), 10 November 1992; Court of Appeal (Civil Division) Transcript No. 1052 of 1992
34 Walker LJ at 2444–2445 cites; *Walker v. Wilsher* (1889) 23 QBD 335
35 Walker LJ at 2445 cites; *Muller v. Linsley & Mortimer* [1996]
36 Walker LJ at 2445 cites; *Cutts v. Head* [1984] and *Rush & Tomkins & Tompkins Ltd v. Greater London Council* [1989] AC 1280

Walker LJ listed an eighth exception but to be more precise this is a 'category of privilege' for protecting 'matrimonial communications' which is 'based on the public interest in the stability of marriage'.[37] The courts will not allow disclosure of 'conciliation' negotiations except where there is a 'clear indication' that the person making the statement has or is 'likely in the future to cause serious harm to the wellbeing of a child'.[38] This special form of privilege for family conciliation has been used to make a case for the development of a wider 'privilege' for the process of mediation in other contexts, which is considered below.[39]

Debate on the boundaries of the without prejudice rule

The categories above provide exceptions for admitting evidence in litigation but there has been a notable division of opinion in the courts about the level of protection that should be afforded, which centred on an analysis of whether the without prejudice rules are confined to admissions of liability or include all communications made in settlement negotiations.[40] The uncertainty surrounding the boundaries of the without prejudice rule was perceived to be problematic for mediation, particularly in view of the apparent 'willingness' of courts to issue witness orders to mediators.[41]

The ambiguity resulted from conflicting opinions in the cases.[42] First in *Muller v. Linsley & Mortimer* Hoffmann LJ adopted a narrow approach by limiting the rule to admissions.[43] Second in *Unilever v. Procter and Gamble* Walker LJ proposed that without prejudice should exclude all statements on the grounds that that the 'distinction' was 'impractical' and would suppress the openness of the settlement negotiations.[44]

The difference in the two approaches was at 'issue' in the House of Lords in *Ofulue v. Bossert* when Ofulue appealed against the decision that the defendant had gained a freehold property though adverse possession.[45] Ofulue's tenants had allowed Bossert to live in the premises from 1983 after which Ofulue began possession proceedings in 1997.[46] In 1992, Bossert had made an offer to buy the house and at the possession hearing admitted Ofulue's title.[47] The proceedings were discontinued in 2002 but renewed in 2003 at which

---

37 *Unilever* [2000] at 23. See *D v. National Society for the Prevention of Cruelty to Children* [1977] AC 171, per Lord Hailsham. *Unilever Plc v. The Procter and Gamble Co* [2000] WLR 2436
38 *D v. National Society for the Prevention of Cruelty to Children* [1977] at 240–2
39 See for example, Koo (2011)
40 See for example, Briggs (2009a); Altaras (2010); Koo (2011)
41 See for example, Briggs (2009a); Wilson (2010)
42 Koo (2011) at 194–5; Altaras (2010) at 152–4
43 *Muller* v. *Linsley & Mortimer* [1996] P.N.L.R. 74 at 79
44 *Unilever v. Procter and Gamble* [2000] at 2448–9. See Koo (2011) at 194–5; Altaras (2010) at 152–4
45 *Ofulue v. Bossert* [2009] UKHL 16; [2009] 1 A.C. 990 (HL) at 8
46 *Ofulue v. Bossert* [2009] at 13
47 *Ofulue v. Bossert* [2009] at 16–17

point Bossert claimed adverse possession relying on s15 of the Limitation Act 1980 (continuous possession for 12 years).[48] Under 29 title to land is not lost if the person claiming adverse possession 'has made a written acknowledgement of the title of the owner of the land'.[49] Ofulue's argument was that adverse possession had been broken by Bossert's acknowledgement of title, which was evidenced by the previous proceedings and the offer to buy the property.[50] The point in contention was whether the without prejudice letter offering to buy the house was an 'acknowledgement of agreed facts' and therefore admissible or an 'admission against liability', which would be protected against disclosure, because if the offer was admissible then it would 'interrupt continuous possession', which required the HL to consider whether the without prejudice rule 'extends to an acknowledgment of what at the time it was made was an agreed fact':[51]

> The issue that is being litigated between the parties now is not the issue that was being litigated when the letter was written in January 1992. In fact it was not an issue that was in dispute between the parties at that time at all. The second is a more subtle aspect of the same point. It is whether the protection that the rule gives in without prejudice negotiations to an admission against interest extends to an acknowledgement of what at the time it was made was an agreed fact.

The majority in the House of Lords in adopting a 'pragmatic approach'[52] were not prepared to accept the distinction on the grounds it was 'too subtle to apply in practice' and held that barring 'exceptional circumstances', all without prejudice statements should be inadmissible other than when they are 'wholly unconnected with the issues between the parties'.[53] The effect of the decision in *Ofulue v. Bossert* is that there is no distinction between acknowledgements and admissions and, although there were dissenting judgments, the majority of the House agreed that 'it would be inappropriate to create further exceptions', although this was not discounted should justice demand it.[54]

Extensions to the Unilever exceptions

The House of Lords in *Ofulue v. Bossert* declined to extend the exceptions to admit 'acknowledgements of facts' but cases have considered the existence of

---

48 *Ofulue v. Bossert* [2009] at 18
49 *Ofulue v. Bossert* [2009] at 32
50 *Ofulue v. Bossert* [2009] at 19
51 *Ofulue v. Bossert* [2009] at 8, 65 & 94
52 Altaras (2010) at 480
53 *Ofulue v. Bossert* [2009] at 98
54 Per Lord Neuberger in *Ofulue v. Bossert* [2009] at 98. See for example, Suter (2011) at 152–3; Higgins (2011); Briggs (2009a)

further categories to those identified in *Unilever*.[55] For example, in *BNP Paribas v. Mezzotero* BNP appealed against the employment tribunal's (ET) decision to permit evidence from a without prejudice meeting with their employee.[56] The defendant had taken out a grievance procedure concerning discrimination on her return to work after maternity leave but was asked to attend a without prejudice meeting where she was informed that the company was terminating her contract but would 'treat' it as a redundancy package separate to her claim of discrimination.[57] The Employment Appeals Tribunal (ETA) held, relying on *Daintrey Re*,[58] that without prejudice only applies when a dispute is in existence between the parties and 'raising a grievance' does not mean the parties are 'necessarily in dispute' but indicates the existence of an 'internal mechanism' where the employee's concerns are 'upheld or dismissed so that the parties may never reach the stage where they could be properly said to be "in dispute"'.[59] Therefore the alleged 'without prejudice' statements made by the company did not 'prevent' them from being 'admissible'.[60] However, the EAT went on to consider in the alternative whether the statements might also be admissible on grounds of 'unambiguous impropriety'[61] before concluding that it is in the public interests that 'allegations of unlawful discrimination are heard and properly determined' because the objective behind 'sex and discrimination legislation is to eradicate' a 'very great evil'.[62] The EAT concluded that this case did not create 'an impermissible extension of the categories of the rule'.[63]

The decision in *BNP Paribas v. Mezzotero* elicited commentary as to whether a new exception existed to permit evidence of sex and racial discrimination or whether this species was included within 'unambiguous impropriety'.[64] The EAT considered this in *Woodward v. Santander* in an appeal against an ET decision not to admit evidence supporting an allegation that an employer had discriminated against an employee by refusing to provide a reference during without prejudice negotiations.[65] Woodward argued for disclosure because it came within the 'new exception' for discrimination cases but although the EAT made reference to *Ofulue v. Bossert*,[66] which gave support to the contention that the 'list of exceptions is not closed', the court concluded

---

55 See Suter (2011)
56 *BNP Paribas v. Mezzotero* EAT 30 March 2004 [2004] I.R.L.R. 508; (2004) 148 SJLB 666
57 *BNP Paribas v. Mezzotero* [2004] at 4
58 *Daintrey Ex p. Holt, Re* [1893] 2 QB 116
59 *BNP Paribas v. Mezzotero* [2004] at 28
60 *BNP Paribas v. Mezzotero* [2004] at 31
61 *BNP Paribas v. Mezzotero* [2004] at 32
62 *BNP Paribas v. Mezzotero* [2004] at 35
63 *BNP Paribas v. Mezzotero* [2004] at 39
64 See for example, Suter (2011) at 150
65 *Woodward v. Santander UK Plc* (Formerly Abbey National Plc) Employment Appeal Tribunal [2010] IRLR 834; (2010) 154(25) SJLB 41
66 *Woodward v. Santander UK Plc* (2010) (Formerly Abbey National Plc) Employment Appeal Tribunal 25 May 2010 at 55. See *Ofulue v. Bossert* [2009] at 38–40, per Lord Rodger

that any extension should be 'scrutinised with care', should be 'consistent' with the policy behind the without prejudice rules and only found 'if justice clearly demands it'.[67]

The EAT in *Woodward v. Santander* declined to accept that *Mezzotero* had established a new exception because the case had been decided on the grounds that there was no dispute between the parties to which the without prejudice rule could apply and the 'employer's alleged conduct' came within the 'abuse principle' (meaning unambiguous impropriety, see below).[68] The appeal tribunal in *Woodward* was of the opinion that the 'without prejudice' rule applies 'with as much force' to employment cases as to other cases and the parties must be 'free within limits' in both 'negotiation or *mediation*' to 'argue their case and speak their minds' without fearing 'subsequent litigation'.[69] The EAT concluded that the boundaries of the rules 'are best stated in terms of the existing exception to impropriety'[70] and rejected a 'wider exception' for alleged race or sex discrimination because it conflicted with the 'policy behind the rule' which is to encourage the parties to 'speak freely' when engaging in 'negotiation or *mediation* settlement.[71]

It is noteworthy that the EAT ruling made specific reference to the relevance of without prejudice in relation to mediation thereby recognising the growing role the process has in employment disputes, but it also indicates further evidence of legalism as parties litigate on the application of legal principles to mediation practice. Litigation is the 'price' of institutionalisation and perhaps it is inevitable that the without prejudice rule, which is an important catalyst for settlement compromises, has become the subject of mediation litigation.[72]

New extension 'to aid construction'

The boundaries of the 'without prejudice' rules came before the Supreme Court (SC) again in *Oceanbulk Shipping & Trading SA v. TMT Asia Ltd* which reversed the decision of the Court of Appeal and extended the categories in *Unilever* to include admissions which aid the court in the interpretation of concluded agreements.[73] In *Oceanbulk*, the parties had reached a compromise agreement but there was a disparity between the parties' 'understanding' of a

---

67   *Woodward v. Santander* [2010] at 55. See *Ofulue v. Bossert* [2009] at 38–40, per Lord Rodger
68   *Woodward v. Santander* [2010] at 58
69   *Woodward v. Santander* [2010] at 60–61
70   *Woodward v. Santander* [2010] at 62
71   *Woodward v. Santander* [2010] at 64
72   Wood (2008) at 15; Bevan (1992)
73   *Oceanbulk Shipping & Trading SA v. TMT Asia Ltd* [2011] 1 AC 662; [2010] 3 WLR 1424. See Ahmed (2010) at 306. The author applauded the CA decision in refusing to extend the exceptions because of the potential negative effect it would have on mediating. See also Suter (2010) at 271

term in the contract (relating to the term 'sleeved').[74] The question before the SC was whether without prejudice emails and discussions could be produced in evidence to explain the 'construction' of the term when it did not come within the *Unilever* exceptions.[75] Clarke LJ, relying on authority from Canada[76] and New Zealand,[77] was persuaded that the without prejudice category permitting evidence to determine whether agreement has been reached encompasses an 'exception as to rectification' because they are 'scarcely distinguishable' and 'no sensible line' can be drawn between the two.[78] Perhaps a practical decision as Wood questions whether any commercial party would opt for mediation if they were unable to appeal to the court to rectify an agreement, which had inaccurately recorded settlement at $600,000 instead of $60,000.[79]

The Supreme Court recognised that the House of Lords in *Ofulue v. Bossert* had accepted that the rule is not confined only to 'admissions of liability' because of the 'importance' of encouraging settlement but held that without privilege should not be 'lightly eroded' by recognising new exceptions.[80] Nevertheless the majority approved statements in *Ofulue v. Bossert* that where 'justice demands'[81] a new 'interpretation exception should be recognised' – but only to 'explain the factual matrix or surrounding circumstances' to aid the court in its 'responsibility' to 'construe' contracts.[82] To have done otherwise, the Court opined, would have introduced an 'unprincipled distinction' between the recognised exceptions (whether a concluded agreement had been reached and rectification) and 'not allowing for the interpretation of the agreement'.[83] The Supreme Court held that whether the 'negotiations were without prejudice or not' the 'same principle' for interpreting language in a contract should be 'applied',[84] which is 'what a reasonable person having all the background knowledge which would have been available to the parties

---

74 *Oceanbulk* [2010] at 9: '"Sleeving" is an arrangement by which one party (party B) will, at the request of another party (party A), enter into a specific FFA [forward freight agreements] trade with a third party (party C) and party B will then replicate that position back-to-back with party A. The usual reasons for such an arrangement are that (i) party C would not be willing to trade with party A (eg because of perceived counterparty risk) and/or (ii) party A does not wish to reveal to the market that he is seeking that position, eg because he is concerned that he will move the market. However, once the contracts have been concluded then (absent eg an agency arrangement), the two contracts are independent and each party acts as a principal: the contracts do not necessarily remain "coupled" '.
75 *Oceanbulk* [2011] at 30
76 *Oceanbulk* [2011] at 33 citing *Pearlman v. National Life Assurance Co of Canada* (1917) 39 OLR 141
77 *Oceanbulk* [2011] at 33 citing *Butler v. Countrywide Finance Ltd* (1992) 5 PRNZ 447
78 *Oceanbulk* [2011] at 33
79 Wood (2008) at 6. Wood cites the USA case of *DR Lakes Inc v. Brandsmart* [2002] 819, So.2nd 971
80 *Oceanbulk* [2011] at 30
81 *Ofulue* [2009] at 57
82 *Oceanbulk* [2011] at 46
83 *Oceanbulk* [2011] at 42
84 *Oceanbulk* [2011] at 40

would have understood them to be using the language in the contract to mean'.[85]

Although the latest HL and SC cases are not directly decided in relation to events in mediation these developments may affect the trust that users have in the confidential nature of the process and may impact on the degree of openness in negotiating which many mediators believe essential for creating settlement.[86] The expansion of the without prejudice rule to 'aid interpretation' has led to concern that this goes beyond 'purely objective facts' to examining the 'basis of negotiations' between the parties, which Suter suggests might involve the courts in investigating the parties' 'subjective negotiating stances'.[87] Others suggest that in practice the new exception is unlikely to be problematic as it only applies when settlement has been reached albeit with remaining 'ambiguities' about the terms, which lawyers are 'warned' to address with careful drafting.[88] Higgins, however, cautiously recommends that legal representatives try to 'contract out' for 'interpretation purposes' in pre-mediation contracts, which the court might accept, as *Oceanbulk* was decided on the basis of the parties' 'presumed intentions', although of course such action would lead to further legalism:[89]

> It is by no means clear whether the English courts would give effect to such an agreement that the courts were not to have recourse to particular communications for the interpretation purposes set out in *Oceanbulk*. However, given that the decision of the Supreme Court is based, at least in part, on the presumed intention of the parties, it is suggested that an explicit agreement to the contrary may have some weight. It may be that such express agreements will become more common as lawyers consider how best to protect their clients from the implications of Oceanbulk.

Application of without privilege rules in mediation

As noted earlier, not all of the identified exceptions to without prejudice have been heard in mediation cases but the courts have indicated a willingness to permit disclosure of information of when the relevant conditions apply.[90]

Without prejudice save as to costs

Negotiations prefaced 'without prejudice save as to costs' are admissible on the costs issue and in *Reed* the Court of Appeal had to consider whether the

---

85 *Oceanbulk* [2011] at 37 citing *Chartbrook Ltd v. Persimmon Homes Ltd* [2009] AC 1101
86 See Ahmed (2010); Suter (2011); Briggs (2009a,b)
87 Suter (2011) at 278–9
88 See Axe (2010); Rawlinson (2011)
89 Higgins (2011) at 195
90 See for example, Koo (2011); Wood (2008) (2009); Koo & Zhao (2011); Cornes (2008); Kallipetis (2009)

parties could be ordered to disclose details of without prejudice negotiations when considering liability for costs, which included whether the cost order should take into account a refusal to use mediation.[91] The court noted that negotiations undertaken on a '*wholly* without prejudice basis' are not admissible, which is called the *Walker v. Wilsher* rule.[92] The Court further 'observed' that CPR rule 44.3.4 provides discretion to take account of 'all the circumstances' when awarding costs and specifically includes an 'admissible offer', which signifies that 'the existing law as to without prejudice' is not affected as it 'assumes some offers to settle are inadmissible'.[93] The Court rejected the claimant's argument that *Halsey* held that 'all circumstances' should be taken into account when examining whether a party should be penalised in costs for unreasonably refusing an offer to mediate because the decision had not 'abrogated' the rule in *Walker v. Wilsher* and 'all circumstances' meant 'any admissible circumstances'.[94] Therefore, the Court of Appeal in *Reed* refused to order disclosure because '*Walker and Wilshire* remains good law' and, although acknowledging that occasionally it will not be possible to determine whether mediation has been unreasonably rejected,[95] no 'adverse inference' should be taken from a party's refusal to permit without prejudice statements because it would be 'clear indirect pressure to permit disclosure'.[96]

Exception to provide evidence that compromise reached

As discussed in Chapter 3, the court had to decide in *Brown v. Rice & Patel* whether the parties had reached an enforceable agreement at the end of mediation.[97] Before the court could establish whether a compromise settlement had been arrived at it had to consider the 'scope' of the without prejudice exceptions in relation to the mediation process.[98] The court was not persuaded that a 'distinct mediation privilege' existed and decided the case on two of the exceptions in *Unilever*.[99] First, whether 'the without prejudice communications in mediation had reached a concluded settlement' and second, 'whether a statement on which the other party is intended to and does in fact act may give rise to an estoppel'.[100] The court held that evidence of

---

91 *Reed Executive Plc & Anor v. Reed Business Information Ltd & Ors* [2004] EWCA Civ 887 at 9
92 *Reed* [2004] at 21 citing *Walker v. Wilsher* (1889) 23 QBD 335
93 *Reed* [2004] at 12
94 *Reed* [2004] at 28 & 31
95 *Reed* [2004] at 34
96 *Reed* [2004] at 36
97 *Brown v. Rice & Patel* [2007] at 51 & 67. The court held that an offer had been made but that it was incomplete because the offer held 'no certainty' as whether the settlement was to be 'effected' through a Tomlin Order or a court judgment and the mediation contract required the settlement to be in writing.
98 *Brown v. Rice & Patel* [2007] at 1
99 *Brown v. Rice & Patel* [2007] at 19
100 *Brown v. Rice & Patel* [2007] at 10

what happened in the mediation was admissible because it 'fell fairly and squarely within the recognised exceptions' in *Unilever* in order to prove that the communication had led to a 'concluded agreement'.[101] The argument that the mediation contract requiring the settlement to be in writing had the effect of 'removing the exception' was rejected because the category 'operates' whether based on the agreement of the parties or 'public policy'.[102] Nor was it accepted that the Patels had 'waived' the requirement for writing or there would be no 'meaning' to an acceptance, which Koo contends is an estoppel:[103]

> On either basis, there is nothing to justify the conclusion that the fact that Mrs Patel's offer was open for acceptance until midday on 17 February means that clause 1.4 was impliedly waived or that to give effect to clause 1.4 would make the existence of the acceptance period 'just verbiage', as counsel for the Applicant submitted.

Disclosure to provide evidence of perjury, blackmail or other 'unambiguous impropriety'

The court will permit evidence of 'perjury, blackmail or other unambiguous impropriety' in order that one party is not given licence to 'abuse' the protection given by the without prejudice rule.[104] *Savings Investments Ltd in Liquidation v. Fincken* reviewed examples of conduct in this category in non-mediation cases.[105] In *Foster v. Friedland*, the defendant felt 'honour bound' about an agreement but his threat to 'deny a legal obligation', if the matter proceeded to litigation, was found to be 'very far from blackmail'.[106] In contrast, 'clear cases of improper threats' include giving perjured evidence if a claim continues or 'bribing others' to perjure themselves.[107] The 'test' for unambiguous impropriety is that it 'should only be admitted in the very clearest of cases', which was not reached in *Fazil-Alizadeh v. Nikbin* when a tape recording of an alleged 'denial of settlement payments' and a forgery cover up were not permitted in evidence.[108]

---

101 *Brown v. Rice & Patel* [2007] at 21
102 *Brown v. Rice & Patel* [2007] at 24–5
103 *Brown v. Rice & Patel* [2007] at 56. See Koo (2011) at 270
104 Koo (2011) at 197. See Suter (2011) at 151. Suter provides examples of conduct, which have reached the required level of 'impropriety' citing for example *Underwood v. Cox* (1912) 4 DLR 66, which involved a threat to reveal discreditable personal information to force a sister to agree to a unfavourable division of property.
105 *Savings Investments Ltd in Liquidation v. Fincken* [2003] EWCA Civ 1630 at 57
106 *Savings Investments Ltd in Liquidation v. Fincken* [2003] citing at 57 *Foster v. Friedland* (unreported) 10 November 1992 CA (Civil Division) No 1052 of 1992
107 *Savings Investments Ltd in Liquidation v. Fincken* [2003] at 57 citing *Greenwood v. Fiss* 29 DLR (2d) 260; *Hawick Jersey International Ltd v. Caplan, The Times*, 11 March 1988
108 *Savings Investments Ltd in Liquidation v. Fincken* [2003] at 47, citing Simon Brown LJ in *Fazil-Alizadeh v. Nikbin* (unreported) 25 February 1993; Court of Appeal (Civil Division) Transcript No 205 of 1993

Where claims of perjury are concerned, the Court of Appeal held in *Savings Investments Ltd in Liquidation v. Fincken* that it is not the 'possibility of an inconsistency between a stated position' which 'may lead to perjury' but the actual 'abuse' of the privilege.[109] The claimant sought to 're-re-amend the statement of claim to include an admission' which 'allegedly' showed the defendant's change on a 'sworn affidavit about ownership of shares'.[110] The Court accepted that it might be considered 'distasteful' to ignore a situation where a party 'appears' to have 'lied on a sworn document' but where two 'competing policies' conflict, without prejudice should take precedent unless the party has utilised the rule to 'abuse the privilege'.[111]

The Court of Appeal in *Berry Trade Ltd v. Moussavi* rejected the trial judge's test of 'serious and substantial risk of perjury' because it was 'too low' and 'nothing less than unambiguous impropriety' suffices to admit evidence.[112] Furthermore, the Court stated that it is wrong to search through 'hours' of without prejudice negotiations to find an 'admission here and an admission there in order to mount a claim of perjury' because it would always be possible to find an 'admission inconsistent with some pleading or sworn assertion' and this would limit the benefits of without prejudice privilege as litigants would need a 'lawyer' or 'script' as they negotiate:[113]

> No litigant could be advised to enter into without prejudice discussions without a lawyer at his elbow or a prepared script approved by his lawyer. To allow such admissions in evidence flies in the face of the public policy justification for the without prejudice rule.

Mediation and unambiguous impropriety

The Court reviewed unambiguous impropriety in relation to mediation in *Hall v. Pertempt Group Ltd* when Hall (and another) sued for the return of documents, an injunction to prevent disclosure of information and for payment for work done on 'quantum meruit' basis.[114] The Court stayed proceedings on several occasions for mediation and 'settlement discussions' to take place and after a Part 36 offer in respect of the payment claim, the parties mediated over two separate days but failed to reach an agreement.[115] 'Eight months' later an action was brought by Pertempt claiming that Hall had breached 'express or implied terms in the mediation agreement' by revealing to a third party that threats had been made during or just after the mediation.[116]

---

109 *Savings Investments Ltd in Liquidation v. Fincken* [2003] at 57
110 *Savings Investments Ltd in Liquidation v. Fincken* [2003] at 1
111 *Savings Investments Ltd in Liquidation v. Fincken* [2003] at 62. See Altaras (2010)
112 *Berry Trade Ltd v. Moussavi (No.3)* [2003] EWCA Civ 715 at 48
113 *Berry Trade Ltd v. Moussavi (No.3)* [2003] at 53
114 *Hall v. Pertempt Group Ltd* [2005] EWHC 3110 (Ch) at 1
115 *Hall v. Pertempt Group Ltd* [2005] at 2–4
116 *Hall v. Pertempt Group Ltd* [2005] at 4

One issue was whether the Court should give consideration in costs to the 'alleged threat' or whether without prejudice prevented disclosure.[117] Lewison J noted that evidence of 'perjury, blackmail or other ambiguous impropriety' could only be given in the 'clearest cases of abuse of privilege'[118] and confirmed the decision in *Savings Investments Ltd in Liquidation v. Fincken* that loss of privilege is not due to the 'possibility' that it would lead to perjury but because the 'privilege was itself abused'.[119] The Court suggested that 'unambiguous impropriety' will only be permitted in 'exceptional circumstances', such as an 'assault', but that most allegations are 'irrelevant to the underlying dispute' but the 'more relevant' the more likely 'without prejudice protection' will be preserved, and where there is no nexus the 'more likely to be disclosed'.[120] The threats relied on in *Hall v. Pertempt* were 'hotly contested' so they were 'not unambiguous' and the Court held that disclosure should be permitted because both parties had 'mutually waived' privilege through the pleadings in 'the satellite litigation', which were 'public documents'.[121]

Waiving without privilege

Without prejudice privilege belongs to the parties and it can only be waived when both parties agree.[122] In *Carleton v. Strutt & Parker*, the litigants were trying to provide the Court with evidence of the reasonableness of their offers in mediation in relation to a costs order.[123] The waiving of privilege gave the Court of Appeal the 'opportunity' to investigate the parties' conduct and to use the same costs principles for assessing an unreasonable refusal to mediate explicated in *Halsey* because it was deemed to be 'in reality the same position'.[124] The court reduced the claimant's costs for exaggerating their claims and for taking 'a plainly unrealistic' and 'unreasonable position' in the mediation.[125] Some commentators caution legal advisors not to recommend waiving privilege to their clients but the cases show that parties will attempt to give courts access to mediation information when there are allegations of more serious conduct, which might reach the threshold of the *Unilever* exceptions.[126]

---

117 *Hall v. Pertempt Group Ltd* [2005] at 6
118 *Hall v. Pertempt Group Ltd* [2005] at 13, citing Walker LJ in *Unilever* at 11
119 *Hall v. Pertempt Group Ltd* [2005] at 11 citing *Fincken* (2003) Headnote
120 *Hall v. Pertempt Group Ltd* [2005] at 14; Brooker (2011) at 156
121 *Hall v. Pertempt Group Ltd* [2005] at 16
122 *Farm Assist (2)* [2009] at 22
123 *Carleton v. Strutt & Parker (A Partnership)* [2008] EWHC 424 (QB) at 23 & 24
124 *Carleton v. Strutt & Parker* [2008] at 72. This is discussed in Chapter 4
125 *Carleton v. Strutt & Parker (A Partnership)* [2008] at 88(2)
126 See for example, Allen (2008)

Muller exception: to show evidence that the party has acted reasonably to mitigate losses

More than one party involved in mediation

Mediation may of course involve more than two parties all of whom are entitled to without prejudice in the mediation. In *Cumbria Waste Management Ltd (1) v. Baines Wilson (A Firm)* the question before the court was whether the defendant could disclose documents from two mediations that had involved a third participant, the Department for Environment, Food and Rural Affairs (DEFRA), which was not party to the litigation proceedings.[127] The claimants were suing their solicitors, who had represented them in the mediation, for negligence in 'negotiating, drafting and preparing documents' for a compromise agreement with DEFRA.[128] The defendant and claimant both waived privilege in the mediation but DEFRA declined as they feared that disclosure of settlement information might prejudice ongoing claims with other parties and they submitted a witness statement that the two mediation agreements entered into had contained confidentiality clauses.[129] The case was decided on the without prejudice exception provided in *Muller* which allows disclosure to show a party has acted reasonably to mitigate losses in their conduct and the compromise agreement.[130]

However, the court held that the facts did not fall within the *Muller* exception because a third party was resisting disclosure, not the plaintiffs and privilege rested not only with the claimants but also with DEFRA.[131] The decision was based on public policy because a third party not involved in the litigation should be able to rely on protection from disclosure, 'which may embarrass them in other disputes', and on the 'express (not just implied)' agreement between the claimant and DEFRA 'that the without prejudice rule applies' in the mediation.[132] Kirkham J was of the opinion the principles of without prejudice and confidentiality 'overlapped'[133] but because of the importance of protecting mediation DEFRA should be allowed 'to rely on the exception to the general rule that confidentiality is not a bar to disclosure'[134] which is 'subject to the statutory and common law exceptions' of which without prejudice is one.[135]

---

127 *Cumbria Waste Management Ltd (1) v. Baines Wilson (A Firm)* [2008] EWHC 786 (QB) at 1
128 *Cumbria Waste Management Ltd (1) v. Baines Wilson (A Firm)* [2008] at 4
129 *Cumbria Waste Management Ltd (1) v. Baines Wilson (A Firm)* [2008] at 12
130 *Cumbria Waste Management Ltd (1) v. Baines Wilson (A Firm)* [2008] at 18
131 *Cumbria Waste Management Ltd (1) v. Baines Wilson (A Firm)* [2008] at 24
132 *Cumbria Waste Management Ltd (1) v. Baines Wilson (A Firm)* [2008] at 24
133 *Cumbria Waste Management Ltd (1) v. Baines Wilson (A Firm)* [2008] at 29
134 *Cumbria Waste Management Ltd (1) v. Baines Wilson (A Firm)* [2008] at 28. Justice Kirkham reviewed the authoritative authors on confidentiality, Toulson & Phipps (2004)
135 *Cumbria Waste Management Ltd (1) v. Baines Wilson (a firm)* [2008] at 30, citing *British Steel Corporation v Granada Television Ltd* [1981] AC 1096. See Toulson & Phipps (2004) at 17.005. The authors note that this rule is 'subject to statutory and common law exceptions' of which without prejudice is one.

Malek et al. in *Phippson on Evidence* criticises the reasoning in *Cumbria* because third party confidentiality is not generally a bar to 'disclosure' if the judge takes 'measures' to protect the future use of the documents in other proceedings.[136] Furthermore he argues the court by not using discretion was speciously 'elevating mediation privilege to a higher status than without prejudice' without acknowledging this when the parties had waived privilege, were not 'relying' on what the claimant said as an 'admission against interests', nor using DEFRA's statements against them as they were not party to the negligence claim.[137]

Cumbria involved the privilege of a third party involved in the mediation but in *Cattley & Anor v. Pollard*, the defendant had not participated in the process but sought disclosure of the settlement arrangement reached between the claimant and the Solicitors Indemnity Fund (SIF).[138] A solicitor's firm had acted as executors of a will and one of the firm's members, Pollard, had misappropriated the estate and later transferred a share to his wife.[139] The claimants began an action for indemnity from Pollard and the solicitors firm (who were not fraudulent) added his wife as a defendant at which time she made an application to the court for disclosure of the mediation settlement on the grounds that they were not entitled to compensation from her as this would 'amount to double recover'.[140]

Master Bragge considered the two diverging principles of without prejudice, one confining privilege only to admissions of liability (*Muller*) and the other extending inadmissibility to any settlement communications (*Unilever*).[141] Whilst recognising that ordering disclosure would require a 'broad view of what an admission was', Master Bragge held there were strong public policy reasons for permitting evidence of 'factually relevant material to Mrs Pollard's legal argument' on double counting and the 'overriding objective to enable the court to deal justly with cases'.[142] *Cattley* indicates that where the two 'competing policies'[143] come head to head, one encouraging settlement negotiations and the other enabling courts to decide cases on the best possible evidence, the later should take priority.

The status of confidentiality in mediation

The disclosure sought in *Cumbria* would have included documents held by the mediator but Kirkham J advised courts to 'be slow' in making orders admitting this information so that mediators are able to conduct mediation

---

136 Malek et al. (2009) at 24–56
137 Malek et al. (2009) at 24–56
138 *Cattley & Anor v. Pollard* [2007] EWHC B16 (Ch)
139 *Cattley & Anor v. Pollard* [2007] at 1
140 *Cattley & Anor v. Pollard* [2007] at 3
141 *Cattley & Anor v. Pollard* [2007] at 20–24
142 *Cattley & Anor v. Pollard* [2007] at 24
143 Briggs (2009a)

in the confidence that others will not be able to access their papers.[144] Some mediators destroy notes after the conclusion of the mediation to limit the usefulness of attendance at court and to protect confidentiality, although Wood argues that where impropriety is claimed the mediator is the best person to help the court – particularly if they are the foil in this abuse.[145]

The lack of notes did not influence the High Court in *Farm Assist Ltd (FAL) v. Secretary of State for the Environment, Food and Rural Affairs (DEFRA)*, when an application was made for a court order for a mediator to attend as a witness in connection with a claim that economic duress had been used by DEFRA to reach the compromise agreement.[146] Both litigants agreed to waive without prejudice and confidentiality agreements 'about the entire conduct of the mediation including private conversations' but the mediator attempted to resist a court order because the parties had signed 'confidentiality and non-attendance' clauses in the mediation agreement and 'the evidence was confidential and/or irrelevant'.[147]

Farm Assist (2) is the leading High Court judgment reviewing the 'overlap' between the without prejudice rules and confidentiality in mediation.[148] The court held that 'without prejudice' in mediation belongs to the parties and not to the mediator and should they elect to waive their privilege the mediator is not in a position to resist a witness order.[149] The court also clarified that when a party reveals other privileged documents in meetings with the mediator, such as legal advice or earlier without prejudice discussions, this does not have the effect of waiving privilege and such information is not admissible.[150]

Ramsey J reviewed the authoritative position given by Toulson and Phipps before concluding that mediation confidentiality is based on two sources.[151] First, the parties may agree to an 'express' 'obligation of confidentiality' in a mediation contract, which applies 'not only between the parties but the parties and the mediator' and second, using the analogy of arbitration,[152] there is an 'implied confidentiality' between the parties and between the parties and the mediator'.[153] Ramsey J opined that confidentiality could only be waived 'with the consent of all the parties', which means that the mediator

---

144 *Cumbria Waste Management Ltd (1) v. Baines Wilson (a firm)* [2008] at 31
145 Wood (2008) at 3
146 *Farm Assist (2) Ltd (FAL) v. Secretary of State for the Environment, Food and Rural Affairs (DEFRA)* [2009] (No.2) [2009] EWHC 1102 (TCC). See Wood (2009)
147 *Farm Assist (2)* [2009] at 22 & 13
148 *Farm Assist (2)* [2009] at 29
149 *Farm Assist (2)* [2009] at 44(2)
150 *Farm Assist (2)* [2009] at 44(3)
151 *Farm Assist (2)* [2009] at 23. See Toulson & Phipps on Confidentiality [2004] at 15-013–15-016
152 *Farm Assist (2)* [2009] at 23. Mr Justice Ramsey noted that Toulson & Phipps describe arbitration as 'the closest parallel of a dispute resolution technique' to mediation.
153 *Farm Assist (2)* [2009] at 23 & 44(1)

can 'enforce a confidentiality provision'.[154] Therefore, in *Farm Assist (2)* the parties, FAL and DEFRA, could not waive their right to confidentiality at the expense of the mediator's 'right'.[155]

The court, however, took a narrow reading to the specific confidentiality clause agreed by the parties and the mediator.[156] The clause stated that the parties would not call the mediator as witness in 'relation to the Dispute', which was read to mean the dispute identified in the 'preamble' to the mediation agreement relating to work performed by FAL.[157] The dispute before the court was not about the work undertaken but about a claim that the mediated settlement had been reached through duress and therefore the parties' 'express' agreement about confidentiality did not apply to calling the mediator as a witness about the alleged conduct in the mediation:[158]

> The dispute with which I am concerned is not that dispute but the dispute whether the settlement agreement was entered into under duress. In this context, I consider that the phrase 'in relation to the Dispute' has been chosen to be narrow and some limited support may be derived from contrasting it with the use of the phrase 'connected with the Dispute' used in paragraph 12 of the Mediation Procedure.

Ramsey J agreed with Toulson and Phipps that 'the basis of mediation would be destroyed' if parties were able to 'publicise' what had gone on between themselves or between themselves and the mediator whether confidentiality was based on their agreement (contractual) or an 'equitable obligation'.[159] The question of whether confidentiality is 'absolute' in mediation was decided with reference to Lord Bingham MR in *Re D (Minors)* when disclosure in family conciliation is only ordered when there has been or is likely to be 'serious harm to the wellbeing' of a child.[160] In other mediation contexts, confidentiality should be protected unless 'after balancing the various interests, it is in the interests of public policy that the communications or information be used or disclosed'.[161] The position was deemed to be 'similar to arbitration' which allows disclosure 'in limited circumstances' when the parties have consented or it is 'in the interests of justice'.[162] In the opinion of Ramsey J there is an 'implied confidentiality' in mediation even in the absence of an 'express provision' but in either case the court may order disclosure in

---

154 *Farm Assist (2)* [2009] at 29 & 44(1)
155 *Farm Assist (2)* [2009] at 29
156 See for example, Allen (2011); Koo (2011); Kallipetis (2009); Wood (2008) (2009)
157 *Farm Assist (2)* [2009] at 47
158 *Farm Assist (2)* [2009] at 48
159 *Farm Assist (2)* [2009] at 24
160 *Re D (Minors) Conciliation: Disclosure of Information* [1993] Fam 231 at 26
161 *Farm Assist (2)* [2009] at 27
162 *Farm Assist (2)* [2009] at 28

'the interests of justice'.[163] In *Farm Assist (2)* it was in the interests of justice that the mediator gave evidence in order that the court could 'properly determine the allegation of economic duress' and the fact the mediator had 'little recollection' should not prevent attendance as 'memories can be jogged'.[164]

Farm Assist (2) provides clarification about the boundaries of confidentiality, which endows some measure of protection to mediators who can resist a witness order unless it is in the 'interests of justice' that they should be compelled to attend court. The recognition that mediators have confidentiality in mediation which the parties cannot override by their agreement to waive privilege may assist in some limited circumstances but the information remains admissible if it fits any of the without prejudice exceptions explored above.[165] Koo observes that 'contractual confidentiality' is no wider than that provided by the without prejudice rule but it may protect disclosure if the court does not 'apply' any of the exceptions or it may form the basis for making an application for an 'injunction' if there is a threat of breaching confidentiality.[166] The narrow reading of the express confidentiality clause failed to help the mediator in *Farm Assist (2)* and presumably would not have assisted either of the parties should they have resisted disclosure on the strength of agreed confidentiality. The practical advice for drafting mediation agreements is that they should use broadly drawn clauses which cover information not only in 'connection with the dispute' but also 'any record or notes relating to the mediation' and that a further clause should clearly state that the mediator will not 'agree to act as a witness'.[167]

Farm Assist (2) is a landmark decision that defines and interprets the position of confidentiality in mediation but it does leave the court with wide discretion when it is deemed to be in the 'interests of justice'.[168] In *DEFRA* the defendants were accused of 'illegitimate pressure and/or bad faith' in the 'conduct of the mediation' because they 'refused or failed to take a structured, reasoned, bilateral or bona fide approach to the valuation of FAL's account' and because of other 'examples' of their 'conduct' in mediation 'and/or the contents of its mediation statement'. In the event the case was not pursued so that it is impossible to gauge whether the conduct in mediation reached the level of economic duress or what, if anything, may have been decided about the parties engaging in 'bad faith' behaviour when mediating.[169]

---

163 *Farm Assist (2)* [2009] at 29
164 *Farm Assist (2)* [2009] at 5
165 Koo (2011) at 200
166 Koo (2011) at 200
167 See Tumbridge (2010) at 148; Brookes (2009)
168 See Allen (2009). See for example, Koo (2011): Kallipetis (2009); Wood (2008) (2009)
169 *Farm Assist (2)* [2009] at 51. See Allen (2009)

Special mediation privilege?

Mediators were reported to be 'considerably' concerned that mediation is only protected to the same degree as that afforded to without prejudice negotiations, particularly when there was confusion surrounding the admissibility of admissions and acknowledgments.[170] Nor has the identification of 'implied' and 'contractual' mediation confidentiality assuaged fears that mediators are vulnerable to court witness orders in view of the wide discretion given to judges to investigate when the 'interests of justice' demand it.[171] There have been calls from judges and leading mediators for a 'broader more comprehensive level' of confidentiality because of the 'public interest in encouraging mediation' such as exists for 'matrimonial' communications'[172] and for a special privilege for mediators similar to that given to legal professionals.[173]

Mediation privilege

In *Re D (Minors)*, the mother had meetings with a clinical psychologist after the breakdown of her marriage, some of which the father attended.[174] She then sought disclosure of a statement made by the psychologist at a hearing for a residency order but the father resisted on the basis that the meetings were privileged.[175] The Court of Appeal recognised an 'unquestioned line of authority' establishing that the courts will not 'compel' disclosure of information 'given to a third party' when it was done 'with a view to conciliation'.[176] Bingham LJ in handing down the judgment stated that it was not 'fruitful' to deliberate on the 'relationship' of this type of privilege with 'without prejudice privilege' because although there was a 'similar underlying basis' it was a 'new category of privilege based on the public interest in the stability of marriage'.[177] The Court observed that it was 'undesirable' for the law to stray from 'best professional practice', which although not 'authoritative' did show the 'inviolability of privilege' given to statements in family conciliation 'in proceedings' with the exception where the statement

170 Briggs (2009a); Allen (2011); Kallipetis (2009); Wood (2008) (2009)
171 Brookes (2009). See also Briggs (2009a); Allen (2011); Kallipetis (2009); Wood (2008) (2009)
172 Briggs (2009b) at 508. See also Cornes (2008); Kallipetis (2009) (2011); Brown & Marriott (2011); Wood (2009)
173 Briggs (2009b). See also Koo (2011). The development of a special mediator privilege is considered in more detail below.
174 *In Re D (Minors) Conciliation: Disclosure of Information*, [1993] Fam 231 at 237
175 *In Re D (Minors)* [1993] citing Lord Hailsham of St Marylebone and Lord Simon of Glaisdale in *D v. National Society for the Prevention of Cruelty to Children* [1978] AC 171 at 237
176 *In Re D (Minors)* [1993] at 238
177 Per Sir Thomas Bingham MR 238 *In Re D (Minors) Conciliation: Disclosure of Information*, citing Lord Hailsham of St Marylebone and Lord Simon of Glaisdale in *D v. National Society for the Prevention of Cruelty to Children* [1978] AC 171 at 231 & 238

indicates 'serious harm' to a child either in the 'future' or the 'past'.[178] The Court, however, elected not to make 'any more general statements' on the law and specifically stated that the decision was given 'to cover this case and no others', which should be decided on 'their own special circumstances'.[179] Both commentators and legal counsel have used this special category of privilege as the basis of legal arguments for extending it to other civil mediation contexts.[180]

Widening mediation privilege

In *Brown v. Rice & Patel*, an argument was forwarded for mediation privilege, which as a 'minimum' should prevent the mediator being called as a witness or producing documents.[181] Counsel for the ADR Group, in court as 'interveners', made reference 'to a budding mediation privilege in this and other jurisdictions' and to judicial comment in *Reed* that there was a 'fuzzy' line 'between a third party assisted ADR and party to party negotiations' though Mr Isaacs QC did not believe that this provided 'support for the existence of a distinct mediation privilege.[182] The case was decided on an application of the without prejudice rules but did recognise the opinions that champion a 'so called mediation privilege' and the probable need for 'future' development by the common law or statute.[183]

Following *Brown v. Rice*, other courts have made passing comment to 'mediation privilege'. In *Cattley* the mediator made an 'application' to 'rescind' an order to provide information to the court about statements made in mediation on the grounds of a 'clear rule of public policy' that the parties should be encouraged to speak 'in a frank and open manner'.[184] In a letter to the court, the mediator contended that the Civil Procedure Rules 'supported and promoted' settlement and ordering disclosure would have a 'profound' negative effect on settlement in mediation.[185] The mediator's counsel make reference to the 'chilling effect on mediation' if disclosure was ordered, but it was accepted that there was 'no special privilege rule in relation to mediations and no special public policy involved over and above the general public policy that was attached to privilege'.[186] Although Master Bragge made reference to a 'distinct mediation privilege' in the future developed either by court or legislation, the decision in *Cattley* was also based on the without prejudice rules (see above).[187]

---

178 *In Re D* [1993] at 241
179 *In Re D* [1993] at 240–1
180 See for example, *Briggs* (2009a, b). See for example, *Brown v. Rice & Patel* [2007]
181 *Brown v. Rice & Patel* [2007] at 19
182 *Brown v. Rice & Patel* [2007] at 19; see *Reed* [2004] at 3 & 5
183 *Brown v. Rice & Patel* [2007] at 20
184 *Cattley* (2009) at 9–10; see Briggs (2009a)
185 *Cattley* (2009) at 9
186 *Cattley* (2009) at 13
187 *Cattley* (2009) at 23

Ramsey J in *Farm Assist (2)* reviewed both authoritative commentary and case comments on mediation privilege before noting that the 'use of the words confidential, privileged and without prejudice' all indicate the importance of a 'general rule that what takes place in a mediation should not be disclosed to third parties outside the mediation'.[188] Ramsay J recognised a 'need' for a 'further privilege' but decided the case on an interpretation of 'implied' and contractual confidentiality and suggested that the privilege defined by Brown and Marriott and *Re D* may be 'no more than a duty of confidentiality and the reference to privilege merely a question of semantics'.[189]

The cases all indicate that the lower courts are unlikely to initiate a new species of privilege and whether the appeal courts will take up the challenge remains to be seen. The Court of Appeal in *Halsey*, although not specifically considering the principle of confidentiality or without privilege accepted that the 'integrity' of mediation requires it to be confidential and that it 'was not a matter for the court' to enquire into the positions adopted by the parties.[190] Brown and Marriott in their most recent edition of *ADR: Principles and Practice* support the call for statutory intervention for mediation privilege, as the process becomes an 'adjunct of the court'.[191] They 'agree' with Cornes that this should not be left to the common law to develop on a 'case by case' basis on the without prejudice rules but should be carefully drafted for a 'consistent approach'.[192] In view of the general reluctance exhibited by the courts for mediation privilege and the unlikeness of statutory intervention, commentators suggest another approach the law could take would be to protect the relationship between the mediator and the parties in the form of a mediator privilege.[193]

Mediator privilege

Mr Justice Briggs argues that the process of mediation is more than engaging in 'without prejudice negotiations' because mediators have a special relationship with the parties when they persuade them in the caucus 'to share information about their views, hopes and fears about the dispute' on the promise that these will be kept 'secret'.[194] This 'unique' role enables them to help the participants reach a successful outcome.[195] Mediation 'magic'[196] is said to

---

188 *Farm Assist (2)* [2009] at 43
189 *Farm Assist (2)* [2009] at 43 citing Brown & Marriott (1999)
190 *Halsey* (2004) at 14
191 Brown & Marriott (2011) at 551–2
192 Brown & Marriott (2011) at 551; Cornes (2008) at 395, 404
193 See for example, Briggs (2009b); Kallipetis (2011); Koo (2011); Wood (2009)
194 Briggs (2009b); See also Kallipetis (2011) at 188–9
195 Kallipetis (2011) at 206; Briggs (2009b)
196 Rute (2010) at 28 'The parties and litigants who have participated in a successful mediation sometimes refer to "the magic" of the mediation process. If sorcery is involved, it is more than likely apparent during and following the mediator's private meetings (caucus) with the individual parties.'

occur 'during and following the caucus' but Mr Justice Briggs believes that the without prejudice exceptions jeopardises the parties' willingness 'to share secrets'.[197] Furthermore, Kallipetis contends that mediators are not sufficiently protected by the without prejudice rule because privilege belongs to the parties, which they can 'waive', or to the discussions between the parties and their lawyers and mediators are in the position of 'legal advisors' in the process.[198] There are concerns that the deficiencies in the common law on mediation confidentiality and without prejudice will negate the effectiveness of the process at an early stage of 'development' because parties will not feel assured that they can participate in an 'open and frank' manner.[199] Commentators suggest that a special mediator privilege, akin to that given to legal professionals, would persuade parties to speak 'openly and frankly' and provide information, which improves the likelihood for settlement.[200]

Legal professional privilege has a long pedigree[201] based on the 'interests of justice' that people can safely 'consult' with lawyers and 'dare tell them' the details of their case.[202] Clients and solicitors have 'absolute'[203] privilege, although the party can waive it, but it can only be 'overridden by statute' or when the client or lawyer 'abuses the confidential relationship to facilitate crime or fraud'.[204] The status of legal privilege information revealed to the mediator during mediation was clarified in *Farm Assist (2)* and sharing privileged 'documents' with the mediator does not act as a 'waiver'.[205]

Briggs maintains that a privilege for 'mediator secrets' would not hamper the without prejudice rules which would continue to apply to 'Shared Information' because people are 'fallible', which may lead to 'misrepresentation,

---

197 Briggs (2009b). See also Koo (2011) at 273; Tumbridge (2010) at 147; Wood (2009) at 7; Kallipetis (2009) at 5
198 Kallipetis (2011) at 187–8
199 Kallipetis (2011) at 187–8
200 See Kallipetis (2011) at 188; Briggs (2009b)
201 *Three Rivers District Council & Ors v. The Governor & Company of the Bank of England* Rev 1 [2003] EWCA Civ 474 (3 April 2003) at 8. Legal privilege is described as being of 'great antiquity'.
202 Per Lord Brougham in *Greenough v Gaskell* (1833) 1 My. & K. 98 citing in *Three Rivers* (2003) at 8 'But it is out of regard to the interests of justice, which cannot be upholden, and to the administration of justice, which cannot go on, without the aid of men skilled in jurisprudence, in the practice of the Courts, and in those matters affecting rights and obligations which form the subject of all judicial proceedings. If the privilege did not exist at all, every one would be thrown upon his own legal resources; deprived of all professional assistance, a man would not venture to consult any skilful person, or would only dare to tell his counsellor half his case. If the privilege were confined to communications connected with suits begun, or intended, or expected, or apprehended, no one could safely adopt such precautions as might eventually render any proceedings successful, or all proceedings superfluous'.
203 Per Lord Brougham in *Greenough v. Gaskell* (1833) 1 My. & K. 98 cited in *Three Rivers* (2003) at 8
204 See Koo (2011); Koo & Zhao (2011) citing Lord Bingham CJ in *Paragon Finance Plc v. Freshfields* 1 WLR 1183; [1999] EWCA 955
205 *Farm Assist (2)* [2009] at 44(3)

fraud, duress and undue influence' and because both oral and written mediation are 'vulnerable to legal uncertainties'.[206] Regardless of this cogent argument, Higgins notes that recent EU and domestic case law points towards a 'restrictive approach' to any extension of legal professional privilege.[207] EU law does not extend legal privilege to 'in-house' legal advisors because lawyers have to be 'independent', although Higgins maintains this is contrary to English law,[208] and the Court of Appeal did not approve privilege to 'other professions' giving legal advice.[209]

At present, it would appear unlikely that the common law will provide mediators with a 'special' legal privilege or develop that of family conciliators to a wider area of practice.[210] Furthermore, not all mediation advocates fully support the proposition that the process or the mediator requires special treatment beyond that already provided by the without prejudice rule or the recently defined rules on mediation confidentiality, particularly if fraud or duress has been perpetrated 'through the mediator' because in the interests of 'fairness' such evidence should be available to the courts.[211] Wood contends that increased litigation about mediation is the inevitable 'price' mediators pay as their profession gains 'maturity' and there should be no special dispensation because courts have a duty to decide cases on the 'best evidence' available:[212]

> If a party is said to have made a fraudulent representation or exerted duress in the presence of the mediator (*a fortiori* where has done so through the mediator) should the mediator not be available and even keen to give his or her evidence? That evidence may simply be indispensable in establishing the truth of these very serious allegations.

European Union developments on confidentiality

The proposals for mediator privilege attracted critical attention when plans for implementing the EU Mediation Directive were publicised.[213] The Mediation Directive required Member States to introduce protection for mediators (and mediator administrators) against being compelled to give evidence except in limited circumstances in cross border disputes. This lead to speculation that an 'opportunity' existed for wider statutory intervention in the area of mediation confidentiality because the EU Directive advised

---

206 Briggs (2009b) at 551
207 See Higgins (2011) at 192
208 Higgins (2011) at 191–2 citing *Akzo Nobel Chemicals Ltd v. European Commission* (C-550/07 P) (2010) 160 NLJ 1300
209 In *R. (on the application of Prudential Plc) v. Special Commissioner of Income Tax* [2010] EWCA Civ 1094. See Higgins (2011) at 189
210 *In Re D* (1993)
211 Wood (2009) at 6–7; See also Koo (2011) at 48; Green (1986); Wood (2009)
212 Wood (2009) at 7–8 at 7
213 Briggs (2009a); Wood (2009); Cornes (2008)

Member States that they might apply any changes in law to 'internal mediation processes'[214] and Article 7(2) of the Directive did not 'preclude' the possibility of 'enacting stricter measures to protect the confidentiality of mediation'.[215]

EU Mediation Directive

The EU Mediation Directive Recitals required each Member State to have a 'minimum degree of compatibility' with their civil procedure rules on how to 'protect' mediation information from later litigation or arbitration proceedings.[216] An earlier EU Directive draft[217] had advocated an 'absolute bar' on calling the mediator to give evidence about party offers or willingness to mediate and had recommended excluding all statements including admissions, party or mediator's suggestions for settlement or a party's readiness to accept a mediator's proposal.[218] The final version of Article 7 however only requires each State to 'ensure' that mediators and administrators are not 'compelled to give evidence' of 'information arising out of or in connection with the mediation in subsequent arbitration or litigation' unless either the parties agree or it is 'necessary for overriding considerations of public policy'.[219] Specific exceptions are given for protecting children or preventing physical or psychological harm to a person or where the evidence is necessary 'to implement or enforce' the mediation agreement.[220]

The UK implemented the requirements by Statutory Instrument in 2011 with regulation 9 providing mediators and mediation administrators with the 'right to withhold mediation evidence' in court or arbitration proceedings but with exceptions provided in reg 10.[221] A court may order mediators or administrators to 'give or disclose evidence' when all the parties agree;[222] or where it is 'necessary for the overriding consideration of public policy in accordance with article 7(1) (a) of the Mediation Directive';[223] or where it is 'necessary to implement or enforce the mediation agreement'.[224] Allen notes that the regulations do not provide an explanation of the meaning of 'overriding public policy',[225] although Article 7 of the Mediation Directive alludes to the 'risk' to children and 'harm' to other persons.

---

214 EU Mediation Directive (2008), Recital at 8
215 See Briggs (2009a); Wood (2009); Cornes (2008)
216 EU Mediation Directive (2008), Recital at 23. See Cornes (2008) at 395
217 Draft Mediation Directive 2004/0251 (COD). See Cornes (2008) at 403
218 See for example, Cornes (2008) at 395; Allen (2011)
219 EU Mediation Directive (2008) at 1 & 1(a)
220 EU Mediation Directive (2008) at 1(b)
221 Cross-Border Mediation (EU Directive) Regulations 2011, No. 1133 regs 9 & 10
222 Cross-Border Mediation (EU Directive) Regulations 2011, Part 2, reg10(a)
223 Cross-Border Mediation (EU Directive) Regulations 2011, Part 2, reg10(b)
224 Cross-Border Mediation (EU Directive) Regulations 2011, Part 2, reg10(c)
225 Allen (2011)

CPR Part 78.24 now provides the procedure for enforcing mediation settlements in cross border disputes.[226] A party who wants to 'obtain evidence' from 'the mediator or the mediation administrator'[227] or requests their 'attendance as a witness' has to provide 'evidence that all the parties agree'.[228] Furthermore, the party must show that 'it is necessary for overriding considerations of public policy, in accordance with Article 7(1) (a) of the Mediation Directive; or the disclosure or inspection of the mediation settlement is necessary to implement or enforce the mediation settlement agreement'.[229] In compliance with the EU Mediation Directive, CPR has given limited protection for the confidentiality of the mediation process in CPR Part 5.4 (Court Documents), which specifically states that 'no document relating to a mediation order can be inspected by a party not party to the proceedings without permission of the court'.[230]

Criticism of EU regulations

The major criticisms of the cross border regulations are that they introduce law and legal principles on mediator confidentiality which may apply different standards depending on the source of the mediation agreement and that they may even negatively effect 'the common law' developments in confidentiality.[231] There is uncertainty whether the current law governing domestic mediations is 'more or less strict' than the EU requirements for cross border mediations, which Allen maintains will in the future 'undermine' the process:[232]

> The point I make as forcefully as I can is that, as the law stands at present, we in England & Wales do not know whether our law on this topic is more or less strict than what the EUMD (European Union Mediation Directive) requires. To enact the provisions of the EUMD without knowing this is extremely dangerous, bearing in mind that confidentiality is the cornerstone of mediation's success and heedless damage to the concept could profoundly undermine its usefulness.

Allen explores whether the regulations would provide 'greater or weaker protection' for mediator confidentiality in *Farm Assist (2)*, which he suggests was influenced by 'both parties' agreeing to the mediator providing evidence and questions whether the court would have made the order had only one party

---

226 CPR r78.24. See Chapter 3
227 CPR r78.26 & 78.27
228 CPR r78.26 at (2) (a); CPR 78.27 at (2) (a)
229 CPR r78.27 at (2) (b) (c) & 78.27 at (2) (b) (c)
230 CPR Part 5 Court Documents at 5.4
231 See for example, Kallipetis (2009) at 5; Allen (2011); Cornes (2008); Phillips (2011)
232 Allen (2011) http://www.cedr.com/articles/?293 downloaded on 28 February 2013

agreed.[233] Should the order have been issued with the consent of only one party then the Cross Border Regulations requiring 'both parties' agreement' would 'strengthen English law', which he contrasts to the decision in *Cumbria* and *Brown v. Rice* where the court refused to admit evidence when one party refused:[234]

> It would seem that the judge only felt able to go that far because *both parties* consented to the mediator being called. What we do not know is whether, if FAL [Farm Assist Limited] had objected but DEFRA persisted, the judge would have felt that he could nevertheless rule that the mediator should be called. If that were to be the case (and we do not know), then the EUMD provision, which requires *both parties* to agree to this would be a strengthening of English law. Contrast *Cumbria Waste*, where the judge found that confidentiality kept 'mediation evidence' from a later interested party (though calling the mediator as witness was not at issue here, and nor was it in *Brown v. Rice*, where the judge did admit 'mediation evidence' despite opposition by the other party and a mediation provider).

This may be one reading of *Farm Assist (2)* but the final point in paragraph 53 is that the mediator has a 'right to rely on the confidentiality provision in the mediation agreement' which was overridden in this case in 'the interests of justice' implying that judicial discretion can be used even when one party is not in agreement:[235]

> Finally, whilst the Mediator has a right to rely on the confidentiality provision in the Mediation Agreement, I consider that this is a case where, as an exception, the interests of justice lie strongly in favour of evidence being given of what was said and done.

The Regulations are also criticised for ambiguity both in drafting and the terminology used because of the transfer of 'language' and principles into the English jurisdiction.[236] Commentators observe that the term 'all parties' does not indicate whether this includes the mediator or other parties not involved in the litigation or arbitration proceedings.[237] Cornes observes that under the Directive 'both parties' may agree that evidence should be given by the mediator or mediation administrator but no explanation is given as to whether this includes evidence from the caucus (which involves only the mediator and one of the parties).[238] However, as Fender-Allison suggests, this

---

233 Allen (2011)
234 Allen (2011)
235 *Farm Assist (2)* [2009] at 53
236 See for example, Allen (2011); Cornes (2008)
237 Allen (2011); Cornes (2008)
238 Cornes (2008) at 404

does imply that the parties' rights prevail over those of the mediator who may be compellable as a witness if both litigants agree.[239] Allen criticises the English legislation for using the term 'mediation evidence', which has a narrower meaning than 'mediation information' (the term used in the EU Directive), because it may be interpreted to 'import the whole law of evidence as to relevance and admissibility':[240]

> In the hands of a subtle judge, encouraged by counsel straining to do the best for a client, might this not lead to an interpretation wholly unintended by the EUMD differently from this English statutory definition, either because of this change of word or generally? 'Evidence' is arguably more restricted in meaning than 'information', as it imports the whole law of evidence as to relevance and admissibility.

There is further concern that the choice of the EU term 'overriding considerations of public policy' is inconsistent with the common law developments in *Farm Assist (2)*, which uses the phrase 'in the interests of justice'.[241] The EU term does not permit evidence unless there is a 'serious threat to a fundamental interest in society';[242] in comparison 'interests of justice' is said to provide judges with a wider discretion to order disclosure on the grounds that it is 'useful'[243] to the court rather than requiring a judicial consideration of 'competing policies'.[244] Allen is critical of the court decision in *Farm Assist (2)*, which was prepared to order disclosure of a 'four-year allegation' of economic duress by a government body with no consideration of the 'interests of justice' in protecting mediator confidentiality and the 'public confidence' in mediation.[245]

Commentators regret that the lost 'opportunity' for enhancing mediation confidentiality or that at the very least that the provisions ensure that the law is the same for both cross border and domestic mediation.[246] Nevertheless, there is some optimism that the regulations may 'stimulate parallel protection' as common law decisions take notice of EU requirements when judges are invited to look at both.[247] However, the judiciary's negative response to the government's proposal to enact similar provisions for domestic mediation settlements suggests that many judges may not be strongly inclined to take particular heed of the EU regulations when considering whether to compel

239 Fender-Allison (2011)
240 Allen (2011)
241 See Phillips (2011) at 738; See also Fender-Allison (2011); Allen (2011); Cornes (2008)
242 Phillips (2011); Allen (2011); Cornes (2008); Fender-Allison (2011)
243 Allen (2011)
244 Briggs (2009a)
245 Allen (2011); See also Fender-Allison (2011)
246 See for example, Allen (2011); Allen & Mackie (2010); Kallipetis (2011)
247 Koo & Zhao (2011) at 277; See also Allen (2011)

mediators to give evidence from domestic mediations.[248] Lord Jackson's response was that such legislation would only add a 'raft of unwelcome rules' and that there is no necessity for 'special rules' because the without prejudice rules make 'evidence' from negotiations settlement inadmissible regardless 'whether a mediator is involved'.[249]

Comparative approaches to mediation confidentiality: the USA, Australia and Hong Kong

The English jurisdiction may regrettably be moving to a dual approach to confidentiality depending on whether the parties have participated in a domestic or cross-border mediation. Conversely, the common law may reconsider the principles circumscribed in *Farm Assist (2)* to take into consideration the rules enacted to implement EU requirements, although statutory intervention is unlikely given the government proposals for mandatory mediation for small claims were curtailed to automatic referral to a mediation consultation.[250] Mediation developments in the UK have been considerably influenced by the experience of other countries further along in their national 'mediation movement' and it may be constructive to consider how other common law jurisdictions have tackled shielding mediation communications orders to encourage the participants to speak openly whilst protecting them from harm or from unjust or unfair settlements.[251]

United States' approach to confidentiality and admissibility

There is no universal approach to mediation confidentiality in the USA and protection may be provided through contractual arrangements, common law principles on compromise agreements, state, federal or court evidential rules, mediation privilege or by adopting the Uniform Mediation Act, which provides for mediator privilege.[252] The myriad number of sources creates 'confusion' not only between states because what is confidential in one state may not be so in another but also because of a lack of clarity over interpretation.[253]

This section provides an overview because the constraints of this work make it impossible to look at the approach each state uses for securing

---

248 Lord Chief Justice Jackson (2011) (http://www.judiciary.gov.uk/JCO%2fDocuments%2f Consultations%2flcj-mr-response-solving-disputes-county-court.pdf   Downloaded   on 28 February 2013
249 Lord Jackson (2011) at 51–4
250 See Ministry Justice Response to the Consultation (2012)
251 Koo says that *Farm Assist (2)* [2009] was 'a fair result'.
252 Cole et al. (2012) at 8.1. For a detailed exploration of confidentiality and privilege in the USA see for example, Cole et al. (2012); Hiers (2005); Kovach (2006); Choquette (2006); Noble Foster & Prentice (2009)
253 Hiers (2005) at 532–3

confidentiality or review the growing jurisprudence in this area.[254] It does, however, provide a more detailed analysis of the Uniform Mediation Act because many UK commentators reference it, particularly when calling for a wider protection in England and Wales[255] and, although only 11 'jurisdictions' at the time of writing have adopted it in the USA, observers note its 'influence' on new legislation in other states.[256]

Contractual arrangements for confidentiality

Parties when entering into contractual arrangements to mediate may agree to clauses attempting to preserve confidentiality but these may fall short, either if the court deems the agreement is contrary to 'public policy', if for example a party is trying to 'suppress evidence', and/or the contract provision may not protect against disclosure by a third person.[257] When a litigant is resisting disclosure from a party not privy to the confidentiality clause, the court may engage in a 'balancing act', for example, the need to 'vindicate a legal position' against protecting the 'privacy interest'.[258] Where the parties have signed confidentiality agreements, Cole et al. indicate USA courts are likely to uphold clauses on contractual or 'unfairness' principles as a party should not be able to renege on agreements to be bound, but the public policy argument will be 'weighed' against the 'harm' to private interests such as 'trade secrets, confidential business matters, or other information'.[259]

Admissibility at common law

Courts in the USA sometimes exclude mediation information by extending the common law rules governing the inadmissibility of 'offers of compromise' in a later court action, which is based on similar policy reasons to the without prejudice rules in the English jurisdiction that parties should be encouraged to settle disputes; but also on the basis of 'low probative weight'.[260] Analogous with the without privilege rules, courts in the USA have taken diverse

---

254 Coben & Thompson (2006); Cole et al. (2012); Kovack (2006)
255 See for example, Wood (2009); Kallipetis (2011); Cornes (2008)
256 Cole et al. (2012) at 8.14; (2011); Kelly (2011). The Uniform Law Commission report that a further three states are listed for 'Introduction Enactment' in 2013 http://www.uniformlaws.org/Act.aspx?title=Mediation%20Act Accessed on 1 February 2013
257 Cole et al. (2012) at 8.37–8.38
258 Cole et al. (2012) at 8.38 citing *Grumman Aerospace Corp v. Titanium Metals Corp of America*, 91 FRD. 84, 32 Fed R Serv 2d 1520 (EDNY 1981). In contrast, Cole et al. (2012) cite *Hinshaw, Winkler, Draa, Marsh & Still*, 51 Cal. App. 4th 233, 58 Cal Rptr 2d 791 (6th Dist 1996), when the court did not permit disclosure of documents giving salary information because the 'public interest' in this matter did not override 'privacy interests'.
259 Cole et al. (2012) at 8.39. Citing for example, *Floral Accounting Systems, Inc. v. Florists' Transworld Delivery, Inc.*, 2008 WL 2224416 (WD La 2008)
260 Cole et al. (2012) at 8.5

approaches to whether admissibility extends to 'all mediation communications' or only to admissions of liability, which means that parties have to verify the position depending on where the mediation took place.[261]

Evidential provision

Some states have implemented legislation to prohibit 'testimonial evidence' from mediation being disclosed at court or arbitral forums but these provisions do not always preclude public 'disclosure' or disclosure at other mediations.[262] For example, Kovach identifies Texas legislation which prevents mediation information from being disclosed in court unless both parties agree but notes that many statutes permit evidence that is already 'discoverable or admissible' or contain specific provisions which obligate information where, for example, child abuse or criminal activity is divulged when mediating.[263] Some statutory provisions ensure that 'discoverable' information remains admissible in order to prevent parties from 'hiding information' in the mediation process but the position may differ as to whether the evidentiary rules apply only to communications in mediation or to communications in preparation for mediation and whether they apply only to written communications or include oral communications.[264]

Kovach notes that federal law through the ADR Act 1998 requires district courts to 'authorise' the use of at 'least one ADR process in civil cases' and to implement local rules, which 'provide for confidentiality and prohibit disclosure of confidential dispute resolution communications'.[265] Similarly, the Administration Dispute Resolution Act 1996 requires each administrative 'agency' to have an ADR policy with provision that the 'neutral' cannot 'voluntarily disclose, or through discovery or compulsory process be required to disclose any dispute resolution communication or confidence'.[266] The Act provides exceptions to confidentiality, which include when all parties agree in writing,[267] where statute requires that the information be public,[268] where it is required to 'prevent manifest injustice,[269] 'to establish a violation of law'[270] or to 'prevent harm to public health or safety'.[271]

261 Cole et al. (2012) at 8.5
262 Kovach (2006) at 435
263 Kovach (2006) at 440–1 citing Texas Civ Proc and Rem s 1540.073.
264 Kovach (2006) at 439. Kovach cites *In re Learjet* 59 SW 3d 842 (Tex Appl 2001) when a Texas Appeal court permitted discovery of a videotape made 'solely for the mediation'.
265 Kovach (2006) at 442; See also Hensler (2003) at 185
266 Administration Dispute Resolution Act 1996, s3
267 Administration Dispute Resolution Act 1996, s574 (1)
268 Administration Dispute Resolution Act 1996, s574 (3)
269 Administration Dispute Resolution Act 1996, s574 (4) (a)
270 Administration Dispute Resolution Act 1996, s574 4(b)
271 Administration Dispute Resolution Act 1996, s574 4(c)

Statutory privilege

Another approach has been for states to implement procedural rules to distinguish between 'testimonial privilege' and confidentiality as two different concepts: confidentiality means that the parties will not 'disclose information' to non-participants of the mediation; whereas privilege signifies that statements are 'not admissible' in court or other tribunals.[272]

> This principle – that statements made in mediation will not be repeated – encompasses two related, but distinct concepts: confidentiality and privilege. The principle of confidentiality provides that the parties will not repeat statements made in mediation to those not present at the mediation. The mediation privilege, on the other hand, is a narrower protection, which provides that statements made in mediation are not admissible in court proceedings, arbitrations or legislative hearings.

Mediation privilege 'protects' against any disclosure regardless of the purpose, which is different to 'evidentiary exclusion' based on 'admissibility' rules for court purposes: 'Thus, most mediation privileges govern use of the mediation information in all forums – not just those judicial hearings governed by the rules of evidence, as with evidentiary exclusions'.[273] Privilege rules derive from a different 'source' to the evidentiary rules and are based on the special 'confidential relationship' between various parties involved in the mediation and 'well established privileges' given to 'attorney-client, doctor-patient and spousal communications'.[274] Kovach observes that many codes and standards of mediation practice in the USA 'operate' under the understanding that there is a confidential privileged relationship between the parties and the mediator but such a 'broad privilege' is not universally applied because it is sometimes perceived to be different to legal privilege.[275]

States in the USA have drafted 'mediation privilege' in divergent ways both in relation to who has the privilege and its extent.[276] Observers illustrate that mediation law only affords privilege to the mediator, whereas other jurisdictions extend this to the parties[277] or to 'non-parties' such as 'expert advisors'.[278] Cole et al. note that the 'scope' of the information protected

---

272 Noble Foster & Prentice (2009) at 164; Kovach (2006) at 436; Hiers (2005)
273 Cole et al. (2012) at 8.6
274 Kovach (2006) at 440. The author cites a Texas statute which provides confidentiality privilege unless the parties agree: *Tex Civ Prac and Rem s 154.073*. See also Hiers (2005) at 532
275 Kovach (2006) at 440–1
276 Hiers (2005); Cole et al. (2012) at 8.12
277 For example, Florida mediation law s. 44.405 provides that 'all mediation communications shall be confidential. A mediation participant shall not disclose a mediation communication to a person other than another mediation participant or a participant's counsel.' See Noble Foster & Prentice (2009) at 163–4
278 See Hiers (2005) at 538–9

by privilege also varies greatly and may 'shield' all mediation information, by providing an 'absolute bar' on disclosure or by being 'qualified' by 'balancing' the need for information against public policy requirements or by only protecting evidence from the mediator.[279]

For example, Florida State Mediation and Confidentiality Act chapter 44.405 takes a 'broad' approach by providing that 'all mediation communication shall be confidential and that a mediation participant shall not disclose a mediation communication to a person other than another mediation participant or participant's counsel'. Similarly, Section 1119(a) of the California Evidence Code excludes admissibility 'of anything said or any admission made for the purpose of, in the course of or pursuant to a mediation or a mediation consultation' and Section 1119(c) states that 'All communications, negotiations, or settlement discussions by and between participants in the course of a mediation or a mediation consultation shall remain confidential'.[280] In contrast to the state Section, Judge Marcus states that the federal courts in California adopt a more 'ad hoc' line to confidentiality by permitting disclosure of threats to life or injury or when mediation has been used to conceal criminal activity and the Eastern District Court allows evidence that is 'required by law' or where the parties agree in writing.[281]

Commentators explore the problems of adopting a 'nearly absolute bar' to information from mediation in California where it has caused 'judicial angst', particularly when 'attorney malpractice' or 'bad faith' has been at issue.[282] For example, Kelly cites the attempts of the appeal courts in California to introduce an exception to allow disclosure of 'attorney malpractice'.[283] However, the Supreme Court reversed the decision holding that under the Evidence Code, ss1119 (a) (b) 'All communication, negotiations or settlement discussion by and between participants in the course of a mediation . . . shall remain confidential', which is an 'absolute bar' that does not permit 'judicially crafted exceptions or limitations even where competing public policies apply'.[284] As Cole et al. observe recent cases in California continue to apply an absolute bar on mediation evidence to prove 'legal malpractice',[285] or for 'any court created exception' for 'coercion and duress'.[286]

---

279 Cole et al. (2012) at 8.12. The authors cite California Evidence Code, Section 1119(a), which provides an 'absolute bar'.
280 Rule 1119(a) of the California Evidence Code
281 See for example, Marcus (2011) at 23
282 Cole et al. (2012) at 8.2 & 8.28; See also Kelly (2011)
283 Kelly (2011). See also Cole et al. (2012) at 8.14. For example, citing the UMA (2003) s6(a) (5) which allows for disclosure of mediation evidence to show 'Professional misconduct or malpractice by the mediator'.
284 *Cassel v. Superior Court of Los Angeles* No S178914 Jan 13 2011 Ct Spp 217B215215 Los Angeles County Super Ct No LC070478 at 2 & 24 California Evidence Code, ss1119 (a) (b)
285 Cole et al. (2012) at 8.28 citing *Gossett v. St. John*, 2011 WL 1797249 (Cal App 2 Dist 2011)
286 Cole et al. (2012) at 8.28 citing *Provost v. Regents of University of Cal.*, 201 Cal App 4th 1289, 1303, 135 Cal Rptr 3d 591, 605 (Cal App 4 Dist 2011) at 9

States sometimes have taken a wrong turn when attempting to introduce a confidentiality provision, as illustrated by Maine, which promulgated a rule of evidence by providing privilege for mediators and for information in the private sessions but making discussions in the joint session admissible.[287] McEwen observed that this would have limited confidentiality to information where the mediator was present[288] but following extensive censure, a new provision was enacted providing a 'qualified mediator privilege' with exceptions based on the Uniform Mediation Act.[289]

Critics report on the complex frameworks for mediation confidentiality in their states, which demonstrate the overlap between these different sources of law and the uncertainty created in the case law, which can sometimes lead to perverse judgments.[290] Shopp cites a case in Western Pennsylvania where a court ordered a mediator to provide evidence of a discussion between one party and her lawyer that had occurred in the caucus despite confidentiality provisions in the court rules and both state and federal evidence statutes.[291] Gatto had rejected an offer to settle at the mediation and disputed that she had authorised her attorney to settle on the same terms afterwards, but the court held that the mediator was the only person who could determine what had been said between Gatto and her lawyer.[292] Shopp suggests that the judge may have 'misunderstood' mediation to be 'one step' in the negotiation process towards settlement rather than as a 'stand alone' procedure, but had mediation been understood as a 'self contained' process with the end result leading to a mediation agreement, then the judge has 'two options': If there is an agreement in writing it can be enforced; if there is no agreement in writing the mediator cannot be called to give evidence about the settlement as it does not exist.[293]

Academic sources in the USA observe that despite the number of statutes dealing with confidentiality, the cases have not been consistent in 'clarification, construction or interpretation', which was a key incentive for consultation and implementation of the Uniform Mediation Act.[294] At the time of drafting the UMA, it was reported that there were over 2,500 statutes concerning mediation, that each state had on 'average' 'five mediation confidentiality statutes' and there were 'approximately 250 state statutes' dealing with 'some form of privilege'.[295]

287 M. R. Evid 514 See McEwen (2009)
288 McEwen (2009) at 514
289 Cole et al. (2012) at 8.16. See 2010 Me. Rules 1
290 See Shopp (2010); Cole et al. (2012)
291 See Shopp (2010). Shopp cites *Gatto v. Verizon Pennsylvania, Inc.* 2009 WL 3062316 (WD Pa)
292 Shopp (2010) at 106–107
293 Shopp (2010) at 107
294 Kovach (2006) at 442
295 See Draft UMA Committee (2001) at 2

Uniform Mediation Act (UMA)

The drafters' objective was to achieve certainty and create 'one comprehensive law' in order to 'help increase the likelihood that the mediation process will be fair'.[296] Under the UMA, privilege applies to mediations where the state or court require mediation;[297] where the parties and mediators agree 'in a record' that there is an 'expectation of privilege';[298] and where the parties have used a mediator or a person who 'holds himself out to be a mediator'.[299] It does not apply to mediations involving collective bargaining;[300] students in primary or secondary schools;[301] residents of correctional institutions[302] or mediation by a judge who might rule on the case[303] nor does it apply where the parties have a written or 'recorded agreement' that the mediation is 'not privileged'.[304]

The UMA protects 'mediation communication', which is 'a statement, whether oral or in a record or verbal or non-verbal, that occurs during a mediation or is made for purposes of considering, conducting, participating in, initiating, continuing, or reconvening a mediation or retaining a mediator.'[305] The commentary to the Act provided an explanation of 'conduct', that is not a communication such as attendance compared to 'nodding' to a question which may be an 'assertion'.[306] One area where there is little uniformity in USA law is on the 'scope' of who holds mediation privilege which s4 addresses by providing that the parties, mediators and 'non-party participants' who have made 'mediation communications' have a 'blocking function' to prevent 'disclosure or admissibility', they are also provided with an 'express waiver'.[307]

The UMA provides an exclusion to mediation privilege when it has been used to 'intentionally attempt or commit a crime or conceal an ongoing crime or ongoing criminal activity' in s4c but further exclusions are provided in s6(a) to show:

- a 'record of agreement' about mediation[308]
- mediations which 'are open to the public or records open by law'[309]

---

296 UMA Draft Committee – Reporters Notes (2001) at 1. See generally for overview, Kovach 2006 at 438–44; Cole et al. (2012) at Chapter 8
297 UMA (2003) s3(a) (1)
298 UMA (2003) s3(a) (2)
299 UMA (2003) s3(a) (3)
300 UMA (2003) 3(b) (1) (2)
301 UMA (2003) 3(b) (4A)
302 UMA (2003) 3(b) (4B)
303 UMA (2003) 3(b) (3)
304 UMA (2003) 3(c)
305 UMA (2003) s2(2)
306 Cole et al. (2012) at 8.28
307 See UMA (2003) Comment on Section 4(b) 'Operation on the s4 privilege' Section 4(b); Cole et al. (2012) at 8.28
308 UMA (2003) s6(a) (1)
309 UMA (2003) s6(a) (2)

- 'threats or plans to inflict physical injury'[310]
- 'communication to plan or commit crime'[311]
- 'professional misconduct or malpractice by the mediator'[312]
- 'professional misconduct or malpractice by a party or representative of the party'[313]
- 'evidence of abuse or neglect'[314]

Under s6(3), privilege may also be excluded where there is a 'demonstration of need' but the party has the 'burden of persuading the court' that the 'need outweighs the policy underlying the privilege' and evidence is only permitted 'for that limited purpose'.[315] The UMA sought to 'preserve' contractual defences such as 'duress' and therefore evidence is allowed to show the 'validity and enforceability of the settlement agreement'.[316]

The UMA 'prohibits' the mediator from providing the court with 'reports, assessment, evaluation, recommendations, findings or other communication regarding the mediation' but is allowed to inform the court whether the mediation took place, was 'terminated' or 'whether settlement was reached and who attended'.[317]

Cole et al. report that some states when adopting the UMA have made specific amendments and in some instances have preserved state legislation or court rules.[318] For example, Nebraska retained its confidentiality statutes, Washington introduced 'unique provisions' providing the court with discretion to permit evidence to assess whether a divorcing party has acted 'in good faith during post-decree mediation' and Ohio is reported to have excluded 'all felony proceedings'; 'child protection proceedings' and 'delinquency proceedings' involving adult felonies.[319]

The relatively low number of states adopting the UMA indicates only limited success in the main objective of creating uniformity[320] but some commentators believe that the Act influences mediation practice, legislative enactments or amendments on confidentiality and can be persuasive on courts

---

310 UMA (2003) s6(a) (3)
311 UMA (2003) s6(a) (4)
312 UMA (2003) s6(a) (5)
313 UMA (2003) s6(a) (6)
314 UMA (2003) s6(a) (7)
315 UMA (2003) at 32–3 s6(b) (2)
316 UMA (2003) at 32 Comment on 11.6(b) (2) provided as an example of duress in *Randle v. Mid Gulf. Inc.,* No. 14-95-01292, 1996 WL 447954 (Tex Appl 1996) where the defendant sought evidence to show that he had asked the mediator to allow him to leave the mediation due to chest pains and medical history of heart problems.
317 UMA (2003) s7(a)
318 Cole et al. (2012) at 8.14
319 See the Uniform Law website. Downloaded on 1 February 2013 http://uniformlaws.org/ LegislativeFactSheet.aspx?title=Mediation Act; See Cole et al. (2012) at 8.14. The authors report on the amendments made by various legislative bodies before enacting the UMA.
320 Kovach (2006) at 444

where it has not been implemented.[321] The success of the UMA is also judged by the relatively few court cases testing the provisions, which Cole et al. suggest is the result of a 'broad categorical approach with exceptions' in contrast to an 'absolute or qualified bar' with no 'exceptions listed'.[322] The few cases reported indicate the main issues involve 'propriety of mediator reports', 'enforcement of oral agreements', 'waiver of privilege' and evidence to show mediation agreements.[323]

Not only has there been little case law on the UMA but Coben and Thompson report that in practice courts have a 'rather cavalier approach' to confidentiality and in their study over 300 cases, heard evidence from mediation without the parties 'raising confidentiality' issues, 67 cases permitted mediator 'testimony' and in only 9 cases was evidence refused.[324] The authors believe that the findings cast doubt on 'conventional wisdom' about the critical importance of confidentiality if 'practitioners, lawyers, and judges' are less disturbed about the principle than academics.[325] However, research by Foster suggests that in Washington state practitioners strongly observe confidentiality.[326] The survey found 'only 65 breaches of confidentiality from a total of 23,114 (0.28%)' and the respondents were strongly opposed to implementing 'Florida-style' legislation or imposing sanctions for breaches on the grounds that this might lead to further litigation.[327]

Confidentiality and admissibility in the Australian jurisdiction

Australia draws a distinction between confidentiality, which concerns the disclosure of information to non-participants, and the admissibility of information from mediation as evidence in courts or tribunals.[328] As a federal system, it faces many of the same problems as the USA with regard to both these matters because there are many different 'sources', which may occur through the common law, contractual or implied provisions, rules for court ordered mediation schemes or through state and federal legislation.[329] A NADRAC review of ADR in 2009 raised specific concerns about the inconsistency of legislative provision for both confidentiality and admissibility of evidence and its later review in 2011 concluded that ambiguity about the 'scope' of both confidentiality and admissibility is detrimental to the

---

321 Kelly (2011); See also Cole et al. (2012) at 8.14. The authors point to mediation confidentiality and privilege provisions in Florida, Maine and Virginia, which have been influenced by the UMA.
322 Cole et al. (2012) at 8.15; see also Kelly (2011)
323 Cole et al. (2012) at 8.15
324 Coben & Thompson (2006) at 48
325 Coben & Thompson (2006) at 48
326 Noble Foster & Prentice (2009) at 170. There were 30 participants in Foster's study.
327 Noble Foster & Prentice (2009) at 170
328 Alexander (2009) at 57
329 NADRAC (2011) at Chapter 3

'integrity' of ADR. It consequently made recommendations for legislation to remedy the problem:[330]

> As is the case in relation to confidentiality, the rules governing what is admissible, and the exceptions to those rules, derive from diverse common law principles and legislative provisions. Potential inconsistencies and confusion arising from this circumstance may harm the integrity of ADR processes, and undermine existing policy directions to have disputes resolved as early as possible and, if practicable, without (or with minimum) recourse to litigation.

Common law rules on admissibility of evidence from mediation

A 'patchwork' of common law rules and statutory provisions from both federal and state sources applies to the admissibility of evidence.[331] The courts recognise that the mediation process is 'analogous to without prejudice discussions' and consequently for policy reasons applies the common law rules in order to promote settlement and encourage discussions.[332] Nevertheless, judicial statements also acknowledge the 'tension'[333] that exists between admitting information as evidence, which may discourage mediation, and applying a 'blanket'[334] rule barring all evidence which could lead to parties admitting all kinds of information to prevent it being used against them in court, which would 'sterilise' the process.[335] In *AWA v. Daniels* a deed, referred to in mediation, was permitted into evidence, first, by Rolfe J who followed the reasoning in *Field v. The Commissioner of Railways for New South Wales* that without prejudice is concerned with admissions and not 'with objective facts' which can be proved by 'admissible factual evidence':[336]

> They do not seek to prove directly or indirectly what was said at Mediation. They seek to prove, by admissible evidence, a fact to which reference was made at Mediation not by reference to the statement but to the factual material which sourced the statement.

---

330   NADRAC (2009) at 6.77; NADRAC (2011) at 42 & 57
331   See NADRAC (2011) at 77. NADRAC cites Limbury (2007). See also Field & Wood (2005); Limbury (2007)
332   See Field & Wood (2005) at 148. *AWA Limited v. Daniels (t/a Deloitte Haskins & Sells)* (1992) 7 ACSR 463. See NADRAC (2011); Field & Wood (2005) at 154; Limbury (2007) at 69
333   Alexander (2009) at 252
334   Field & Wood (2005) at 153. See *789TEN v. Westpac Banking Corporation* [2004] NSWSC at 18
335   *AWA Limited v. Daniels (t/a Deloitte Haskins & Sells)* (1992) 7 ACSR 463 at 9–10; also see *Pihiga Pty v. Roche* [2011] FCA 240. See Alexander (2009) at 252. See also Alexander for an analysis of confidentiality in a comparative international context. Alexander (2009) at 245–90
336   *AWA Limited v. Daniels* (Rolfe J, 5029 of 1991, 18 March 1992, unreported: BC 9201994) at 12, citing *Field v. Commissioner of Railways for New South Wales* [1957] HCA 92; (1957) 99 CLR 285 at 291 & 292.

As Angyal observes, if the 'fact or document' can be proved by 'independent evidence' such as a 'serving notice' on the other party, then it is irrelevant that it was raised in the mediation, but a party cannot rely on what was 'said or done at the mediation to prove the fact or document'.[337] In a later hearing, Rogers CJ permitted the deed into evidence, because the mediation only confirmed the defendant's knowledge about its existence and it should have been disclosed during discovery.[338] His Honour supported the application of a 'wider view'[339] than that of Rolfe J by suggesting that information raised in mediation, which one party has 'no inkling about' and would not become aware of 'in the normal progress of litigation', should not be disclosed even should the 'fact or document be capable of being established by objective evidence'.[340]

NADRAC suggests that 'more contemporary decisions' adopt the wider approach in line with 'evolving public policy' and cites *Lukies v. Ripley* where Young J stated that if the parties agree 'either expressly or impliedly' not to disclose 'communications made during those discussions, then public policy makes those discussions privileged from disclosure in a court of law or equity'.[341] However, more recently in *789TEN v. Westpac*, McDougall J followed the approach taken by Rolfe J by concluding that the common law should not be extended from 'statements and documents' to 'information contained in documents' because of the 'sterilising effect' on mediation and the costs if courts have to establish where the party got the 'sources of the information' from.[342]

The Australian courts have applied many of the exceptions to without prejudice to mediation, which are consistent to those highlighted in *Unilever*.[343] Limbury and NADRAC list cases where the courts have admitted evidence from mediation to show that the parties had arrived at a settlement agreement,[344] in cases involving 'professional misconduct',[345] 'unconscionable conduct',[346] 'oppression'[347] or 'misleading conduct'.[348]

---

337 Angyal (1998) at 6
338 Rogers CJ. *AWA Ltd v. Daniels* (1992) 7 ACSR 463; See McDougall J in *789TEN v. Westpac* [2004] at 16–31. See for example, Field & Wood (2005) at 153–4; NADRAC (2011) at 46, 59 & 60
339 Spencer & Brogan (2006) at 320
340 per Roger CJ. *AWA Ltd v. Daniels* (1992) 7 ACSR at 467–8
341 NADRAC (2011) at 46 & 59 citing *Lukies v. Ripley* (1994) 35 NSWLR at 283.
342 *789TEN v. Westpac* [2004] at 18; See Spencer & Brogan (2006) at 320–4. See also *Williamson v. Schmidt* [1998] 2 QD R 317 cited by Spencer & Brogan (2006) at 331–2
343 NADRAC (2011) at 60–61; Limbury (2007); Alexander (2009) at 280–5
344 NADRAC (2011) at 60 citing *Barry v. City West Water Ltd* [2002] FCA 1214
345 NADRAC (2011) at 61 citing *Tapoohi v. Lewenberg and Ors* (No 2) [2003] VSC 410 (21 October 2003)
346 NADRAC (2011) at 60. *Pittorino v. Meynert* [2002] WASC 76
347 NADRAC (2011) at 60 citing *Abriel v. Australian Guarantee Corporation Ltd* [2000] NSWSC 965 cited by Limbury
348 NADRAC (2011) at 60 citing *Quad Consulting Pty Ltd v. David Bleakley & Associates Pty Ltd)* (1990–1991) 98 ALR 659

The Federal Court of Australia reviewed the exceptions in *Pihiga Pty v. Roche* when the applicant argued that a deed was 'void or void *ab initio*' because it had been obtained by 'misleading and deceptive' representations about the valuation of shares.[349] It was also claimed that the deed should be 'set aside' because the misrepresentations 'contravened' various statutory provisions from the 'Corporation Act 2001, the Australian Securities and Investments Commission Act 2001 and the Trade Practices Act 1974'.[350]

Landers J did not approve the defendants' argument that misrepresentations were not sufficient for an exception because there was 'no ambiguity' in Walker LJ's judgment in *Unilever*,[351] which was consistent with the 'Australian authorities' where 'misleading or deceptive representations' used in without prejudice negotiation are admissible.[352] Nor could the respondents rely on 'express agreements' in the mediation contract which conferred without prejudice on 'the communications' because the clauses did not provide 'greater protection than that given by the common law'[353] and a party should not be able to 'avoid' the statutory provisions or else 'private agreements' would 'oust public policy statutes'.[354]

Furthermore, Lander J declined to consider the effect of s53B of the Federal Court Act, which creates an 'absolute bar' on the admissibility of evidence from court ordered mediation, because the parties had not been mandated to mediate, despite counsel's argument that this created an 'anomaly' depending on how the process was commenced.[355] His Honour refused to 'judicially craft'[356] the common law rules notwithstanding legislative policy although conceding that it might be 'a matter for the High Court':[357]

> He (counsel) also said the common law should be developed by reference to the policies evidence in the legislation enacted by those Parliaments and in the *Evidence Act*. Having regard to the state of the authorities to which I have referred, that is a matter for the High Court not for a Judge of this Court.

---

349 *Pihiga Pty v. Roche* [2011] FCA 240 at 62. The applicant also claimed that the deed should be 'set aside' because the misrepresentations 'contravened' various provisions of the Corporation Act 2001, the Australian Securities and Investments Commission Act 2001 and the Trade Practices Act 1974.

350 *Pihiga Pty v. Roche* [2011] at 95

351 *Unilever plc v. Procter & Gamble* [1999] EWCA Civ 3027, per Robert Walker LJ at 2448–9

352 *Pihiga Pty v. Roche* [2011] at 98, citing *Quad Consulting Pty Ltd v. David R Bleakley & Associates Pty Ltd* (1990) 27 FCR 86

353 *Pihiga Pty v. Roche* [2011] at 111

354 *Pihiga Pty v. Roche* [2011] at 112, citing Lockhart J in *Henjo Investments Pty Ltd v. Collins Marrickville Pty Ltd (No 1)* [1988] FCA 40; (1988) 39 FCR 546

355 *Pihiga Pty v. Roche* [2011] at 114

356 *Cassel v. Superior Court of Los Angeles* No S178914 Jan 13 2011 at 24

357 *Pihiga Pty v. Roche* [2011] at 115

Statutory provision for admissibility

As noted above, the Federal Court Act provides an absolute bar on evidence from court ordered mediations and numerous other state and federal provisions deal with admissibility.[358] However, the NADRAC review highlighted cases which demonstrate the inconsistency of statutory legislation.[359] For example, the report notes that s131 of the Evidence Act 1995 prohibits evidence from settlement negotiations but in *Silver Fox Co Pty Ltd v. Lenard's Pty Ltd*[360] mediation evidence was sanctioned because it was covered by the costs exception in s131(h).[361] In contrast, the Federal Court of Appeal in *Pinot Nominees Pty Ltd v. Commissioner of Taxation*[362] refused to allow evidence on costs because the mediation had not been court ordered under s54A of the Federal Court Act and therefore the 'absolute bar' did not apply.[363] These conflicting provisions and other ambiguities about the extent of admissibility led NADRAC to recommend that 'inadmissibility' of ADR evidence should be the 'default position' because it will protect mediation from 'fishing expeditions' and 'satellite litigation' and because of the benefits of 'frank' negotiations, which support the parties in constructing 'flexible and creative solutions'.[364] The perceived potential of mediation sometimes exceeds the reality, with the majority of empirical studies recording that monetary outcomes far surpass 'creative' settlements and reflecting growing evidence that the involvement of lawyers introduces tactical and more adversarial conduct.[365]

NADRAC's proposals are confined to federal enactment because the Commonwealth can legislate on admissibility in 'federal courts or tribunals' but not for 'state and territorial courts and tribunals', unless the parties have been ordered to mediate by a 'federal court or tribunal'.[366] The 'general inadmissibility' of ADR communications were provided for in two recommendations: One for 'federally mandated ADR' in any 'federal, state or territorial' court or proceedings and the second, for any other ADR process in a federal court or tribunal.[367]

---

358 NADRAC (2011). See Appendix 4.1 (Federal Legislation) & Appendix 4.2 (state legislation)
359 NADRAC (2011) at 62–6
360 *Silver Fox Co Pty Ltd v. Lenard's Pty Ltd* [2004] FCA 1570
361 See NADRAC (2011) at 62
362 See NADRAC (2011) at 63 citing *Pinot Nominees Pty Ltd v. Commissioner of Taxation* [2009] FCA 1508
363 See NADRAC (2011) at 63. For a discussion on the limitation of statutory confidentiality see Spencer & Brogan (2006) at 328–42.
364 NADRAC (2011) at 66
365 See discussion on evaluative mediators in Chapter 1. See for example, Baruch Bush & Pope (2002); Lowry (2000); Lande (2000); Stulberg (1997); Kovach & Love (1996) (1998); Menkel-Meadow (1997); Clark (2012); Clark & Mays (1996). For a review in England and UK see for example, Roberts (1992) (1993); Brooker (2007)
366 NADRAC (2011) at 66
367 NADRAC (2011) Recommendations 4.7.1 & 4.7.4 at 68–9

Where the ADR communication comes from a 'federally mandated process', such as a court-ordered mediation, the recommendation is that it is inadmissible without the 'disputants' consent', subject to the leave of the court, in any 'federal, state or territorial' court or proceedings.[368] If the ADR communication 'occurs' from another 'confidential ADR source', such as 'private mediation', the recommendation is that it should be inadmissible before a 'federal court or federal tribunal'.[369]

However, because of the 'constitutional restraints', NADRAC did not advise that the Commonwealth should legislate for state or territorial rules but recommended that the Attorney General 'liaise' between state and territories to introduce 'uniform admissibility provisions across Australia'.[370] Nor was it recommended that 'multiple unqualified exceptions' be enacted but the court when considering leave for disclosure should 'take into account the recommendations for the exceptions to confidentiality, 'the general public interest' in 'maintaining mediation confidentiality' and 'whether admission or disclosure would serve the administration of justice'.[371]

Confidentiality in mediation

Just as admissibility stems from different sources, so does confidentiality and NADRAC state it can be provided through the common law, statutory provision, rules from institutional providers, professional bodies and the Australian National Mediators Standards, which require accredited mediators to observe 'confidentiality obligations'.[372] Although the courts have recognised 'express confidentiality' in contracts, NADRAC reports such clauses have not been 'extensively considered' in the jurisprudence but are decided on a 'case-by-case' approach dependent on the contractual language used – but that generally contract clauses will not 'override' legislative provisions unless 'preserved' in the statute.[373]

Field and Wood commented on the narrow approach taken to the express confidentiality and privilege clauses in *789TEN v. Westpac Banking Corporation* and warned mediation participants not to take even 'comprehensive' confidentiality clauses for granted.[374] The parties agreed to privilege under Clause 12 which included several sub-clauses concerning proposals, concessions and 'statements and documents', but the court held that the 'matter' did not come 'within any of the subsections'.[375] The English jurisdiction took a similar

368 NADRAC (2011) Recommendation 4.7.2 at 69
369 NADRAC (2011) Recommendation 4.7.4 at 69
370 NADRAC (2011) Recommendation 4.7.8 at 69
371 NADRAC (2011) Recommendation 4.7.3 at 69
372 NADRAC (2011) at 50. NADRAC traces the various sources of confidentiality in Australia.
373 NADRAC (2011) at 45
374 Field & Wood (2005) at 151 citing *789TEN v. Westpac Banking Corporation* [2004] at 5
375 *789TEN v. Westpac Banking Corporation* [2004] at 12

narrow approach in *Farm Assist (2)*, when the Court held that the express clause in the contract providing confidentiality for the mediation 'dispute' did not involve the 'matter' before the court which was the compellability of the mediator in an alleged claim of duress.[376] In *789Ten v. Westpac* the evidence sought was 'information disclosed' at the mediation, which was in an 'affidavit'.[377] McDougall J held that the parties had chosen to draw a 'distinction' between 'information and documents' in Clauses 11 and 12 indicating an 'intentional' awareness of the difference:[378]

> ... the contrast between Clauses 11 and 12 is, in my judgment, significant. Clause 11 requires the mediator to keep confidential, and not disclose or use, 'confidential information' (the exceptions are irrelevant). It also requires the mediator, at the conclusion of the mediation, to return all 'documents' provided to him. The distinction between information and documents is clear and, I think, intentional. It shows that the parties to the mediation agreement understood the distinction. I see no reason to impute to them any intention to blur the distinction in the very next clause of their agreement.

Commentators suggest that the courts will recognise implied confidentiality in mediation by 'analogy' to privilege given to without prejudice negotiations (discussed below) which is conferred on the negotiations during the mediation process but indicate that it unlikely to cover situations where litigation is not pending.[379]

Confidentiality provisions in legislation

NADRAC records the vast array of legislation 'imposing confidentiality'. However, the weaknesses of many provisions are such that they rarely protect disclosure of information to parties not involved in the mediation and for the most part only address admissibility at later court hearings.[380] Many examples of state legislation provide for confidentiality[381] but these provisions are observed to differ on to whom they apply ('any person, only the mediator or only the parties or the mediator and the parties'); what information is confidential ('any information which may or may not include preparatory information for the mediation'); and the exceptions that apply ('by consent

---

376 *Farm Assist (2)* [2009] at 48
377 *789TEN v. Westpac Banking Corporation* [2004] at 10
378 *789TEN v. Westpac Banking Corporation* [2004] at 14
379 NADRAC (2011) at 45 citing *AWA Ltd v. George Richard Daniels T/A Deloitte Haskins and Sell* (1992) 7 ACSR 463. See also Field & Wood (2005) at 152
380 NADRAC (2011) at 61. NADRAC, however, identify two federal statutes, the Native Title Act 1993 and the Family Law 1975, which make provision for wider admissibility. NADRAC (2011) at 49
381 NADRAC (2011) at 48. See fn 121 & Appendix 3.2

of the parties, when needed by law, or in accordance with the law of the territory').[382]

In order to provide a 'consistent standard' of confidentiality, NADRAC recommends the enactment of legislation, which clearly defines the 'scope and application of the obligations, the persons bound by it, and the exceptions to it'.[383] Its report concluded that the benefits of legislation would outweigh the objections, which centred on the adequacy of the current provision, the possibility of 'unintended consequences' and the lack of 'empirical evidence' supporting the 'need' for further action.[384]

The legislation proposed would provide confidentiality for the parties and ADR practitioners in the 'federal justice system' where mediation is mandated, and would be subject to defined exceptions to prevent disclosure 'to non-participants'.[385] The proposals suggest that courts should maintain 'discretion' over 'enforcement' and breaches 'as they think fit'.[386]

NADRAC provided a number of reasons for confining the proposals to mandatory mediation :[387] first, the parties elect to use mediation voluntarily and this 'freedom and flexibility should be preserved'; second, there was no evidence to indicate that confidentiality in 'private mediation' was 'unsatisfactory'; third, there would be difficulties in 'identifying a constitutional head of power'.[388] Finally, NADRAC maintained that legislation might diminish the 'voluntariness and flexibility of ADR' in the private sector, but recommended that comparable clauses recommended for mandatory mediation should be introduced into mediation agreements and institutional rules.[389]

Exceptions to confidentiality obligations

After reviewing the submissions, NADRAC recommended a wide 'range' of exceptions to confidentiality. First, legislation should provide a waiver for 'all the persons in the dispute' but not the mediator because mediation is the 'parties' process' and they should have power over.[390] This is at variance with the approach taken by the English courts in *Farm Assist (2)* (see above), which held that the mediator could rely on a confidentiality clause even when both parties had waived their right, although this should be subject to 'the interests of justice'.[391]

---

382 NADRAC (2011) at 49 and Appendix 3.2. See also Spencer & Brogan (2006) at 328–30
383 NADRAC (2011) at 52 & 50
384 NADRAC (2011) at 51
385 NADRAC (2011) Recommendation 3.9.1 at 55
386 NADRAC (2011) Recommendation 3.9.1 at 55
387 NADRAC (2011) at 54
388 NADRAC (2011) at 54
389 NADRAC (2011) at 54
390 NADRAC (2011) at 55
391 *Farm Assist (2)* [2009] at 28

Second, their recommendations for exceptions to confidentiality include:[392]

- Permitting information to enforce a mediation settlement agreement;
- Disclosing mediation communications when this will 'lessen or prevent threats' to 'life or health or safety of persons', 'public health or public safety' or 'damage to property';
- When it is 'required by law';
- To enable mediators or parties to get 'legal, medical or psychological advice';
- To facilitate reports of 'misconduct' to professional bodies;
- 'To inform those with a legitimate or direct interest in the process' (examples given were if the Federal Government were a disputant or to family members); and
- Anonymous information for 'administrative, research, supervisory or educational purposes'

The final 'catchall provision'[393] proposed that the court should admit evidence when it is 'necessary to protect the administration of justice or the public interest', which might include when the settlement has been 'affected by fraud, or by misleading or unconscionable conduct, and where that conduct has caused damage to a disputant'.[394] This exception would provide the court with a similar discretion to that afforded by the EU Mediation Directive, the Uniform Mediation Act and newly enacted legislation in Hong Kong.

Hong Kong confidentiality and privilege

After the introduction of the Civil Justice Rules (CJR) in Hong Kong, the government took further steps to promote mediation by setting up a Working Group to review implementing a Mediation Ordinance, which came into force in January 2013.[395] There was particular concern at that time that professional institutions, such as the Law Society, were overstating the true protection provided by the common law principles of without prejudice or not specifying or providing sufficient information on the legal exceptions.[396] For example, it was reported that the International Arbitration Centre's rules state that 'nothing that transpires' in the process will be used against the parties in later court action and the Mediation Practice Directive was criticised for stating that 'mediation being without prejudice communications, is protected by privilege. It must be emphasised that there is no question of the court undermining the protection afforded privilege.'[397] Koo and

---

392 NADRAC (2011) Recommendation 3.9.2 at 55
393 Keady & Ganesh (2011) at 3
394 NADRAC (2011) Recommendation 3.9.2 at 55
395 Hong Kong Working Party Report (2010)
396 Koo & Zhao (2011) at 272
397 Hong Kong International Arbitration Centre (HKIAC) The mediation rules 12(ii). See Koo & Zhao (2011) at 274

Zhao contended that participants were mediating in Hong Kong under a misapprehension of the true position of confidentiality or without prejudice and the exceptions to both rules:[398]

> Unless clarification [is given] by individual mediators, these mediation rules encourage general members of the public to mediate with a mistaken belief that what they say in the process can never be used against them or disclosed to any third party. This situation is certainly unsatisfactory to the healthy development of alternative dispute resolution processes in Hong Kong.

Without prejudice

Following common law principles, the Hong Kong courts acknowledge that mediation is a form of without prejudice negotiation protected by privilege to which the exceptions apply.[399] In *Wu Wei v. Liu Yi Ping*, the defendant sought to use information from the mediation to explain non-compliance with an injunction requiring the transfer of money from Mainland China to Hong Kong but the court, after considering without privilege and the exceptions, concluded that 'justice requires that she be allowed to explain'.[400]

Confidentiality

A number of judgments in the Hong Kong jurisdiction underscore the importance that the courts afford to the principle of confidentiality. In *Champion Concord Ltd v. Lau Koon Foo* the appellants were seeking to rectify the mediation agreement claiming that the mediator had drafted the settlement incorrectly, but the court of final appeal held a 'different case' was being argued and the appeal court was not the 'appropriate forum' to hear the matter.[401] After dismissing the appeal, the court made specific note that it should 'not be taken' that the case was 'accepting' 'disclosure' from mediation because confidentiality was of 'fundamental importance', which should only be lifted in 'exceptional circumstances'.[402]

This view was reiterated in *S v. T*, which involved the admissibility of documents at a custody proceeding some of which involved what was 'said or not said in the course of mediation'.[403] In giving the judgment, Roger VP noted the 'fundamental' importance of confidentiality, which would make it 'wholly wrong' for any person to disclose what was 'said or not said' until

---

398 Koo & Zhao (2011) at 274
399 *Wu Wei v. Liu Yi Ping* [2009] HKEC 139 at 73–6. See Hong Kong Working Party Report (2010) at 7.116; See also Yu (2012)
400 *Wu Wei v. Lui Yi Ping* [2009] at 76
401 *Champion Concord Ltd v. Lau Koon Foo* [2011] HKEC 699 at 7 & 10
402 *Champion Concord Ltd v. Lau Koon Foo* [2011] at 17
403 *S v. T* [2011] 1 HKLRD 534 at 2. See Kallipetis (2011) at 201

settlement.[404] The court observed that both parties together can waive confidentiality but also asserted that the principle is so central to the process, that it must be 'adhered to' or the 'whole mediation system will come to naught', because parties would 'tactically' use it in order to find evidence for later litigation purposes:[405]

> It is not a simple question of one party waiving privilege because it is a matter for both parties. I regard this as extremely important because it goes to the root of the mediation process which, as I have said, is now part of the court's process. Unless this is adhered to the whole mediation system will come to naught and people will use mediation as a tactical advantage and then seek to introduce evidence which has come from an unsuccessful mediation and somehow bring that into court proceedings. That is quite contrary to anything which was envisaged in the process of mediation. This applies just as much to matrimonial and custody proceedings as it does to any other proceedings.

S v. T was considered by the High Court in *Chu Chung Ming v. Lam Wai Dan* when, after reviewing both confidentiality and without prejudice, an application was refused to permit evidence from two sections of a letter read out in mediation.[406] Queeny Au-Yeung J held that *Farm Assist (2)* provides that when confidentiality is agreed between the parties then the person wishing to rely on the evidence has the 'burden' of 'proving' whether there are 'other public interests overriding the general principles', which the respondents had not been able to do.[407] The court confirmed that confidentiality 'will apply to all communications' and not only 'admissions or remarks'[408] and applying *Farm Assist (2)* held that disclosure was 'not necessary for the fair disposal of the case'.[409]

Consideration was then given to the without prejudice rules in negotiation which Queeny Au-Yeung J said applies to admissions and to 'all communications' unless there has been an 'abuse' of the privilege, and although the excerpts from the letters were found to be 'self-serving assertions' and not admissions, they were protected.[410] The claim that they were 'independent facts' unconnected to the underlying dispute was dismissed because parties should be able to 'speak freely about all issues in the litigation both factual and legal' and the letters were written for the mediation and therefore were covered by the without prejudice rules.[411] Nor was it accepted that the

404 *S v. T* [2011] at 3
405 *S v. T* [2011] at 4
406 *Chu Chung Ming v. Lam Wai Dan* [2012] HKLRD 897 at 11 &13
407 *Chu Chung Ming v. Lam Wai Dan* [2012] at 18 & 19
408 *Chu Chung Ming v. Lam Wai Dan* [2012] at 19–20
409 *Chu Chung Ming v. Lam Wai Dan* [2012] at 26
410 *Chu Chung Ming v. Lam Wai Dan* [2012] at 25–8, 33
411 *Chu Chung Ming v. Lam Wai Dan* [2012] at 33–6

petitioners had waived privilege through 'pleading that the respondents did not seek approval' (for fire prevention work) or by 'excluding them from management', since if this was a waiver it would apply to every unsuccessful mediation.[412] Finally, the petitioners were not found to have 'abused the privilege' by 'simply listening to or reading' the letters and there was no evidence of 'fraud or other vitiating conduct'.[413] The court concluded that it was not a suitable case to 'depart' from the 'general principles governing confidentiality and without prejudice'.[414]

Government review of confidentiality and privilege

After reviewing the common law position on confidentiality, legal privilege and without prejudice, the government justice review recommended that the Mediation Ordinance should provide an explicit provision for 'mediation confidentiality and privilege'.[415] The Sub-group provided a number of reasons for taking this step. First, the objective behind the mediation ordinance is to provide a 'legal framework' and 'confidentiality and privilege' are crucial to its practice.[416] Legislation on these issues would incentivise use and instil confidence in mediation.[417] Both principles rely on case law, which was 'undesirable' from a policy perspective[418] and there were legal uncertainties surrounding the parameters, which taking legislative action would clarify.[419] Specific doubts were cast on the ability of the without prejudice rules to promote mediation development because of the debate surrounding protection for communications other than admissions and the extent of the exceptions, which could be clarified by the enactment of a 'general mediation privilege subject to exceptions'.[420]

After wider consultation, HK implemented the Mediation Ordinance with the stated aim to 'protect the confidential nature of mediation communication'.[421] Mediation communication is broadly defined as '(a) anything said or done; (b) any document prepared (c) or any information provided' but specifically excludes agreements to mediate or the mediated settlement (2), which has led to advice that lawyers should organise the parties to sign mediation settlements containing confidentiality clauses.[422]

The ordinance provides broad exceptions to the general rule that a person is precluded from disclosing mediation communications.[423] Permission from

---

412 *Chu Chung Ming v. Lam Wai Dan* [2012] at 37–8
413 *Chu Chung Ming v. Lam Wai Dan* [2012] at 44
414 *Chu Chung Ming v. Lam Wai Dan* [2012] at 46
415 Hong Kong Working Party Report (2010) Recommendation 38 at 13
416 Hong Kong Working Party Report (2010) at 7.130
417 Hong Kong Working Party Report (2010) at 7.131
418 Hong Kong Working Party Report (2010) at 7.132
419 Hong Kong Working Party Report (2010) at 7.133 & 7.134
420 Hong Kong Working Party Report (2010) at 7.135–7.136
421 Mediation Ordinance (2012) 2(b)
422 Mediation Ordinance (2012) 1(a) (b) (c). See for example, Menachem et al. (2011)
423 Mediation Ordinance (2012) Provision 8 (1)

the court for disclosure is not required when the parties, the mediator or mediators and the person making the mediation communication give consent[424] or when it is 'lawfully in the public domain'[425] or when it is 'otherwise subject to discovery'[426] or where there are 'reasonable grounds to believe' that disclosure will 'prevent or minimize' the danger of injury to a person or 'wellbeing of a child'[427] or where the information is anonymously used for 'research, evaluation or education'[428] or, finally, when it is 'in accordance with a requirement imposed by law'.[429]

Section 8(3) circumscribes when mediation communications are discoverable with the 'leave of the court or tribunal under section 10', which includes for the 'purposes' 'of enforcing or challenging settlement agreements',[430] 'establishing allegations of professional misconduct made against the mediator' or others involved in the mediation[431] or, when the 'court or tribunal considers it justifiable in the circumstances of the case',[432] which is analogous to the 'interests of justice' defined in *Farm Assist (2)*.[433] Before giving leave for disclosure, the court 'must take into account' a number of matters specified in 10, which includes whether the 'mediation communication' has already or 'may be' disclosed under s8(2), whether it is in the 'interests of the administration of justice' and, 'any other circumstances or matters' that should be considered.[434] Consequently, the courts are required to engage in a balancing act between mediation confidentiality and policy or justice reasons much as the courts do in the English jurisdiction under the common law. Where there are allegations of 'unambiguous impropriety' such as economic duress, blackmail, or misrepresentation during mediation, judges have to consider whether it is 'justifiable in the circumstances' to permit disclosure, although as commentators note, before the Mediation Ordinance Hong Kong courts would only permit disclosure in 'highly exceptional circumstances' – so are likely to adopt the same rigorous approach.[435]

---

424 Mediation Ordinance (2012) at s8(2) (a) (i), (ii) & (iii). See Keady & Ganesh (2011) at 2
425 Mediation Ordinance (2012) at s8(2) (b)
426 Mediation Ordinance (2012) at s8(2) (c)
427 Mediation Ordinance (2012) at s8(2) (d)
428 Mediation Ordinance (2012) at s8(2) (e)
429 Mediation Ordinance (2012) at s8(2) (f)
430 Mediation Ordinance (2012) at s8(3) (a)
431 Mediation Ordinance (2012) at s8(3) (b)
432 Mediation Ordinance (2012) at s8(3) (c). See Keady & Ganesh (2011)
433 *Farm Assist (2)* [2009] at 28. See Keady & Ganesh (2011)
434 Mediation Ordinance (2012) at s10(2) (a), (b) & (c)
435 Keady & Ganesh (2011) citing *Champion Concord Ltd & Another v. Lau Koon Foo & Another* FACV (2011) See also Koo & Zhao (2011). See also Thomas & Kiesselbach (2013). Thomas and Kiesselbach report on the first case following the Mediation Ordinance, which refused to permit evidence from mediation. The reporters cite *Lincoln Air-conditioning & Engineering Company Ltd. v. Ngan Sui Yeung and other,s* Action No 527 OF 2010 at 3 & 5. The court held that under s9 the 'mediation communication' cannot be used without the permission of the court and, furthermore it was not 'required for the fair disposal of the case' because the plaintiffs had not participated in the mediation – therefore it was 'not binding' on them.

Some critics in Hong Kong criticise the 'conservative' approach taken by the Working Group on Mediation for its failure to stipulate a 'specific' privilege for mediation and for not taking a more 'comprehensive' approach.[436] Yu voiced concern that the proposed Ordinance retained the involvement of the courts in 'overseeing the mediation' when parties continue with litigation and that the mix of confidentiality and privilege rules do not address the practical problems the courts have in 'enforcing without prejudice privilege' when considering costs under CJR:[437]

> The Mediation Bill has not addressed the more difficult issues in the practice of mediation as a court-encouraged procedure under the Civil Justice Reform . . . the wording on the confidentiality provisions in the Mediation Bill may indicate an approach that is too lenient for considera- tion of cost issues, for it does not envisage the difficulty that courts encounter in enforcing the without prejudice privilege following the event when parties are contesting the cost consequences based on their conduct during the litigation – now that mediation is intended to be a mechanism of private dispute resolution overseen by the judiciary.

Commentary

As legal policies in England and Wales incrementally use more 'coercive pressure'[438] to encourage mediation through the threat of costs penalties, the desirability of undertaking a review of the appropriate level of confidentiality afforded to the process and mediators intensifies. Mediation law in the USA reveals that inroads into the level of protection provided but have been made perhaps more importantly, the high profile given to conflicting cases applying the plethora of evidentiary and privilege rules is a timely forewarning for future developments in the English and Welsh jurisdiction. Problems with inconsistent and overlapping law on confidentiality and admissibility, which is evident in the federal legal systems explored above, are perhaps less likely to occur in the English jurisdiction but the implementation of the EU Directive has raised the spectre of different rules applying to mediation depending on whether it involves cross border or domestic disputes. Mediators usually begin the process by reminding the parties about confidentiality or 'without prejudice' and informing them that what they say to the mediator in the caucus is confidential and will not be revealed to the other side without specific permission. That said, in England and Wales it is difficult to provide a 'definitive' explanation of the law, which is further complicated by the EU context.[439] Such a position is unlikely to enhance the reputation of

---

436 Koo & Zhao (2011) at 275
437 Yu (2012) at 368, 369–70
438 Brunsdon-Tully (2009) at 219
439 Kallipetis (2011) at 209; See also Koo (2011) at 192; Allen (2008)

mediation in the eyes of users in England or as a commercial centre for dispute resolution.[440]

There are other problems associated with an imprecise understanding of where the boundaries lie on confidentiality, which also potentially diminishes the confidence that users have in the mediation. In Australia, the vast array of confidentiality and admissibility legislation raises concerns about the 'ethical marketing' of mediation.[441] ADR providers and state law societies were reported to be making statements leading to assumptions that information cannot be used in later court hearings and that the process is a 'safe' haven in which to negotiate disputes.[442] Information given to users in England and Wales is not immune from adopting an overly simplistic explanation about mediation confidentiality. For example, the Civil Mediation Council (CMC) states on its website; 'Mediations are completely confidential and the information discussed within them cannot be used in Court or in any other legal action issued at a later date'.[443] However, the CMC does provide a 'guidance note' with further information on the more complex position and the difficulties mediators face in providing an accurate picture to participants.[444] It is commonplace now for parties who engage in mediation, including the mediator and legal representatives to sign a contract prior to commencing, with specific clauses covering confidentiality and disclosure.[445] Brookes recommends that clauses should continue to 'specify' without prejudice and confidentiality and not 'restrict circumstances' when a mediator can be compelled as a witness because of the effect of the confidentiality clause in *Farm Assist (2)*.[446] However, observers note that mediation contracts now contain clauses with complex legal terms and rules specifying conditions of engagement show levels of 'creeping legalism', which is likely to intensify the reliance of legal support.[447]

There are many mediation advocates, who would like a broader approach to confidentiality and who contend that the law should clarify the complexity surrounding mediation in order to support the policy of encouraging settlement away from the courts.[448] Some argue that English courts have given insufficient judicial consideration to 'balancing' the interests of settlement against

440 Kallipetis (2011) at 206–9
441 Field & Wood (2005) at 148
442 Field & Wood (2005) at 145–6
443 Civil Mediation Council Webpage Information downloaded on 15 February 2013 at http://www.civilmediation.org/about-mediation/29/what-is-mediation
444 Brookes (2009); See also Wood (2009); Newmark (2011)
445 See Koo (2011) at 193
446 Brookes (2009). Sir Henry Brookes provides advice on what clauses should be contained in mediation contracts following the decision in *Farm Assist (2)* [2009]. Sir Henry observes the change in CEDR's mediation contract to provide for confidentiality 'arising from or in connection with the dispute'.
447 Nolan (2010) at 3 & 11. See also Brooker (2011) at 38. Brooker reports that there is 'a high degree of legalistic language' in some mediation contracts and rules for engagement in England and Wales.
448 See for example, Kallipetis (2011); Cornes (2008); Briggs (2009a, b)

the sufficiency of evidence when electing not to develop mediation or mediator privilege.[449] Kallipetis is critical of the decision in *Farm Assist (2)* for declining to accept mediator privilege and only 'recognising' mediation confidentiality, which the parties can waive, particularly when the party claiming economic duress did so seven years after mediating and was legally represented by 'senior counsel, junior counsel and their solicitor'.[450] Furthermore, he criticizes the court for not considering the case of *Fincken* where both 'competing policies' were weighed before giving preference to the 'public interest in settlement'.[451] A number of states in the USA have taken a broad approach to confidentiality by barring nearly all mediation information and despite judicial attempts to ameliorate the effect, particularly when evidence is required to show mediator or lawyer impropriety, the superior courts have rejected 'judicially crafted' exceptions, which may have led some sectors of the 'public' to regard mediation as a 'lawless process'.[452] Professor Green argued against a 'blanket' confidentiality policy in the USA as early as 1986 because he believed that the law governing 'compromise agreements' and evidential rules adequately protected mediation, and stronger measures would risk a 'public backlash against a "secretive" type of dispute resolution'.[453]

The argument that mediators have a special role to receive 'secrets', which is of such importance that it should be protected by privilege, is currently taking shape in England but it is not universally accepted because others make a case that 'justice' or fairness necessitates that the mediator provides the required 'probative evidence'.[454] This is particularly so when the mediator may have unwittingly been the conduit of impropriety.[455] And as Professor Green contends, the position of mediators is little different to other professionals involved in mediation who do not wish to be embroiled in litigation.[456] Furthermore, the evidence from one of the largest reviews of mediation case law in the USA found that judges, practitioners and participants were less troubled about confidentiality than academics, which raises questions about the necessity of greater protection and the centrality of the principle to the effective working of the process:[457]

Mediator privilege is also problematic when based on the contention that the mediator's 'unique' role makes it possible 'for him or her to promote a

---

449 Briggs (2009b). Mr Justice Briggs noted disclosure orders were made in both *Cattley* and *Brown v. Rice & Patel* despite the 'reasoned arguments given by interveners' (ADR group in *Brown v. Rice & Patel* and the mediator in *Cattley*). See also Kallipetis (2011) at 188
450 Kallipetis (2011) at 188–9
451 Kallipetis (2011) at 189
452 *Cassel v. Superior Court of Los Angeles* No S178914 Jan 13 2011 at 2 & 24. See Franklin (2013) at para 5; Clark (2012) at 120
453 Green (1986) at 11
454 Cole et al. (2012) at 8.5; Deason (2001) at 99; Zimmerman (2009) at 369; Wood (2009)
455 Wood (2009) at 15; see also Green (1986) at 5; Deleissegues (2011)
456 Green (1986) at 5
457 Coben & Thompson (2006) at 48

compromise route which would not occur to either party'[458] because this challenges the principle of 'self determination'. Moreover, it is questionable whether privilege should protect the mediator over a participant who has been unjustly disadvantaged, particularly when the process 'belongs' to the parties.[459] Affording mediators a privilege of the same kind given to the lawyer–client relationship endows new professionals with a legal 'status', which may further erode the facilitative approach of encouraging the parties to explore their own settlement options to one of evaluating the best outcome, as participants come to expect them to adopt an authoritative function.[460]

At present in England, in view of the relatively low numbers mediating, it is doubtful that public awareness about confidentiality has reached the level of distrust that is reported in the USA. However, as mediation use increases its profile will be raised, which may necessitate formal steps demarcating the boundaries. There is a strong body of opinion favouring statutory intervention to provide mediation or mediator privilege but with appropriately drafted exceptions rather than relying on the vagaries of the common law on a 'case-by-case basis'.[461] A number of academic and mediation practitioners favour developments along the lines of the Uniform Mediation Act, discussed above, with carefully designed exceptions such as to permit evidence of fraud, impropriety, injury or potential injury to persons or criminal activity and in some cases with proposals for a discretionary power in the 'interests of justice'.[462] Statutory intervention may be the best option as the judicial response to government proposals to extend the EU directive to domestic mediation suggests the unlikelihood of movement through the case law to create 'special rules' for mediators to prevent them being called as witnesses. Lord Jackson in his reply for the judiciary stated that this was 'rarely an issue' since the without prejudice rules make 'evidence' from negotiations settlement inadmissible 'whether a mediator is involved or not'.[463] It is hard to dispute that a need for clarity exists given that as a minimum, users should be in a position to know the limitations of confidentiality or privilege before commencing mediation; otherwise there is lack of informed consent, which may in the future harm its reputation and the reputation of mediators.[464]

Both the number of cases involving confidentiality and the prospect of future statutory intervention makes further inroads into the legal involvement

---

458 Briggs (2009b)
459 Green (1986) at 5; Wood (2009); Deleissegues (2011)
460 See discussion in Chapter 1. Many scholars contend that the institutionalisation of mediation brings an increased interest from legal professionals and more evaluative practice. See for example, Kovach & Love (1996); Stipanowich (1996) (2004); Wissler (2004); Rogers & McEwen (1998); Clark (2012)
461 Cornes (2008) at 404. See also Kallipetis (2009) (2011); Brown & Marriott (2011) at 550–1
462 See for example, Kallipetis (2009) (2011); Brown & Marriott (2011); Cornes (2008)
463 Lord Jackson (2011) at 8
464 Alexander (2008b) at 2; Gould et al. (2010) at 66; Riskin (1996); Brooker (2007) (2011)

of mediation practice and the process of juridification deepens. According to Blichner and Molander, one feature of juridification occurs as the law expands into 'unregulated activity' as decisions are made in 'reference to the law'.[465] The uncertainty created by using the principles of without prejudice and confidentiality results in areas of 'indeterminacy and a lack of transparency' in mediation, which leads to another feature of juridification described by Blichner and Molander: an 'increase of judicial power'.[466] 'Indeterminacy' surfaces when there is uncertainty about the application of the 'legal rules', which leads to an 'increase in discretionary power' and hence more 'judicial power', which Blichner and Molander do not limit to the judiciary but extend to other 'experts in and out of the legal system'.[467] Uncertainty about the law connects to a 'lack of transparency' resulting in parties relying on those who have an expertise over the matters in contention, as Blichner and Molander observe, 'Indeterminacy and lack of transparency increase the importance and independence of legal advice and in court settlement'.[468]

Conclusion

This chapter has reviewed the current position on confidentiality and considered whether further judicial or statutory actions will be essential in future to shield the practice of mediation. The necessity of greater protection of information is a question of maintaining the equilibrium between fairness to parties who may face considerable injustice and the interests of settlement. An overly broad approach may fail to safeguard participants particularly when there is substantial legal pressure for engagement or may protect against the dangers of facilitating a cynical use of confidentiality to prevent later disclosure at court, which may discourage genuine negotiation. Potential users should know the position of their negotiations in order to mediate with full consent. Currently there may be misunderstandings and confusion but it should be borne in mind that any legislative intervention has the potential to lead to further legalism and juridification of the process, and furthermore might foster a progressive move away from mediation's facilitative origins and the core principles of mediation.

The final chapter draws together the themes of juridification explored in the preceding chapters, as mediation progresses from a voluntary process to the institutionalization of its practice supported by an emerging mediator profession dominated by lawyers.

---

465 Blichner & Molander (2005) at 16–17 citing Habermas (1987)
466 Blichner & Molander (2005) at 19
467 Blichner & Molander (2005) at 19
468 Blichner & Molander (2005) at 19

6 Conclusions

Mediation law: journey to juridification through institutionalisation

Introduction

Alexander observes that mediation law includes 'legislation, case law, contractual terms and other legally binding standards that set the legal framework for mediation'.[1] The primary purpose of this book has been to provide a comprehensive examination of mediation law in the English and Welsh jurisdiction with the objective of analysing how the law legalises mediation practice.[2] The aim of this chapter is to draw together the main themes discernible from the developing body of mediation law. Previous chapters explored how the 'modern mediation movement'[3] began either through the voluntary choice of the parties, after a dispute arises or through an agreement to mediate in a pre-dispute contract clause, to achieving its status as an institutionalised part of the formal system which progressively occurs through judicial and government policies.[4] As the mediation movement gained momentum, there has been a further incursion of law into matters relating to the sanctioning powers of the judiciary to penalise unreasonable refusals to mediate and the development of rules on confidentiality, which further regulates practice.[5]

Mediation law first emerged in England and Wales when parties sought the courts' power to enforce contractual obligations to mediate and mediation outcomes, thereby creating a close relationship with the formal system, where the law provides mediation with a 'legal status'[6] and (some contend) the resource pressures on the civil justice system are relieved.[7] When mediating, the participants use the law as a barometer for settlement and

---

1 Alexander (2008b) at 12
2 Alexander (2008b) at 13, 12–13; Allen (2008); Alfini & McCabe (2001); Coben & Thompson (2006). Developing mediation law in the USA jurisdiction is explored for example by Alfini & McCabe (2001) and Coben & Thompson (2006)
3 Alexander (2006) at 1
4 See for example; Press (2003–2004); Sanders (2007)
5 See Blichner & Molander (2005) at 31; Alexander (2008b) at 2
6 See for example; Alexander (2008b) at 13; Hong Kong Working Party (2010) at 116; Sidoli del Ceno (2011) at 192; Carroll (2002) at 168; Zamboni (2008) at 69
7 Genn (2010); Shipman (2006). See Chapters 2 & 3.

'bargain in the shadow of the law'[8] but the majority of disputants, even experienced commercial people, are unable to predict the likely outcome of going to court and frequently decide to seek advice from lawyers to assist their settlement negotiations.[9]

The Civil Procedure Rule were designed to address the shortcomings of litigation and when implemented endowed mediation with a pivotal role in promoting settlement thus limiting access to court determination.[10] Furthermore, the judiciary was given legal powers to pressurise, albeit not compel, the parties, to attempt an ADR procedure through the introduction of costs sanctions for unreasonable conduct in litigation, which includes cooperating in settlement by exploring alternatives.[11] These rules have been instrumental in inextricably connecting mediation to the formal system of litigation through a process of institutionalisation.[12] However, this progression has lead to an exponential increase of mediation cases coming before the courts as the law encompasses this 'previously unregulated area' of dispute resolution activity.[13]

This final chapter first reviews the institutionalisation of mediation as civil procedure reform interweaves the process with litigation. Following this, an analysis is made of the effect of institutionalisation on the escalation of lawyers' interest in mediation either as advisers or lawyer–mediators or mediation advocates – and the consequence of this is an emerging mediator profession.[14] Finally these strands are drawn together to consider the juridification process of mediation in England and Wales.

Institutionalisation of mediation

Modes of institutionalisation

The mediation movement, as described in Chapter 1, shows a sequence of stages from experimentation, implementation, institutionalisation and regulation.[15] Clark's review of common and civil law jurisdictions shows that mediation does not 'thrive' unless there is 'some form of institutionalisation' but the route across different countries or even sometimes states within

---

8 Mnookin & Kornhauser (1978–79); See Genn (2010) at 21 & 35
9 See for example, Holmes (1897) at 154–5
10 Roberts (2000) (2002). See also Genn (2010) (2012)
11 Brunsdon-Tully (2009). Chapter 4 reviews CPR rules on costs sanctions.
12 A number of jurisdictions evidence an increase in mediation law as it has become institutionalised. See for example, Alfini & McCabe (2001); Alexander (2006); Coben & Thompson (2006)
13 Blichner & Molander (2005) (2008) at 12 & 14. See Coben & Thompson (2006). The authors explore the increase of mediation cases in the USA jurisdiction.
14 For an excellent analysis of lawyers' involvement in mediation across many jurisdictions, including England and Wales, see Bryan Clark's book: Clark (2012)
15 See for example, Press (2003–2004); Kovach (2006); Menkel-Meadow (1991); Goldberg et al. (1985)

federal systems has not been homogenous.[16] These approaches include financial incentives such as increased court fees[17] or tax benefits,[18] judicial referral[19] or judicial powers to stay proceeding for ADR to be attempted,[20] court mediation programmes,[21] court sanctions,[22] specialist mediation schemes[23] or mandating the parties to mediate before permitting access to the courts.[24] England and Wales has also followed this progression and has integrated mediation in the formal system through various interventions: judicial encouragement, staying proceedings at the parties' request, court schemes, and finally through the application of cost sanctions. Although it is difficult to state the number of mediations taking place annually in England and Wales, evidence exists to indicate that it is increasingly becoming a mainstream dispute process in a number of non-family contexts. For example, research in the TCC found that litigants in construction disputes 'routinely' use the process at several points during the litigation process and substantial mediations take place in the small claims arena.[25] In both contexts, the parties are enmeshed with the court system as proceedings have usually been initiated and furthermore, many participants of mediation, particularly those representing commercial entities, are likely to have sought legal help or legal representation.[26]

Institutionalisation and civil justice reform

A review of the present mediation phenomenon suggests that the institutionalisation of ADR and mediation occurs usually as a way of tackling deficiencies in stretched formal systems, which are unable to cope with perceived litigious behaviour in modern societies where litigation involves complex

16 Clark (2012) at 5; Alexander (2006)
17 See Chapter 1. The courts in England and Wales considered but discounted implementing court fees. Commercial Court Working Party (1998)
18 Clark (2012) at 140. Clark reports that this approach is used in Italy (Article 20 Decree 28).
19 Clark (2012) at 140. Clark observes that in the Scottish jurisdiction judges are empowered to recommend mediation in family cases. See Aibinu et al. (2010). The authors describe the referral systems used by many Australian courts.
20 Chapter 2 reviews Court Stays.
21 Aibinu et al. (2010) at 29–30. Aibinu et al. (2010) observe that legislation in Australia supports tribunals, which have mediation programmes such as the Victorian Civil and Administrative Tribunal Act 1998, and the Commercial and Consumer Tribunal Act 2003 in Queensland.
22 See for example, Alexander (2006); Clark (2012)
23 Wilkinson (2010) at 111 in Brooker & Wilkinson (2010). New Zealand has set up a mediation programme to deal with compensation claims for leaky buildings under the Weathertight Homes Resolution Services Act 2006.
24 See Clark (2012) at 140–1
25 See for example, Gould et al. (2009) (2010). The authors of the report found that mediation is common practice during proceedings in the TCC. The government reports that over 10,000 mediations have taken place for small claims. Ministry of Justice News Release 29 March 2011 http:// www.justice.gov.uk/news/newsrelease290311a.htm Accessed on 7th April 2011
26 See for example, Gould et al. (2009) (2010); Roberts (2012). Participants in mediation projects for small claims often find the parties are legally represented: see for example, Genn (1998)

procedures, which cause profligate costs and reliance on a high-priced legal profession.[27] Specific to common law countries are the problems associated with the adversarial system, which cultivates excessive procedural costs, delay and legal expenditure.[28] Jurisdictions have adopted ADR as part of 'efficiency' plans to ameliorate the problems challenging litigation and many advocates of mediation, perhaps disappointed by its lack of use, either canvassed or supported this move.[29]

Clark asserts that the partnership between 'mediation believers' and those who wish to align the process to the formal system for efficiency motives is a crucial point because there may be a clash between the civil justice agenda and the qualitative arguments for mediating.[30] Where the institutionalisation of mediation has formed part of a policy to reform an ailing civil justice system evaluations of court-sponsored schemes usually attribute settlement as signifying success but accuse these projects of lacking sufficient focus on the other advantages of mediating:[31]

> By virtue of such goals, settlement and economic efficiency may become overarching aims, with the quality dimensions to such schemes receiving less attention. This is an important issue not least because the key benefits which participants may receive from mediation may be lost in an efficiency driven species of the process.

This matter becomes even more crucial given that mediation increases with institutionalisation and a competitive market develops where one of the key promotional tools is the percentage of successful settlements achieved by mediators.[32] This has led to accusations from some quarters that those who practise mediation become 'settlement junkies' who are more concerned with their 'batting average'[33] and less concerned about other benefits such as improved relationships or exploring creative outcomes.[34] However, as noted

---

27 Genn (2010). Research refutes that there has been a litigation 'explosion'. See for example, Galanter (1983) (1992) (1998) (2006); Auerbach (1984); Markesinis (1990); and Genn (2010)

28 See for example, Jacob (1985); Auerbach (1984); Jolowicz (1996): Woolford & Ratner (2008)

29 Clark (2012) at 5. Clark cites Welsh (2001b). See also McAdoo & Welsh (2005); Genn (2010) (2012)

30 Clark (2012) at 143

31 Clark (2012) at 142; Genn (2010) at 114–19

32 Genn (2010) at 117

33 McGillis (1997). In the USA McGillis observed that evaluations of community programmes in the USA in 1997 looked at the importance of settlement outcome and 'batting averages' as indicators.

34 Agapiou & Clark (2011) at 166 cite Genn (2010) & Pollack (2007); Clark (2012) at 114; See also the recent seminar at Linklaters, 'The Commercial Mediation Group, The American Bar Association and Jams International invite you to an evening seminar to discuss and dissect the evolving field of mediation: Title: Settlement Junkies; Fight 'em or Feed 'em? Exposing the Myths, Method and Clichés of Modern Mediation' October 17, 2012 6:00–8:00 p.m. (BST) http://www.jamsinternational.com/events/jams-international-participates-in-mediation-week Downloaded on 19 April 2013

in Chapter 4, it should be borne in mind that most empirical surveys find that mediation outcomes are financial and in some commercial and construction contexts, parties rarely want to work together on new ventures.[35]

Institutionalisation and the legal professions

Another underlying matter associated with institutionalisation is that as the law connects mediation to the courts, studies here and elsewhere find that there is an increase in the involvement of lawyers. As they are required to be familiar with the process they become less sceptical, but they also become instrumental in when and how the process is used.[36] In the USA, for example, many mediators in court schemes come from the legal profession and there has been an increase in mediation advocacy, which is replicated in the English jurisdiction.[37] For example, lawyers were found to be active in many of the small claims mediation pilot schemes.[38] Furthermore in the commercial and construction sectors most appointments are with lawyer–mediators, which is perpetuated as 'repeat players' select the same mediators or lawyer-recommend ones they have already worked with.[39] Additionally there is an emergent market for legal representation in mediation, particularly when disputes are of high value financially or complex.[40] In England 'The Standing Conference of Mediation Advocates' exists, is a trade organisation with membership predominantly made up of 'solicitors, sets of barristers' chambers and individual legal, surveyor and construction professionals' and innumerable organisations offer courses on how to act for clients in mediation.[41]

Institutionalisation and legalism

While institutionalisation ensures that the legal professions are more prepared to be involved in mediating, many lawyers are observed to be bringing adversarial practices to the process, either as lawyer–mediators or as mediation advocates.[42] This involvement though poses a challenge to the facilita-

---

35 See for example, Genn (2010) at 113; See Brooker & Lavers (2005a) at 198–200

36 See for example, Brooker (2007); Clark (2012); Genn (2010); Clark & Mays (1996)

37 See for example, Genn (1998)

38 Gould et al. (2009) (2010); See also Brooker (2007) (2011); Agapiou & Clark (2011)

39 See for example, Guild et al. (2010) at 68; Brooker (2007) (2011); CEDR Mediators Audit (2012); Clark (2012); Gould et al. (2010)

40 Sternlight (1999). Sternlight reported that parties in the USA increasingly brought legal representatives to complex and relatively large financial disputes.

41 Clark (2012); Brooker (2011); Mason (2012). See for example, The Mediators Advocates Organisation http://www.mediationadvocates.org.uk/79/downloaded on 3 December 2012. See for example ADR Group http://www.adrgroup.co.uk/product/222/mediation_advocacy_training downloaded on 4 December 2012 or the London School of Mediation course http://www.schoolofmediation.org/lsm-launches-mediation-advocacy-training/ downloaded on 4 December 2012

42 See for example, Baruch Rush & Pope (2002); Lowry (2000); Lande (2000); Stulberg (1997); Kovach & Love (1996) (1998); Menkel-Meadow (1997); Clark (2012); Clark &

tive mode of practice because it jeopardises party self-determination and raises concern about the mediation model selected which becomes more reflective of how lawyers negotiate problems.[43]

Langer applies a 'Habermasian Analysis' to the practice of mediation when describing how parts of the 'legal regime' in Canada utilised the process to deflect dissatisfaction away from the courts.[44] She contends that as the legal system assimilates mediation there is a 'new focus on technical solutions' and settlement outcomes, as the process becomes a 'technique to be applied to problem-solving'.[45] The 'technicalisation' of mediation removes the 'values' of 'genuine empowerment' and 'consensus' and replaces them with those of litigation, which are 'accountability, reviewability and boundness'.[46] When mediation functions as part of litigation it becomes a 'precursor or preliminary stage of legal dispute resolution' making an additional hurdle to accessing the courts and bringing 'increasing scrutiny and pressure to rationalise and develop legalistic qualities such as certainty, predictability, reviewability and finality'.[47]

Langer observes how new professionals who are trying to extend their practice play a role in the 'technicalisation' of mediation by endorsing procedures or processes which best suit their 'skills-set and knowledge'.[48] Moreover, Langer contends that when the formal legal system co-opts mediation it becomes 'associated with the practices of lawyers and the courts', which contributes to its 'crystallisation into a technology': 'Lawyers have a pre-disposition to dispose of cases in certain ways, for example settlement. Standardised training will also increasingly contribute to this, as it concentrates on a settlement-driven model'.[49] Finally, mediation becomes a 'contested area' as different professions seeking to extend their practice vie for dominance, which sharpens as 'stakeholders', such as government bodies, begin to regulate and standardise training and practice.[50]

An analogy has already been drawn to Flood and Caiger's analysis of arbitration, where lawyers were able to assert their position because they

Mays (1996). For a review in England see Roberts (1992) (1993); Brooker (2007); Clark & Mays (1996); Mason (2012)

43   See for example, Kovach & Love (1996) (1998); Menkel-Meadow (1997)
44   Langer (1998) at 169–70. Langer's analysis is based on ADR developments in family, 'victim offender' and the 'young offenders'. See Blichner & Molander (2005) at 2. The authors provide a brief explanation of Habermas's theory of 'juridification' as an 'increase in formal law'. Habermas (1987)
45   Langer (1998) at 186 & 183
46   Langer (1998) at 185
47   Langer (1998) at 181. See also Paleker (2006) at 338–9. Paleker describes how the institutionalisation of mediation in South Africa has led to its juridification by failing to distinguish the process from a 'pre-adjudication procedure' of 'interview and investigation'.
48   Langer (1998) at 183
49   Langer (1998) at 182
50   Langer (1998) at 183

were able to 'translate the technical discourse into a legal one' and therefore appropriate it:[51] 'Lawyers are in a strong position to effect colonisation: because of their power over the discourse of legalism they have the power of appropriation.' Lawyers were also in a position to influence how arbitration developed procedurally and historical reviews, both here and in other countries, showing how what began as a flexible procedure began to 'mimic'[52] litigation through 'creeping legalism'[53] as clients brought their lawyers along to represent them.[54] Commentators eventually alleged arbitration in England and Wales was as costly, slow and procedurally complex as litigation which led to its overhaul by the 1996 Arbitration Act with the aim of providing a system 'untrammelled by technical or formalistic rules' and where under s33(1)(b) the tribunal is to 'adopt procedures suitable to the circumstances of the particular case'.[55] Reform may have come too late for arbitration to reverse the stranglehold that the legal profession have over legalism but the process is an adjudicatory one, which may be too similar to litigation to offer a genuine alternative, particularly when there has been a long history of embracing comparable procedures.[56] Arbitration is not the only alternative process to be criticised for legalistic tendencies and employment tribunals[57] and judicial boards have also been found to be overly formulaic and legalistic, which often means that they fail to provide the benefits to users that they were set up to achieve:[58]

> Dispute resolution exists in the shadow of the civil justice system . . . Design choices affect system performance and define the nature of justice a system delivers. The more similar alternative dispute resolution becomes to adjudication, the fewer its benefits. The more legalistic it becomes, the higher the costs, the greater the need for specialized legal representation, and the longer the conflict goes unresolved.

---

51 Flood & Caiger (1993) at 414
52 Phillips (2003) at 37
53 Daintith (1989) at 360. Daintith observes that the *Oxford English Dictionary's* first entry for 'legalism' was 'a disposition to exalt the importance of law or formulated rule in any department of action'.
54 See for example, Searle (1953); Warns (1960); Nolan (2010); Zirkel & Krahmal (2001); Hensler (2003)
55 Department Advisory Committee on Arbitration (1996) at 166; See s34(g) of the Arbitration Act 1996
56 In the construction industry, statutory adjudication may have effectively filled the gap left by the perceived failure of arbitration to provide an efficient alternative to litigation but reform in 1996 may have come too late to recover its position. After a review of the problems in construction, the Latham Report introduced statutory adjudication. See Latham (1994). However, doubt is expressed that adjudication has successfully fulfilled its intended role. See Agapiou & Clark (2011) at 159–60
57 See for example, Sanders (2009)
58 Bingham et al. (2010) at 150

ADR providers and mediators often publish their own procedural 'rules' for mediation, some of which replicate or loosely model the litigation process.[59] Mediation agreements usually require the parties to provide within a time-frame 'positional papers' and evidence, albeit not as much as is required for litigation.[60] ADR Chamber's 'Mediation Rules' for example say that each party should 'prepare a mediation brief' which includes the 'outline of the facts' and 'the issues in dispute' but also any 'legal arguments and important case law'.[61]

These 'mediation rules' on occasions stipulate how the process will proceed with 'opening statements' which may be reminiscent of a truncated court procedure. Furthermore, research shows as the parties bring solicitors to mediation and match others who bring their barristers, there are accusations that lawyers begin to treat mediation as if it were litigation, using case law to prove their point, or giving long legal arguments at the beginning of the process and counter arguing with legal precedent.[62] My own research with commercial and construction lawyers found interviewees blaming each other for 'using legalistic practices' such as:[63]

- Using the opening session to present legal arguments;
- Citing cases;
- 'Tooling up' with legal counsel;
- 'Acting to the mediator to make him convey messages';
- Adopting aggressive attitudes;
- Being entrenched in legal positions.

This is not to say that lawyers do not have an important function or any role in mediation as their clients' legal advisors and of course, the parties have the choice over representation.[64] Clark observes that lawyers sometimes have a positive role to play by 'protecting' their clients from procedural or 'power-balances'; or helping them to have the 'confidence' to mediate or by assisting the mediator in explaining any weaknesses that become apparent; or even protecting their clients from mediators who pressurise for settlement.[65]

---

59 See for example, Brooker (2011)
60 See for example, ADR Group's 'Mediation Procedure and Rules http://www.adrgroup. co.uk/images/library/files/family/Mediation_Procedure_and_Rules.pdf downloaded on 3 December 2012
61 ADR Chambers 'Mediation Rules' at 3.1 http://adrchambers.com/ca/mediation/mediation-rules/downloaded on 3 December 2012
62 See for example, Brooker (2007); Clark and Dawson (2007); Macfarlane (2002); Mulcahy (2001b)
63 Brooker (2007) at 230–1
64 Clark (2012); Brooker (2011)
65 Clark (2012) at 114–16. Clark reviews the literature and research findings in the area of 'lawyer advocacy' in mediation.

CEDR in their Mediation Procedure Rules underscore the importance of legal representation:[66]

> Such advisers play an important role in the exchange of information and opinion on fact, evidence and law; in supporting their clients (particularly individuals) in the negotiations; in advising clients on the implications of settlement; and in drawing up the settlement agreement and any consent order.

The danger, however, is that if the process of mediation gradually resembles parts of the litigation procedure or mediators are unable to counter the negotiation strategies of lawyers then the process and its outcomes may become effectively nullified. Unfortunately, arbitrators were not able to manage these matters in arbitration and although in mediation it is the parties' role to select the design of the process and only settle with an outcome they can accept, they may 'abdicate' this responsibility to their lawyers or be unable to stop them from taking control.[67]

Legal professional interests in mediation

Lawyers' negative attitudes

While mediation remained a voluntary option outside the formal system, a lack of knowledge by the public, judges and the legal profession has been used to explain the low uptake.[68] Here and elsewhere, lawyers were blamed for hindering the development of mediation because they either held negative attitudes about mediating, fearing that it showed a weakness in a case or might reveal litigation strategies – or more resentfully, that they apprehended an 'alarming drop in revenue'.[69] Some held lawyers responsible for its limited application because they used 'defensive marketing' or 'lip-service' to protect their role as dispute resolvers.[70]

Legal professions gaining control

Bryan Clark describes how the legal professions in both civil and common law countries have positioned mediation within the sphere of professional practice through a calculated approach of 'asserting ownership' which

---

66 CEDR Model Mediation Procedure (2010) 12th Edition at Clause 7
67 Brooker (1999) at 36
68 See for example, Lord Jackson (2009) Part 6, 36 at 1.2
69 It became common practice to suggest that the lawyers viewed the acronym ADR to mean an 'alarming drop in revenue'. See for example, Leathes (2009)
70 See Miles (1992) at 313; Clark (2012) at 85–6; Genn (1998)

becomes heightened at the institutionalisation phase because this is often followed by regulation of practice.[71] Clark observes the strategies that lawyers engage in, such as: 'mobilising' the profession to take control over arrangements in court-annexed schemes; and 'lobbying policymakers' to introduce preferential rules for lawyer–mediators[72] – although he states that the most influential way is through 'shopping' for lawyer-mediators on behalf of their clients.[73] The legal professions are placed in an ideal position to influence developments, as many mediation policies take place in the 'shadow of the courts', which Clark describes as the 'lawyers' turf'.[74]

Lawyers have been involved in mediation from its inception in England and Wales, first as enthusiastic newly-trained mediators and then through their involvement in setting up ADR organisations.[75] ADR providers advertising mediation on the Web are dominated by the legal professions, for example, ADR Chambers was established when the CPR were introduced in 1999 and its members are solicitors or barristers. Furthermore it has a 'judicial panel' made up of 'Law Lords, Lords of Justices, High Court, Circuit and other retired judges'.[76] In the construction field, both sides of the legal profession have their own organisations for lawyers acting in the TCC, which provide lists of mediators: TECBAR (Technology and Construction Bar) and TeCSA (Technology and Construction Solicitors Association). CEDR's Mediator Audit in 2012 reported that lawyers 'continue to dominate' with 62 per cent of the respondents from the legal professions.[77] Research confirms an increasing trend for mediator appointments from the legal professions as lawyers make 'repeat' appointments to 'tried and tested' lawyer–mediators.[78]

Lawyers' involvement in evaluative mediation practice

As described in Chapter 1, after the legal professions undertook reviews of ADR in England, lawyers began to train as mediators and 'colonise' the market, which led to concern about their suitability for a role in a 'facilitative' process.[79] Particular criticism of lawyers' interests centres on the influence they have over their client's choice of mediator, which also links to a rise in evaluative rather than facilitative mediation approaches.[80] The difference

---

71 Clark (2012) at 85 & 87
72 Clark (2102) at 90–95. Clark charts the attempts of legal professions in some countries to utilise policies of unauthorised practice of law to limit non-lawyers from mediator practice.
73 Clark (2012) at 84–6
74 Clark (2012) at 84
75 Roberts (1993) at 464
76 See Brooker (2011) at 37–8
77 CEDR Mediators Audit (2012) See at 4
78 Gould et al. (2010) at 68
79 Roberts (1992) at 261
80 Riskin (1996). See for example, Stulberg (1997); Love & Kovach (1996) (1998); Stemple (2000); Lowry (2000); Lande (2000); Stipanowich (2001); Oberman (2005); Noce et al. (2002)

between these two 'styles' was explored in detail in Chapter 1, but to summarise in facilitative mediation, the mediator does not determine the outcome but 'facilitates communication and problem solving by the parties'[81] whereas those who adopt an evaluative 'orientation'[82] use their 'professional expertise' to 'provide additional information, advice and persuade the parties' towards a particular outcome.[83] Evaluative interventions may include analysing the 'strength or weakness' of each party's case, making settlement proposals, or predicting court outcomes and in 'extreme cases' pressing for a particular outcome.[84] Kovach and Love describe how the presence of evaluative mediators 'discourage(s) understanding and problem solving' as the parties 'try to persuade' the mediator towards their point of view in an increasing 'adversarial climate'.[85]

Furthermore, the arrival of evaluative mediation has met with significant criticism because it 'undermines' the parties' self-determination as legal representatives take over decisions on the choice of mediator, how the process is conducted and the settlement outcome achieved, which Welsh argues is often based on 'legal norms' rather than underlying interests: [86]

> However, as mediation has been institutionalized in the courts and as evaluation has become an acknowledged and accepted part of the mediator's function, the original vision of self-determination is giving way to a vision in which the disputing parties play a less central role. The parties are still responsible for making the final decision regarding settlement, but they are cast in the role of consumers, largely limited to selecting from among the settlement options developed by their attorneys. Indeed, it is the parties' attorneys, often aided by mediators who are also attorneys, who assume responsibility for actively and directly participating in the mediation process, invoking the substantive (i.e., legal) norms to be applied and creating settlement options.

Mediation practice in the English jurisdiction has not escaped the facilitative/evaluative debate, and there are a number of studies suggesting that mediators employ 'eclectic' techniques including evaluative interventions, and additionally lawyers may have a preference to appoint lawyer–mediators who once appointed are more 'directive'.[87] It is not surprising that lawyers will

---

81 Menkel-Meadow (1993) at 372
82 Riskin (1996) at 7
83 Boulle et al. (1998) at 29
84 See for example, Riskin (1996) at 28. For an analysis of mediator style in England and Wales see for example, Brooker (2007)
85 Kovach & Love (1996), at 31
86 Welsh (2001b), at 4–5
87 Genn (1998) at 10. See for example, Brooker (2007); Roberts (2000); Dolder (2004); Genn (1998); Mulcahy (2001a); Clark & Mays (1996); Emery et al. (2005); Goriely et al. (2002). See more recently, Clark (2012)

feel more effectual in a process where they are able to use their legal training but it should be recognised that institutionalising mediation confers the legal professions with the power to influence its practice:[88]

> What is equally clear is that as mediation processes have often shifted in their location from outside to within court processes, the lawyer – as mediator or representatives – becomes a more natural participant within it than may hitherto have been the case. Yes, mediation models have been developed and honed by lawyers to better fit their professional cultural and practice norms, but such new modules have also developed because of the court location within which mediation exits and different process requirements that this entails.

In the lead up to CPR, lawyers may not have had significant understanding about ADR but it is now part of the curriculum for the professional training for both sectors of the legal profession.[89] Lawyers have an obligation under CPR to advise their clients about the alternatives to litigation and the legal professions (solicitors and barristers) are expected to have knowledge, although perhaps as yet not practical experience, of mediation. Nevertheless, reports at the highest level still observe that lawyers, and it is intimated some judges, lack knowledge about the 'benefits of mediation' and are blamed for its negligible application.[90] The extent to which lawyers in the English jurisdiction appreciate the theoretical and practical implications of the different approaches to mediation may be embryonic but the legal professions have ensured that their members are in prime position, not only in terms of developing new areas of practice, but also in the nascent professionalism of mediator practice.[91]

Professionalisation of mediation practice

Institutionalisation and a developing mediator profession

Most countries which have experienced recent mediation developments have also found with institutionalisation that a mediator profession begins to emerge or gain pace.[92] In England and Wales as a body of mediation law raises the profile of mediation and its 'legal status' this nurtures aspirations

---

88 Clark (2012) at 96
89 *Solicitors Regulation Authority LPC Training Course Information* (updated March 2012) src. org.uk/lpc downloaded on the 26 April 2012; *Bar Standards Board Bar Professional Training Course* (2011) includes mediation in the skills framework 2.1.1 (3).
90 Lord Jackson (2009) at 362. Lord Jackson called for a 'serious campaign' to ensure that 'all litigation lawyers and all judges (not some litigation lawyers and some judges) are properly informed about the benefits which ADR can bring'.
91 Boon et al. (2007); Brooker (2011); Clark (2012) at 176–80
92 See for example, Alexander (2006); Boon et al. (2007)

on the part of mediators to professionalise their practice.[93] Professionalisation occurs when a group endeavours to prevent others from practising in particular fields by advancing 'restrictive accreditation', which is usually attended by developing 'codes of ethical practice'.[94] Although Alexander suggests no one profession has been able to 'monopolise' mediation in her international review,[95] there have been attempts by legal professions in various jurisdictions to restrict practice to lawyers.[96] For example, Ilter and Dikbas report that one of the most hotly contested areas during the drafting of Turkey's proposed Mediation Act was limiting practice to members of the law bar associations, although this did not prove successful.[97] In Germany, only lawyers are permitted to 'provide legal services', however mediation is not classed as a 'legal service' if the mediator does not provide a 'legal solution'– which Hillag and Huhn note prevents non-lawyers using evaluative interventions or being involved in drafting mediation agreements at the conclusion of the process.[98] Bryan Clark documents how the 'unauthorized practice of law doctrine' has been employed in some court-annexed mediation settings in the USA which only permit lawyer–mediators to practise when 'legal advice' is given and distinguishing this from 'legal information' which is not the practice of law, consequently non-lawyer mediators cannot use evaluative interventions such as applying the law or predicting the likely success of a party's case at court.[99]

Accreditation in England and Wales

In England and Wales, there is no doctrine of unauthorised practise of law and mediation remains an unregulated area of practise, which means anyone could claim expertise and attempt to gain clients.[100] There are, however, features of a developing mediator profession, where groups are pressing to become involved with various organisations are striving for a leading role in setting training standards and regulating or accrediting practice.[101]

Mediators who work in the commercial or workplace sectors usually undertake training from a number of organisations such as the ADR Group,

---

93 See for example, Boon et al. (2007); Brooker (2011); Gould et al. (2009) (2010); Menkle-Meadow (2009); Grossman (2003); Miles (2004); Brady (2009); Nolan-Haley (2002); Clark (2012)

94 Menkel-Meadow (2009) at 195. See also Clark (2009) (2012); Alexander (2006) at 32–5; Brooker (2011) at 26

95 Alexander (2006) at 32

96 See for example, Clark (2012) at 86–91

97 Ilter & Dikbas (2010) at 141

98 Hillag & Huhn (2010) at 56; See *Rechtsdienstleistungsgesetz* 2008 (Legal Services Act), § 2 Abs 3 Nr 4; see Clark (2012) at 94 & 86. Clark notes that only legally qualified people can practise mediation in Greece.

99 Clark (2012) at 93 citing the 'Virginia Guidelines on Mediation and Unauthorized Practice of Law'.

100 Evans (2006); Fry (2006); Brooker (2007); Boon et al. (2007)

101 See Boon et al. (2007) at 49; See Brooker (2011); Brady (2003) (2009); Gould et al. (2010); Clark (2012); CEDR Mediators Audit (2012)

CEDR or the College of Mediators.[102] The Civil Mediation Council (CMC) was set up in 2003 to promote mediation and at the time of writing had accredited 85 organisations and 350 individual members who have 'qualified' to the level required for CMC status.[103] To be accredited by the CMC a training organisation must meet the 'minimum benchmarks' set by the Council covering such issues as mediation theory, ethics and roleplay, and, where trainees are not from the legal professions the mediator course must contain an element of contract law.[104] There are still mediation groups which either train or provide mediators which do not have membership with the CMC, but such organisations are unable to register on 'The Civil Mediation Directory', that is under the auspices of the Ministry of Justice and through which the public can search the online National Mediation Helpline.[105]

Other professional bodies such as the Law Society, the Bar Council and the Royal Institute of Chartered Surveyors[106] also facilitate accreditation schemes for their members who have to undertake a recognised course and must comply with specific codes of practice.[107] Many groups, associations and professional bodies have panels of recognised mediators such as the Royal Institute of British Architects, Institute of Chartered Engineers, the Academy of Experts, The Institute of Chartered Accountants, IRDS Ltd (division of the Chartered Institute of Arbitrators) and the Association of Northern Mediators.[108] Organisations offering mediation services have been found to either have a sizeable number of lawyer–mediators or are specifically set up to represent the legal professions such as Clerksroom Mediation or Law South Mediation.[109]

EU Mediator Code of Practice and Civil Mediation Council

Members of the CMC are required to follow a code of practice, which at a minimum incorporates the EU Mediator Code.[110] This EU code was implemented in 2004 and contains a set of principles that can be voluntarily adopted but does not preclude organisations or mediators 'developing more detailed codes which fit the specific context or type of mediation service

102 See Brooker (2011). In 2011 there were 50 ADR organisations registered with the CMC
103 Information accessed from the Civil Mediation Council website on 27 November 2012 http://www.civilmediation.org/
104 Brooker (2010b) at 162–3; Brooker (2011)
105 Ministry of Justice website http://www.civilmediation.justice.gov.uk/accessed on 27 November 2012 http://www.justice.gov.uk/courts/mediation accessed on 30 November 2012
106 RICS are accredited members of the CMC. Accredited Mediation Provider Organisations 2012 accessed on 28 November 2012
107 See for example, Brooker (2011); Boon et al. (2007)
108 Brooker (2011); Boon et al. (2007)
109 See Brooker (2011) at 34
110 CMC Code of Conduct for Mediators (2009)

which they offer'.[111] However, there is little evidence that organisations or mediators have gone further than recognising the EU Mediators Code.[112] The CMC accreditation scheme stipulates that training must be at 'least 40 hours face-to-face tuition' which incorporates at least 50 per cent roleplaying and panel members are required to undertake six hours of Continual Professional Development (CPD) annually.[113] A number of commercial mediators and mediator organisations now register with the International Mediation Institute (IMI), which provides for an international standard of 'mediator competency' and the expectation for membership is that certification would require at least 200 hours or experience of 20 mediations.[114] Members are required to state which code of practice they adopt.[115] Both the CMC and the IMI require that their members have a complaints system in place and in the case of the IMI, mediators are required to inform the parties of which code of practice the mediator uses.

Regulation debate

The regulation of mediation probably involves one of the most intense debates in the modern mediation movement because it centres around two conflicting 'interests': that of mediators who wish to maintain control over how they practise and the perceived need to protect users from poor standards, which Alexander calls the 'diversity–consistency dilemma'.[116] Those who make a case for regulation are concerned about 'consumer protection' by ensuring that users are informed about 'personnel, procedures and costs' and that mediator practice is 'standardised' with processes in place to prevent incompetent people from practising.[117] Those who argue against regulation contend that there is no evidence of deficient standards in England and Wales at present and that 'market demand' adequately manages any potential problem, as repeat users will not reappoint inept mediators.[118] Furthermore, there are concerns that regulation will 'stifle' flexibility, 'exclude talent', lead to the monopoly of one style of mediating and in the long run will cost participants more as 'qualification' becomes more expensive for mediators.[119]

Fundamental to regulation is arriving at a 'consistent' definition of mediation, which encompasses the evaluative and facilitate divide.[120] Defining

---

111 EU Mediators Code of Practice (2004) at Preamble. See for example, Allen (2008); Brady (2009); Brooker (2011)
112 Brooker (2011)
113 CMC Provider Accredited Scheme (2012)
114 See Meyer & Leathes (2008)
115 The code is available at http://imimediation.org/imi-code-of-professional-conduct Accessed on 27 November 2012
116 Alexander (2008b), at 2
117 See for example, Boon et al. (2007) at 34
118 Boon et al. (2007), at 48–9; Gould (2010), at 66
119 Boon et al. (2007), at 43; South (2009)
120 Alexander (2008b), at 2; Mills (2005)

mediation in a way that only describes specific models can potentially result in some mediators being barred from practice. Neither the EU nor the IMI codes of practice do more than give a basic definition of mediation as a process where the mediator assists the parties to reach a settlement.[121]

The CPR and pre-action protocols do not define mediation, although lawyers are required to advise clients on the benefits of using alternatives. Nor do the courts recommend any procedure or style of mediation over another.[122] The Queen's Bench Guide indicates that advice is available from the National Mediation Helpline, which then gives directions to the Ministry of Justice where an explanation is given in the following terms:[123]

> Mediation, in particular, can be a flexible, speedy and cost effective way to resolve disputes. It is a confidential process that enables both parties to explain and then discuss what their needs and concerns are to each other in the presence of an independent third party – the mediator – so that they reach an agreement between themselves. The individuals concerned have greater control and responsibility in resolving disagreement.

Court Guides often indicate where litigants can get advice from, for example the TCC guide advises that more information is available from the CMC, TeCSA or TECBAR, which the latter two are professional associations for lawyers working in the specialist court.[124] There is substantial evidence in England and Wales indicating that mediation is in the hands of a relatively small group of mediators and although the choice of mediator and the style adopted remains in the hands of the parties, this may be illusory as it is likely to be based on the recommendations of their lawyers (therefore casting doubt on participants' experience of self-determination).[125]

Party self-determination in mediation

The cornerstone of mediation is said to be parties' self determination, which distinguishes it from adjudication[126] but many 'purists'[127] argue this is weakened by evaluative practice.[128] The evaluative–facilitative debate however is

---

121 See Brooker (2011) at 29–30
122 See Brooker (2011) at 27
123 Ministry of Justice website http://www.justice.gov.uk/courts/mediation accessed on 25 November 2012. See Brooker (2009) (2011)
124 TCC Court Guide (2010) at 7.3.4
125 Gould et al. (2010); Brooker (2011) at 27
126 Alfini (2008) at 830
127 Menkel-Meadow (1993) at 372
128 See for example, Alfini (2008); Kovach and Love (1996); Stulberg (1997); Welsh (2001a, b)

undermined to some extent because there is little consensus on the 'demarcation' of mediator activities and some techniques such as 'reality testing' or challenging parties on the strength or weakness of their case are claimed as 'legitimate facilitative tools'.[129] Many now acknowledge that mediation may include evaluation provided informed consent supports self-determination, perhaps because it would be too difficult to change direction.[130] However, this begs the question as to the extent parties are aware of the differences of styles before engaging in the process and to what degree codes of practice, which many mediators and mediation organisations adhere to, give prominence to self-determination.[131]

Mediator codes of practice: party self-determination and informed consent

Neither the EU Mediators Code nor the IMI codes of practice spell out the principles of self-determination or informed consent.[132] The EU code requires that 'The mediator shall satisfy himself/herself that the parties to the mediation understand the characteristics of the mediation process and the role of the mediator and the parties in it' and that at the conclusion of the mediation 'any understanding is reached through knowing and informed consent'.[133] The IMI code places slightly more responsibility on registered mediators by requiring that they 'explain the process to the parties and their advisors', are satisfied that they 'consent to the process being used' and 'ensure that all parties have adequate opportunities to be heard' and are 'involved in the process'.[134] Perhaps more significant in guaranteeing that parties enter the mediation with informed consent is the requirement that IMI-certified mediators direct the parties to their profile on the website, which contains information on their 'background' and 'experience' but also the 'style' used.[135]

Other approaches to regulation

Regulation of Mediation in Australia

Other countries which are further along in the 'regulation phase' of mediation have more stringent or demanding codes underpinning practice or place

---

129 Brooker (2007) at 226. See McDermott and Obar (2004) at 77–8; Stulberg (1997) at 1003–4; Kovach & Love (1998); Love (1997) at 78–9
130 See Brooker (2011) at 39; See for example, Cooley (2000); Imperati (1997); Nolan-Haley (1999)
131 See Brooker (2011)
132 See Brooker (2011) at 39–40
133 EU Mediators Code (2004) at 3.1 & 3.3
134 IMI Code of Practice at 3.2.1.
135 IMI Code of Practice at 1.3. The search facility on the IMI website includes evaluative, facilitative, transformative or 'any styles'. See Brooker (2011) at 40

more responsibility on mediators for ensuring that self-determination forms the basis of mediating.[136] In 2008, Australia introduced a voluntary National Mediator Accreditation Scheme (NMAS) for accrediting mediators, which is registered with a Recognised Mediator Accreditation Body (RMAB).[137] A separate body has been instituted, the Mediation Standard Board (MSB), which has responsibility for 'implementing the NMAS and maintaining and developing standards of practice and training'.[138] The Australian National Mediator Standards state that mediation 'maximises self-determination' and that 'mediators do not advise upon, evaluate or determine disputes', although it recognises that some mediators use a 'blended approach' by providing 'advisory' or 'expert information'.[139] However, if adopting such an approach mediators must show evidence that they have the 'professional qualifications' to provide such advice and must obtain 'clear consent' from the participants.[140]

Regulation of mediation in USA

The Uniform Mediation Act (UMA) in the USA elected not to enact a law that would 'diminish the creative and diverse use of mediation' and the choice of process remains part of the parties' agreement through 'informed choice'.[141] The UMA does not provide mediation standards nor does it prescribe mediator qualifications or require that practitioners are legally qualified, although it does state that mediators must provide information on their credentials on request.[142] This verification process is 'delegated' to states and courts to organise through 'local rules'.[143] The ADR Act 1998, which requires litigants in the federal district courts to consider alternatives, does not legislate on qualifications or training either, but delegates this to the relevant courts, which means there is a great variance in the approaches to mediation standards and mediator qualifications in the USA.[144]

Various associations have developed mediator 'codes of ethics' such as 'Model Standard of Conduct for Mediators: Joint Standards' promulgated by the American Arbitration Association, the ABA and the Association of Conflict (Previously the Society for Professionals in Dispute Resolution).[145] Standard 1A of the 'Joint Standards' places a requirement on the mediator

---

136 Alexander (2008b)
137 See Sourdin (2006) at 31. See NADRAC website http://www.nadrac.gov.au/what_is_adr/ NationalMediatorAccreditationSystem/Pages/default.aspx accessed on 28 November 2012
138 MSB website http://www.msb.org.au/about-us/msb-objectives accessed on 28 November 2012
139 Australia National Mediator Standards (2007) at 2.5 & 2.7
140 Australia National Mediator Standards (2007) at 10.5. See Alexander (2008b) at 119
141 UMA 2003 Comment at 39
142 UMA 2003, s9 (c) and (d)
143 UMA 2003, Prefatory note at 6
144 Cole et al. (2012) at 11.4
145 See Kovach (2006) at 425–30 at 426

that mediation is 'conducted' with regard to party 'self-determination'. Some states have introduced their own codes or Model standards.[146] Association, court and state codes are similar and cover the same issues which Kovach identifies as: 'Competency, Neutrality and Impartiality, Conflicts of Interest, the Mediator's Role, Confidentiality, Party Self-determination, Quality of Process, Duties to the Profession, Qualifications, Advertising and Fees'.[147] Kovach has been particularly critical of the eroding of self-determination by mediators who 'coerce parties into settlement'[148] but this may have been addressed by the latest revision of the 'Joint Standards', which stipulates that mediators must not 'undermine party self-determination for any reason' specifically not to improve 'settlement rates or egos'.[149]

Some states in the USA approach standards through the certification of mediation providers.[150] A task group from the ABA undertook a review of the 'feasibility' of a national certification programme in 2006 but concluded that it was not practicable. Cole et al. report on the findings of another ABA group which indicated that users were very much in favour of mediators taking an evaluative stance by proposing 'suggestions', giving court predictions and questioning the strength and weaknesses of the case.[151]

The problems of mediation and mediator consistency across the USA are unlikely to be resolved through a national system not least because of the size of such an operation. Kovach believes that the weaknesses of the current systems are the lack of effective procedures for 'enforcement', which she advocates could be addressed through state 'licensure' or 'accreditation strategies'[152] and Cole et al. recommend non-compliance should result in 'decertification'.[153] However, this would require 'overarching' bodies to undertake a 'supervisory' role. Until such time Kovach doubts that a mediator profession can truly be said to exist in the USA.[154]

Regulation of Mediation in Hong Kong

Hong Kong also does not have a central accreditation system or single training requirements although the Department of Justice Working Group on Mediation recommended this for the future and suggested a review five years after the report.[155] A number of organisations provide training and

---

146 See Cole et al. at 11.9. The authors reference Oklahoma and Louisiana codes of conduct.
147 Kovach (2006), at 426–7
148 Kovach (2006), at 427
149 Model Standards of Conduct for Mediators (2005), at 1B
150 Cole et al. (2012), at 11.5. The authors refer to certification programmes from Florida and North Carolina
151 Cole et al. (2012), at 11.5
152 Kovach (2006), at 426
153 Cole et al. (2012) 11.9
154 Kovach (2006), at 430
155 Report of the Working Party Group Executive Summary (2010). See for example, Wall (2009); Cheung (2010a, b)

accreditation such as the Hong Kong International Arbitration Centre (HKIAC),[156] or the Law Society, and some international groups have established programmes such as England's CEDR.[157] However, the Task Group noted that presently not all groups have 'disciplinary mechanism' in place nor do all training organisations provide CPD.[158] The Working Party recommended that the 'emphasis' should be on providing 'appropriate information' to prospective users to 'enable' them to appoint a 'competent person'. The Task Group did prepare and publish the Hong Kong Mediation Code in 2010, which is intended to 'provide a common standard' for mediators and operates as a 'quality function'.[159]

The Hong Kong Mediation Code does not use the term self-determination but under section 3 ('Informed Consent') the mediator is required to 'explain the nature of the process, the procedures utilised and the role of the mediator'. The code also does not prescribe a particular model of mediation. However, under section 7 ('Defining the Process') the mediator must consider whether a party who is not represented by a lawyer or an 'expert advisor' should be advised to obtain such support. The only reference to qualifications of mediators in the code is that they must be 'competent and knowledgeable' and should 'have regard to relevant standards and/or accreditation scheme'.[160] At present mediators working in Hong Kong are reported to mainly adopt a facilitative approach. However, Wall suggests that this may change as the civil procedure reforms begin to change mediation practice.[161] Lawyers are now found to dominate in many specialist settings and one of the most effective mediator techniques in construction mediation is said to be 'reality testing'.[162]

Mediator codes of practice in UK

Although most mediators and mediation organisations in England and Wales adhere to the EU Mediators Code of Practice, there is little evidence suggesting that they have gone further to make clear the importance of self-determination or informed consent by developing more explicit codes or adopting more 'inspirational language'.[163] This is not to imply that those who work in the field of mediation do not ensure that before mediating participants are aware of the approach, and indeed many organisations

156 See for example, Wall (2009); Cheung (2010a,b)
157 CEDR website information http://www.cedr.com/about_us/international/list.php? param=64 accessed on 30 November 2012
158 Report of the Working Party Group Executive Summary (2010) at 22
159 Report of the Working Party Group Executive Summary (2010) at 24 & 25
160 Hong Kong Mediator Code at 9
161 Wall (2009) at 79
162 Cheung (2010b) at 69
163 Alfini (2008) at 837. See also Oberman (2008). See Brooker (2011) for a review of codes of practice in England and Wales.

provide information online including their mediation agreements, which sometimes govern how the process will be conducted.[164] A review of websites of organisations offering mediation services found that some agreements or 'mediation rules' contained a 'high degree of legalistic language' stipulating that parties 'comply' with mediator 'directions' or giving mediators 'absolute discretion' on the 'conduct of the mediation'.[165] The websites often imparted little or no explicit acknowledgement of self-determination or informed consent and, although many mediation agreements did suggest that the approach would be by 'consultation' with the participants, the research concluded that much could be done to give more 'transparency' to the principles of self-determination and informed consent.[166] Taking such steps would go some way to 'raise the bar' of 'ethical' practice and would protect the informed choice of participants but would fall short of introducing regulation which some fear might stifle the creativeness of mediator practice.[167] The dangers of parties entering mediation without being fully informed of what to expect may lead to 'disillusionment' which will do little to encourage its use.[168]

Regulation of mediation in England and Wales

It is yet to be seen how mediators will respond to regulation of their practice in England and Wales, although attempts to influence how mediation is conducted met with resistance when the CMC consulted on a new Code of Practice in 2009, which proposed practice 'under the principle of party self-determination'.[169] There were objections because the proposal was 'too prescriptive' and overlooked evaluative or adjudicatory ADR procedures.[170] The 2012 CEDR Mediator Audit reported that mediators are in favour of a standard of training rather than a 'free market' approach of voluntary accreditation and significant numbers would like to see a single body or organisation to take this function.[171] Whilst the Civil Mediation Council remains marginally in the lead to undertake both the role of training and professional standards, mediators in the 2012 audit articulated a preference for a new independent body, although not a 'worldwide' or 'European-wide' organisation.[172]

---

164 See Brooker (2011) at 38
165 Brooker (2011) at 38
166 Imperati (1997) at 705; Alfini (2008) at 831. See Brooker (2011) at 40
167 Brooker (2011) at 41. See Cooley (2000) at 77–8; Imperati (1997) at 705. There is a call for codes of practice for mediation advocates in England and Wales. See Mason (2012)
168 Brooker 2011 at 41; See Cooley (2000) at 79
169 See Brookes (2009)
170 For a commentary on the CMC proposals see Sir Henry Brookes (2009) at 52–3
171 CEDR Mediators Audit 2012 at 9. Significant numbers of mediators in the 2012 survey would like to see a single body or organisation responsible for 'training, regulation and complaints'.
172 CEDR Mediator Audit (2012) at 10

England and Wales may not have travelled as far along the mediation journey as other jurisdictions but government proposals in 2012 to make it mandatory for disputes below £5,000 (with the suggestion that litigants should attend mediation information sessions if their disputes are valued up to £100,000), provides a stronger argument for closer supervision or regulation of practice.[173] Commentators indicate that it is likely that there will be a vigorous 'lobby' from influential quarters against 'over restrictive' regulation because it preserves party choice[174] but equally clear arguments exist for reinforcing the fundamental principles of 'self-determination' and 'informed consent' on which mediation was founded.[175]

Mediation in England and Wales has come a significant way from offering a voluntary alternative to litigation but when litigants face financial penalties for not mediating then they should expect that the process they are being directed to be appropriately regulated. The next section considers how institutionalisation has brought about the juridification of mediation.

Juridification

'Dimensions of juridification'[176]

Chapter 1 reviewed a framework for juridification designed by Blichner and Molander of which three features are specifically relevant to mediation development in England and Wales.[177] First, there is the 'expansion of law' into mediation activity.[178] Second, this escalation of law is connected to the juridification process by deciding new areas of dispute about aspects of mediating by 'reference to the law' and through 'legal reasoning'.[179] Third, the growth in mediation law is attended by an increase in 'judicial power' whereby judges and lawyers are involved in interpreting the law when there are areas of 'indeterminacy' or 'transparency', which is linked to the reliance of disputants on the legal professions.[180]

---

173 The consultation did not come out in favour of making mediation mandatory although it did support making it a compulsory step for parties to be 'automatically referred' to a session with a mediator to consider its use. A pilot automatic referral mediation scheme was introduced for small money claims (less than £5,000) in October 2012 under PD51H. The 61st Amendment to CPR introduced an extension to the scheme.
174 See South (2009); Gould et al. (2010); Clark (2012)
175 For a discussion on these issues see for example, Brooker (2011); Gould et al. (2010); South (2009); Boon et al. (2007)
176 Blichner & Molander (2005) at 1
177 Blichner & Molander (2005) (2008)
178 Blichner & Molander (2005) at 31. Blichner & Molander cite Habermas (1987) at 356–63. See also Ruben (2002)
179 Blichner & Molander (2005) at 6
180 Blichner & Molander (2005) at 19 fn 43. The authors state that 'judicial power' is often referred to as 'judicialisation'. They cite Neal & Vallinder (1995)

Expansion of law

The main process of juridification is said to be the 'expansion of law' and the chapters of this book have explored how the process has increasingly come within the legal sphere.[181] The current mediation phenomenon began in England and Wales as an ADR mechanism in community or neighbour disputes but the potential for using it in a commercial context was recognised as newly qualified mediators began to offer their services as mediations.[182] Mediation in England shows a similar pattern to arbitration, which began as a forum for business people seeking decisions from experienced neutrals based on commercial practice, but arbitration law illustrates that parties sought the help of the courts to uphold agreements to arbitrate or settlement outcomes or to overturn or enforce arbitrators' decisions.[183] The practice of drafting ADR clauses into contracts stimulated the expansion of law into the domain of mediation. At first, this was through the inability of some parties to get those who had contractually agreed to mediate prior to any dispute arising to take part in mediation or seeking help from the courts to enforce the agreements reached through mediating. Thus, lawyers and the law attained a 'propriatorial interest' in the process as these issues about mediation practice, which had previously been 'unregulated areas of activity', came before the courts.[184]

Formal systems interest in mediation: court practice statements to CPR

The judiciary was also quick to recognise the benefits of ADR to the courts and introduced court practice directions to encourage parties to seek other ways to resolve their disputes. Following these judicial actions, Lord Woolf's reform of civil litigation put into practice a legal framework to more vigorously direct cases to ADR, which operated through penalising unreasonable refusals to mediate through costs sanctions. Mediation, as the most prominent ADR mechanism, has undergone a process of juridification as the law has expanded into this previously 'unsupervised' area of activity.[185] Chapter 4 explored how the law integrated mediation with litigation thereby delineating practice by defining appropriate cases for mediating but also by indicating the most suitable timing within the framework of the formal system, which the courts have often decided is after the accumulation of sufficient evidence to defend a case. The CPR and the judicial application of

---

181 Blichner & Molander (2005) at 12 & 14. The authors cite Tuebner (1997). See also Harker et al. (2011) at fn191. Harker, Peyer and Wright contend this is the most general usage of juridification.

182 See Roberts (1992) (1993)

183 See for example, Arthurs (1984); Lane (1986)

184 Roberts (1993) at 464

185 Roberts (2000) at 747

those rules firmly established mediation in the litigation process, which has led to tactical interplay between the two.

Juridification through 'reference to the law'[186]

Disputants who either could not get others to the mediation table; or found their mediated agreements not honoured or who faced costs sanctions for not mediating; or questioned the confidentiality of their compromise negotiations – found themselves with little option than to seek legal advice about the law and then to access the courts for 'authoritative' judgments.[187] Once these cases come before the courts they are decided by 'reference' to either existing common law principles which are extended to deal with new areas of activity, or their claims are dealt with through judicial discretion of the CPR rules, which have led to court guidelines regulating practice.

As disputants rarely have the expertise to engage in 'legal reasoning'[188] and most negotiation is done in the 'shadow of the law',[189] when mediation raises new areas requiring the application of legal rules to new sets of circumstances then this results in party dependence on lawyers who begin to 'monopolise' and 'juridify' the process to prevent competition from non-legal experts.[190] Mediation in the English jurisdiction presents a similar chronology to arbitration where the legal professions sought a hold over a new area of practice from non-lawyers.[191]

Juridification through 'judicial power'

Mediation as a 'juridical field'

When mediation began to be offered as a way of resolving commercial disputes this brought its practice into what Bourdieu calls a 'juridical field' where groups with specific 'technical' proficiencies compete to dominate the 'right to determine law'.[192]

> The juridical field is the site of a competition for monopoly of the right to determine the law. Within this field there occurs a confrontation among actors possessing a technical competence which is inevitably social and which consists essentially in the socially recognized capacity to

---

186 Blichner & Molander (2005) at 6
187 Fuller (1978) at 368
188 Blichner & Molander (2005) at 16
189 Mnookin & Kornhauser (1978–79); See Genn (2010) at 21 & 35
190 Flood & Caiger (1993) who cite Bourdieu (1987) at 817: 'The juridical field is the site of a competition for monopoly of the right to determine law'.
191 Roberts (1992) (1993) (2000). See also for example; Genn (1998); Brooker & Lavers (2001); Clark (2012); Flood & Caiger (1993)
192 Bourdieu (1987) at 817

interpret a corpus of texts sanctifying a correct or legitimized vision of the social world.

'Juridical language' in mediation

Within this 'space', legal professionals protect their 'economic interests' by using 'juridical language' in order to exclude the 'non-specialist'.[193] They achieve this by 'redefining problems' presenting in 'ordinary language' into a 'legal problem' and then 'translating them into the language of law', thus lawyers are able to take the role of appraising the likelihood of succeeding with 'different strategies' such as mediation:[194]

> The professionals create the need for their own services by redefining problems expressed in ordinary language as legal problems, translating them into the language of the law and proposing a prospective evaluation of the chances for success of different strategies.

Bourdieu uses the experience of the labour field to illustrate how the legal profession 'appropriates' a new field of activity by excluding 'lay people' and thereby completing a 'circular' process of 'juridicization'.[195] Labour arbitration boards were set up to provide 'simplified' procedures based on principles of fairness with specialist arbitrators who were experts. However, subsequently disputes in this field were 'annexed by the juridical realm' and then appropriated by certain members of the legal profession into their field of specialism.[196] As Bourdieu explains there was an escalation of appeals from arbitral awards to the 'legal system' which promotes a reliance on the legal profession who then intensify the 'formalism of procedures' which requires further legal expertise until eventually the 'complainants and defendants' come 'under the jurisdiction of the courts':[197]

> In short, a process of circular reinforcement goes into action: every step toward the 'juridicization' of a dimension of practice creates new 'juridical needs,' and thus new juridical interests among those who, possessing the specific qualifications necessary (knowledge of labor law in this case), find in these needs a new market. Through their intervention, such practitioners cause an increase in the formalism of legal procedures, and thereby contribute to increasing the need for their own services and products, to the practical exclusion of laypeople. Laypeople are obliged to have recourse to the advice of legal professionals, who little by little

193 Bourdieu (1987), at 818, 819 & 829
194 Bourdieu (1987), at 834
195 Bourdieu (1987), at 835–7 at 836
196 Bourdieu (1987), at 836
197 Bourdieu (1987), at 836–7

will come to replace the complainants and defendants. The latter in their turn become nothing more than a group of individuals who have fallen under the jurisdiction of the courts.

Just as Flood and Caiger observed the 'struggle' between lawyers and non-lawyers in the field of construction through the juridification of arbitration, mediation has witnessed the legal professions in England and Wales seeking to control practice as it becomes a 'juridical field'.[198] This has intensified as the CPR have institutionalised mediation by integrating it with the formal system and as disputes have emerged over contractual arrangements surrounding mediation practice, upholding mediated agreements, confidentiality or the judicial application of the costs rules sanctioning unreasonable refusals to mediate.

Conclusion

This book has explored the modern phenomenon of mediation in England and Wales and has seen the progression from a voluntary process after experimentation, to institutionalisation; moves towards regulation of training and practice; and finally how these developments result in juridification. When people are unable to resolve disputes themselves, it is to be expected that on occasions on their own volition or the advice of their lawyers they choose to consult, they will seek judicial determination. Therefore, at the invitation of litigants, albeit through the control that the legal professions exert over dispute resolution, the courts have been required to define mediation rules, first on the principles governing contractual relationships or the uncertainties created by the CPR and then the protection given to negotiations when mediating.

Legal history shows that it may be impossible for any alternative to remain outside the law, some argue because the formal system will not allow challenges to their jurisdiction.[199] Perhaps mediation is not able to exist on a 'parallel'[200] independent track to litigation because both processes originate from conflict or dispute and if commercial practices or social values do not assist resolution, then most settlement will be done in the 'shadow of the law'[201] with the assistance of lawyers which inevitably leads to juridification.

198 Flood & Caiger (1993) at 413. See also Roberts (2000)
199 See for example, Auerbach (1984)
200 *Burchell v. Bullard* (2005) per Lord Justice Ward at 43. See Genn (2010) at 79
201 Mnookin & Kornhauser (1978–79); Genn (2010) at 21 & 35

References

Abel R. (1982) *The Politics of Informal Justice: The American Experience*, Vol. 1 Academic Press Inc; First Edition, (Feb 1982)

Abrahams B. (1988) The Origins of Arbitration, *Arbitration* November, 54, 4

Admiralty and Commercial Court Guide (2011) 9th Edition

ADR Chamber's *'Mediation Rules'*, at http://adrchambers.com/ca/mediation/mediation-rules/ Accessed on 3 December 2012

ADR Group's *'Mediation Procedures and Rules'* at http://www.adrgroup.co.uk/images/library/files/family/Mediation_Procedure_and_Rules.pdf Accessed on 3 December 2012

Agapiou A. & Clark B. (2011) Scottish construction lawyers and mediation: An investigation into attitudes and experiences, *International Journal of Law in the Built Environment* Vol. 3 Issue 2, 159

Ahmed M. (2010) Reinforcing the need to protect the without prejudice rule, *Civil Justice Quarterly*, Vol. 29, No. 3, 303

Ahmed M. (2012) Implied compulsory mediation, *Civil Justice Quarterly* 31(2), 151

Aibinu A., Akin-Ojelabi L. & Gardiner B. *Construction mediation in Australia* in Brooker P. & Wilkinson S. (2010) (Editors) *Mediation in the Construction Industry: An International Review* Spon Press (imprint of Taylor & Francis Group)

Alexander N. (2006) (ed.) *Global Trends in Mediation* 2nd Edition, Kluwer Law International, Netherlands

Alexander N. (2008a) Mediation metamodels: understanding practice, *Conflict Resolution Quarterly* Vol. 26, No. 1, 97

Alexander N. (2008b) Mediation and the Art of Regulation, *Queensland University of Technology Law & Justice Journal* 8, 1

Alexander N. (2009) *International and Comparative Mediation: Legal Perspectives*, Kluwer Law International, The Netherlands

Alfini J. (2008) Ethics in the expanding world of ADR: Considerations, conundrums, and conflict, *South Texas Law Review* Vol. 49, 829

Alfini J. & McCabe C. (2001) Mediating the Shadow of the Courts: A Survey of the Emerging Case Law, *Arkansas Law Review* 54, 171

Allen T. (2008) Implementing the EU Directive on Mediation, *CEDR Article* available at: www.cedr.com/index.php?location=/library/articles/20081006_244.htm Accessed 13 February 2009

Allen T. (2009) Calling all mediators? A review of *Farm Assist v DEFRA, CEDR Article*, at http://www.cedr.com/index.php?location=/library/articles/20090705_263.htm Accessed on 25 September 2009

Allen T. (2011) The Mediation Directive now implemented, *CEDR Article* available at: http://www.cedr.com/articles/?293 accessed on 15 November 2011

Allen T. (2012) Don't ignore a request to mediate *Halsey* applied!: A note on *PGF II SA v. OMFS Company* [2012] EWHC 83 (TCC) *CEDR Article* http://www.cedr.com/articles/?301 25 October 2012, accessed on 6 July 2012

Allen T. & Mackie K. (2010) Higher resolution – why is there no more mediation?, *CEDR Article* available at http://www.cedr.com/articles/?284, accessed on 12 December 2010

Allen T. & Mackie K. (2010) Moves in mediation: confidentiality, the EU Directive and regulation, http://www.barristermagazine.com/archive-articles/issue-43/moves-in-mediation-confidentiality-the-eu-directive-and-regulation.html, accessed on 15 November 2011

Alschuler A. (1988) Mediation with a mugger: The shortage of adjudicative services and the need for a two tier trial system in civil cases, *Harvard Law Review* 99, 1808

Altaras D. (2010) The without prejudice rule in England, *Arbitration* 76(3), 474

Angyal R. (1998) Legal issues in the mediation process *ADR Bulletin*: Vol. 1: No. 6, Article 1. Available at: http://epublications.bond.edu.au/adr/vol1/iss6/1 accessed on 26 April 2013

Angyal R. (1994) The Enforceability of Agreements to Mediate, *Australian Construction Law Newsletter* Issue 34, 35

Armstrong A. (1995) Making Tracks in *Reform of the Civil Procedure Essays on 'Access to Justice'*, Edited by A. Zuckerman & Cranston, R. Clarendon Press, Oxford

Arthurs H. W. (1984) *Special Courts, Special Law: Legal Pluralism in Nineteenth Century England*, Law and Economy and Society. Edited by Rubin and Sugarman

Auerbach J. (1983) *Justice Without Law*, Oxford University Press

Australian Law Commission, Final Report on *Evidence Law* (2005)

Australia National Mediator Standards (2007) (2008)

Australian National Mediator Standards: Commentary on Approval Standards. Accessed from the WWW on 3 March 2010 at http://www.nswbar.asn.au/docs/professional/adr/documents/Commentaryonpracticestndrds.pdf

Axe, M. (2010) Exception chat proves the rule – Supreme Court extends exception to Without Prejudice Privilege http://www.rawlinsonbutler.com/news/the_exception_that_Interpretation_to_without_prejudice_privilege

Baker J. H. (2007) *An introduction to English Legal History*, 4th Edition, Oxford University Press

Baker J. H. (1988) *An Introduction to English Legal History*, 2nd Edition, Lexus Nexus: Butterworth, England

Bar Standards Board Bar Professional Training Course (2011) at https://www.barstandardsboard.org.uk/media/1435625/bptc_081112.pdf accessed 26 April 2013

Barrett K. (2008) The Pre-Action Protocol for Construction and Engineering Disputes: satisfactory performance, *Construction Law Journal* 24(8), 687

Baruch Bush R. (2002) Substituting mediation for arbitration: the growing market for evaluative mediation and what it means for the ADR field, *Pepperdine Dispute Resolution Law Journal* Vol. 3, 111

Baruch Bush R. (2008) Staying in orbit, or breaking free: The relationship of mediation to the courts over four decades, *North Dakota Law Review* 84, 705

Baruch Bush R. & Folger J. (1994) *The Promise of Mediation: Responding to Conflict Through Empowerment and Recognition*, San Francisco, Jossey-Bass

Baruch Bush R. & Folger J. (2005) *The Promise of Mediation: The Transformative Approach to Conflict*, San Francisco, Jossey-Bass

Baruch Bush R. & Pope S. (2002) Changing the quality of conflict interaction: the principles and practice of transformative mediation, *Pepperdine Dispute Resolution Journal* Vol. 3, 67

Beatson J. *Anson's Law of Contract* (2002) 28th Edition Oxford University Press

Behrens J. (2002) The history of mediation of probate disputes, *Arbitration* 68: 138

Beldham L.J. (1991) *Report of the Committee on ADR* (General Council of the Bar, Committee on ADR)

Bevan A. (1992) *Alternative Dispute Resolution*, Sweet & Maxwell, London

Bingham T. (1992) Judgment Ways, *Building*, 20 November

Bingham T. (2008) Keeping Mum about Mediation, *Building* 7, 63–5

Bingham L., Raines S., Hedeen T. & Napoli L. (2010) Mediation in employment and creeping legalism: implications for disputes systems design, *Journal of Dispute Resolution* Vol. 10, No 1, 129; Indiana University School of Public & Environmental Affairs Research Paper No. 2011-05-03, available at SSRN: http://ssrn.com/abstract=1827063

Birch E. (2006) The historical background to the EU Directive, *The International Journal of Arbitration, Mediation and Dispute Management*, Vol. 72, No. 1, 57

Blichner L. & Molander A. (2005) What is Juridification? *Centre for European Studies* https://www.sv.uio.no/arena/english/research/publications/arena-publications/workingpapers/working-papers2005/wp05_14.pdf, accessed on 26 April 2013

Blichner L. & Molander A. (2008) 'Mapping Juridification' (2008) *European Law Journal* 14 Vol. 1, 36

Boon A., Earle R. & Whyte A. (2007) Regulating mediators?, *Legal Ethics* 10(1), 26

Boulle L. (2001) Revisiting the mediation referral order, *The ADR Bulletin* Vol. 4 No 4, accessed on 26 April 2013

Boulle L. (2005) *Mediation: Principles, Process, Practice* (2nd edn) Chatswood: LexisNexis Butterworths

Boulle L. & Nesic M. (2001) *Mediation: Principles, Process, Practice*, London, Butterworths

Boulle L., Jones J. & Goldblatt V. (1998) *Mediation: Principles, Process, Practice*, (New Zealand Edition) Wellington, Butterworths

Bourdieu P. (1987) The Force of Law: Towards a Sociology of the Juridical Field, *Hastings Law Journal*, July, 38, 805 Translated by Richard Terdiman

Brad Reich J. (2002) Attorney v. client: creating a mechanism to address competing process, *Southern Illinois University Law Journal* Vol. 26, 183

Bradney A. & Cownie F. (2000) *Living without Law*, Ashgate, England

Brady A. (2003) *Alternative dispute resolution (mediation) development for non-family civil disputes in England and Wales*, World Jurist Association 21st Biennial Conference on Law of the World, August, WJA Publication, Sydney

Brady A. (2009) Mediation developments in civil and commercial matters within the European Union, *Arbitration* Vol. 73, No. 3, 390

Briggs (Mr Justice) (2009a) Mediation Privilege *New Law Journal* 159, Issue 7363, 506

Briggs (Mr Justice) (2009b) Mediation Privilege *New Law Journal* 159, Issue 7363, 550

Brooker P. (1997) PhD Unpublished Thesis, Factors which impact on the choice of ADR in the Construction Industry Oxford Brookes University

Brooker P. (1999) Juridification of ADR, *Anglo-American Law Journal* 28(1), 1

Brooker P. (2002) Construction lawyers' attitudes and experience with ADR, *Construction Law Journal* Vol. 18, No. 2, 97

Brooker, P. (2007) An Investigation of Evaluative and Facilitative Approaches to Construction Mediation, *Structural Survey* Vol. 25, Number 3/4, 220

Brooker P. (2009) Criteria for the Appropriate Use of Mediation in Construction Disputes: Judicial Statements in the English Technology and Construction Court, *International Journal of Law in the Built Environment,* Vol. 1, Issue 1, 82

Brooker P. (2010a) Judging Unreasonable Litigation Behavior at the Interface of Mediation in the English Jurisdiction, *Journal of Legal Affairs and Dispute Resolution in Engineering and Construction* Vol. 2, No. 3, August, 2010, 148

Brooker P. (2010b) Construction Mediation in England and Wales in Brooker P. and Wilkinson S. (2010) *Construction Mediation: An International Review* Spon Press (imprint of Taylor & Francis Group)

Brooker P. (2011) Towards a code of professional conduct for construction mediators, *International Journal of Law in the Built Environment* Vol. 3, Issue 1, 24

Brooker P. & Lavers A. (2000) Issues in the Development of ADR for Commercial and Construction Disputes, *Civil Justice Quarterly* Vol. 19, 353

Brooker P. and Lavers A. (2001) Commercial and construction disputes: Lawyers' attitudes and experience, *Civil Justice Quarterly* 20(Oct), 327

Brooker P. & Lavers A. (2002) Commercial Lawyers' Attitudes and Experience with ADR, 4 *Web JCLI (Web Journal of Current Legal Issues)*

Brooker P. and Lavers A. (2005a) Mediation Outcomes: Lawyers' Experience with Mediation, *Pepperdine Dispute Resolution Journal* Vol. 2, 161

Brooker P. and Lavers A. (2005b) Construction Lawyers' Experience with Mediation Post-CPR, *Construction Law Review* No 1, 19

Brooker P. & Wilkinson S. (2010) *Construction Mediation: An International Review,* Spon Press; Taylor & Francis, Abingdon, England & New York, USA

Brookes H. (2009) *Chairman's Report on Consultation CMC,* available at: www.civilmediation.org/files/pdf/Responses"to"the"Consultation"Process% 20final.pdf Accessed 6 July 2010

Brown A., Anderson I., Nixon J. & Hunter C. (2003) *The role of mediation in tackling neighbour disputes and anti social behaviour,* Scottish Executive, Social Research Responding to Community Conflict: A review of neighbourhood mediation. Joseph Rowntree Publication

Brown H. (1989) Sizing up ADR, *The Law Society Gazette* Number 46, December 20

Brown H. (1991) *Alternative Dispute Resolution,* A report prepared by Henry Brown for the Courts and Legal Services Committee, Law Society Legal Practice Directorate, July

Brown H. & Marriott A. (1999) *ADR: Principles and Practice,* 2nd Edition, Sweet & Maxwell, London

Brown H. & Marriott A. (2011) *ADR: Principles and Practice,* 3rd Edition, Sweet & Maxwell, London

Brunet E. (1987) Questioning the Quality of Alternative Dispute Resolution, *Tulane Law Review* 62, 1

Brunsdon-Tully M. (2009) There is an A in ADR but does anyone know what it means any more?, *Civil Justice Quarterly* 28, 218

Bucklow A. (2006) The law of unintended consequences, or repeated patterns?, *Arbitration* 72(4), 348

Bucklow A. (2007) The 'Everywhen' mediator: the virtues of inconsistency and paradox: the strength, skills, attributes and behaviours of excellent and effective mediators, *International Journal of Arbitration, Mediation and Dispute Management* Vol. 73, No. 1, 40

Burnley R. & Lascelles G. (2004) Mediator confidentiality: conduct and communication, *Arbitration* 70(1), 28

Burns R. (1986) The enforceability of mediated agreements: An essay on legitimation and process integrity, *Ohio State Journal on Dispute Resolution* 2, 93

Burr A. & Honey H. (2001) The Post-Woolf TCC: Any change?, *Construction Law Journal* 17(5), 378

Carroll E. (1989) Are We Ready for ADR in Europe?, *International Financial Law Review* 8, Part 12, 11 (December)

Carroll R. (2002) Trends in Mediation Legislation: 'All for One and One for All' or One at All?, *University of Western Australia Law Review* 23, 2

CEDR Civil Justice Audit (2000) at http://www.cedr.com/library/articles/CJAreport. pdf Accessed on 27 April 2013

CEDR Mediators Audit 2012 available at http://www.cedr.com/docslib/TheMediator Audit2012.pdf Accessed on 27 November 2012

CEDR Model Mediation Agreement (2012) 13th Edition at http://www.cedr.com/ about_us/modeldocs/?id=20 Accessed on 4 January 2012

CEDR Model Mediation Procedure (2010) 12th Edition, http://www.cedr.com/about_ us/modeldocs/?id=21 accessed on 19 April 2013

CEDR Statistics (2003), http://www.cedr.com/press/?item=CEDR-Solve-mediation-statistics-2003, accessed on 27 April 2013

Chancery Court Guide (2001) amended in (2011) & (2013)

Cheong K. (2008) A persisting aberration: The movement to enforce agreements to mediate, *Singapore Academy of Law Journal*, 20, 195

Cheung S. (2010a) Construction Mediation Landscape in the Civil Justice System in Hong Kong, *Journal of Legal Affairs and Dispute Resolution in Engineering and Construction* 2(3), 169

Cheung S. (2010b) *Construction Mediation in Hong Kong* in Brooker P. & Wilkinson S. *Mediation in the Construction Industry: An International Review* Spon Press, an imprint of Taylor & Francis, London & New York

Chitty on Contracts (2004) Beale H. 29th Edition, Vol. 1

Choquette S. (2006) Alternative Dispute Resolution Colorado Law on Mediation: A primer, *Colorado Lawyer* 35, 21

Civil Mediation Council (2009) Code of Good Practice for Mediators at http:// www.civilmediation.org/files/pdf/The%20CMC%20Code%20of%20Good%20 Practice%20for%20Mediators%202009.pdf, assessed on 21 October 2009

Civil Mediation Council *Information what is mediation?*, accessed on 15 February 2013, at http://www.civilmediation.org/about-mediation/29/what-is-mediation

Clark B. (2003) A time for change? The Development of commercial ADR in Scotland, *Scottish Law Times* (SLT) No 20, 169

Clark B. (2009) Mediation and Scottish lawyers: past, present and future, *Edinburgh Law Review* Vol. 13, No. 2, 252

Clark B. (2012) *Lawyers and Mediation*, Springer, London

Clark B. & Dawson C. (2007) ADR and Scottish commercial litigators: a study of attitudes and experience, *Civil Justice Quarterly* 26 (April), 228

Clark B. & Mays R. (1996) Regulating ADR – the Scottish experience, 5 *Web JCLI* at http://webjcli.ncl.ac.uk/1996/issue5/clark5.html, accessed on 26 July 2010

Clark K. (2002) The philosophical underpinning and general workings of Chinese mediation systems: What lessons can American Mediators Learn?, *Pepperdine Dispute Resolution Law Journal*, 2, 117

Clarke D. (1991) Dispute Resolution in China, *Journal of Chinese Law* 5, Issue 2, 245

Clarke LJ (Lord Clarke of Stone-cum-Ebony) *The Future of Civil Mediation* (speech delivered to 2nd conference of the Civil Mediation Council, May 8, 2008), at http://www.judiciary.gov.uk/media/speeches/2008/speech-clarke-lj-mor-08052008, accessed on 24 April 2013

CMC Code of Conduct for Mediators (2009) http://www.civilmediation.org/downloads.php?f=63%20%20assessed%20on%20the%2013%20August%202013-08-12.pdf, accessed on 10 May 2010

Coben J. & Thompson P. (2006) Disputing Irony: A Systematic Look at Litigation about Mediation, *Harvard Negotiation Law Review* 11, 43

Cole R., McEwen C., Rogers N., Coben J. & Thompson P. (2012) *Mediation: Law, Policy and Practice*, Thomson Reuters

Colvin A. (2010) The new mediation in Italy *Arbitration*, Vol. 76, Issue 4, 739

Commercial Court Working Party on ADR (1998), *ADR Orders in the Commercial Court*

Consumer Focus *Consumer Experience of the Small Claims Court* (2010), at http://www.consumerfocus.org.uk/files/2010/10/Research-Report.pdf Accessed on 11 January 2012

Cooley J. (2000) Mediators and advocates ethics, *Dispute Resolution Journal* Vol. 55, 73

Cooper C. (1992) Mediation: The Experience of the United States in Fenn P. & Gameson R. (eds), *Construction Conflict Management and Resolution* RN Spon, London, 1992

Cornes D. (2007) Commercial mediation: the impact of the courts, *Arbitration* 73(1), 12

Cornes D. (2008) Mediation Privilege & the EU Directive: An Opportunity?, *Arbitration* 74(4), 384

Costello E. (1998) To Mediate or not to Mediate, *The Arbitration and Dispute Resolution Law Journal* Part 1, March, 25

Daintith T. (1989) Legal Research and Legal Values, *Modern Law Review* 52, 352

Davies R. (1992) *Construction Conflict – The Specialist Contractor's View*, Proceedings of the First International Construction Management Conference, UMIST

Deason E. (2001) Enforcing mediation settlement agreements: Contract law collides with confidentiality, *U.C. Davis Law Review* 35, 33

Deason E. (2005) Procedural Rules for Complementary Systems of Litigation and Mediation – Worldwide, *Notre Dame Law Review* 80, 553

Deason E. (2006) The need for trust as a justification for confidentiality in mediation: A cross-disciplinary approach, *University of Kansas Law Review* 54, 1387

Debattista C. (2005) Drafting Enforceable Arbitration Clauses, *Arbitration International* 21.2, 238

Dehn C. (1995) 'The Woolf Report: Against the Public Interest?' in *Reform of Civil Procedure: Essays on Access to Justice*, Edited by Zuckerman A. & Cranston C. Clarendon Press, Oxford

Deleissegues C. (2011) Mediation Confidentiality: Has It Gone Too Far?, *University of La Verne Law Rev.*, 33, 123

Department Advisory Committee on Arbitration (1996)

Department of Constitutional Affairs (DCA) (1999), *Discussion Paper on Alternative Dispute Resolution*, November 1999

Dignan J., Sorsby A. & Hibbert J. (1996) *Neighbour Disputes: Comparing the Cost Effectiveness of Mediation and Alternative Approaches*, University of Sheffield, Centre for Criminological and Legal Research

Dixon G. & Carroll E. (1990) ADR Development in London, *International Construction Law Review* Vol. 7, 436

Dobbins R. (2005) The layered dispute resolution clause: From boilerplate to business opportunity, *Hastings Business Law Journal* 1, 161

Dolder C. (2004) The contribution of mediation to workplace justice *Industrial Law Journal*, Vol. 33, No. 4, 420

Dominguez D. (2007) Atlantic Pipe: A Harbinger Decision Leading to Mandatory Mediation, *American Law Institute – American Bar Association Continuing Legal Education Court of Study*, at http://files.ali-cle.org/thumbs/datastorage/skoobesruoc/pdf/CM090_chapter_25_thumb.pdf, accessed on 26 April 2013

Douglas G. (1989) Report of the Newcastle Conciliation Project Unit, *Anglo American Law Review* Vol. 18, 1, 26

Doyle M. (2006) *Department for Constitutional Affairs Manchester Small Claims Mediation Scheme Evaluation*, (DCA, 2006)

Draft UMA Committee (2001), at http://uniformlaws.org/Narrative.aspx?title= |Why States Should Adopt UMA published at Mediate.com, accessed on 6 December 2011

Dreadon K. (2005) Mediation: English Developments in an International Context, *Arbitration* 71, 112–17

Dundas H. (2002) CPR has teeth, *Arbitration* 68(3), 290

Dundas H. (2004) Mediation and the Court's Recent Developments, *Arbitration* 70(2), 150

Dundas H. R. (2010) Court-compelled mediation and the European Convention on Human Rights, Article 6 *Arbitration* 76(2), 343

Dwyer D. *The Civil Procedure Rules Ten Years On*, Oxford University Press

Dyke R. (2001) Roses and Horses for FDR & ADR, *New Law Journal*, 1562, 7031, 678

Dyson L. J. (2011) A Word on Halsey (A Talk Given at the CIArb's Third Mediation Symposium in October 2010), *Arbitration* 77(3), 337

Edge P. & Loughrey J. (2001) Religious charities and the juridification of the Charity Commission, *Legal Studies* 21, 36

Effron J. (1989) Alternatives to Litigation: Factors in Choosing, *Modern Law Review* Vol. 52, No. 4, 480

Emery R., Sbarra D. & Grover T. (2005) Divorce Mediation in the USA, *International Family Law Journal View* 64, 43(1), 22

Enterkin J. & Sefton M. (2006) *An Evaluation of the Exeter Small Claims Mediation*, Department of Constitutional Affairs Research Series (DCA Research Series, December 2006)

EU Mediators Code (2004) http://ec.europa.eu/civiljustice/adr/adr_ec_code_conduct_en.pdf Accessed on 26 April 2013

Evans G. (2006) Elements of Confusion: Education and Training Supplement, *New Law Journal* 156, (7215), 404

Expensive Arbitration (1920) *The Journal of the Institute of Arbitrators*, Vol. 1, no 4, 9

Fender-Allison J. (2011), Cross border mediation, *Cons. Law* 22, 5, 17

Fenn P. (1991) Alternative Dispute Resolution, *Construction Law* 2(3), 99

Ferguson R. (1980) Adjudication of Commercial Dispute and the Legal System in Modern England, *British Journal of Law and Society* 7(2), 141

Field R. & Wood N. (2005) Marketing Mediation Ethically: The Case of Confidentiality, *Queensland University of Technology Law & Justice Journal* 5, 143

Fisher R., Patton B. & Ury R. (1991) *Getting to yes: Negotiating agreements without giving in*, 2nd Edition, Penguin, New York

Fiss O. (1984) Against Settlement, *The Yale Law Journal* Vol. 93, Issue 6, 1073

Flood J. & Caiger A. (1993) Lawyers and Arbitration: The Juridification of Construction Disputes, *Modern Law Review* 56, 412

Folberg J. & Taylor A. (1984) *Mediation*, Jossey-Bass, San Francisco.

Foster K. (2003) A study in mediation styles: A comparative analysis of evaluative and transformative styles, at www.mediate.com/articles/fosterK1.cfm accessed on 4 November 2009

Franklin C. (2013) Mediation Confidentiality Controversy, *The Daily Journal Corporation*, at http://www.dailyjournal.com/cle.cfm?show=CLEDisplayArticle&q VersionID=80&eid=872569&evid=1, accessed on 26 April 2013

Fry E. (2006) It's Good to Talk, *New Law Journal*, 156, 132

Fuller L. (1971) Mediation – Its Forms and Functions, *Southern California Law Review* 44, 305

Fuller L. (1972) *Talks on American Law*, Voice of America Forum Lectures.

Fuller L. (1978) The forms and limits of adjudication, *Harvard Law Review* 92, 353

Funding Code Criteria (2011) at http://www.justice.gov.uk/legal-aid/funding/ funding-code, accessed on 27 April 2013

Gaede A. H. (1991) ADR – The USA Experience and some suggestions for International Arbitration: The Observations of an American Lawyer, *The International Construction Law Review* 5

Gaitskell R. (2005a) Adjudication: its effect on other forms of dispute resolution – the UK experience www.keatingchambers.co.uk/resources/publications/2005/rg_ kl_adjudication_its_effect.aspx, accessed on 13 February 2009

Gaitskell R. (2005b) Current trends in dispute resolution, *Arbitration* Vol. 71, No 4, 288

Galanter M. (1983) Reading the Landscape of Disputes, *U.C.L.A. Law Review* Vol. 31, 4

Galanter M. (1986) The day after the litigation explosion, *Maryland Law Review* 46, 1

Galanter M. (1992) Law abounding around the North Atlantic, *Modern Law Review* Vol. 55, 1

Galanter M. (1996) Real world torts: An antidote to anecdote, *Maryland Law Review* 55

Galanter M. (1998) An oil strike in hell: Contemporary Legends about the Civil Justice System, *Arizona Law Review*, 40, 717

Galanter M. (2006) A world without trials, *Journal of Dispute Resolution*, Vol. 26, 1, 7

Gardiner S. (2006) *Sports Law and Legislation*, 3rd Edition, Cavendish Publishing, London

Gardiner S. & Felix A. (1995) Juridification of the football field, *Marquette Sports Law Review* Vol. 5, Issue 2, 4

Genn H. (1998) *Central London County Court Pilot Mediation Scheme: Evaluation Report* (Lord Chancellor's Department), Research Series No 5/98. July 1998

Genn H. (2002) *Court-based ADR Initiatives for Non-family Civil Disputes: the Commercial Court and the Court of Appeal*, Department of Constitutional Affairs (DCA) Research Series, 1/02

Genn H. (2010) *Judging Civil Justice: The Hamlyn Lecture 2008*, Cambridge University Press

Genn H. (2012) What is Civil Justice for? Reform, ADR and Access to Justice, *Yale J. L. & Human* 24, 397

Genn H., Fenn F., Mason M., Lane A., Bechai N., Gray L. & Vencappa D. (2007) *Twisting Arm: court referred and court linked mediation under judicial pressure*, Ministry of Justice Research Series, 1/07 May 2007

Gilvarry L. S. G. (1989) Talk First – Avoid Action, *The Law Society Gazette* 86(26), 6

Goldberg S., Green E. & Sander F. *Dispute Resolution* (1985), Little Brown and Company, Boston & Toronto

Goriely T., Moorhead R. & Abrams P. (2002) *The Impact of the Woolf reforms on pre-action behaviour*, at http://www.law.cf.ac.uk/research/pubs/repository/557.pdf, accessed on 28 February 2013

Gould, N. (2007) *Mediation in construction disputes: an interim report*, at: www.fenwick-elliott.co.uk/articles/ADR/mediation_interim_report.htm, accessed on 2 November 2007

Gould N. and Cohen M. (1998) Appropriate dispute resolution in the UK construction industry, *Civil Justice Quarterly* 17, 103

Gould N., King C. and Hudson-Tyreman A. (2009) *The Use of Mediation in Construction Disputes: Summary Report of the Final Results*, May 2009, Kings College London, at: http://www.ciarb.org/information-and-resources/2009/07/29/Summary%20Report%20of%20the%20Final%20Results.pdf

Gould N., King C. and Britton P. (2010) *Mediating Construction Disputes: An Evaluation of Existing Practice*, Kings College London, Centre of Construction Law and Dispute Resolution, London.

Mediating Construction Disputes: An Evaluation of Existing Practice, Kings College London, Centre of Construction Law and Dispute Resolution, London.

Green E. (1986) Heretical View of the Mediation Privilege, *Ohio State Journal on Dispute Resolution* 2, 1

Greenslade D. (1996) Objections to Woolf, *New Law Journal*, Vol. 146, Issue 6757, 1252

Grossman A. (2003) Professionalising commercial mediation: discarding the baggage of idealised professions, Mediate.com, at: www.mediate.com/articles/grossmanA.cfm#bio, accessed on 6 May 2010

Guill J. & Slavin E. (1989) Rush to Unfairness: The Downside of ADR, *The Judges Journal* Vol. 28, 8

Habermas J. (1987) *The Theory of Communicative Action*, Vol. 2 Beacon Press, Boston

Harker M., Peyer S. & Wright K. (2011) Judicial scrutiny of merger decisions in the EU, UK and Germany, *International & Comparative Law Quarterly* 36, 60(1), 93

Harrington C. (1982) *Delegalization of Reform Movement: An Historical Analysis* in Abel R. *The Politics of Informal Justice*, Vol. 1, Academic Press, New York

Henderson D. (1996) Mediation Success: An Empirical Study, *Ohio State Journal on Dispute Resolution* 11, 105

Hensler D. (2002) Suppose it's not true: Challenging Mediation Ideology, *Journal of Dispute Resolution* 3, 81

Hensler D. (2003) Our Courts Ourselves: How the Alternative Dispute Resolution Movement Is Reshaping Our Legal System, *Penn. State Law Review* 108, 165

Hensler N. (2001) Making deals in court connected mediation: what's justice got to do with it?, *Washington University Law Quarterly* Vol. 79, 787

Hiers R. (2005) Navigating Mediation's Uncharted Waters, *Rutgers Law Review* 57, 531

Higgins I. (2011) Recent Developments in the law of privilege, *Journal of International Banking Law and Regulation* 26(4), 188

Hill R. (1996) Dispute Avoidance and Resolution Mechanisms, *The Arbitration and Dispute Resolution Law Journal*, Part 4, December, 287

Hillag J. & Huhn M. (2010) *Construction Mediation in Germany*, in Brooker P. & Wilkinson S. (2010) (eds) *Mediation in the Construction Industry: An International Review* Spon Press (imprint of Taylor & Francis Group)

Holdsworth W. (Sir) (1922) *A History of English Law* Vol. 15 London, Methuen

Holdsworth W. (Sir) (1938) *A History of English Law* Vol. 12 London, Methuen

Holland D. (1992) ADR in Construction, *Arbitration* 58(1), 57

Holmes O. W. (1897) The Path of Law, *Harvard Law Review* 10, 457

Hong Kong Mediator Code at http://www.jointmediationhelpline.org.hk/pdf/pdf4.pdf Accessed on 19 April 2013

Hong Kong Working Group on Mediation (2010) Department of Justice, the Government of Hong Kong Special Administrative Region, February http://www.justice.gov.uk/courts/mediation, accessed on 25 November 2012

Hong Kong Working Party (2010) *Report of the Working Party Group Executive Summary*, at http://www.doj.gov.hk/eng/public/pdf/2010/medexe20100208e.pdf, accessed on 30 November 2012

Hunter-Schulz T. & Boulle L. (2006) Alleging Mistake after Mediation, *ADR Bulletin* Vol. 8, No. 7, Article 2 http:/epublications.bond.edu.au/adr/vol8/iss7/2, accessed on 29 December 2012

Ilter D. and Dikbas A. (2010) Construction Mediation in Turkey in Brooker P. & Wilkinson S. *Mediation in the Construction Industry: an International Review* Spon Press

IMI Code of Professional Conduct http://imimediation.org/imi-code-of-professional-conduct Accessed on 27 November 2012

Imperati S. (1997) Mediator practice models: the intersection of ethics and stylistic practices in mediation, *Willamette Law Review* Vol. 33, 703

Irish Law Commission Report (2010) *Consultation Paper on ADR, Conciliation and Mediation* LRC 98-2010

Jackson (Lord Justice) (2009) *Civil Justice Costs Review The Final Report*

Jackson LJ (2011) *Proposals for Reform of Civil Justice Litigation & Costs in England and Wales Lord Jackson's Response* at http://www.judiciary.gov.uk/JCO%2fDocuments%2fConsultations%2flcj-mr-response-solving-disputes-county-court.pdf, accessed on 28 February 2013

Jacob J. (1985) *Justice Between Man and Man. Towards a Code of Civil Procedure*, Current Legal Problems, Oxford University Press

Jaffe P. (1989) Judicial supervision of commercial arbitration in England, *Arbitration* 55(3), 184

Jarrett B. (2009) The future of mediation: a sociological perspective, *Journal of Dispute Resolution* 49, 74

Johnson M., Thomas G. & Lewis G (Herbert Smith Freehills LLP) (2010) *Mediating in Hong Kong: Issues you will need to consider* at http://www.lexology.com/

library/detail.aspx?g=bd64783e-7d38-4a67-85dc-6ce7d877ce1f assessed on the 13 August

Jolowicz J. (1996) The Woolf Report and the Adversary System, *Civil Justice Quarterly* Vol. 15, 198, 208

Jones D. (2009) Dealing with multi-tiered disputes resolution process, *Arbitration* 75, 188

Kakalik J., Dunworth T., Hill L., McCaffery D., Osguri N., Pace N. & Vaiana M. (1996) *Just speedy and inexpensive? An evaluation of judicial case management under the Civil Justice Reform Act*, Institute for Civil Justice RAND

Kallipetis M. (2009) Mediator Privilege at http://billwoodmediation.com/articles/privelage.pdf, accessed on 26 April 2013

Kallipetis M. (2011) *Mediation Privilege and Confidentiality and the EU Directive* in Pointon G. *ADR in Business: Practice and Issues Across Countries and Cultures*, Vol 2 Kluwer Law International, The Netherlands

Katz L. (1988) Enforcing an ADR Clause: Are Good Intentions All You Have?, *American Business Law Journal* 26, 576

Katz L. (2008a) Getting to the Table, Kicking and Screaming: Drafting an Enforceable Mediation Provision, *Alternatives to High Cost Litigation* 26, 183

Katz L. (2008b) Keep it Simple: Developing the Legal Lessons for more Effective Mediation Enforcement, *Alternatives to the High Cost Litigation* 26, 206

Keady R. & Ganesh W. (2011) Mediation Bill introduced into Hong Kong Legislation *Dispute Resolution Update November*, at http://www.clydeco.org.uk/uploads/Files/Publications/2011/Dispute%20Resolution%20Update%20(Nov%202011).pdf, accessed on 28 February 2013

Kelly, J. (2011) The Uniform Mediation Act turns 10 this month, JAM Dispute Resolution Alert, http://jamsadr.com/files/uploads/documents/DRA/DRA-2011-06.pdf accessed on 18 July 2013

Kendall J. (1993) Ousting the jurisdiction, *Law Quarterly Review*, Vol. 109, 385

Kendall J. (2000) Choosing a system for resolving commercial disputes, *International Company and Commercial Law Review*, Vol. 11, 82

Kennedy P. and Milligan J. (2008) *Adjudication Reporting Centre 9th Report*, at http://www.adjudication.gcal.ac.uk/report9.pdf, accessed on 21 October 2009

Kennedy P., Mulligan J., Cattanach L. & McCluskey E. (2010) Paper at COBRA 2010 Paris at http://www.adjudication.gcal.ac.uk/COBRA%20conference2010.pdf, accessed on 11 January 2013

Koo A. (2011) Confidentiality of Mediation Communications, *Civil Justice Quarterly* 30(2), 192

Koo A. & Zhao Y. (2009) *International and Comparative Mediation: Legal Perspectives*, Wolters Kluwer Law and Business, The Netherlands

Koo A. & Zhao Y. (2011) The development of legal protection for mediation confidentiality in Hong Kong, *Common Law World Review*, 40, 263

Kovach K. (2006) *The evolution of mediation in the United States: Issues ripe for regulation may shape the future of practice*, in Alexander N. (2006) *Global Trends in Mediation*, 2nd Edition, Kluwer Law International, The Netherlands

Kovach K. & Love P. (1996) Evaluative Mediation is an Oxymoron, *Alternatives to High Cost Litigation*, 14, 31

Kovach K. & Love L. (1998) Mapping Mediation: The Risks of Riskin's Grid, *Harvard Negotiation Law Review* 3, 71, 109

Kritzer H. (2004) Disappearing trials, A comparative perspective, *Journal of Empirical Legal Studies* 1, 3, 735

Lande J. (2000) Towards a More Sophisticated Mediation Theory, *Journal of Dispute Resolution* 321, 331

Lane W. (1986) The role of the Legislature and Courts in the Development of the Arbitration Process, *Arbitration* 52(3), 195

Langer R. (1998) The Juridification and Technicalisation of Alternative Dispute Resolution Practices, *Canada Journal of Law & Society* 13, 169

Latham M. (1994) *Constructing the Team*, Final Report HMSO, London

Lavers A. (1992) *Construction Conflict: Management and Resolution – Analysis and Solutions*, Proceedings of the First International Construction and Management Conference UMIST

Leasure S. (2008) Summary Judgement for failure to mediate: Is it really that simple?, *Journal of the Kansas Bar Association* 77, 22.

Leathes M. (2009) A perfect storm is gathering at http://www.mediate.com/articles/a_perfect_storm_is_gathering.cfm, accessed on 18 April 2013

Lee J. (1999) The Enforceability of Mediation Clauses, *Singapore Journal of Legal Studies* July, 229

Lightman Mr Justice (2007) *Mediation: An Approximation of Justice*, at http://www.judiciary.gov.uk/Resources/JCO/Documents/Speeches/berwins_mediation.pdf, accessed on 24 April 2013

Limbury A. (2007) Should there be a distinct 'Mediation Privilege'?, *LEADR Update* 3, September 2007 at www.leadr.com.au/update/update14sept07.htm, accessed on 19 January 2012

Lind. E (2002) In the matter of ADR v CPR, *New Law Journal* 152 (7049), 1430

Lind E., MaCoun P., Ebener P., Felstiner W., Hensler D., Resnik J. & Tyler T. (1989) *Litigants views of trial, court annexed arbitration, judicial and settlement conferences*, Rand Report

Linden J. (2001) Mediation styles: The purists vs the toolkit at http//:www.mediate.com/articles/linden4.cfm, accessed on 26 April 2013

Lord Chancellor's Department (2001) *Civil Justice Reform: Emerging Findings. An Evaluation of the Civil Justice Reforms*

Lord Chancellor's Department (2002) *Civil Justice Reform: A Continuing Evaluation of the Civil Justice Reform*

Love P. (1997) The Top Ten Reasons Why Mediators Should Not Evaluate, *Florida. State University Law Review* 24, 937

Lowry R. (2000) Training Mediators for the 21st Century: To Evaluate or Not: That is not the Question!, *Family and Conciliation Courts Review* 38, 48

McAdoo B., Welsh N. & Wissler R. (2003) Institutionalisation: what do empirical studies tell us about court mediation, *Journal of Dispute Resolution* 9, No. 2, 8

McAdoo B. and Hinshaw A. (2002) The Challenge of Institutionalising ADR: Attorneys' Perspectives on the Effect of Rule 17 on Civil Litigation in Missouri, *Missouri Law Review* 67, 473

McAdoo B. & Welsh N. (2005) Look Before You Leap and Keep on Looking: Lessons from the Institutionalization of Court-Connected Mediation, *Nevada Law Journal* 5, 399

McDermott P. & Obar R. (2004) What's Going On in Mediation: An Empirical Analysis of the Influence of Mediator's Style on Party Satisfaction and Monetary Benefit, *Harvard Negotiation Law Review* Spring 9, 75

McEwen C. (2009) Maine's new rule of evidence 514 – An issue of mediation confidentiality, *Maine Bar Journal* 2, 44

McEwen & Maiman R. (1984) Mediation in small claims court: Achieving compliance through consent, *Law and Society* Vol. 18, No 1, 19

McGillis D. (1997) *Community Programmes: Developments and Challenges*, NIJ USA Department of Justice, Office of Justice Programmes, National Institute of Justice

Macfarlane J. (2002) A culture for change? A tale of two cities and mandatory court connected mediation, *Journal of Dispute Resolution*, 241, 266

Mack K. (2003) *Court Referral to ADR: Criteria and Research*, NADRAC Publication http://www.nadrac.gov.au/publications, accessed on 27 April 2013

Mackie K. (1992) *ADR and construction disputes*, Proceedings of the First International Construction Management Conference, Manchester, UMIST

Mackie K. (2003) The future for ADR clauses after Cable and Wireless v. IBM, *Arbitration International* Vol. 19, No. 3, 345

Mackie K., Miles D., Marsh W. & Allen T. (3rd Edition, 2007), *The ADR Practice Guide: Commercial Dispute Resolution*, Tottell, England

Malek H., Auburn J. & Bagshaw R. (2009) *Phippson on Evidence*, 17th Edition, Sweet & Maxwell, England

Marcus M. (Judge) (2011) What happens in mediation, *Los Angeles Lawyers* December 2011, 17

Markesinis B. (1990) Litigation Mania in England, Germany and the USA, *The Cambridge Law Review* Vol. 49, Part 2, 233

Mason J. (2012) How might the adversarial imperative be effectively tempered in mediation, *Legal Ethics* 15(1), 111

Mead P. (1996) Enforceability of ADR Clauses Revisited, *Australia Construction Law Newsletter* Issue 42, 32

Meggitt G. (2010) The CPR and the CJR – applying English Legal Authorities on civil procedure in Hong Kong, *Civil Justice Quarterly* 29(2), 235

Menachem M., Hasofer S. & Harris J., The Mediation Bill: Hong Kong Takes Another Small Step (13 December 2011) at http://www.mayerbrown.com/publications/article.asp?id=11958, accessed on 17 January 2012

Menkel-Meadow C. (1991) Pursuing Settlement in An Adversary Culture: A Tale of Innovation Co-Opted or The Law of ADR, *Florida State Law Review* 19, 1, 6–17

Menkle-Meadow C. (1993) Lawyer Negotiation: Theories and Realities – What we learn from Mediation, *Modern Law Review* Vol. 56, 362–79

Menkle-Meadow C. (1997) When Dispute Resolution Begets Disputes of its own: Conflicts among dispute professionals, *UCLA Law Review* 44, 1871

Menkle-Meadow C. (2009) Are there systematic ethics issues in Dispute Systems Design?, *Harvard Negotiation Law Review* 14, 195

Meyer J. & Leathes M. (2008) How mediators can obtain professional certification and thereby elevate their profession: A look at IMI's voluntary credentialing programme, *Dispute Resolution Journal* Vol. 63, Issue 3, 22

Miles D. (1992) The problems of using ADR in Construction, in Fenn P. and Gameson G. (eds.) *Construction Conflict and Management*, Spon, London

Miles R. (2004) Mediation: a fledgling profession or a pot puri of good intentions?, *ADR News: The NADR Quarterly Newsletter* Vol. 4, No. 3, 1

Mills K. (2005) Can a single ethical code respond to all models of mediation?, *Bond Dispute Resolution News* Vol. 21, 5

Mills A. & Loveridge R. (2011) The Uncertain Future of Walford and Miles, *Lloyd's Maritime and Commercial Law Quarterly* Vol. 4, 529

Ministry of Justice (2011) *Solving disputes in the county courts: creating a simpler, quicker and more proportionate system: A consultation on reforming civil justice in England and Wales, Consultation paper* CP6/2011, accessed on 11 April 2011

Ministry of Justice (2012) *Solving Disputes in the County Court: Creating a simpler, quicker and more proportionate response The Government Response*

Mistelis L. (2001) ADR in England and Wales *American Review of International Arbitration* 12, 167

Mistelis L. (2006) *ADR in England and Wales: a successful case of public private partnership* in Alexander, N. (Ed.) *Global Trends in Mediation* 2nd edn., Kluwer, Alphen aan den Rijn

Mnookin R. & Kornhauser L. (1978–1979) Bargaining in the Shadow of the Law: The case of Divorce, *Yale Law Journal* 88, 950

Model Standard Case Management Direction allocating cases to the Multi Track Form MT3 (CHY) (2012)

Model Standards of Conduct for Mediators (2005) Joint Committee of American Arbitration Association, American Bar Association & Association for Conflict Resolution

Mosten F. (2004) Institutionalisation of Mediation, *Family Court Review* Vol, 42, No 2, 292

Mulcahy L. (2000) The devil and the deep blue sea?: A critique of the ability of community mediation to suppress and facilitate participation in civil life, *Journal of Law and Society* 27(1), 133

Mulcahy, L. (2001a) The Possibility and Desirability of Mediator Neutrality – towards an Ethic of Partiality?, *Social and Legal Studies* Vol. 10(4), 505

Mulcahy L. (2001b) Can Leopards Change Their Spots? An Evaluation of The Role of Lawyers in Medical Negligence Mediation, *International Journal of the Legal Profession* 8, 3, 203

Nader L. (1988) ADR Explosion: Implications of Rhetoric in Legal Reform, *Windsor Yearbook Access to Justice* 8, 269

Nader L. (1993) Controlling processes in the practice of law: Hierarchy and Pacification in the movement to reform disputes ideology, *Ohio State Journal on Dispute Resolution* 9, 1

NADRAC (2006) *Legislating for ADR. A Guide for Government Public Policy Makers and Legal Drafters*

NADRAC (2009) *Resolve to Resolve – Embracing ADR to improve Access to Justice in the Federal Jurisdiction Report to the Attorney General*

NADRAC (2011) *Maintaining and Enhancing the Integrity of Mediation*, February 2011 accessed 20 January 2012

National Mediator Accreditation Standards (2008) (Australia) Practice Standards

Nesic M. (2001) Mediation – On the Rise in the United Kingdom?, *Bond Law Review* Vol. 13, Issue 2, 427

Neuberger LJ Lord Neuberger of Abbotsbury (2010) *The Gordon Slynn Memorial Lecture 2010: Has mediation had it day* (November 11, 2010)

Newman P. (1997) Does business need arbitration and litigation, *Arbitration* 63(2) Supp, 35

Newmark C. (2011) (Spenser Underhill Newmark LLP) *Mediator Do mediators do what they say?*, CMC Academic Seminar Series April 6

Noble Foster T. & Prentice S. (2009) The promise of confidentiality in mediation: Practitioners' perceptions, *Journal of Dispute Resolution* 1, 163

Noce D. (2008) Communicating Quality Assurance: A case study of mediation profiles on a court roster, *North Dakota Law Review* 84, 769

Noce D., Baruch Bush R. & Folger F. (2002) Clarifying the Theoretical Underpinnings of Mediation: Implications for Practice and Policy, *Pepperdine Dispute Resolution Law Journal* 3, 39

Nolan D. (2010) Disputatio: Creeping Legalism as a Declension, Myth *Journal of Dispute Resolution*, 1, 5

Nolan-Haley J. (1998) Lawyers, clients and mediation, *Notre Dame Law Review*, Vol. 73, 1369

Nolan-Haley J. (1999) Informed consent in mediation: a guiding principle for truly educated decision making, *Notre Dame Law Review* Vol. 74, 775

Nolan-Haley J. (2002) Lawyers, Non-Lawyers and Mediation: Rethinking the Professional Monopoly from a Problem-Solving Perspective, *Harvard Negotiation Law Review* 7, 235 (Spring)

Nolan-Haley J. (2004) The Merger of Law and Mediation: Lessons from Equity Jurisprudence and Roscoe Pound *Cardozo Journal, Conflict Resolution* 6, 57, 59

Nolan-Haley J. (2012) Mediation: The 'New Arbitration', *Harvard Negotiation Law Review* 17, 61

Noll D. (2001) A Theory of Mediation, *Dispute Resolution Journal* 56, 78

O'Connor P. (1992) ADR: Panacea or Placebo?, *Arbitration* May, Vol. 58(2), 107

Oberman S. (2005) Mediation Theory vs. Practice: What are we Really Doing? Resolving a Professional Conundrum, *Ohio State Journal on Dispute Resolution* 20, 775

Oberman S. (2008) Style vs model: why quibble?, *Pepperdine Dispute Resolution Journal* Vol. 9, 1

Oyre T. (2004) CPR and the use of mediation/ADR, *Arbitration* 70(1), 19

Paleker M. (2006) *Mediation in South Africa Here: But Not all There* in Alexander N. *Global Trends in Mediation* 2nd Edition, Kluwer Law International

Palmer M. & Roberts S. (1998) *Dispute Processes: ADR and the Primary Forms of Decision Making*, Butterworths, UK

Parke J. & Bristow D. (2001) The Gathering Storm of Arbitrators' and Mediators' Liability, *International Arbitration Law and Review* 4(5), 135–42

Parker LCJ (1959) *History and Development of Commercial Arbitration*, Lionel Cohen Lecture, Hebrew University of Jerusalem

Parris J. (1978) *The Law and Practice of Arbitration*, Goodwin Ltd, London

Pei C. (1999) The origins of mediation in traditional China, *Dispute Resolution Journal* Vol. 54, Issue 2, 32

Peysner J. & Seneviratne M. (2005) *The Management of Civil Cases: The Courts and Post-Woolf Landscape*, DCA Research Series 9/05 November

Phillips D. (2011) At Cross Purposes, *New Law Journal* 161, 735

Phillips G. (2003) Is Creeping Legalism Infecting Arbitration? *Dispute Resolution Journal* 58, 37

Phillips LJ (Lord Phillips of Worth Matravers) *Alternative Dispute Resolution: An English View* (2008), at http://www.judiciary.gov.uk/Resources/JCO/Documents/Speeches/lcj_adr_india_290308.pdf, accessed on 26 April 2013

Pollack C. (2007) The Role of the mediator. A user's guide to mediation, *Arbitration* 73(1), 20

Press, S. (2003) Institutionalization of mediation in Florida: At the crossroads, *Penn State Law Review*, Vol. 108, 43

Press S. (2003–2004) Institutionalization: Saviour or Saboteur of Mediation?, *Florida State University Law Review*, 24, 903

Prince S. & Belcher S. (2006) *An Evaluation of the Small Claims Dispute Resolution Pilot at Exeter County Court: Final Report for the Department of Constitutional Affairs* (September 2006) University of Exeter

Pryles M. (1998) Assessing disputes resolution procedures, *Arbitration* 64(2), 106

Rau A. (2005) The Culture of American Arbitration and the Lessons of ADR, *Texas International Law Journal* 40, 449

Rawlinson (2011) Exception that proves the rule: Supreme Court endorses new interpretation of exception to the without prejudice rule, at http://www.myashurst.com/en/Events/documents/Confidentially%20yours_recent%20cases%20on%20privilege.pdf), accessed on 25 October 2011

Resnik J. (1998) Trial as error jurisdiction of injury: Transforming the meaning of Article 111, *Harvard Law Review* 113, 928

Resnik J. (2000) Trial as error, jurisdiction as injury: Transforming the meaning of Article 111, *Harvard Law Review* 113, 25

Riggs L. & Schenk R. (1990) Arbitration: Survey on User Satisfaction, *Journal of Performance of Constructed Facilities* Vol. 4, No. 2, 88

Riskin L. (1996) Understanding Mediators' Orientations, Strategies and Techniques: A Grid for the Perplexed, *Harvard Negotiation Law Review* 1, 7

Riskin L. (2003) Retiring and replacing the grid of mediator orientations, *Alternatives to the High Cost of Litigation* April, 21, 69

Roberts R. (2009) Listing Concentrates the Mind, *Oxford Journal of Legal Studies* 29(3), 457

Roberts S. (1992) Mediation in the Lawyers' Embrace, *Modern Law Review* 55, 258

Roberts S. (1993) ADR and Civil Justice: An Unresolved Relationship, *Modern Law Review* 56, 452

Roberts, S. (2000) Settlement as Civil Justice, *Modern Law Review* 63(5), 739

Roberts S. (2002) Institutionalised Settlement in England: A contemporary panorama, *Willamette Journal of International Law and Dispute Resolution* 10, 17

Roberts S. (2012) The Mayor's & City of London Court Mediation Scheme; A Review of the Scheme's first 5 Years at http://www.citydisputespanel.org/media/downloads/The%20Mayors%20and%20City%20of%20London%20Court%20Mediation%20Scheme.pdf, accessed 26 April 2013

Robertshaw P. & Segal J. (1993) Milking of ADR, *Civil Justice Quarterly* 12, 23

Roebuck D. (2006) The pre-history of dispute resolution in England, *Arbitration* 72(2), 93

Rogers N. & McEwen C. (1998) Employing the law to increase the use of mediation and to encourage direct and early negotiations, *Ohio State Journal of Dispute Resolution* 13, 831

Royce N. (1989) Conciliation in Business Disputes: Has it a future?, *Construction Law Journal* Vol. 15, No. 1, 34

Ruben G. (2002) United Kingdom Military Law: Autonomy, Civilisation, Juridification, *Modern Law Review* 65, 1, 36

Rute L. (2010) The evolution of commercial mediation in the Midwest: Best practices, confidentiality and good faith, *Journal of the Kansas Bar Association* 79, 24

Sanders A. (2009) Legislative Comment: Part one of the Employment Act 2008: 'better' dispute resolution?, (2009) *Industrial Law Journal* 38(1), 30

Sanders F. (2000) The future of ADR The Earl F. Nelson Memorial Lecture 1999, *Journal of Dispute Resolution* 3, 5

Sanders F. (2007) Developing the MRI (Mediation Receptivity Index), *Ohio State Journal on Dispute Resolution* 22, 599–610

Saunders D. (2002) 'Within the orbit of this life': Samuel Pufendorf and the autonomy of law: The Juridification of Religious Conflict *Cardozo Law Review* 23, 13, 2173

Schmitz A. (2004) Refreshing contractual analysis of ADR agreements by curing bipolar avoidance of modern common law, *Harvard Negotiation Law Review* 9, 1

Searle A. (1953) Arbitration Versus Litigation, *Arbitration* 19(1), 32

Second Report of the Commercial Court Committee Working Party on ADR (1998)

Shapiro D. (1999) Alternative Dispute Resolution under the new civil Rules – some guidelines for lawyers and judges, *Litigation* 18(7), 2

Shipman S. (2006) Court Approaches to ADR in the civil justice system, *Civil Justice Quarterly* 25, (April), 181

Shipman S. (2011) Compulsory mediation: the elephant in the room, *Civil Justice Quarterly* 30(2), 163

Shopp J. (2010) Mediation: Confidentiality, *Pennsylvania Bar Association Quarterly* 81, 101

Sidoli del Ceno J. (2011) An investigation into lawyer's attitudes towards the use of mediation in commercial property disputes in England and Wales, *The International Journal of the Law of the Built Environment*, Vol. 3, Issue 2, 182

Sime S., Blake S. & Brown J. (2010) *Professional Ethics in Negotiation and Mediation*, Oxford Online Resources, England

Simmons R. & Howell-Richardson P. (2001) ADR, Update on the impact of CPR on ADR, Smith H. (2011), accessed on 7 April 2011 *Journal of ADR, Mediation and Negotiation* 1(1), 8

Solicitors Regulation Authority LPC Training Course Information (updated March 2012) src.org.uk/lpc, accessed on 26 April 2012

Soo G. (2000) Working through Unworkable Mediation, *Arbitration* Vol. 66, No 3, 207

Sorabji J. (2008) Costs – further developments from *Halsey*: *Nigel Witham Ltd v. Smith & Isaacs* and *S v. Chapman*, *Civil Justice Quarterly* Vol. 27, No. 4, 427

Sourdin T. (2007) Australian National Mediator Accreditation Scheme Report on the Project, at www.nswbar.asn.au/docs/professional/adr/documents/Accreditation ReportSept07.pdf, accessed 3 March 2010

Sourdin T. (2006) *Mediation in Australia: Impacts on Litigation* in Alexander N. (2006) *Global Trends in Mediation*, 2nd Edition, Edited by Alexander N., Kluwer Law International, The Netherlands

South J. (2009) Development of Mediator Training in England and Wales, at http://www.mediate.com/articles/southJ1.cfm, accessed 30 May 2009

Spain L. & Paranica K. (2001) Considerations for mediation and alternative dispute resolution in North Dakota, *North Dakota Law Review* 77, 391

Spencer D. (1995) Mediation: Notice of motion for a stay of arbitration to allow for mediation, *Australia Construction Law Newsletter*, Issue 2, 57

Spencer D. (2005) Enforcing Mediation Settlement Agreements in Australia, *World Arbitration and Mediation Report* 16(4), 124

Spencer D. & Brogan M. (2006) *Mediation Law and Practice*, Cambridge University Press

Stemple J. (1996) Reflections on Judicial ADR and the Multi-Door Courthouse at Twenty: Fait Accompli, Failed Overture or Fledgling Adulthood, *Ohio State Journal on Dispute Resolution* 11, 297

Stemple J. (2000) Identifying Real Dichotomies Underlying the False Dichotomies: 21st Mediation in an Eclectic Regime, *Journal Dispute Resolution* 371, 94

Sternlight J. (1999) Lawyers Representation in Mediation: Using Economics and Psychology to Structure Advocacy in a Non-adversarial Setting, *Ohio State Journal on Dispute Resolution* 14, 269

Stewart D. (2002) Can the Court Force Parties to Use ADR?, *Commercial Law* 54, 72

Stipanowich T. (2001) Contract and conflict management, *Wisconsin Law Review* (3), 831

Stipanowich T. (1996) Beyond Arbitration: Innovation and Evolution in the United States Construction Industry, *Wake Forest Law Review* 31, 1, 65

Stipanowich T. (1998) The multi-door contract and other possibilities, *Ohio State Journal on Dispute Resolution* Vol. 13, 303

Stipanowich T. (2004) ADR and the Vanishing Trial: The Growth and Impact of Alternative Dispute Resolution, *Journal of Empirical Legal Studies* 1, 3, 843

Stipanowich T. (2007) The Arbitration Penumbra: Arbitration Law and the Rapidly Changing Landscape of Dispute Resolution, *Nevada Law Journal* 8, 427

Stulberg J. (1997) Facilitative versus evaluative mediator orientations: piercing the grid, *Florida State University Law Review* Vol. 24, 985

Sussman E. (2006) A brief survey of USA case law on enforcing mediation settlement agreements over objections to the existence or validity of such agreements and implications for mediation confidentiality and mediator testimony, *Mediation Committee Newsletter* April 2006, 32

Suter E. (2009) The progress from void to valid for agreements to mediate *Arbitration* 75(1), 28

Suter E. (2010) Case Comment: Is there any reasonable prospect of a successful mediation? *Corby Group v Corby DC (Costs)*, *Arbitration* 76(1), 176

Suter E. (2011) Discrimination without prejudice: *Woodward v. Santander UK Plc (formerly Abbey National Plc)*, *Arbitration* 77(1), 147–54

Suter E. (2011) Building towards compulsory mediation, *Arbitration* 77(3), 375

Suter E. (2009) The progress from void to valid for agreements to mediate, *Arbitration* 75(1), 28

Tate C. & Vallinder T. (1995) *The Global Expansion of Judicial Powers*, New York University Press

TCC Court Guide (2010) 2nd revision http://www.justice.gov.uk/downloads/courts/tech-court/tech-con-court-guide.pdf, accessed on 25 November 2012

Teubner G. (1997) (ed.) *Juridification of Social Spheres*, Berlin, de Gruyter

Thomas G. & Kiesselbach P. (2013) Hong Kong First Case on Mediation Ordinance, at http://hsfatadrnotes.com/2013/01/25/hong-kong-first-case-on-new-mediation-ordinance, accessed on 27 April 2013

Thompson P. (2004) Enforcing rights generated in court connected mediation – tension between the aspiration of private facilitative process and the reality of pubic adversarial justice, *Ohio State Journal on Dispute Resolution* 19, 507

Thornberg E. (2011) Reaping what we sow: anti-litigation rhetoric, limited budgets, and declining support for civil courts, *Civil Justice Quarterly* 30(1), 74

Toulson R. & Phipps C. (2004) *On Confidentiality*, Sweet & Maxwell, England

Toulson R. & Phipps C. (2006) *On Confidentiality*, Sweet & Maxwell, England

Treital, (2003) *Law of Contract* (11th Edition) Sweet & Maxwell, England

Tronson B. (2006) Mediation Orders: do the arguments against them make sense?, *Civil Justice Quarterly* 25 (July), 412

Tumbridge J. (2010) Mediators: confidentiality and compulsion to give evidence – issues in England, *International Company and Commercial Law Review* 21(4), 144

Turner D. & Gammack D. (2003) Mediation: Where Does It Fit Into The Civil Justice System?, *Corporate Briefing* 17(1), 2

Turner R. (2000) New Rules for the Millennium, *New Law Journal* 150, 49, 6919

Tyler T. (1988) Client Perceptions of Litigation: What Counts: Process or Results?, *Trial* 7, 40

Underhill D. (2000) I.R.S. Case Comment Court Order for Alternative Dispute Resolution, *Civil Justice Quarterly* 19(Apr), 106

Underhill D. (2003) The English Court and ADR – Policy and Practice, *European Business Review* 14, Issue 3, 259

Uniform Law website, accessed 1 February 2013 at http://uniformlaws.org/Legislative FactSheet.aspx?title=Mediation Act

Van Canegegem R. (1988) *The Birth of the English Common Law*, 2nd Edition, Cambridge University Press

Waldman E. (1998) The evaluative-facilitative debate in mediation: Applying the lens of therapeutic jurisprudence, *Marquette Law Review* 82, 155

Wall C. (2009) Mediation in the civil justice system in Hong Kong, *Arbitration* 75(3), 425

Warns C. (1960) Arbitration and the Law, *Arbitration* 26(2), 85

Weixia G. (2010) Civil Justice Reform in Hong Kong: Challenges and Opportunities for Development of Alternative Dispute Resolution, 43 *Hong Kong Law* Vol. 40, No. 1, 43

Welsh N. (2001a) Making Deals in Court Connected Mediation: What's Justice got to do with it?, *Washington University Law Quarterly* Vol. 79, 787

Welsh N. (2001b) The Thinning Vision of Self-Determination in Court Connected Mediation: The Inevitable Price of Institutionalisation?, *Harvard Negotiation Law Review* 6, 1

White Book, (2013) Sweet & Maxwell, UK

Wilcock S. (2002/2003) When Is It Safe to Say No?, *The Commercial Lawyer* 58, 44

Wilkinson S. *Construction Mediation in New Zealand* (2010) in Brooker P. and Wilkinson S. (2010) (eds) *Mediation in the Construction Industry: An International Review*, Spon Press (imprint of Taylor & Francis Group)

Williams R. (1987) Should the State Provide ADR Services, *Civil Justice Quarterly* 6(Apr), 142

Wilson J. (2010) ADR Professional: Stand and Deliver! The Mediator and the Witness Summons, *Family Law* 40 (Sep), 1010

Wissler R. (2004) Barriers to Attorneys' Discussion and Use of ADR, *Ohio State Journal on Dispute Resolution* Vol. 19(2), 460

Wood, B. (2008) When girls go wild: The debate over mediator privilege, *The Mediator Magazine*, September

Wood, B. (2009) Mediator Privilege at http://billwoodmediation.com/articles/privelage.pdf, accessed 16 April 2013

Woolf (1995) (The Right Honourable The Lord Woolf, Master of the Rolls) *Access to Justice: The Interim Report*, London: HMSO

Woolf (1996) (The Right Honourable The Lord Woolf, Master of the Rolls) *Access to Justice: The Final Report*, London: HMSO

Woolford A. & Ratner R. (2008) *Informal Reckonings: conflict in mediation, restorative justice and reparations*, Routledge Cavendish, Abingdon

Xuereb P. (1988) The Juridification of Industrial Relations through Company Law Reform, *Modern Law Review* Vol. 51, Issue 2, 156

Yarn D. (2004) The Death of ADR: A cautionary tale of isomorphism through institutionalization, *Penn State Law Review* 108, 929

Young R. (1989) Neighbour Dispute Mediation Theory and Practice, *Civil Justice Quarterly* 8, 319

Yu H. (2012) The Draft Mediation Bill, *Hong Kong Law Journal* Vol. 1, Part 2, 351

Zamboni M. (2003) Confidentiality in Mediation, *International Arbitration Law Review* 6(5), 175

Zamboni M. (2008) The 'social' in social law: An analysis of a concept in disguise, *Journal of Law in Society* 9, 63

Zander M. (1995a) Why Lord Woolf's Proposed Reforms of Civil Litigation should be rejected; in *Reform of Civil Justice* Edited by Zuckerman A. & Cranston C. Clarendon Press, Oxford

Zander M. (1995b) Are there any clothes for the Emperor to Wear? Objections to Woolf, *New Law Journal* August, 145, 154

Zander M. (1996) Consistency in the exercise of discretionary powers, *New Law Journal* 146, 1590

Zander M. (1997) The Woolf Reforms: forward and backwards for the new Lord Chancellor, *Civil Justice Quarterly* Vol. 17, 208

Zander M. (2009) More Harm than good? Professor Zander QC reflects on 10 years of the Woolf Reforms, *New Law Journal* Vol. 159, 7360

Zimmerman S. (2009) Judges gone wild: Why breaking the mediation confidentiality privilege for acting in 'bad faith' should be re-evaluated in court ordered mandatory mediation, *Cardozo Journal of Conflict Resolution* 11, 353

Zirkel P. & Krahmal A. (2001) Creeping Legalism in Grievance Arbitration: Fact or Fiction?, *Ohio State Journal on Dispute Resolution* Vol. 16, 243

Zuckerman A. (1996a) Lord Woolf's Access to Justice: *Plus a change, Modern Law Review* 59, 6, 773

Zuckerman A. (1996b) *Reform in the Shadow of Lawyers' Interests* in *Reform of Civil Procedure*, Edited by Zuckerman A. & Cranston R., Oxford University Press

Zuckerman A. (2003) *Civil Procedure*, Lexis Nexis Butterworth, London

Index